Guns and
College Homicide

D0768219

Guns and College Homicide

The Case to Prohibit Firearms on Campus

STEPHEN K. BOSS

McFarland & Company, Inc., Publishers

Jefferson, North Carolina

LIBRARY OF CONGRESS CATALOGUING-IN-PUBLICATION DATA

Names: Boss, Stephen K., 1959– author.
Title: Guns and college homicide : the case to prohibit firearms on
campus / Stephen K. Boss.
Description: Jefferson, North Carolina : McFarland & Company, Inc.,
Publishers, 2019. | Includes bibliographical references and index.
Identifiers: LCCN 2018053973 | ISBN 9781476676098 (softcover :
acid free paper) ∞
Subjects: LCSH: Campus violence—United States. | School
shootings—United States. | Gun control—United States. |
Universities and colleges—Security measures—United States. |
Homicide—United States. | Firearms and crimes—United States.
Classification: LCC LB2345 .B66 2019 | DDC 371.7/82—dc23
LC record available at https://lccn.loc.gov/2018053973

BRITISH LIBRARY CATALOGUING DATA ARE AVAILABLE

ISBN (print) 978-1-4766-7609-8
ISBN (ebook) 978-1-4766-3488-3

Front cover image of *University of Arkansas—Old Main*, watercolor
on paper, 15.5" × 21.5", 2012 (Beth Woessner, bethwoessner.com).

Printed in the United States of America

McFarland & Company, Inc., Publishers
  Box 611, Jefferson, North Carolina 28640
  www.mcfarlandpub.com

Table of Contents

Preface

Books of nonfiction are usually written to tell the story of something that has happened or is happening or is likely to happen. Nonfiction books are written to describe historical events or the lives of those individuals who influenced history in some way. Nonfiction books are written to argue forcefully, through careful documentation, for political action or implementation of policies intended to improve civilization, or to document some interesting aspect of civilization from empirical studies. Nonfiction books document the heroic stories of those who struggle for civil rights or battle and vanquish oppressors, or they tell of great moments of scientific discovery or exploration or feats of human daring. Nonfiction books use science and tangible results of scientific inquiry to detail phenomena happening all around our planet and how those physical processes impact environmental and human dimensions of our existence. Nonfiction books are narratives of the dynamics of humanity interacting in the environment.

This nonfiction book is different because it tells the story of something that, for the most part, does not happen, is not happening, and is unlikely to happen. More correctly, it documents a phenomenon that occurs only rarely or not at all. In this book, I document the low incidence of homicides and, in particular, gun-related homicides on university and college campuses in the United States. I do not intend to minimize those incidents that occur annually. Every year, there are about seventeen homicides (including around a dozen with guns) on college campuses nationwide. No one reading this book should imagine that I am callous or unfeeling regarding those who fall to bullets or other means of homicide in our nation's post-secondary institutions. Quite the contrary—I am aghast that our society accepts any acts of violence, including gun violence, as a condition of our freedom or as a consequence of constitutional privilege.

I am a professor at a major state-sponsored university: the University of Arkansas. I know your sons and daughters, and I understand my obligation to you, their parents, and to them to do whatever I can to ensure their safe

1

passage through the halls of my academy. I understand my responsibility to ensure the quality of their educational experience and to help them realize their intellectual potential and aspirations. I am their mentor, their teacher, their advisor, their confidant, their friend, their surrogate parent, and (albeit rarely) their inspiration. For me, I cannot accept any policy that permits even one gun homicide on a college campus anywhere in the United States. And that is my point with this book.

I want you to know what I know. My entire adult life has been affiliated with a university in some capacity. First, I was an undergraduate student. Then I earned a master's degree. I taught for three years as a college instructor; then I returned to two of our nation's great public universities to pursue my doctorate. Upon earning my doctorate, I served briefly as an instructor again, substituting for a faculty member who had been granted a research sabbatical. I served two more years as a post-doctoral researcher at a major research university before finally joining the faculty at the University of Arkansas in August 1996. I began as an assistant professor and worked my way up through the ranks to professor. I've been in college more than twice as long as a typical college freshman has been alive. That's right—I'm in my 41st year of college! My experience extends across four decades at eight universities across the United States. And I think I've learned something in that time. I certainly have experienced a great deal, and my experience overall was a wonderfully positive one. Such will be your experience if you are a college student, or your daughter's or son's experience if you are a parent. That is my expectation based on my experience.

During my undergraduate career (1977–1981), no shots were fired on my campus. I would know; I was there. How many of you reading this book had the same experience? (No shots fired, I mean.) I am certain that the correct answer is almost all of you. During my graduate studies for the Master of Science degree at a different university, no shots were fired on campus. Following completion of my master's degree, no shots were fired on another campus during three full years of employment as a college instructor. I completed my doctorate, served as a temporary instructor and completed two years as a post-doctoral research scientist at four more universities, and no shots were fired. Ever. I joined the University of Arkansas in 1996, and all was well until the first day of fall semester: 28 August 2000. On that day, two gunshots were heard emanating from an office in an academic building on the university campus. That is the only time I experienced a shooting on a university campus, across eight universities scattered over the width and breadth of the United States during a 41-year career. This incident has been the only incident of gun homicide at the University of Arkansas since its founding in 1871—a span of 147 years. Just this one incident of murder-suicide. In contrast, 7,280 people in the general public were murdered with guns in the states where I resided during the intervals of my various academic stints: 7,280 to 1. That is the point of this book.

Again, I do not desire to minimize the cruel tragedy of gun violence in our nation. Just as public health professionals do, I find the epidemic of gun violence among the American public a legitimate public health crisis that should be addressed with the same energy, focus, and resources with which we have addressed other public health crises during my lifetime (e.g., polio and other debilitating or fatal childhood diseases; smoking and its connection to respiratory afflictions; unsafe automobiles; air and water pollution; HIV/AIDS; etc.). Nor do I wish to minimize the horror of gun homicides that occur from time to time on our nation's college campuses. But I wish to bring the reality of those incidents to public consciousness. We are shocked, paralyzed, and horrified whenever we hear of a campus shooting. That is because the uncommon nature of those incidents is truly shocking, paralyzing, and horrific. Gun homicides on college campuses are so rare that we don't actually expect them to occur, and, indeed, they rarely do. When this phenomenon does occur, we take notice because it shocks our senses, and that shock creates a perceptual bias. We remember selected incidents of this phenomenon because they are horrific in nature. And we should never get over that horror, because it is a valid and legitimate human reaction to a rare event that is truly awful and disturbing. Gun violence on university and college campuses resonates with us because it reminds us of our inner darkness. The loss of bright, energetic sons and daughters as they strive to enter adulthood and the prime of their lives strikes at our parental instincts.

I want to begin this book by disclosing that I am neither a social scientist nor an expert in public health, nor even an expert on the origins and causes of gun violence in our society. I am a physical scientist by training. By writing this book, I am exposing myself to skepticism and perhaps criticism from some who will argue that I am not qualified to be writing on this topic. You may be wondering, then, why I would take this risk. I've been at this job for 41 years, and I'm pretty good at it. I know what I'm doing, and I know how to do it. I'm writing this book because I want everyone in the general public to know what I know. I want to explain what I have experienced on college campuses during a four-decade career, and I want you to relate my experience to your own college experience (in all probability, one that was also gun-free and without gun incidents while you were attending that institution). I want you to be aware that our society has created a grand social experiment and conducted that experiment for quite a few decades. In this experiment, we have sequestered those individuals who are most at risk of becoming victims of gun violence in our society into thousands of gun-safe enclaves distributed across every state in the nation—our universities, colleges, and technical institutions. The results of that experiment are available if we are willing to look for them. We have the data, and those data are available in a publicly accessible archive. I spent the last few years poring over these data as I engaged with others in a political battle in my home state to keep lethal weapons off our college campuses statewide. I will present these data to you, and I will document how you can access the information and fact-check my results. I will provide the results of my analysis for your inspection. I am completely confident that you will reach the same conclusion I have if you examine the same data that I did. That is how scientists operate. What is more, I believe we can draw important conclusions from those data, which demonstrate conclusively the efficacy of gun-safe colleges.

Those who have not examined the data speak incessantly on the grave danger that gun-safe zones pose to our society, telling you they are "magnets for murderers." The data I will present (which you can review for yourself) tell a stunningly different story. Gun-safe college campuses do not attract murderers—they are sanctuaries from them. I will repeat this statement often, and I will provide you with its empirical justification. Those who oppose my conclusions will do so with histrionic assertions, but they will provide no data to validate their hysteria, because the available data don't support their arguments. *Guns and College Homicide: The Case to Prohibit Firearms on Campus* tells of something that happens rarely or not at all. That is the point of this book.

1

My Journey to Sanctuary

"We must always take sides."

—*Elie Wiesel*

On 28 January 2013, I became an activist. I was not born to that métier. In fact, I never self-identified as an activist growing up or throughout my adult life until I wrote the first sentence of this chapter. I am the child of a very conservative Republican household with roots in New England puritanism. There is a long-standing family tale that we are related to notable Pilgrims and historic founders of Rhode Island and Hartford, Connecticut. I have seen several genealogies that purportedly trace those relations. These genealogies also suggest convoluted familial connections to several other famed Americans of the Puritan tradition in the 18th and 19th centuries, or so I am told. And maybe it's true or maybe it's not, but they're good family yarns either way, just like your family's legends.

I suppose the seeds of activism were planted within me several times during my life, but they took more than half a century to germinate and sprout. I remember the assassinations of Martin Luther King and Robert F. Kennedy in 1968, though vaguely. I remember evening news reports of the 1969 Cuyahoga River fire in Cleveland, Ohio.[1] I remember the first Earth Day observance in 1970,[2] and then, two weeks later, evening news footage of turmoil and violence as the Ohio National Guard ran amok at Kent State University.[3] I remember the ecology symbol and flag from the early 1970s. In junior high school, I discovered the books of the American conservationist John Muir at the public library in Huntington Beach, California. In the summer of 1974, my family traveled in a rented recreational vehicle from southern California to Concord, California, where my older brother was to participate in an athletic competition. I persuaded my parents to let me take my bicycle so I could go exploring rather than sit in the bleachers for the entire event. On one of those days, I rode my bike from Concord to Martinez, California, where I stumbled onto John Muir's house, a National Historic Site administered by the National Park Service. I suppose something there stuck with me.

For college, I chose to study environmental sciences at a small state university in the pristine environment of a town in far northern Minnesota, barely 100 miles from the international border with Canada. While there, I marveled almost every day at the freshness of that place and the abundant wildlife that lived practically within the city limits—deer, owls, bald eagles, porcupines, coyotes and foxes, as well as rivers and lakes full of fish of all kinds—and the seeming harmony in which those creatures coexisted with the local development. It was a great revelation to a young man who had spent half of his sentient life in southern California exurbs. My undergraduate curriculum required that every course I took had some component of conservation theory or practice as part of the course content. In that way, I was introduced to the conservation literature of Aldo Leopold and the more obscure (yet more profound) Sigurd F. Olson—activist, wilderness philosopher, and champion of the Boundary Waters Canoe Area and Voyageurs National Park. I read Rachel Carson's opus, *Silent Spring*,[4] and I learned about cross-country skiing through the Northwoods in deep fluffy snow on below-zero days of the long northern winter. Though I later changed my major to geology, I did not forget my early training in conservation or the serenity of solitude in my northern Minnesota sanctuary. All in all, that experience taught me a great deal and shaped my adult life.

I am a physical scientist by training, with bachelor's and master's degrees in geology and a doctorate in marine sciences (that is, oceanography). These academic pursuits were chosen simply because I found them interesting, was curious about the world around me and how it worked, and was fortunate to have opportunities to engage in earth science research in exotic places (Theodore Roosevelt National Park in western North Dakota, Big Bend National Park, Yellowstone National Park, the U.S. Virgin Islands, Jamaica, and the Bahamas) at the right times in my life to influence my future decisions: "Hey, this is a pretty cool place! Someone will pay me to study it? Neato!"

None of the foregoing information, of course, has anything whatsoever to do with guns or gun-safe colleges, but it has a great deal to do with my conceptualization of "sanctuary." For me, sanctuary is a place where tranquility and harmony coexist. It's a place conducive to contemplation and reflection, where discussion is stimulating, vigorous, and challenging while also being dignified and respectful. It's a place where ideas dominate over practices. Sanctuary exists for me as a place of youthful exuberance and optimism for better futures. It is a place of hopeful beginnings and successful outcomes. It is a place of magnificent beauty where the body, mind, and soul commune with the extraordinary nature of our planet—where we feel a part of all of it. In my sanctuary, reason prevails. Here facts are presented and interpretations of those facts are defended with logic and analysis. In my sanctuary, opinions are valued and respected, but only insofar as those opinions are based in fact-based evidence. In my sanctuary, lying is not permitted; those caught lying are banished. My sanctuary is an ideal space that I choose to inhabit. It does not exist in its ideal state in the real world, but I can imagine it in my mind's eye. Universities, though they are far from perfect realizations of sanctuary, for me are nonetheless the tangible manifestations of sanctuaries in our society. New York University president John Sexton delivered an eloquent discourse on "University as Sanctuary"[5] in 2004 in which he presented his own thoughts on the nature of sanctuary as represented by our great universities:

> Our great universities are modern sanctuaries, the sacred spaces sustaining and enhancing scholarship, creativity and learning. I use the word sanctuary here not to signal detachment from the world, for our universities increasingly are in and of their surroundings; rather I use the term to signal both the specialness of what our great universities do, and the fragility of the environment in which it is done.

"Fragility of the environment in which it is done." I know a thing or two about fragile environments. I have conducted research on coral reefs and in our national parks. My early academic scholarship was filled with words about fragility from our nation's greatest writers on the subject. "Sanctuary" is indeed fragile.

Continuing, President Sexton elaborates on the concept of sanctuary:

> What makes these sanctuaries special is the core commitment to free, unbridled and ideologically unconstrained discourse in which claims of knowledge are examined, confirmed, deepened or replaced. In this regard, I emphasize the importance of acting aggressively and with every means at our disposal to secure and protect every element essential to the general enterprise of free inquiry, the centrality of standards and the reciprocal commitments attendant to citizenship within the sanctuary.

Sexton also quotes Cardinal Newman, the 19th-century Anglican and Oxford professor, stating that a true university is a place

> in which the intellect may safely range and speculate, sure to find its equal in some antagonistic activity, and its judge in the tribunal of truth. It is a place where inquiry is pushed forward, and discoveries verified and perfected, and rashness rendered innocuous, and error exposed, by the collision of mind with mind, and knowledge with knowledge.

It is no coincidence that I and many of my colleagues regard the university as a sanctuary. Centuries ago, grand universities in England were established on a principle that is now known as the Anglo-Saxon University Model.[6] In this model, universities and university education were developed and administered by the clergy, often in monastic refugia, giving rise to the common architecture of many universities as campuses set apart from the communities they serve. In the monastic university architectural vernacular, students and faculty cohabitate on the campus, where they can, as President Sexton puts it, commit themselves to "understand and engage, through reasoned and civil intercourse, even the most provocative challenges to one's point of view."[7] American universities and colleges, in particular, employ this model. Many of our historic colleges and universities were established as "sanctuaries" dedicated to intensive intellectual development of the individuals within their walls, purposely removed from the distractions of everyday life in order to maximize the learning of their inhabitants and provide the tranquility necessary for deep thought and insightful investigation of our physical and metaphysical universes. Despite the current societal, political, and economic pressures to utterly overhaul higher education in the United States, we should all consider the purposeful construction of our universities and colleges as "learning sanctuaries" and the overwhelming, demonstrable success of this system during centuries of human enlightenment and progress. Our universities and colleges are indeed "sacred sanctuaries of thought" and deserving of our unyielding effort "to protect the university's sacred space," for failing to do so "would carry great risks that could threaten the very existence of our institutions and the character of our society."[8]

Given my stated view of sanctuary and my general agreement with President Sexton's address, it is no surprise that I was attracted to universities and have spent my entire adult life engaged in universities in some capacity, first and forever as student, but also as professor. Each day, I participate with many others as we strive to actualize the visions of sanctuary expressed above, and the closest we come is the university. I love universities and the ideal of sanctuary they represent to me despite their failings. My love of the university as a tangible expression of my ideal of sanctuary lies at the core of my activism to prevent the incursion of lethal weapons onto our nation's university and college campuses. You may agree or disagree with me. I can respect your disagreement so long as your disagreement is founded in reason and evidence (that is, data).

I became an activist on 28 January 2013, because our sanctuary was under assault from barbarians. See what I did there? "Sanctuary" is not my exclusive domain. Sanctuary is *ours*. You are deserving of it, too. I will welcome you if you want to be here with me. I will engage you as I have engaged literally thousands of students—others just like you—over my extensive career nurturing this sanctuary. Sanctuary belongs to all of us—the royal "we."

On 28 January 2013, the hordes were massing at the boundaries of our sanctuary, preparing to pour through the gates with guns. I made a decision to stand against them to defend our sanctuary. I fight for no other reason than because it's worth fighting to preserve sanctuary in our society. Not only should we fight to preserve it, but we should also be fighting to expand it. Everyone should have the privilege I have to experience sanctuary. And that is how I became an activist.

On that day in January, I responded to a request from a colleague at my university to sign an online petition informing the Arkansas General Assembly, our state's legislative body, that I was opposed to their efforts to introduce and pass legislation permitting the carrying of concealed, lethal weapons on college campuses statewide. I posted the following comment to my signature on that petition:

> I oppose legislation permitting carrying of concealed weapons on any campus of the University of Arkansas system or any other institution of higher learning in Arkansas. Current Arkansas law prohibiting concealed weapons on university campuses DOES NOT infringe the 2nd Amendment guarantee of citizens to keep and bear arms. This was made evident and unambiguous by the Supreme Court of the United States majority ruling in the landmark case of *District of Columbia vs. Heller* (2008). Presenting the majority opinion in that case, Justice Antonin Scalia wrote "Like most rights, the Second Amendment right is not unlimited. It is not a right to keep and carry any weapon whatsoever in any manner whatsoever and for whatever purpose: For example, concealed weapons prohibitions have been upheld under the Amendment or state analogues. The Court's opinion should not be taken to cast doubt on longstanding prohibitions on the possession of firearms by felons and the mentally ill, or laws forbidding the carrying of firearms in sensitive places such as schools and government buildings...." By specifically mentioning "schools" in this statement, the Supreme Court of the United States draws explicit attention to precedent indicating (for instance) that current Arkansas law prohibiting concealed carry on university campuses is a valid "regulation" of the 2nd Amendment under *District of Columbia vs. Heller*. Public safety on our state's university and college campuses is adequately provided by professional security forces. All citizens of Arkansas working at, attending courses at, or visiting our institutions of higher learning should rely on our duly-empowered peace officers to ensure tranquility and safety. Thank you for your learned and thoughtful consideration of this objection to proposed legislation permitting carrying of concealed weapons on campuses of Arkansas universities.

A day or so later, another colleague at the university approached me and requested that I co-sponsor a resolution to the faculty senate proclaiming opposition to an armed campus. I agreed.

The following Monday, 4 February 2013, I informed my institution's executive leaders, the chancellor and the provost, of my absolute moral opposition to any provision to permit guns on campus and my pledge to resist through noncooperation in the following email message:

Dear [Chancellor and Provost]:

I am taking a moment today to make you both aware of my absolute opposition to any efforts permitting weapons of any kind on our campus. While I am aware you both share my opposition to proposed efforts to repeal the long-standing prohibition to weapons on our campus, my statement to you both today is given with utmost respect as my formal declaration that I consider myself a "conscientious objector" on this topic. I hope you both will accept that I am not trying to rabble-rouse, but instead that I am attempting to develop a proactive strategy to work around legislation that I feel undermines the integrity of higher education. In the event that legislation permitting weapons of any kind on our campus becomes law, I will desire to meet with both of you to discuss how I might continue to serve the University of Arkansas while also honoring my absolute moral opposition to weapons on our campus. At this time, I share my current thoughts with you below.

With respect to courses I teach, I intend to take them all into the online domain should concealed weapons be permitted on campus. I feel it is my personal responsibility to ensure that students who do not want to be in classrooms with guns are not forced into that predicament. I don't want to be in a classroom with a gun either, and I would not want my daughters to attend an institution where it is permitted. While I do not necessarily desire to teach courses online, I see this as my only recourse to continue to meet my teaching obligations at the university.

The more challenging aspect will be participation in on-campus events (including commencement ceremonies), campus committees, faculty meetings, and other meetings. If faculty and staff are permitted to carry concealed weapons, I will ask at the beginning of each meeting if anyone is carrying a concealed weapon. If there is an affirmative answer, I will excuse myself from the meeting. If I am aware in advance that someone will be carrying a concealed weapon, I will request accommodation to "attend" the meeting via video feed (e.g. via Skype or alternative video conferencing capability).

I know you both are working hard to ensure that concealed weapons are not permitted on campus and I want you to know that you have my full support. However, I also wanted to make you both aware of my current state-of-mind and thoughts regarding my personal response if we should fail in this endeavor.

Respectfully submitted,
Steve
Stephen K. Boss, PhD, PG
Director, Environmental Dynamics Program

Into the breach I went. That is how my activism began. During the next few days, I met primarily with two university faculty colleagues to organize for nonviolent action. One, a professor of English, specialized in the literature of nonviolence and peace studies; the other was a professor of political communications. What could the physical science guy do to assist these people in creating an effective message opposing pro-gun legislation that was on the rocket rails to passage in a gun-loving, ultra-conservative state with gun-loving, ultra-conservative majorities in both chambers of the state legislature? I became "the data guy." My role in this unlikely academic alliance was acquiring and summarizing data related to guns, gun violence across the United States and in colleges nationwide, and other violent crimes on college campuses and in society at large. I provided fact-based information that the more-articulate-than-me English professor could translate into words and the more-politically-savvy-than-me communications professor could translate into effective public messages. And so we three sallied forth like Cervantes' paragons. Did we think we could possibly win this fight? Yes, we did. Just like Don Quixote of old.

2

A Grand Social Experiment

"...an infringement of the rights of an individual..."
—Francis Peyton Rous (editor, Journal
of Experimental Medicine, *1941)*

This book is a summary of research I began in 2013 (and continue today) to document the nature and incidence of homicides on college campuses nationwide. More generally, I will recount what I have learned regarding all collegiate homicides in the United States, with special reference to the incidence of gun homicides.

I want you to imagine a grand social experiment. Imagine a society awash with guns and drowning in gun violence. A society where the fear of becoming a victim of gun violence is tangible—every day. A place where that fear induces millions of citizens annually to purchase guns of all calibers and styles, presumably for self-protection. Imagine a society stoked on fear of being shot every day, where elected officials simultaneously respond and contribute to that fear with multiple, repeating legislative acts making it easier for citizens to own guns and permitting citizens to carry those guns in more and more public spaces. You want to own guns with unlimited firing capacity? Enacted. You want armor-piercing ammunition for your gun? Enacted. You want to carry those guns concealed or openly in public? Enacted. You want to carry those guns without permits? Enacted. You want to carry your gun at the grocery store? Enacted. Carry a gun at the shopping mall? Enacted. Carry a gun at a movie theater? Enacted. Carry a gun at an elementary school? Enacted. Carry a gun at any public school? Enacted. Carry a gun at the state capitol? Enacted. Carry a gun at a bar? Enacted. Carry a gun at a restaurant? Enacted. Carry a gun at a courthouse? Enacted. Carry a gun at the post office? Enacted. Carry a gun at a gas station? Enacted. Carry a gun to church? Enacted. Carry a gun in a national park? Enacted. Carry a gun in a municipal park? Enacted. Carry a gun to a children's sporting event? Enacted. Carry a gun to your workplace? Enacted. Carry a gun in your car? Enacted. Carry a gun in a hospital?

Enacted. Carry a gun at a mental institution? Enacted. Carry a gun to a mass shooting? Enacted. Carry a gun on a college campus? Not so fast, gunslinger!

Since 2007, bills to permit the carrying of concealed handguns on college campuses have been introduced in nearly 40 states.[1] In a number of states, bills permitting citizens to carry concealed handguns appear in every legislative session, year after year after year. When they fail, they simply get reintroduced the next year. Do college administrations want to permit guns on their campuses? No.[2] Do campus police want to permit guns on their campuses? No.[3] Do college faculty want guns on their campuses and in their classrooms? No.[4] Do college students want guns on campus? No.[5] Do college mental health professionals want guns on campus? No.[6] Does the general public want guns on college campuses? No.[7] It's perfectly obvious that no one engaged in the collegiate endeavor wants guns on campus. Still, in 2013, the year after the mass shooting at Sandy Hook Elementary School, 19 state legislatures considered bills to permit lethal, concealed weapons on college campuses. Two states passed versions of "guns on campus" bills that year.

In Kansas, a law was enacted in 2013 that permitted the carrying of concealed handguns in any public building statewide. Guns could be prohibited from a public building if (and only if) that facility had adequate security at each entrance and exit to the building. In this case, "adequate security" meant a metal detector staffed by trained security personnel. Of course, very few public buildings can accommodate this legislative requirement, and such an arrangement would be virtually impossible at a university. Consider all the buildings on a single campus and all the entrances and exits that would require a metal detector and security staff. The framers of the bill understood that impossibility. That's why they included it. The framers "generously" granted a 4-year moratorium on implementation of the law to give public facilities an opportunity to acquire adequate security if they chose to do so. Most government buildings have no mechanism to do this—they depend on state allocations of funds for their operating expenses, and the Kansas legislature was in no mood to appropriate additional funds for "adequate security." See how that works? Courthouses, jails, prisons, airports, and other such buildings that generally already had metal detectors and the corresponding security staff may still prohibit guns in Kansas. However, everyone else had a deadline to permit concealed handguns in their public facilities beginning on 1 July 2017. Did I mention that the on-campus residences of university and college presidents in Kansas are public buildings and those people are required by state law to permit visitors to carry concealed handguns into their homes?[8]

The other state to authorize "guns on campus" in 2013 was Arkansas—

my state. However, in Arkansas, Act 226 was enacted with a significant concession by its sponsor. He offered this concession at the 11th hour because his signature legislation was going to lose in committee without it. Whereas Act 226 permitted only faculty and staff with Arkansas Concealed Handgun Licenses (ACHLs) to carry their lethal weapons on campus, the governing board of each institution could vote on an annual basis to opt out of the law—that is, the board of trustees of each higher education institution in the state could vote to overrule the law and continue the long-held statewide tradition of prohibiting guns and other lethal weapons on campus. In other words, the Arkansas General Assembly passed a law in 2013 requiring college campuses to comply with the law unless their boards of trustees vote every year to ignore the law. That, right there, is what we call "fancy legislatin.'"

How did that go in Arkansas? In 2013, all 52 institutions of higher education (private and public 4-year universities and colleges, private and public 2-year colleges, and private and public technical institutes) voted to opt out of the law and prohibited guns on their campuses. In 2014, all 52 institutions once again voted to opt out of the law and continued to prohibit guns on their campuses. In 2015, for the third consecutive cycle, every higher education institution in the state voted to opt out of the law, and guns remained banned on campuses. In 2016, it was another clean sweep: every institution of higher education in the state (all 52 individual campuses) voted unanimously to opt out (i.e., ignore this law) and ban guns on campus. Do you think Arkansas universities and colleges were sending a message to the Arkansas General Assembly?

So, recapping the above information, two states passed "guns on campus" laws in 2013, but neither state actually permitted guns on campus in 2013. No other bills passed state legislatures that year.

In 2014, only 6 state legislatures put forward bills to permit lethal, concealed weapons on college campuses—primarily because a number of legislatures (such as Arkansas) don't convene for legislative action during even-numbered years. Nonetheless, of the 6 legislatures that considered "guns on campus" bills in 2014, only the Idaho legislature enacted one over the vociferous and well-publicized objections of higher education professionals (administrators, faculty, students, police—just about everyone).[9] The Idaho campus-carry law forced public universities statewide to allow persons with Idaho "enhanced" concealed handgun permits to carry their guns onto campus and into classrooms. Did anyone ask the parents of Idaho college students if they wanted guns on college campuses? I don't think so. Imagine how you might have felt as a parent reading the news that your daughter was one of 19 students in chemistry class at Idaho State University when the professor with the enhanced CHL shot himself in the foot with the gun he was licensed to carry in his pants pocket.[10] You can't make that up. And you can't recount that story often enough to illustrate the clear and present danger that armed, inexperienced civilians pose to all of us with their concealed handguns.

In 2015, 15 state legislatures took up "guns on campus" bills, and Texas passed one, despite the vociferous objections of the public,[11] college communities,[12] and law enforcement statewide.[13] "Guns on campus" bills failed in all 14 remaining states.

In 2016, 18 states considered "guns on campus" bills and two bills passed their legislatures, but only one was enacted. Georgia passed a bill that was vetoed by Governor Nathan Deal, and the legislature was unable to muster sufficient votes to override the governor's veto. By contrast, Tennessee passed a bill and Governor Bill Haslam allowed it to become law without his signature. In Tennessee, full-time employees (but not students) at public institutions of higher education are now permitted to carry concealed handguns at most campus facilities if they have a valid concealed weapons permit. The law requires persons carrying concealed weapons to register with campus public safety officials and exempts the institution from monetary liability should one of these licensed, registered carriers fire their weapon in self-defense.

Across the United States in recent years, laws expanding permission to carry guns into more and more public places have been passed in almost every state. Yet few states have adopted laws permitting lethal, concealed weapons on college campuses. That fact makes the premise of this book pertinent and increasingly relevant. What is the motivation for state legislatures to force guns onto college campuses? Some states have been trying to pass this type of legislation almost every year since 2008 (I'm talking to you, Arizona, Michigan, Ohio, Oklahoma, and Virginia)—and so far they have failed. People don't want guns on college campuses. So let's get back to the purpose of this book.

The premise of the book is straightforward and elegantly simple. At the opening of this chapter, I asked that you imagine a grand social experiment. I asked you to imagine a society awash with guns and drowning in gun violence. Do you have this image in your mind? Okay, so here's the experiment: Into this society awash with guns and drowning in gun violence, let's create a nationwide archipelago of "gun-safe zones"—spaces where guns are prohibited outright. Scatter those gun-safe spaces across every state. Put them in urban centers, rural areas, suburbs, affluent communities and communities wracked with poverty. Put them in communities dominated by white people, or African Americans, or people of Hispanic or Asian descent, or any other group you can imagine. Put them in crime-ridden inner cities. Put them on sprawling estates. Put them among farm fields, in deserts, near beaches, on lakeshores, and in the mountains. Make sure they are scattered throughout the land in all conceivable environments. Now populate those gun-safe zones with tens of millions of unarmed citizens drawn from the general population. Just imagine this scenario—tens of millions of your countrymen, unarmed and defenseless in isolated enclaves surrounded by a society awash with guns and drowning in gun violence. Now, let that experiment run for many decades and observe what happens to the experimental subjects. What do you predict will happen? Will the criminals running amok in the society surrounding every gun-safe zone descend en masse on the poor, defenseless subjects in this experiment? Will those heavily armed thugs rob, rape, and murder every one of those people? Will there be a merciless, unrelenting slaughter? Who would even volunteer to participate in this experiment? Would you? What kind of society would even permit such an experiment? Surely it's illegal to purposefully, knowingly, and willfully endanger that many people across any nation? If anyone ever attempted to carry out such an experiment, they would certainly be prevented from doing so. If I tried to design this experiment and conduct it as a research project, my institution would never approve it. The risks of harm to the experimental subjects are just too great. And yet…

What I have described is precisely the experiment that is "on" across our nation. Embedded in our gun-ridden society, we have created a nationwide archipelago of gun-safe zones, represented in part by our universities, colleges, and technical institutes. Think about that. Very likely it never occurred to you that this is a grand social experiment. Now you know. I am one of the experimental subjects; I have been involved directly in this experiment for 41 years. By writing this book, I became the documentarian of the experiment.

Remember, I'm a physical scientist by training. I understand experiments and experimentation. I know an experiment when I see one. I am an expert in the scientific method. You probably learned about the scientific method for the first time in a middle school science class. What are the elements of the scientific method? In the grade-school version, the scientific method has a series of steps. Do you remember them?[14]

The scientific method begins with an observation. I made an observation at the outset of this book. In the preface, I noted that I've been involved in higher education for my entire adult life—4 decades. I also noted that in my career, crossing the United States at a number of universities, I never encountered gun violence personally. I noted that it seemed very few other people affiliated with colleges and universities had personally encountered gun violence on their campuses and that, overall, gun violence seemed to be a rare occurrence on college campuses across America. That experience appears to contrast with the prevalence of gun violence in the U.S. general public. On balance, it seemed to me that college campuses are relatively peaceful, safe enclaves with low rates of violent crime.

However, as I recounted above, there are members of our society who currently present a very different view. Conservative politicians across the nation suggest that college campuses are not safe. They believe that everyone is in grave danger and, at any moment, anyone might appear on campus to do great harm to the innocent inhabitants. They argue that we need to permit those inhabitants to carry concealed, lethal weapons for their own protection from the criminals stalking their campus. They argue that society, on the whole, is so dangerous that every one of us should consider carrying a concealed handgun all the time, everywhere we go, including into my university classrooms.

So now I have two observations that don't comport with each other. Indeed, they seem mutually exclusive. College campuses are either safe or unsafe. My personal experience of 41 years in the academy is challenged directly by elected representatives in at least 40 states where legislation has been introduced to permit people to carry guns for their own protection on college campuses. Well, which is it? Safe or unsafe? Dangerous or not dangerous? This raises a lot of questions in a scientist's mind. Is my experience on campus unusual? Have I just been extraordinarily lucky throughout my entire adult life on campus? Are campuses actually much more dangerous than I perceive? Or are college campuses much safer than my opponents understand? Perhaps the truth lies in the middle somewhere? How do I respond to those who claim our nation's higher education system is inherently violent and dangerous? Perhaps I should just shout back, "No, it isn't!" To which they will likely respond "Yes, it is!" "No, it isn't!" "Yes, it is!" This method won't resolve anything. The scientist recognizes the nature of the scientific question to be asked.

Are college campuses in the United States safe or unsafe? That is the foundational question being asked as the premise for this book. More to the point, are you more or less likely to be murdered on a college campus or in the general public in the United States? Now we have a question that can be answered with research. We've stated some observations and we've posed relevant questions. We're applying the scientific method. The next step is to formulate a hypothesis from those questions—a hypothesis that can be tested experimentally with data.

We wish to know whether colleges are more safe or less safe than society at large. However, that's not a very useful formulation because it's rather vague. "More safe or less safe"—safe from what? Perhaps you might answer, "Safe from criminals," but that's vague, too. Criminals come in many forms. Do you mean safe from all criminals, or safe from certain classes of criminals? My opponents nationally suggest that colleges are unsafe from criminals in general, but one of their primary concerns is that colleges are especially unsafe from murderers armed with guns. That's the main reason why they want to permit others to carry guns—so they can defend themselves from the gun-wielding murderers who are coming to the campus. We want to know whether colleges are more safe or less safe from murderers than society at large.

Okay, here's how we would state the hypothesis we want to test. We make an assertion that the incidence of homicides on college campuses is no different from the incidence of homicides in society at large. That is a testable assertion. We can test it by gathering data for homicides in society at large and data for homicides on college campuses and comparing them. There are three possible outcomes to this test: (1) we discover that the incidence of homicides on college campuses really is no different from the incidence of homicides in society at large; (2) we discover that the incidence of collegiate homicides is different from the incidence of homicides in society at large; or (3) the results are inconclusive. In the first outcome, my opponents are correct and the prospect for gun violence on college campuses is the same as it is throughout the United States. In the second outcome, there are two possibilities: First, homicides (and, specifically, gun homicides) on college campuses have a significantly higher incidence than in U.S. society—a revelation that would likely substantiate my opponents' claims that we need to arm people for their own protection while attending college. The alternative outcome would demonstrate that the incidence of homicide (and gun homicide) on college campuses is significantly lower than in society at large, substantiating my personal experience during the last 41 years of my professional life in college, and supporting my argument that we should continue to prohibit lethal weapons on college campuses because these campuses are sanctuaries from violence. In the third case, in which we have an inconclusive result, we may need to reconsider the nature of the question or restate it with different criteria in order to find the answer we seek.

At any rate, we have made an observation, we've asked some questions that might be answered with research, and we've hypothesized what the answers might be when we complete that research. Those are the first three steps in the scientific method. Now it remains for us to define an experiment and devise the experimental protocol that will yield data bearing on the answers we seek.

So it is that I will detail for you the results of this experiment. In the pages to follow, I will first describe the general state of gun violence in the United States in this century and the gun culture that gave rise to it. Using the best available data documenting the nature and incidence of gun violence in the United States, you will become aware of the present state of our society and know the facts regarding gun violence to provide context for understanding the same phenomenon on college campuses. Following that, I will tell you how I gathered my data regarding homicides in general, and gun homicides in particular, on college campuses nationwide. Then I will complete this book with several chapters of data documenting every known homicide on a college campus from 2001 to 2016 (the full period of data availability).

I'm here to report the results of the experiment. You will need to decide for yourself what those results mean and how society should respond. I am merely the documentarian. I'll provide you with the results of the experiment, as well as the data and where I sourced it. You'll be able to fact-check me if you want to. One way or another, the truth will out.

3

Gun Violence
in the United States

"Welcome to ... Thunderdome!"

We have a daunting task ahead. We need to document the prevalence of homicides and gun homicides in U.S. society at large. Then we need to do the same for college campuses nationwide. Next, we need to compare those two sets of statistics and determine whether they are the same, different, or inconclusive. How do we begin? Here's how a scientist would do it.

We're going to search for data detailing U.S. homicides in general and gun homicides in particular. I'm going to tell you what we know about gun violence and the gun culture that spawns it in the United States. It's going to be a rough, bumpy ride, so buckle up. What's coming is a brutal statistical beat-down that will exhaust you. I'm sorry for that. But it's necessary to really comprehend the state of U.S. society in the 21st century. It's a hard read. It's overwhelming. It's grotesque. It's awful. It's 21st-century America. I expect that many readers won't like this. In reality, no one should like this. Every one of us should read what follows and recoil in horror at the end of every sentence. It's sickening. Again, I'm sorry, but I want you to know what I know. I want you to see the background violence across the general public so you too, have a thorough understanding of the nature of gun violence in America. Once you've acquired that understanding, we'll do the same for homicides and gun violence incidents on college campuses nationwide. Then you will be able to accurately compare the two. Then, maybe, at the end of this book, you'll see a way forward. Perhaps you'll join me in a nationwide struggle to preserve sanctuary on our college campuses. You'll join me in a nationwide effort to expand sanctuary across society for every person. You deserve it. We all deserve it. We need to fight for it, because there are those in our society who want to take it away and guarantee that you never feel safe. Ever. They can't be allowed to win. So let's get on with it. Let's have a look at gun violence in the United States. If you find that you need to take a break while reading this chapter, do it. I know as well as anyone that statistics can be ponderous and stultifying. Put the book down for a few minutes. Walk away for a bit. But then come back and finish this chapter. Get through it. You need to know, and, I promise, it gets better.

Our nation is awash in guns. There are more guns in the United States than people. In 2013, the Congressional Research Service estimated that there were 114 million handguns, 110 million rifles, and 86 million shotguns in the United States.[1] Currently, there are more than 120 guns for every 100 people in the United States.[2] And the guns are proliferating faster than the people. According to the World Bank,[3] population growth in the United States since 2010 averaged about 0.8% annually, meaning that we add about 2.6 million people each year.[4] How many guns did we add? Unfortunately, total gun sales in the United States are unknown, so it is not possible to document with certainty how many guns are purchased annually. Sales records of individual guns are not directly tracked (an act of willful ignorance by our nation). Tabulations of criminal background checks nationwide provide only an estimate of gun transactions.

The National Instant Criminal Background Check System (NICS) may be activated for reasons other than gun purchases. For instance, NICS background checks are used by states to check qualifications for explosives permits. In 2016, there were 89,512 background checks for explosives permits; 1,810 explosives permit applications were denied. NICS background checks are also used by states to check qualifications for concealed handgun licenses, which aren't necessarily related directly to gun sales. In many instances, persons applying for concealed handgun permits already own guns. In addition, multiple guns may be purchased for each criminal background check, so there isn't necessarily a one-to-one correlation there. Further, NICS checks will apply to an individual buying a new gun or a used one from a federal firearms licensee (FFL). In the case of a new gun purchase, this transaction results in an additional gun in circulation in America. For a used gun purchase, it simply transfers ownership from one gun owner to another—a zero-sum outcome. Finally, not all gun sales require background checks. Well-known loopholes for purchasing guns without background checks (such as at gun shows, from online sellers, or through private transactions) account for an unknown number of the total annual gun transactions in the United States. A lesser-known factor is that 26 states exempt persons with concealed handgun licenses from background checks.[5] In more than half the states, a concealed handgun license holder can purchase as many guns as they want without background checks! Nonetheless, NICS checks indicate extraordinary gun-related transactions in the United States.

The FBI reported that the National Instant Criminal Background Check System (NICS) processed 27,538,673 background checks in 2016. On average, that's 2,294,889 background checks per month; 75,448 background checks per day; 3,134 background checks per hour; 52 background checks per minute; or almost 1 background check every second!

The FBI reported 27,538,673 background checks in 2016 and approved 27,418,176.[6] A mere 0.44% of applications (120,497 applicants) were denied. The other 99.56% presumably followed through with their gun-related transaction, most of which were likely gun purchases. On a single day in 2012 (21 December 2012, to be exact), the FBI's NICS system received 177,170 requests for criminal background checks.[7] It is notable that this single-day record for criminal background checks was one week to the day after the mass shooting at Sandy Hook Elementary School in Newtown, Connecticut. It was also the same day that NRA executive vice president Wayne LaPierre delivered this infamous declaration: "The only thing that stops a bad guy with a gun is a good guy with a gun."[8] Coincidence? In the week following Sandy Hook, from Sunday, 16 December 2012, to Saturday, 22 December 2012, the NICS processed slightly less than 1 million (953,653) background checks,[9] and we must presume the great majority of those resulted in gun sales.

So the NICS is an imperfect source of information on the total number of attempts to purchase guns from federal firearms licensees, and it doesn't let us know how many guns were purchased from a single background check (or if the background check was even for a gun purchase), and you can legally buy guns without a background check in most states through a variety of loopholes. It's a diabolical system of deliberate stupidity specifically intended to prevent accurate accounting and obfuscate gun ownership in America.

Are there other means to determine how many guns are sold in the United States annually? We might look at total gun production reported by gun manufacturers. What do those data reveal? The U.S. Bureau of Alcohol, Tobacco, and Firearms (ATF) reports annually on U.S. gun production, exports, and imports. In 2013, the year following the Sandy Hook Elementary School mass shooting (which occurred on 14 December 2012), U.S gun manufacturers produced a record 10,349,650 firearms: 725,282 revolvers, 4,441,726 semi-automatic pistols, 3,979,570 rifles, and 1,203,072 shotguns.[10] I'm not a particularly good capitalist, but I'm smart enough to know that record production is the business response to record demand. Gun manufacturers didn't produce those weapons to remain in inventory. We should assume that those guns were produced in response to orders for guns. Of the weapons produced in 2013, only 370,373 were exported (21,236 revolvers, 167,653 semi-automatic pistols, 131,718 rifles, 49,766 shotguns). An additional 5,539,539 guns were imported to the United States that year (3,095,528 handguns, 1,507,776 rifles, 936,235 shotguns). In total, 15,564,816 new guns appeared in America and were likely sold in 2013—nearly 6 new guns for each new member of the U.S. population that year. To be fair, the commerce statistics reported by the ATF include firearms purchases by domestic law enforcement agencies but exclude military firearms orders. The 2012 Small Arms Survey[11] estimated, however, that U.S. law enforcement agencies (municipal and state police plus federal law enforcement) possessed a mere 1,150,000 firearms nationwide, and they weren't all replaced with new purchases in 2013. So there's that.

Domestic manufacturing production and imports might account reasonably well for sales of *new* guns,[12] but we have no way of tracking sales of used firearms in the United States. If we assume that each NICS background check was for the purchase of a single new gun produced in 2013, there remains a surplus of more than 5 million NICS background check applications for 2013, and it's not unreasonable to suggest that most of those remaining checks were for gun sales. Considering that it isn't possible to know what fraction of the more than 15 million guns arriving in the United States in 2013 were sold and that we have no reliable estimates of the commerce in new and used guns sold without background checks through various legal loopholes and that we don't know how many firearms are purchased when a background check is approved for gun purchase, I'm going to argue that there were between 16 million and 20 million new and used guns sold in the United States in 2013. I think that's a conservative estimate. Prove me wrong.

A decade ago, 35% of all guns in the world were owned by residents of the United States. If guns owned by military and law enforcement entities were excluded from the total above, American residents (who constituted little more than 5% of the global population) owned almost half of all guns in civilian hands worldwide.[13] The U.S. military forces and combined law enforcement agencies nationwide owned approximately 4.2 million guns.[14] Civilians in the United States owned 74 times more guns than the military and police—74 guns for every military and law enforcement weapon. General Custer wouldn't stand a chance. And that was 10 years ago. Between 2007 and 2014, no fewer than 72 million additional guns were introduced to the United States.[15] It is estimated, then, that there are 380 million to 400 million guns in civilian hands across our nation,[16] and that's probably a conservative estimate.

Increasingly, it's perfectly legal to display that firepower in public everywhere in America. In at least two instances in the last few years, individuals legally carrying semi-automatic rifles modeled after military weapons opened fire on an unsuspecting public: in Colorado Springs, 3 people plus the shooter were killed,[17] and in Dallas, 5 police officers plus the shooter were killed and 7 other people wounded.[18]

Gun ownership by civilians in the United States (>100 guns per 100 people) is the highest in the world. The nation with the next highest gun ownership rate is Serbia, where there are 58 guns per 100 people. The situation in Serbia translates to a total number of guns in civilian possession of about 3,050,000 compared to 380,000,000–400,000,000 in the United States—in other words, there are more than 100 times more guns here than in Serbia.

In a nation awash with guns, it is no surprise our society is drowning in gun violence. More than 100,000 Americans are shot every year. More than thirty thousand Americans die from gunfire every year. Annually, more than 19,000 commit suicide by gun or are killed in negligent shootings; more than 11,000 are victims of gun homicide.[19] Every year in America.

Each year, gun violence in the United States kills a number of people equivalent to the population of College Park, Maryland, or Wake Forest, North Carolina, or Walla Walla, Washington. Since 2001, so many Americans have perished in acts of gun violence that it is as if we eliminated every resident of Manchester, Connecticut; Kingman, Arizona; Key West, Florida; Kennesaw, Georgia; Highland Park, Illinois; Valparaiso, Indiana; Mason City, Iowa; Gloucester or Northampton or Watertown, Massachusetts; Albert Lea and Brainerd, Minnesota; Kearney, Nebraska; Williamsport, Pennsylvania; Waxahachie, Texas; Petersburg, Virginia; and Laramie, Wyoming. Try to imagine vanquishing every living person in Englewood, Colorado, or Poughkeepsie, New York, next year. This is the toll that gun violence exacts on American society. Every year.

If the loudly crowed warnings of the National Rifle Association, National Shooting Sports Foundation, and National Association for Gun Rights make you fearful of the possibility of a mass shooting in the United States, you need to understand that 21st-century America *is* a mass shooting in progress! A 2013 report from the nonprofit organization Mayors Against Illegal Guns documented 93 mass shootings nationwide between 2009 and the Washington Navy Yard incident in September 2013[20]—an average of almost 2 mass shootings every month during that time period. However, that's a gross underestimate. Following the mass shooting at Sandy Hook Elementary School in December 2012, the Gun Violence Archive (GVA; http://www.gunviolence archive.org/) was established to accurately track and document incidents of gun violence across America. Privately financed, GVA is a major source of information for all acts of gun violence in the United States, including mass shootings. Mass shootings are defined by the FBI as a single incident in which 4 or more individuals are shot, being either killed or wounded. In its first full year of reporting (2014), GVA documented 277 mass shootings across America—an average of 1 mass shooting every 1.3 days. In 2015, the documented number of mass shootings rose to 333, or nearly 1 mass shooting daily. In 2016, there were 383 mass shootings, including what is now the second worst mass shooting in U.S. history in Orlando, Florida, on 12 June 2016 (49 murdered, plus the shooter killed by police, and 53 wounded). In 2017, GVA recorded 346 mass shootings, including the worst mass shooting in U.S. history on 1 October 2017 in Las Vegas, Nevada (59 killed and 441 wounded in a single incident as a man opened fire on a country music concert from the 32nd floor of a Las Vegas hotel). For the last 3 years, America averaged more than 1 mass shooting every day. EVERY DAY! Be warned: In our "shining city on a hill," those "thousand points of light" are muzzle flashes!

Every day, 342 Americans are shot, and 96 of those Americans die from that daily gunfire: 59 commit suicide by gun, 34 are murdered, 1 is killed by negligent discharge of a gun, and 1 is gunned down by police. Every day, 246 Americans survive shootings: 183 are shot in gun assaults, 49 are victims of negligent shootings, 11 survive an attempted suicide by gun, and 4 survive police shootings.[21] Every day in America.

Every hour, 4 Americans die from gunfire. Another 10 survive a shooting. In the time it takes an average American to read this chapter,[22] one of our fellow citizens will fall to bullets. Every 15 minutes in America.

On 14 December 2012, Americans let out a collective horrified gasp as we learned that 20 precious children aged 6–7 years old had been gunned down with 6 of their courageous teachers at Sandy Hook Elementary School in Newtown, Connecticut. Their assailant took his own life by gun. Twenty-seven people perished in a hailstorm of 155 bullets in 5 minutes.[23] Then we learned the shooter had already killed his mother earlier that day. Twenty-eight lives ended with guns.

In truth, 14 December 2012, was just another day in gun-ridden America, where the blood flows from sea to shining sea. Can we muster a collective horrified gasp every day?

Gun violence is so pervasive in America that it took less than six months following Newtown for more daughters and sons to be slain with guns than were felled in 11 years of combat and military occupation in Iraq.[24] Ask yourself where the real war zone is.

So pervasive is gun violence in America that on 14 December 2012 we created a grim new unit of measure to help us cope with the overwhelming quantity of gun violence facing us every day. It is the "Newtown." We now measure gun violence relative to the number of precious souls lost in the mass shooting at Sandy Hook Elementary School. Twenty-six innocent women and children plus one perpetrator and his mother dispatched by gun violence equals one Newtown. This new unit of measure assigns a small numerical value to a large number of gun victims so we are less traumatized … for a while. Every day in America, ninety-six Americans die from gunfire, or 3.4 Newtowns—ho hum. Every month in America, we experience almost 103 Newtowns … hmmm. Every year, gun homicides in America amount to 393 Newtowns. Gun suicides and negligent shootings slay another 679 Newtowns. That's 1,072 Newtowns every year in America … are you paying attention yet?

The gun carnage afflicts every demographic in the United States. The Centers for Disease Control and Prevention maintains a searchable, interactive online database known as the Web-based Injury Statistics Query and Reporting System (WISQARS, pronounced "whiskers") to document injuries to persons from many sources, including fatal injuries due to violence.[25] From 2000 to 2016, 6,938 children between 0 and 14 years old were killed by firearms—almost 248 Newtowns in 17 years. During the same interval, 112,930 teens and young adults (ages 15–24 years old) were victims of gun violence throughout the United States—more than 4,033 Newtowns. That's 237 Newtowns per year, or one Newtown every 37 hours among America's 15–24-year-old daughters and sons.

People older than 24 years were almost equally likely to be victims of gun play, though the total number of victims falls with age. Of course, this tally reflects, in part, fewer numbers of individuals in higher age groups; nonetheless, no group in U.S. society is immune from gun violence. From 2000 to 2016, 108,560 Americans aged 25–34 years were killed with guns (3,877 Newtowns); 86,937 people aged 35–44 years old were murdered, committed suicide, or were negligently killed by gun (3,104 Newtowns); 84,193 adults aged 45–54 years succumbed to gun violence (3,006 Newtowns); 61,660 folks nearing retirement age (55–64 years old) were prematurely "retired" in gun-related incidents (2,202 Newtowns); 39,598 senior citizens aged 65–74 years died by gunfire (1,414 Newtowns); and 30,722 of our elders aged 75–84 years (1,097 Newtowns) and 11,948 persons older than 85 years all died from guns in some manner (427 Newtowns). In total, 543,663 individuals—the equivalent of nearly 19,417 Newtowns—were dispatched in acts of gun violence in 17 years. What a mind-numbing number of gun fatalities! It's difficult to make that value register in one's consciousness. It's unfathomable. It's as if we made every resident of Albuquerque, New Mexico; or Tucson, Arizona; or Milwaukee, Wisconsin, disappear. You knew these people. They had families and friends. In America, 50% of people know someone who was victimized by gun violence.[26] Among those polled, 22% claim to know someone killed by another person with a gun, and an additional 28% knew someone who committed suicide with a gun.

Annually, 2,868 children and teens (ages 0–19) die from gunfire,[27] or 102 Newtowns. Teens and young adults (ages 15–24) are the age group most at risk of being victimized by gun violence. Firearm-related homicides, suicides and negligent shootings affecting 15–24-year-olds in the United States outnumber total mortality from the next nine causes listed in official records.[28] Annually, almost 6,700 girls and boys—young women and young men, our sons and daughters—in this age group are killed from various forms of gun violence (homicide, suicide, negligent shootings), totaling 239 Newtowns every year.

If we become frightened by the total number of Newtowns annually in America, we can adopt a new unit of measure—perhaps the "Las Vegas." On 1 October 2017, 58 people were murdered at an outdoor country music concert in Las Vegas, Nevada. The perpetrator opened fire on the venue from the 32nd floor of a luxury hotel almost a quarter-mile away. He used multiple assault rifles modified to discharge rounds at a rate commensurate with that of a fully automatic weapon. He killed 58 people and wounded nearly 500 others. It takes almost 2.1 Newtowns to equal a Las Vegas. Well, rounding down, it is two Newtowns for 1 Las Vegas. So let's start measuring our gun-related fatalities by the "Las Vegas" unit. That will make it all seem better—for a while, anyway.

Critics of the preceding recitation of statistics demonstrating widespread gun violence in United States society will argue that the presentation of raw numbers is misleading because it does not adequately allow for direct comparison with raw numbers derived from populations of differing sizes. For example, in 2009 around 16,800 Americans were victims of homicide through any method (guns, knives, beatings, etc.)[29] among a population of about 300,000,000. By comparison, during the same year about the same number of people were murdered in South Africa (16,800)[30] among a population of 50,000,000. In absolute numbers, the number of people killed in South Africa and the United States in 2009 was the same. However, the population of South Africa is only one-sixth that of the United States. So how should we compare deaths due to violence in South Africa and the United States?

Demographers make comparisons using normalization schemes such that numerical values become directly comparable, for instance, on a per capita or per cent or "per something" measure of population. Of course, I am able to recast the numbers presented in this chapter in those terms so we can evaluate the occurrence of acts of gun violence in the United States relative to their frequency across demographic groups, which can be more meaningful depending on the context of the discussion. Most often, crime statistics of all types, including statistics on gun homicides, are reported as the number of incidents per 100,000 members of the nation's population. This is a relatively simple value to derive. To calculate this number, one simply divides the total number of occurrences of a particular crime by the total national population. This calculation yields the observed frequency of the crime per person within the nation of interest. Multiplying the value of crime frequency per person by 100,000 will then yield the number of observed incidents of that crime (i.e., its frequency) per 100,000 people in the population. In our example above, we concluded that the absolute number of people murdered in South Africa and the United States in 2009 was the same: approximately 16,800 persons in each country. And this value is correct in absolute terms. If we consider, however, the observed frequency of murder per 100,000 population in each country, we arrive at a very different conclusion. Dividing the number of persons killed in each nation by that nation's population, and then multiplying the result by 100,000, yields the following values:

South Africa: (16,800 murders ÷ 50,000,000 people) × 100,000 = 33.6
United States: (16,800 murders ÷ 300,000,000 people) × (100,000) = 5.6

The above calculations show that the South African homicide rate in 2009 was 33.6 persons per 100,000, or six times higher than the homicide rate of 5.6 persons per 100,000 in the United States during the same year.

The method described above is "scalable," meaning that we can use it to describe crimes across a variety of spatial scales. Above, we compared homicides in South Africa and America—that is, at a national scale. However, we could use this same method to describe violent crime rates within U.S states (state scale) or even to describe crime rates at the scale of individual municipalities. Let's see how that might work.

During the last decade or so, much media attention in the United States focused on the rate of gun homicides in Chicago. Of course, Chicago is a big city, and it has many issues that most of us associate with big cities, one of which is a reported crime rate significantly higher than the national norm. But how high is it? What if we compared Chicago's gun homicide rate to that of another city? There is a lot of national press handwringing about the rate of gun homicide in Chicago, but much less about the rate of gun homicide in New Orleans. So let's compare the two cities using the most recent data available.

As stated earlier, the Gun Violence Archive (GVA) is a privately funded, nonpartisan, nonprofit organization tasked with tracking incidents of gun violence across the United States.[31] Its data are publicly available from a website, and you can obtain customized gun violence statistics on request in some instances. GVA began tracking U.S. gun violence incidents on 1 January 2014, so this date provides a convenient starting point for our comparison of gun homicides in Chicago versus those in New Orleans. From 1 January 2014 to early September 2016, GVA documented 1,340 gun homicides in Chicago and 461 in New Orleans—nearly three times more gun murders in Chicago than New Orleans! Clearly, Chicago is much more dangerous than New Orleans, and the national press is rightly focused on gun violence in the "City of Big Shoulders," right? No.

To comprehend the gun violence in either city, comparatively, we need to make a valid comparison. Apples to apples, and all that. To be sure, the total number of gun murders in Chicago is almost three times higher than total gun deaths in New Orleans—1,340 to 461. But Chicago is a city of almost 2.7 million people, whereas New Orleans is a city of about 380,000 people (which is equal to 0.38 million). In other words, Chicago has more than 7 times more people than New Orleans. In a nation awash with guns and drowning in gun violence, we should expect there to be more gun murders in Chicago than New Orleans simply because Chicago has so many more people than New Orleans. Indeed, this is true. Dramatically so. Chicago has almost three times more gun murders than New Orleans, but we need to scale those murders against the population somehow in order to make a valid comparison. We need to normalize the count of gun homicides against a common population, as we did above in comparing homicides in the United States and South Africa. When we do that, we discover that the rate of gun homicides in Chicago is about 16.5 per 100,000 population. That's pretty high—about three times higher than the overall homicide rate in America (5.6 per 100,000), and more than four times higher than the national gun homicide rate (3.9 per 100,000).[32] Calculating the same statistic for New Orleans, however, yields an observed gun homicide rate of 40.4 per 100,000 from 2014 to the present day. Despite New Orleans' much lower population, the rate of gun homicides there is nearly 2.5 times higher than in Chicago!

You may wonder why crimes are normalized to 100,000 population? It is an established convention for reporting and a convenient way of expressing crime rates in whole numbers rather than decimal fractions. Simply dividing the number of homicides above by the population of South Africa and the United States yields values of 0.000336 and 0.000056, respectively. Similarly, we get values of 0.000165 for Chicago and 0.000404 for New Orleans. It's simply easier to report values in whole numbers as opposed to decimals. Of course, there is nothing magical about reporting crimes per 100,000 population. We could also have chosen to report them per million population, or per 10 million, if we chose. However, demographers and criminologists long ago settled on reporting crimes per 100,000 population, and this convention holds.

Examining data for the frequency (or rate) of gun violence in the United States helps us understand these gun crimes across subpopulations of the U.S. public. From 2001 to 2016, the overall gun-related death rate in the United States (including murders, suicides, negligent shootings, etc.) varied from a high of 11.96 persons per 100,000 in 2016 to a low of 10.10 persons per 100,000 in 2004, averaging 10.56 persons per 100,000 over the 16-year period.[33] Gun-related homicides are a subcategory of all gun-related deaths (other subcategories are suicides and deaths from negligent shootings) in the United States and, as such, were calculated to have slightly lower incidence rates and displayed somewhat lower variation between the highest and lowest rates per 100,000. During the 2001–2016 interval, the highest rate of gun homicides occurred in 2016, with 4.5 gun homicides per 100,000; the lowest rate was observed during 2009, with 3.75 gun homicides per 100,000.[34] We even know the total numbers and rates of people murdered by different types of guns. Total handgun murders in the United States averaged more than 7,400 per year from 2001 to 2006, resulting in handgun homicide rates ranging from 2.4 to 2.6 persons per 100,000. Beginning in 2007, however, there was a decrease in homicides from handguns, with total recorded handgun murders peaking in 2007 at 7,398 (2.5 homicides per 100,000), and between 6,800 and 5,500 murders every year thereafter (rates averaging about 2.0 homicides per 100,000).[35]

Overall rates of gun homicide in the United States don't tell the entire story, though. Even overall rates of gun-related deaths from different types of guns are not particularly revealing of the plague of gun violence afflicting the United States. What we really desire to know is how rates of gun murder in the United States compare across demographic groups. If we examine trends of gun violence among various demographic groups, there are some very stark realities that confront us.

First and foremost, we discover that gun violence in America afflicts every age group, every race and ethnicity, and both sexes. Gun violence is rightly referred to as a national public health crisis by professionals who study it.[36] Gun violence statistics available from the Centers for Disease Control and Prevention tell a grim story of brutality across our population, but they also show conclusively that guns do not afflict demographic groups equally. Examination of detailed violent injury statistics from the Centers for Disease Control and Prevention[37] reveals startling disparities in total numbers and rates of gun deaths per 100,000 people across racial and ethnic categories, as well as between men, women, and, sadly, children.

Let us examine trends in gun homicide among different age groups in the United States, for instance, as we did earlier in this chapter. Starting with the youngest among us, children aged 0–14 years old have a gun homicide rate of 0.4 per 100,000. Elsewhere in the world, among the twenty-five nations that are industrial counterparts to the United States, the observed gun homicide rate is 0.06 per 100,000.[38] The gun homicide rate for children in the United States is almost 7 times higher than the observed rate in the other 25 industrial nations of the global north.

Those in the next age group, 15–24-year-olds, are the people most at risk for gun violence in the United States and worldwide. I reported earlier that from 2000 to 2016 there were 112,930 deaths from all gun-related causes among this age group. That's more than 6,500 teens and young adults killed with guns every year. In the United States, a 15–24-year-old is killed by gun every 79 minutes. The total number of gun homicides among 15–24-year-olds during the interval years from 2000 to 2016 was 71,113, with an average gun homicide rate of 9.8 per 100,000. Among the other 25 nations of the industrial north, the average gun homicide rate among this age group was 0.23.[39] Thus, the observed gun homicide rate among 15–24-year-olds in the United States was almost 43 times higher than in other countries. Let me say that again—43 times higher!

Pre–middle age adults in the United States don't fare much better than their youthful counterparts. Among the 25–34-year-old age group, there were 60,281 gun murders from 2000 to 2016, translating to an average murder rate of 8.65 per 100,000.[40] The observed gun murder rates for Americans begins to decline in higher age groups, principally because there are fewer of them to kill.

Among 35–44-year-olds, the observed murder rates in the United States ranged from 4.07 persons per 100,000 (in 2010) to 4.76 persons per 100,000 (in 2007), averaging 4.63 persons murdered by gun per 100,000[41] during the interval 2000–2016. For 45–54-year-olds, the observed gun murder rates ranged from 2.37 per 100,000 in 2001 to 3.32 per 100,000 in 2016, averaging 2.65 per 100,000 from 2000 to 2016.[42] In the 55–64-year-old age group, rates of gun murders fall even further, ranging from 1.32 per 100,000 (2005) to 1.78 per 100,000 (2016) and averaging 1.49 per 100,000 from 2000 to 2016.[43] U.S. senior citizens (65–74 years old) had gun homicide rates ranging from 0.82 per 100,000 (2006) to 1.06 per 100,000 (2005) and averaged about 0.94 per 100,000 from 2000 to 2016.[44] Even these murder rates among our aged population are more than 4 times higher than observed rates for the most at-risk age group (15–24 years old) in other industrialized nations![45]

Everyone in the United States is at risk of gun violence every day, and that risk is substantially higher than in any other industrialized nation.[46] However, there are groups decidedly more at risk than others of being victimized by gun violence. Just as I have already demonstrated showing variable rates of gun homicides across age groups, rates of gun homicide vary significantly across other demographic variables. For example, men are more likely to be murdered by gunfire than women. From 2000 to 2016, 171,046 men were murdered with guns compared to 31,301 women.[47] The observed number of gun murders translates into observed frequencies of gun homicide of 6.75 per 100,000 for men and 1.19 per 100,000 for women; thus, men were almost 6 times more frequently murdered with guns than women.

We can also examine the total number and frequency of gun homicides for various racial and ethnic groups in the United States. Among Americans of Asian and Pacific Island descent, there were 3,614 gun homicides from 2000 to 2016, yielding an observed frequency of 1.32 per 100,000. Asian and Pacific Island men were nearly 4 times more frequently murdered (total = 2,848 for observed frequency of 2.17 per 100,000) than their female counterparts (total = 766 for observed frequency of 0.54 per 100,000).[48] Documented gun homicides among Native Americans (American Indian and indigenous Alaskan groups) totaled 1,923 between 2000 and 2016, for an observed frequency of 2.90 per 100,000.[49] Native American men were more frequently victims (total = 1,563; 4.70 per 100,000) relative to Native American women (total = 363; 1.10 per 100,000).[50] Note that documented frequencies of gun homicide among Asian, Pacific Island, and Native American populations in the United States are comparable to documented frequencies of gun homicide among Caucasian Americans. From 2000 to 2016, 85,036 white Americans (66,104 men; 18,932 women) lost their lives in acts of gun homicide across the nation, yielding an observed frequency of 2.06 per 100,000 (3.24 per 100,000 for men and 0.91 per 100,000 women).[51]

Contrasting with relatively low observed quantity and frequency of gun murders among the groups listed above, Hispanic Americans and African Americans are significantly more victimized by guns. Hispanic Americans had an observed rate of gun homicide of 4.48 per 100,000 (total documented gun homicides = 35,915) from 2000 to 2016. Men of Hispanic heritage were more frequently victims (total = 31,859; 7.81 per 100,000) than Hispanic women (total = 4,056; 1.03 per 100,000).[52] Among the African American population in the United States, gun homicide may be considered epidemic.[53] The total number of African Americans murdered by guns from 2000 to 2016 was 111,771, resulting in an observed gun murder rate of 16.03 per 100,000.[54] As with other groups, African American men (100,531 total gun homicides; 30.19 per 100,000) were more frequently victims than African American women (11,240 total gun homicides; 3.09 per 100,000) by a ratio of 10 to 1. African American men were also nearly 15 times more frequently killed by guns than Caucasian Americans.[55] Within the African American population, though, there were extreme incidences of gun homicide among particular age groups. For example, African American male children (aged 0–14 years) displayed a gun murder rate of 1.34 per 100,000, which was more than 3 times the observed rate of gun homicide for this age group among all population groups in the United States but relatively low when compared to the observed rate of gun homicide of 71.05 per 100,000 among male African Americans in the adolescent to young adult category (15–24 years old). Within the dominant college age group (18–24 years old), the gun murder rate among African American men soars to 88.87 per 100,000! In the United States from 2000 to 2016, 36,029 college-aged African American men were murdered with guns; one college-aged African American man was murdered with a gun every 4 hours and 8 minutes every day for 17 years. This is our national crisis.

If statistics documenting the human toll of gun violence in the United States aren't sufficient to overwhelm you, perhaps the economic costs of gun violence will do the trick. A study by the Pacific Institute for Research and Evaluation[56] released in 2013 estimated the total economic costs of gun violence in 2010 by examining costs associated with gun homicides and gun injuries, including hospitalization costs, emergency room/trauma center care, lost work wages, medical care costs, mental health care costs, costs for emergency transport, police work, expenses in the criminal justice system, insurance claims processing, expenses for employers, and impacts on quality of life. This study concluded that each gun homicide in the United States has a societal cost in excess of $5 million and each firearm injury has a societal cost of about $430,000. Tallied over the total number of gun homicides and firearm injuries annually, the report determined that the total costs of gun violence in the United States exceeded $174 billion in 2010.[57] To put this number into perspective, the total estimated cost of gun violence in 2010 was equal to 42% of U.S. Medicaid spending during the fiscal year 2011. Additionally, the total estimated cost of gun violence in the United States in 2010 was more than the estimated war-related costs in Iraq and Afghanistan and other Global War on Terror operations ($171 billion) in the same year.[58] The $174 billion cost of gun violence represents extraordinary opportunity cost to U.S. society, being 6.7 times more than the entire budget of the U.S. Department of Agriculture or the Department of Energy, 4.0 times larger than the 2010 budget of the Department of Homeland Security, 3.6 times higher than the entire budget of the Department of Housing and Urban Development, nearly 13 times greater than the budget for the Department of Labor, 2.2 times more than the Department of Health and Human Services budget, 3.7 times more than the Department of Education budget, almost 16 times greater than the budget for the U.S. Environmental Protection Agency or the Department of Interior, 3.3 times greater than the budget for the Department of State, 3.1 times more than the budget of the Department of Veterans Affairs, 2.4 times more money than appropriated to the Department of Transportation, 6.4 times more than appropriated to the Department of Justice, 12.6 times greater than the budget of the Department of Commerce, and 9.2 times more than NASA's budget.[59] This is why we can't have nice things.

The total cost accounting analysis of emergency room/trauma center visits alone amounted to more than $4 billion. That cost was more than the Medicaid spending of 17 individual states (Alaska, Delaware, Hawai'i, Idaho, Iowa, Kansas, Maine, Nebraska, Nevada, New Hampshire, New Mexico, Rhode Island, South Dakota, Utah, Vermont, West Virginia, and Wyoming) and the District of Columbia during the 2011 fiscal year. The $174 billion total costs of gun violence in 2010 equaled almost 52% of the total expenditures for higher education in the United States in 2011, and the $4 billion spent on emergency room/trauma center treatments of gun injuries was more than the total expenditure for higher education in 25 individual states during 2011 (Alaska, Arkansas, Connecticut, Delaware, Hawai'i, Idaho, Iowa, Kansas, Maine, Mississippi, Montana, Nebraska, Nevada, New Hampshire, New Mexico, North Dakota, Oklahoma, Oregon, Rhode Island, South Carolina, South Dakota, Utah, Vermont, West Virginia, and Wyoming). Amortizing the estimated total costs of gun violence ($174 billion) over the estimated 310 million guns in the United States yields an average societal cost of $561 per gun. Gun owners may have a constitutional right to keep and bear arms, but it is less clear that they have a right to cost society $561 for each gun they own. In the United States, a minority of the population owns guns; recent surveys indicate that only 32–37% of Americans possess firearms of any kind.[60] However, those individuals who do own guns have 6 in their possession, on average.[61] So the average gun owner in America costs our society $3,366 annually. Remarkably, 62% of gun owners report owning more than one gun, and 50% may own more than 8 guns (a societal cost in excess of $4,400 annually); 3% of gun owners report that they possess more than 25 guns,[62] thereby increasing their societal cost of gun ownership to more than $14,025 annually. In one extreme instance reported in 2013, an individual in Connecticut was arrested when found to be in possession of 250 guns, tens of thousands of rounds of ammunition, explosive devices, and chemicals necessary to manufacture explosives.[63] Gun ownership in the United States continues to decline; yet gun sales are increasing, indicating that those who own guns are actually stockpiling them!

A more conservative study by the Urban Institute[64] documented only costs of emergency room care and hospitalization due to firearm injuries using data from 2010 (the most recent year available at the time) and published the results in 2013.[65] The study documented 36,341 emergency room visits related to firearm injuries requiring 25,024 hospitalizations with a total cost of almost $630 million. Hospitalizations resulting from firearm injuries in this study had average costs of $23,497 ($14,000 more than other hospitalizations), resulting in $588 million of the $630 million total documented costs. These hospital and emergency room costs alone were more than the total costs of the Medicaid program in Wyoming.[66] The staggering costs of gun violence year after year in the United States saps the economy of financial resources that could be used to improve national infrastructure, or create jobs and reduce unemployment, or improve education opportunities for every American, or reduce poverty, or increase agricultural production and food subsidies, or so many other worthy social advances; instead, this money is wasted on wanton violence because we lack the courage to rein in guns.

So pervasive is gun violence in America that we are implored by gun rights advocates to engage in more gun violence as the only practical solution! You heard it, and so did I: "The only thing that stops a bad buy with a gun is a good guy with a gun."[67] Just one week after the mass shooting at Sandy Hook Elementary School in Newtown, Connecticut, the executive vice president for the National Rifle Association, Wayne LaPierre, told a grieving nation that the only solution to gun violence was committing another act of gun violence. Get yourself a gun and be prepared to use it—this was LaPierre's advice. The invocation that "the only thing that stops a bad guy with a gun is a good guy with a gun" has gained wide acceptance among the American public if you read newspaper letters to the editors, blog posts, and online discussion threads or watch television interviews with gun rights advocates nationwide. Never mind that there are already more guns in America than people to shoot them. Never mind that individual citizens regularly stockpile thousands to tens of thousands of rounds of ammunition,[68] quantities routinely dismissed by gun advocates as "not that much."[69] The American public was implored to buy guns in order to protect themselves from everyone else who was implored buy guns in order to protect themselves! Following the mass shooting at the Washington Navy Yard in September 2013, LaPierre appeared on television once again, exhorting that "more guns are needed to protect civil society." He even went so far as to claim that while there were some "good guys with guns" at the Washington Navy Yard, there weren't nearly enough of them! He then proposed that the nation needed to create "multiple layers of security" at all military installations. It is madness of the first order to suggest that military installations need additional armed security.

So inured are we to gun violence in America that gun-speak figures prominently in our everyday colloquialisms.[70] A partial list of common gun-related idioms reads like this: gun shy, gun sure, gunner, gun tough, gunning for bear, young guns, trigger happy, trigger point, hair trigger, under the gun, silver bullet, give them ammo, don't give them ammo, on target, in the crosshairs, straight shooter, hip shot, take aim, shooting blanks, magic bullet, gunslinger, shotgun approach, shotgun formation, facing the barrel of a gun, drawing fire, locked and loaded, shot in the dark, bite the bullet, sweating bullets, eat lead, spit bullets, dodged a bullet, ride shotgun, stick to our guns, jump the gun, go ballistic, she's a pistol, trigger man, six shooter, hot shot, son of a gun, take a shot at, long shot, shot across the bow, shoot the messenger, shooting fish in a barrel, shoot your mouth off, shoot from the hip, shoot yourself in the foot, shoot the breeze, shoot to kill, shoot first (ask questions later), sure as shooting, shoot it down, shooting blind, just shoot me, bulletproof, loose cannon, take your best shot, sniping, keep it in the sights, fire away, caught in the crossfire, pull the trigger, itchy trigger finger, trigger event, triggered a response, rapid fire, draw a bead, under fire, both barrels, guns blazing, big guns, set your sights, stick to your guns, point blank, holding a gun to your head, misfire, rapid fire, quick draw, dead eye, keep your powder dry, firing line, firing squad, looking down the barrel of a gun, taking careful aim, half-cocked, high caliber, friendly fire, taking flak, big shot, smoking gun, top gun, into the line of fire, cocked and locked, drop the hammer, the whole nine yards, shot through and through, the whole shooting match, lock, stock, and barrel … and on and on and on. American gun culture provides salvo after salvo in an almost endless barrage of gun metaphors from our colloquial language arsenal!

Guns, guns, guns, guns, guns, and more guns across the United States. There are guns in almost every aspect of American life. You see guns on TV, in movies, in department stores, in discount retail stores, in sporting goods stores, in mail-order catalogs, on online shopping sites, and, let's not forget, in 51,438 retail gun stores and 7,356 pawn shops selling guns[71] nationwide. There are literally thousands of individual places to purchase guns in every state. In 2012, there were a mere 37,053 grocery stores in the United States[72]—less than 741 in each state on average—but thousands of stores in each state to purchase guns. In the same year, there were 14,157 McDonald's restaurants in the United States[73]—only one-quarter the number of retail gun stores and pawn shops selling guns.

Indeed, America is a nation awash with guns and drowning in gun violence. Is that the society you want? What if I told you it didn't have to be that way? What if our society had inadvertently engaged in an extraordinary social experiment demonstrating that gun violence can be arrested? What if I told you that there was an archipelago within our blood-inundated country where gun violence almost never occurs? What if we decided, collectively, to sequester our young people in the age group most at risk of becoming victims of gun violence (ages 15–34) into isolated enclaves where guns were prohibited? Would you want to conduct that experiment? Would these gun-safe zones become "magnets for murderers"? Would we be endangering the lives of our young people, leaving them defenseless against criminal savages? Would you want to see the evidence? Would you want to learn more? Would you ask where these islands of tranquility are and how you can navigate to one? Would you be curious to see the results of this grand social experiment? Would those data convince you that we can have a better society and a better world without guns?

The remainder of this book will document precisely the results of such a social experiment. It has been ongoing for decades, and the results are available to every person with a computer and an internet connection. All that is required is for us to look for the data and examine them objectively. The rest of this book will show you where these sanctuaries scattered across America are located. They are remarkable places of peaceful reflection and learned thought. They are places where the dreams and aspirations of your daughters and sons take form and substance. Sanctuaries! They are our nation's postsecondary education campuses: private and public four-year universities and colleges, private and public two-year colleges, and private and public technical institutes. The great majority of these campuses are zones where gun violence only rarely occurs. Subsequent chapters outline real data on the frequency of homicide (generally) and gun violence (specifically) on college campuses nationwide during the 21st century (2001–2016) to demonstrate the astonishing results of a grand social experiment. We cloistered our young people, the dominant age group most likely to be victimized by gun violence, and provided environments that were among the safest sanctuaries from gun violence on our planet. Hands down. Throughout the remainder of this book, gun homicides will be rare incidents, but those incidents that do occur will inform us of the nature of these crimes. If we look at these incidents in detail, there is much to learn about how we might best reduce even these rare tragedies. If you want to know precisely how rare these incidents are on our nation's college campuses, then read on.

4

The Clery Act

"I'm for truth, no matter who tells it."
—Malcolm X

You've now been briefed on the backdrop of gun violence in the United States. It's not very uplifting, is it? More than 32,000 people die from gunfire every year in our country—approximately two-thirds from suicides and negligent shootings and one-third in homicides. I don't want to belabor that point, and you've read enough statistics in the previous chapter to be an expert on the topic. Unfortunately, that is the society we've built.

"An armed society is a polite society." Opponents of sensible gun regulation in our nation love that quote from a 1942 science-fiction novel, *Beyond This Horizon*, by Robert Heinlein.[1] "An armed society is a polite society"—with 32,000 victims of politeness every year. "An armed society is a polite society"—if by "polite" you actually mean "belligerent." If "an armed society is a polite society," why don't the victims ever say "thank you"? For comparison, let me show you what an unarmed society looks like. Then you can decide which society you prefer.

The remainder of this book is an exploration of the nature and incidence of collegiate homicides in the United States. Going forward, I'll compare the documented homicides on campuses of higher education to the gun-created bloodbath across America. That was the stated intent of this book: to provide details of our grand social experiment of creating small gun-safe islands embedded in our armed society and documenting the results. At first glance, this may seem like an easy task. Just count the homicides in society at large across America, and then count the homicides on college campuses and compare. Of course, it's not that easy. If it were, this wouldn't be a book—it would be a sentence.

To begin, you might ask a straightforward question (because all research begins with a straightforward question): How many college students are murdered on college campuses every year? See, simple! So let's think about it.

Who are "college students"? Are students the only ones murdered on college campuses? What about faculty? Or staff? Or administrators? Or sports coaches? What is the specific affiliation of the homicide victims to the institution? Is there an affiliation? Truly, who are the victims every year and how do we find out?

Beyond those issues, what is the "college campus" where these incidents take place? Is it the classrooms? The laboratories? The sports facilities? The dormitories? The administration buildings? The maintenance buildings? The open spaces across the university? My university has a farm and agricultural research stations scattered statewide. Are those part of "the campus"? What about parking lots? Or the streets adjacent to university property? What about fraternity and sorority houses across the street from my university? What about the restaurants in the student union? My university has a parking deck where the public can pay to park. The first floor of the parking deck has retail space leased to private commercial enterprises. Are those private enterprises part of "the campus"? My university also leases space in a number of privately owned and managed buildings in the city. Is that part of "the campus"? There is undeveloped, forested land in my city owned by the university but far removed from the academic buildings. Is that part of "the campus"? In addition, students live in apartments all over town. Are those part of "the campus"? My institution leases apartments it owns directly to students. Are those part of "the campus"? My university likewise contracts with private real estate management firms to provide student housing. Are those privately owned and managed apartments part of "the campus"? If someone is murdered in all those places, were they murdered on "the campus"? There are legal consequences to the answers to those questions. Are the victims of crimes in those locations "students" or otherwise affiliated with "the campus"? How should we account for crimes that may occur in all these places? Which crimes should be counted? Who will do the counting? Is there even an obligation to count these crimes? If you count them, to whom are they reported? How frequently should they be reported? Should they be reported immediately? Daily? Once a week? Monthly? Annually? Who compiles the reports? Who has access to the reports? Who can read the reports? Can the general public have access to the reports? Can state-owned institutions of higher education be compelled to gather crime statistics? Can privately owned institutions be compelled to gather crime statistics? If we gather all these crime statistics, what good is it? Why bother? From a simple question—"How many college students are murdered on college campuses every year?"—so many additional questions emerge.

These questions and many others were asked three decades ago and addressed through the passage of the Jeanne Clery Disclosure of Campus Security Policy and Campus Crime Statistics Act. The Clery Act, as it has come to be known, is a federal statute requiring any post-secondary institution participating in federal student financial aid programs to report crime statistics to the U.S. Department of Education annually. Post-secondary institutions are private or public 4-year universities and colleges, private or public 2-year colleges (commonly referred to as community colleges), and private or public technical institutes (formerly referred to as vocational colleges, vocational schools, or "vo-techs"). The qualifying requirement for reporting campus crimes is participation in federal student financial aid programs. Institutions that don't participate in such programs are not required to report crimes under the Clery Act. This is an important fact to note. In the United States, most post-secondary institutions participate in at least one federally managed student financial aid program, so reporting is somewhat ubiquitous, but understand there are some institutions that do not report and universal reporting of campus crimes is not mandated. Understand also that uniform crime reporting from college campuses is a relatively recent regulation. Prior to passage of the Clery Act, there was virtually no reporting on the status of campus security or public safety on college campuses in the United States. To better understand how college crime reporting became regulated, it is perhaps informative to briefly review the incident that spawned the Clery Act.

Jeanne Clery was a first-year student enrolled at Lehigh University, a private 4-year institution in Bethlehem, Pennsylvania, during the 1985–1986 academic year. During the spring semester of 1986, she was murdered on campus in her dormitory room. Out of respect for the victim and her family, I will not recount the details of her murder. Nor will I name her assailant and provide him with any additional notoriety. Those who want to know the details of this crime can easily find out with a quick search on the internet using the referenced links for this chapter. All the grim facts are there, and there are many articles written about Jeanne Clery's death and her parents' efforts afterward. Her assailant, another student, was captured, tried, and sentenced to death for first-degree murder and other crimes in 1987.[2] In 2002, 15 years after his conviction and while awaiting execution on death row, his death sentence was thrown out on appeal and he was awarded a new trial that might have concluded with reaffirming the death penalty. Before that trial began, however, the assailant agreed before the court to abandon the retrial and all future appeals in exchange for a sentence of life in prison without the possibility of parole.[3] He remains incarcerated today.

During the murder trial, the family became aware of a relatively large number of violent crimes on the Lehigh University campus—38 committed over a three-year interval leading up to their daughter's murder.[4] Note that 38 violent crimes over three years (an average of just under 13 per year) represented a campus crime wave. How many violent crimes are committed in your town every year? And over three years? I'll wager that for cities with more than 50,000 residents, the numbers are commonly quite a bit higher. However, information regarding the crimes on the Lehigh campus was not publicly available; there was no requirement at that time for any postsecondary institutions to report crimes to any centralized repository. Incredibly, the Clery family had chosen Lehigh as a safer alternative for their daughter's college experience after learning secondhand of the homicide of a student (also a woman) at their daughter's first choice, Tulane University in New Orleans, in 1984.[5] Once again, despite a good deal of publicity in New Orleans and New York City (the victim's home state),[6] the Tulane incident was not widely known, as there was no requirement for institutions to report crimes at that time and no way for the general public to be aware of the campus security status or ongoing issues of public safety. It simply wasn't the norm of the day. Indeed, the Clerys found out about it only through an offhand comment by a university administrator. That state of affairs would change with Jeanne Clery's murder in 1986.

Following the revelations of significant security lapses at Lehigh University, including locking doors that were frequently propped open, unlocked rooms in dormitories, rising campus crime rates, and an institutional administration that failed to appreciate the relatively serious campus security situation, the Clery family led lobbying efforts to impose regulatory requirements that would ensure accurate reporting of collegiate crimes. In 1988, Pennsylvania passed Act 73,[7] the College and University Security Information Act, requiring Pennsylvania post-secondary institutions to report "information relating to crime statistics and security measures and to provide similar information to prospective students and employees upon request." This law was a precursor to the federal Student Right-to-Know and Campus Security Act (U.S. Public Law 101–542, Title I)[8] and the Crime Awareness and Campus Security Act of 1990 (U.S. Public Law 101–542, Title II).[9] Both statutes were later combined, amended, and renamed the Jeanne Clery Disclosure of Campus Security Policy and Campus Crime Statistics Act. Many of the foundational regulations of the Clery Act were established in the Pennsylvania and 1990 federal statutes. In recent years, reporting requirements have expanded to intersect with provisions in Title IX,[10] the Family Educational Rights and Privacy Act (FERPA),[11] and the Violence Against Women Act (VAWA).[12]

As a result of these laws, crime reporting on college campuses in the United States is becoming standardized, more extensive, and more reliable, but also ever more complex. This is good news for families, students, and members of academic communities working on these campuses. The bad news is that campus crime reporting remains rather incomplete. The reporting protocols under the Clery Act are highly detailed (the 2016 *Handbook for Campus Safety and Security Reporting* is 265 pages long),[13] and extensive training is required for authorized and mandated reporters. In addition, campus crime reporting statutes, as currently written, prioritize reporting *the number of crime victims* over reporting of *the number of criminal victimizations.*[14] This accounting protocol is a very important distinction and also controversial, as you will discover. However, crime accounting under the Clery Act must be understood to properly assess information contained in annual reports submitted by higher education institutions in compliance with the law. To understand the effort being expended nationally to quantify crimes on college campuses, it's necessary to look at the types of crimes that must be reported, how those crimes are reported in the context of prioritizing reporting on the number of crime victims, and the geographic boundaries of required crime reporting by individual institutions (so-called "Clery geography").

Let's begin our exploration of the Clery Act with descriptions of the types of crimes that must be reported. These crimes are actually quite limited in number and scope. Compliance with the Clery Act requires post-secondary institutions to report property crimes (arson, automobile theft, and burglary) as well as crimes against persons (criminal offenses, in order of increasing severity, of aggravated assaults, robbery, sexual assault, negligent manslaughter, non-negligent manslaughter and homicide). In recent years, sexual assaults have been further defined to include specific reporting of rape, fondling, incest and statutory rape. In addition to criminal offenses, institutions are required to report separately any of these criminal offenses if they are determined to be hate crimes (that is, crimes committed against persons or property motivated by bias against various classes of people). In 2014, crimes defined by VAWA were added,[15] so institutions must now report instances of stalking, dating or acquaintance violence, and domestic violence. Finally, institutions must report referrals for disciplinary action related to weapons violations, drug or liquor violations, or other serious disciplinary actions to appropriate campus authorities, and this information must be conveyed in annual reports to the U.S. Department of Education. A chapter of the Clery Act reporting handbook is dedicated to defining the crimes above and how authorized reporters should record individual crimes. The focus of this book is homicides on college campuses, but it is informative to understand the definitions of other crimes relevant to Clery Act compliance in order to properly interpret institutional security and crime reports submitted to the Department of Education.

Once again, I emphasize at the outset that crime reporting in compliance with the Clery Act prioritizes reporting of crime victims over criminal victimizations. The distinction between these categories will become apparent as the discussion develops in this chapter, so if the distinction seems odd or confusing at this stage, keep reading. It will become quite clear before we're done.

The emphasis on tabulating crime victims over criminal victimizations is codified in the Clery Act through establishment of a "hierarchy rule" regarding crime reporting. When more than one crime is committed during a single incident, the Clery Act generally specifies that only the most serious crime must be reported. The "most serious" crime is determined by reference to the Clery Act reporting handbook, which provides a list of hierarchical crimes in order of decreasing severity or reporting priority. The most serious crimes are those committed against persons, which will always be reported before crimes against property. Homicide and non-negligent manslaughter, of course, rank as the most serious crimes in the hierarchy (as the taking of another's life by force should always be considered the most serious offense). In order after homicide and non-negligent manslaughter are negligent manslaughter, sexual assault, robbery, aggravated assault, arson, burglary, and automobile theft. However, the hierarchy rule results in undercounting criminal acts or criminal victimizations, and therein lies the controversy over Clery Act crime reporting. Imagine a single incident, an armed robbery (crime #1) in which the victim is stabbed (crime #2, aggravated assault) and later succumbs to the stabbing injury and dies (crime #3, homicide). Using the hierarchy rule, this incident will be reported under the Clery Act as a homicide. In most cases, the aggravated assault and robbery are not required to be reported. I think most reasonable people would say that's undercounting crimes. But under the Clery Act reporting protocol, there is only one victim, and the victim was murdered. The other crimes are incidental but not reported because Clery Act reporting prioritizes the number of victims (one) and, under the hierarchy rule, the most serious crime committed against the victim (homicide). See how that works? However, there are exceptions to the hierarchy rule.

All arsons are reported under the Clery Act, regardless of other crimes that may accompany an act of arson. In the event of additional crimes accompanying the arson incident, only the most serious crime (ranked according to the hierarchy rule) is required to be reported. Deaths resulting from arson are categorized as homicide or non-negligent manslaughter or negligent manslaughter.

Sexual assaults reported under the Clery Act intersect with definitions of sexual assault in Title IX and VAWA, and they are reported according to definitions in those statutes. A sexual assault resulting in the death of the victim is reported as homicide or non-negligent manslaughter, but the sexual assault is also reported. Overall, however, the hierarchy rule combined with Clery Act prioritization of counting only victims results in collegiate crimes being undercounted.

With respect to crimes against property, those that must be reported in compliance with the Clery Act are arson, burglary, and automobile theft. As mentioned above, arsons are always reported. Burglaries are defined as "the unlawful entry of a structure to commit a felony or a theft," including "unlawful entry with intent to commit a larceny or felony; breaking and entering with intent to commit a larceny; housebreaking; safecracking; and all attempts at these offenses."[16]

Burglaries are, strictly speaking, crimes against property. Only fixed structures can be burglarized, and a fixed structure is defined as having walls, a roof, and at least one door. Any attempt to unlawfully enter such a structure for the purpose of committing a felony or theft, whether using force (i.e., forcible entry) or not, constitutes burglary for the purposes of Clery Act reporting. A foundational aspect of the definition of burglary is that of trespass with intent to commit theft or another felony. Under the Clery Act definitions, a person who forcibly enters a building to sleep is not committing a felony or theft, and this incident would not be reported as burglary. A student forcibly entering a campus apartment because they forgot their key is not committing burglary as defined by the Clery Act; they may be committing other offenses, but those are not required reporting under the Clery Act. Unsuccessful attempts at forcible entry should be coded as burglaries if there is clear evidence that theft was the intent of the forced entry. Interestingly, thefts from breaking and entering into vehicles (whether locked or not) are not classified as burglaries under the Clery Act because vehicles are not fixed structures; theft from vehicles is larceny and not a crime that triggers Clery reporting unless it is larceny associated with a hate crime (more on hate crimes later). Shoplifting from commercial establishments (such as a campus bookstore) is not burglary if committed during business hours; under those circumstances, shoplifting is larceny and not required reporting under the Clery Act. However, if merchandise is stolen from a commercial property after hours as a consequence of a forced or unforced entry, that is burglary and reported. Thefts from open access areas of the campus are also classified as larceny and not required reporting under the Clery Act. So, if a student leaves a laptop or tablet computer at a library table (for instance) and it is stolen, this incident is not required to be reported under the Clery Act. Finally, individual rooms in dormitories or student rooms in multi-room suites (which have become common dwelling modes on college campuses) are considered separate structures for Clery Act reporting. Thus, if one unlawfully enters multiple rooms in a dormitory or suite during a single incident, each unlawful entry is counted as a burglary. However, individual offices in academic buildings are not considered separate structures. So when a burglary occurs in an academic building, it is counted as a single incident regardless of the number of rooms entered or the number of items stolen in the building during that time frame; if multiple rooms are entered across multiple days, representing multiple break-ins, then each separate unlawful entry into the building is counted as one burglary.

You see that the reporting requirements of the Clery Act for burglary appear somewhat complicated. They can be understood more easily if we recall that Clery Act crime reporting prioritizes victims, not victimizations. In the case of burglary, if a person unlawfully enters five dorm rooms (each room is considered a separate structure under the Clery Act), then five burglaries are reported because there are five victims (one victim in each room that was burglarized). Contrast that tabulation with an institutional building in which five faculty offices are burglarized. This incident is tabulated as one burglary because the "victim" in this instance is the institution, not the individual faculty members whose institutional offices were burglarized. The logic here is that someone entered the institutional building with the intent of committing a felony or larceny by stealing institutional property, not the personal property of the faculty members who occupy the offices. Do you think this is an example of undercounting crimes? Under the Clery Act, it is not. The Clery Act guidelines for reporting crimes developed over many years from incidents and questions related to those incidents regarding how they should be reported. The overall objective has been creating a system of standardized reporting so people may understand how to interpret annual campus crime reports; one needs to have confidence that a "burglary" on one college campus is describing a similar crime of "burglary" on another college campus.

Motor vehicle thefts must be reported under the Clery Act. However, motor vehicles are strictly defined as "any self-propelled vehicle that runs on the land surface and not on rails, such as sport utility vehicles, automobiles, trucks, buses, motorcycles, motor scooters, trail bikes, mopeds, all-terrain vehicles, self-propelled motor homes, snowmobiles, golf carts and motorized wheelchairs."[17] Specifically excluded from this definition are "farm equipment, bulldozers, airplanes, construction equipment, water craft (motorboats, sailboats, houseboats or jet skis)."[18] Theft of these vehicles is not required under the Clery Act. Does this result in underreporting of crimes? Of course. But the Clery Act permits it. Furthermore, theft of a motor vehicle during a car-jacking should be reported as robbery and not motor vehicle theft because car-jacking is defined as the unlawful taking of a motor vehicle from another person by force with a weapon or other threat or intimidation.[19] Since robbery (a crime against a person) is more serious than vehicle theft (a property crime) in the hierarchy of crimes, only the robbery (car-jacking) is reported in most cases.

Crimes against persons, in order of increasing severity, that require reporting under the Clery Act are aggravated assaults, robbery, sexual assaults, negligent manslaughter, and homicide/non-negligent manslaughter. Hate crimes are separate offenses, and all hate crimes must be reported regardless of their severity in the ranking of crime hierarchies. Reporting crimes against persons and hate crimes in general can be quite complicated, so adherence to the detailed definitions of these crimes is particularly important to ensure standardized reporting nationwide. In order for anyone to make sense of campus crime reports and the reported crimes against persons, we all need to know what, exactly, is being reported.

Aggravated assaults are the most frequently reported crimes against persons at colleges nationwide. This is not to say that the number of aggravated assaults on college campuses is extraordinary or that every aggravated assault gets reported. Is every fistfight in a fraternity house an aggravated assault? No, not necessarily. Many may be categorized as simple assaults, which are not reported under the Clery Act. The defining feature of an aggravated assault is "an unlawful attack by one person upon another for the purpose of inflicting severe or aggravated bodily injury. This type of assault usually is accompanied by the use of a weapon or by means likely to produce death or great bodily harm."[20] In some instances, hands, feet, teeth, and so on may be considered "weapons" under this definition, so severe beatings will always be categorized as aggravated assaults. Aggravated assaults include attempted homicide, assault with dangerous or deadly weapons, maiming or mayhem (defined in criminal law as an "act of maliciously disabling or disfiguring the victim permanently"),[21] assault with explosives, and assault with disease. (The last item refers to instances in which a person infected with a deadly disease—such as HIV/AIDS or other sexually transmitted diseases—attempts to infect another person through any means.) In instances in which weapons (e.g., guns, knives, clubs, etc.) are used in an assault, it is not necessary that an injury resulted from the assault. It is sufficient that there is a threat of great bodily injury from these weapons, so the assault will be categorized as an aggravated one; thus, a person who merely draws a gun or other lethal weapons on another individual commits an aggravated assault under the Clery Act. Attempts to subdue victims with drugs are counted as aggravated assaults under the Clery Act, as are serious injuries resulting from one person administering illicit drugs to another person. In cases when injuries are incurred during an assault, the seriousness of the injuries and the intent of the attacker must be evaluated to determine whether the assault is an aggravated assault or a simple assault. Again, the Clery Act doesn't require the reporting of most simple assaults.

The ambiguity involved in some instances of establishing the actual motive of an attacker in an assault or judgment regarding the severity of injuries creates contention in the reporting of some campus assaults. Undoubtedly, some underreporting of aggravated assaults and other crimes occurs when they are miscoded or are not reported to law enforcement authorities.[22] In addition, aggravated assaults may be underreported because the Clery Act prioritizes counting the number of victims, not victimizations. Here's an example: Suppose there is a brawl following a collegiate sporting event. During this brawl, there may be hundreds of participants actively engaged in fighting. Many of the assaults that occur during this brawl are simple assaults, which are not reported under the Clery Act. Suppose, however, that part of this mob descends on several individuals and inflicts serious injuries—maybe nine people are seriously injured in this manner. Authorities, however, are unable to identify the total number of persons participating in the assaults that injured those nine persons. Under the Clery Act, there are nine victims, and thus nine aggravated assaults are reported, regardless of whether each person was severely beaten by one or ten assailants. For the purposes of the law as it is written, there are nine victims who suffered nine aggravated assaults. This is potential undercounting of crimes. Codified in the law. If one of the victims was also robbed during this incident, then the robbery is counted (because it is a more serious crime than the aggravated assault) and the aggravated assault is dropped from the official Clery Act record. Under the Clery Act, there are still nine victims and nine crimes— one robbery and eight aggravated assaults. I think most of us would likely agree that there were at least nine aggravated assaults, one of which included robbery as an additional crime. Still nine victims in total, but ten crimes committed during the incident. Under the Clery Act, your accounting is incorrect! See? Undercounting!

The Clery Act requires reporting robberies at higher education institutions. Robbery is defined as "the taking or attempting to take anything of value from the care, custody, or control of a person or persons by force or threat of force or violence and/or by putting the victim in fear."[23] Robbery is a crime against a person and is distinguished from larceny (or theft, which is a property crime) by the application of force or violence against a victim to cause them harm or great fear for their well-being in order to take their property. For instance, theft of an unattended smartphone from a library table is larceny whereas taking a smartphone directly from the student by knocking them to the ground and snatching the phone is robbery. Knocking a person to the ground might also be aggravated assault (depending on circumstances), but that won't get reported under the Clery Act—only the robbery will be reported. We just went over that. Please pay attention! But I'll go over it again, just to be clear. According to the Clery Act reporting handbook,[24] the essential conditions to categorize a crime as robbery are (1) the crime is committed in the presence of the victim, (2) the victim is directly confronted by the perpetrator, (3) force (or the threat of force) is employed to make the victim fear for their well-being, and (4) the intent of the force or threatened force is to commit larceny. According to this definition, however, assault of some kind (either simple or, potentially, aggravated assault) is a required element of a robbery.[25] The hierarchy rule described in the Clery Act handbook requires that the robbery take precedence over the assault in these instances, so the crime is reported as a robbery and the assault is not reported as a separate criminal act (recall the example of robbery and assault following a sporting event). If the assault during the robbery results in the death of the victim, the hierarchy rule requires that the crime be elevated to homicide or non-negligent manslaughter and so reported, leaving out the robbery aspect.[26]

Once again, I think most reasonable people would prefer to report all the crimes committed during an incident. After all, if our objective is to document and record crimes on college campuses, we should count all the crimes committed during a given incident, not just the most serious one. But the Clery Act only demands recording one crime per victim (in most cases), so undercounting is permissible and accepted. If you don't like that accounting method, then you need to contact your congressional representatives and senators and demand that they amend the law to prioritize criminal victimizations over crime victims. I wonder how long it will take to pass that legislation? If the accounting method specified by the Clery Act seems perfectly reasonable, then read on. Maybe you will change your mind in the next section.

Collegiate sexual assaults are crimes that must be reported under the Clery Act. There are four primary sexual crimes that must be reported: rape, incest, fondling, and statutory rape. In addition, other provisions of the Clery

Act related to its intersection with VAWA require reporting dating violence, domestic violence, and stalking. VAWA crimes are exempted from the hierarchy rule, meaning that any VAWA crime must be reported in the criminal complaints reporting for the Clery Act, as well as reported in the VAWA sections of Clery Act reporting.

The most serious sexual assault is rape, defined as "the penetration, no matter how slight, of the vagina or anus, with any body part or object, or oral penetration by a sex organ of another person, without the consent of the victim. This offense includes the rape of both males and females."[27] The nonconsensual nature and frequently violent aggravated assault accompanying rape elevates it to the highest priority among sexual assaults. Incest is "sexual intercourse between persons who are related to each other within the degrees wherein marriage is prohibited by law,"[28] and statutory rape is "sexual intercourse with a person who is under the statutory age of consent."[29] Incest may be consensual, but it is a criminal act because there is a legal prohibition regarding sexual behavior with another person owing to familial relationship. In statutory rape, the victim is considered too young to give legal consent, so by definition it is nonconsensual sexual activity. Statutory rape and incest are further complicated by varying state laws establishing different standards for each, often times mandating different ages of consent or defining different familial boundaries of sexual contact. When reporting incest or statutory rape, institutions are bound to report any incidents falling under the established laws of their own state. This leads to nonstandardized reporting nationally and, undoubtedly, some underreporting of these crimes.

Fondling is "the touching of the private body parts of another person for the purpose of sexual gratification, without the consent of the victim, including instances where the victim is incapable of giving consent because of his/her age or because of his/her temporary or permanent mental incapacity."[30] Fondling is frequently an element of other sexual assaults detailed above, so the hierarchy rule means that the more serious crime is reported; fondling is only reported when it is the sole aspect of the reported sexual assault. As a result, fondling is a grossly underreported sexual crime on college campuses.

As with other criminal violations under the Clery Act, the reporting of sexual assaults follows the hierarchy rule and prioritizes the number of victims over the number of victimizations. Thus, if a person is sexually assaulted during the course of an armed robbery, the sexual assault takes precedence in the hierarchical reporting, so it gets reported, whereas the armed robbery does not. Once again, the total number of crimes is underreported in favor of reporting only the most serious crime committed against the victim.

Then there is this undercounting outrage presented as a scenario in *The Handbook for Campus Safety and Security Reporting 2016 Edition*: "Scenario 5: Three female students report that they were each raped by five male students at an off-campus fraternity house owned by a recognized fraternity. Each male raped each of the female students. Include this as three non-campus Rapes [*sic*]."[31] Read that again, and read it carefully. Five men each raped three women at an off-campus fraternity house. Five men times three rapes each equals fifteen rapes, right? I think everyone would agree with that total. I read that scenario, read it again, and again. I did the math. I came up with fifteen rapes. However, that's not how the handbook describes the appropriate recording of these crimes under the Clery Act. I read it again. I thought about it, I slept on it, and then I thought, "Surely this is a typographical error in the handbook. It must be fifteen rapes, not three." I sent an email to the Department of Education Clery Act reporting help desk for clarification, certain that I had identified an error in the handbook that required correcting. I received a response in less than 24 hours (kudos to the Department of Education staffer who provided such a timely answer to my query)! Below is the actual verbatim text of the response:

> The scenario and the counts are correct as written. As stated on page 3–3 of the Handbook, the Clery Act requires institutions to use the definition and guidance provided by the FBI's Uniform Crime Reporting (UCR) Program. As stated on page 3–6 of the Handbook, Rape is to be counted by the number of victims. The example provided in Scenario 5 is considered to be a single incident. Even though there were multiple offenders the offense occurred within the same time and space. The incident must be counted by the number of victims. Unless the FBI changes its guidance, institutions must continue to count in this way.

So, there you have it—the ultimate expression of Clery Act preference for reporting numbers of crime victims over numbers of criminal victimizations. Three rapes reported out of fifteen committed during the incident described above. Codified, legally permissible underreporting of 80% of the sexual assaults committed during this single incident.

If you are a woman, I can't begin to imagine what you might be thinking right now. I'm a man—a father of two daughters, both of college age. I am simply aghast that this is how campus sexual assaults are reported under the Clery Act. At a time when higher education institutions nationwide are under intense scrutiny for underreporting sexual assaults, we discover here that they are legally encouraged to do so. I don't get it. We know that sexual assaults are among the most underreported crimes on college campuses anyway (and in society at large), largely because so many victims never come forward with allegations or reports of their assaults. Now we find that even if they do, the institution will likely undercount them—legally, because it's about the number of victims, not the number of victimizations. What's more, the scenario presented above describes five men who are serial rapists. It might be good to know that there's a serial rapist on your college campus, let alone five. Seriously, dear readers, it's time to write your congressional representatives and senators and demand that they amend the Clery Act to actually report every criminal victimization on our college campuses, not the number of crime victims. If you really want to know how many crimes occur on college campuses, you must count all that are reported.

Reporting of sexual assaults is further complicated by the inclusion of VAWA crimes in Clery Act reporting. The reauthorization of VAWA in 2013 included adding several new crimes against persons in Clery Act reporting for higher education institutions. Under VAWA, institutions must now report crimes of domestic violence, dating violence, and stalking. Note that reporting these crimes is required under VAWA, but these crimes are not exclusive to women; anyone who is a victim of dating violence, domestic violence, or stalking is protected under the law.

Domestic violence is defined as "a felony or misdemeanor crime of violence committed by (1) a current or former spouse or intimate partner of the victim, (2) a person with whom the victim shares a child in common, (3) a person who is cohabitating with, or has cohabitated with, the victim as a spouse or intimate partner, (4) a person similarly situated to a spouse of the victim under the domestic or family violence laws of the jurisdiction in which the crime of violence occurred, (5) any other person against an adult or youth victim who is protected from that person's acts under the domestic or family violence laws of the jurisdiction in which the crime of violence occurred."[32] Domestic violence requires the persons involved to presently be in, or historically have had, an intimate relationship, which is not required or implicit in the description of dating violence.

Dating violence is defined under VAWA as "violence committed by a person who is or has been in a social relationship of a romantic or intimate nature with the victim. The existence of such a relationship shall be determined based on the reporting party's statement and with consideration of the length of the relationship, the type of relationship, and the frequency of interaction between the persons involved in the relationship."[33]

Stalking under VAWA is defined as "engaging in a course of conduct directed at a specific person that would cause a reasonable person to (1) fear for the person's safety or the safety of others; or (2) suffer substantial emotional distress."[34] For reporting purposes under the Clery Act, only the first instance of stalking behavior occurring within the institutional geographic boundaries defined under the Clery Act (the so-called Clery geography) must be reported; there is no requirement to report each instance of stalking activity by a perpetrator against a single victim. If the same stalker targets more than one victim, then the stalking activity against each victim should be reported, but not the total number of stalking activities directed against each victim. Here again we see how campus crimes may be underreported even as an institution complies with the law.

VAWA crimes are exempt from the hierarchy rule, but they are reported in a separate section of the annual Clery Act report submitted by higher education institutions (and these crimes have only been included since 2014). For example, if there was a weapon involved in the three sexual assaults reported in "Scenario 5" above, those are aggravated assaults committed during rapes and are crimes against women. The Clery Act requires three of the fifteen rapes to be reported in the criminal offenses portion of its annual campus security report, and the aggravated assaults must be reported under the VAWA section of the annual report. So, in the example described above, three rapes are reported in the criminal offenses section and three aggravated assaults are reported in the VAWA section of the annual security report submitted to the Department of Education. This tally complicates our understanding of collegiate crimes because it decouples the rapes from the aggravated assaults. In the published campus security report, compliant with the Clery Act, all we will see is a tabulation of three rapes in the criminal offenses section and three aggravated assaults in the VAWA section of the report. There will be no suggestion that these crimes were related to each other. Furthermore, the aggravated assaults documented in the VAWA section are not included among the aggravated assaults in the criminal offenses section because the hierarchy rule excludes them—they were trumped by the rapes that were reported instead. Furthermore, the weapons used during commission of the crimes must be reported under the weapons violations section of the institutional annual security report. But those weapons violations aren't reported under the criminal offenses section because there is no reporting of weapons use under the criminal offenses section of the report. That section includes only the number of victims experiencing one of the criminal offenses as the most serious crime committed against them (three of the 15 rapes described above for the reasons previously discussed).

At this time, you may be getting the idea that annual campus security reports published by higher education institutions may not provide as much information as one might expect or information that doesn't mean what you think it means. That would be the correct interpretation!

Moving on from sexual assaults and the known underreporting of these crimes, the final and most serious offenses reported under the Clery Act are those crimes against persons involving loss of life—negligent manslaughter, non-negligent manslaughter and homicide. Negligent manslaughter is "the killing of another person through gross negligence."[35] This category is often difficult to assign because determining "gross negligence" on the part of an assailant is not easy. Many cases of negligent manslaughter might easily be investigated as accidental deaths from various causes, deaths due to a person's own negligence, or traffic fatalities—none of which are reportable under the Clery Act. Negligent manslaughters are very rarely reported. In my research for this book, there was only one reported negligent manslaughter incident on a college campus in the United States since 2001.

Non-negligent manslaughter or homicide is "the willful (non-negligent) killing of one human being by another."[36] Thus, there is a distinction of intent with non-negligent manslaughter or homicide versus negligent manslaughter. The "willful killing" aspect distinguishes the former category from "killing through negligence." Any instance of homicide and non-negligent manslaughter on college campuses should always be reported under the Clery Act because it is the most serious criminal offense under the hierarchy rule. For this reason, I have chosen to write this book with special reference to collegiate homicides in the United States. Virtually every other collegiate crime is underreported (sometimes dramatically so, as I've discussed). But homicides should always be reported. In the words of 2016 edition of *The Handbook for Campus Safety and Security Reporting*, "Count one offense per victim."[37] Even if an institution fails to report a homicide, "the truth will out," as it is very difficult to hide a murdered person. Someone will eventually notice that their daughter or son or friend is not responding to messages; staff people failing to appear for work will be noticed; faculty failing to appear for their classes will be noticed. Homicide simply can't be hidden. But, remarkably, it can be underreported.

The Clery Act requires that homicide and non-negligent manslaughter or negligent manslaughter be reported. However, the Clery Act does not require the reporting of non-criminal deaths. Suicides, accidental deaths from any accidental cause (for instance, a fall from a building or down a flight of stairs or an accidental overdose of a prescribed drug), traffic fatalities, fetal deaths, situations in which a person succumbs to a heart attack as a result of being criminally victimized, and homicides committed in self-defense or to prevent the commission of some other crime (i.e., justifiable homicides by private citizens or police) aren't reported. So, for the most part, homicide statistics are accurate, but there are caveats. If a person is found dead on a campus and it may reasonably be asserted that it was suicide or some form of accidental death or any of the situations described above, there is no obligation to report the death because those forms of death aren't crimes. But consider this scenario: If a person dies from a fall, was the person pushed, or was it an accidental fall, or was it a purposeful suicide? If there are no witnesses, who can say? How will we ever know? The only scenario of those three that should be reported is the first. If there are no witnesses, it may reasonably be asserted that the second or third scenario was the cause of death. It's problematic. Are there actual, documented instances of this type of underreporting occurring in campus security reports? No, of course not. Think that through carefully.

The final class of criminal offense that must be reported under the Clery Act is hate crimes. These crimes are exempt from the hierarchy rule, so all hate crimes must be reported, not just the most serious hate crime. Unfortunately, hate crimes are challenging issues in society and on college campuses. To qualify as a hate crime, there must be evidence that bias against the victim was part of the motivation for the crime.[38] However, demonstrating bias can be difficult. Further, the Clery Act only recognizes eight classes of bias: race, religion, sexual orientation, gender, gender identity, ethnicity, national origin, and disability. What if the College Socialists office was burglarized and the burglar spraypainted "I HATE SOCIALISTS" and "KILL ALL SOCIALISTS" on the walls? Burglary is a reportable criminal offense under the Clery Act, and there is evidence that the burglary was motivated by bias against socialists. However, the burglary is not a hate crime because "political affiliation" is not a protected class under the law. How does the law define bias against the protected classes?

Racial bias is "a preformed negative attitude toward a group of persons who possess common physical characteristics, e.g., color of skin, eyes, and/or hair; facial features, etc., genetically transmitted by descent and heredity which distinguish them as a distinct division of humankind, e.g., Asians, blacks or African Americans, whites."[39] What about biracial or multiracial people, who represent an increasing demographic in America's melting pot? Are biracial or multiracial people a "distinct division of humankind"?

Hate crimes directed toward individuals' and groups' sexual orientation are the second-most common type of hate crime recorded on college campuses (with crimes motivated by racial bias being most common). Bias toward sexual orientation is described as "a preformed negative opinion or attitude toward a group of persons based on their actual or perceived sexual orientation."[40] Individuals manifest their sexual orientation in many ways. Most people are familiar with the designations *heterosexual, homosexual, lesbian, gay,* and *bisexual.* Fewer people in the general public are fully cognizant of the orientation of individuals as *queer, questioning,* or *asexual,* and even fewer comprehend *transgender* or *intersex identity.* Nonetheless, crimes targeting homosexuals and persons identifying as transgender are among the most common hate crimes on college campuses in the United States.[41] Not surprisingly, hate crimes manifesting bias against sexual orientation are associated with hate crimes targeting gender and gender identities. Gender bias is "a preformed negative opinion or attitude toward a person or group of persons based on their actual or perceived gender, e.g., male or female," whereas bias toward gender identity is defined as "a preformed negative opinion or attitude toward a person or group of persons based on their actual or perceived gender identity, e.g., bias against transgender or gender non-conforming individuals."[42] As discussions regarding the gender binary, gender fluidity, and the gender spectrum have emerged on college campuses, the number of reported hate crimes targeting gender and gender identity has increased, primarily due to increased awareness of this crime category.

Religious bias is bias manifesting "preformed negative opinion or attitude toward a group of persons who share the same religious beliefs regarding the origin and purpose of the universe and the existence or nonexistence of a supreme being, e.g., Catholics, Jews, Protestants, atheists."[43] Historically, a number of religious groups in the United States have experienced bias and bias-motivated crimes on college campuses: Catholics, Jews, members of the Church of Jesus Christ of Latter-day Saints (i.e., Mormons), and so forth. More recently, bias-motivated crimes have targeted persons practicing the tenets of Islam, and these crimes have found their way onto the campuses of higher education institutions nationwide.[44]

Hates crimes targeting ethnicity (i.e., bias "toward a group of people whose members identify with each other, through a common heritage, often consisting of a common language, common culture ... and/or ideology that stresses common ancestry")[45] and national origins (i.e., bias "toward a group of people based on their actual or perceived country of birth")[46] must also be reported under the Clery Act. Finally, hate crimes may be directed at persons with disabilities, defined as "physical or mental impairments, whether such disability is temporary or permanent, congenital or acquired by heredity, accident, injury, advanced age or illness."[47]

Hate crime reporting is an important amendment to the Clery Act, as it captures a class of collegiate crimes that has long been ignored. In addition, the types of criminal offenses reported as hate crimes are more expansive than for other crime categories in the Clery Act. This is partly due to the seriousness ascribed to the emotional aspects of these crimes as expressions of real hatred for various peoples attending higher education institutions.

The crimes that must be reported in the hate crimes section of annual campus security reports are as follows: (1) murder and non-negligent manslaughter, (2) sexual assault, (3) robbery, (4) aggravated assault, (5) burglary, (6) motor vehicle theft, (7) arson, (8) larceny-theft, (9) simple assault, (10) intimidation, and (11) destruction/damage/vandalism of property. (Note that the last four offenses are only reported as elements of hate crimes.)

Hate crimes reporting under the Clery Act is exempt from the hierarchy rule. If multiple criminal offenses are committed and motivated by hate in a single incident, all criminal offenses are counted in the hate crimes section of the annual security report from the institution. Further, each crime is described with the corresponding category of bias (for example, aggravated assault motivated by racial bias, or larceny and arson motivated by religious bias). It's of interest to note that amending the Clery Act to report hate crimes included a legitimate effort to identify and categorize all bias-motivated offenses. It seems that this strategy could easily be extended to non-bias-motivated crimes in order to provide our nation with more complete records of the totality of criminal victimizations on college campuses.

The preceding pages provide just a glimpse of the complexity involved in reporting collegiate crimes under the Clery Act. As I mentioned previously, the 2016 handbook for reporters is 265 pages long. It takes a good deal of training to ensure that campus crimes are properly underreported in accordance with the law (I'll be in trouble for writing that, but it's true)! Progress in collegiate crime reporting has been incremental. The addition of VAWA and hate crime offenses has improved reporting overall (particularly because VAWA and hate crimes are exempt from the hierarchy rule), but criminal victimizations in our nation's colleges remain underreported. If nothing more emerges from this book than a discussion of what we should do to better report all crimes on college campuses, I will view that as a success. We deserve to know how safe our college campuses are.

The discussion so far in this chapter focused on *which* crimes get reported under the Clery Act and *how* they get reported. We have not yet explored the geographic boundaries of crime reporting for higher education institutions. At the outset of this chapter, I posed a number of questions regarding the geographic limits of "the campus." The 2016 *Handbook for Campus Safety and Security Reporting* includes a chapter describing what is known as "The Clery Act Geography"—that is, the geographic limits for which crimes must be reported at institutions. As with the types of crimes that must be reported, understanding the geography of college crime reporting is necessary to know how to interpret annual security reports published by higher education institutions.

Generally speaking, the Clery Act requires crime reporting from four specific geographic locations related to an institution: (1) on campus, (2) on-campus residential facilities, (3) public property on or adjacent to the campus, and (4) non-campus facilities owned or controlled by the institution.[48] The Clery Act defines "on-campus" locations as "any building or property owned or controlled by an institution within the same reasonably contiguous geographic area and used by the institution in direct support of, or in a manner related to, the institution's educational purposes, including residence halls; And any building or property that is within or reasonably contiguous to the area identified in paragraph (1) of this definition, that is owned by the institution but controlled by another person, is frequently used by students, and supports institutional purposes (such as a food or other retail vendor)."[49]

For institutions in the United States that were constructed according to the Anglo-Saxon University Model described in the first chapter, identifying "the campus" is relatively easy. There is usually a clear institutional footprint with a distinct geographic boundary, and it is plainly evident when one is on campus and when one is not. However, over the years, many communities have grown up around college campuses, diffusing the boundary somewhat. Or colleges have expanded into the surrounding communities through acquisition of properties that weren't originally part of the "monastic campus." My institution has a very distinctive core campus with obvious physical boundaries (public roads that adjoin the property). However, the university has expanded rather dramatically in 20 years to properties quite remote from the central core. This situation is very common nationally. In addition, many urban college campuses have rather indistinct boundaries. For example, the Massachusetts Institute of Technology (MIT) has an original campus that is quite distinct, but over the years MIT has also acquired a number of buildings within the downtown metro area of Cambridge, Massachusetts, so the campus "boundary" has become very obscure. So the concept of "contiguity" in the definition above refers in part to geographic (spatial) contiguity but also, and more important, extends to contiguity of ownership or control of properties. With respect to geographic contiguity of the institution, a rule of thumb is that properties controlled or owned by the institution within one mile of the campus are considered contiguous. However, there are many exceptions to this rule. My institution owns and controls properties several miles from campus; these are sufficiently far away that the university operates a motor shuttle to and from the facilities from the central core campus. Those facilities are considered "on campus" for purposes of Clery Act reporting. "On campus" also relates to property owned by the institution but not controlled by it. An example at my institution is retail spaces leased by the institution in the student union and on the first floor of our parking decks. The institution leases these spaces to private retailers and concessionaires, who control them. However, these spaces are also considered "on campus" under the Clery Act. On-campus residential facilities are a subset of on-campus locations for which crimes must additionally be reported under the Clery Act. If a Clery-classified crime occurs in an on-campus residential facility, it is reported under "on-campus student housing" and also in the overall "on campus" portion of the annual campus security report. It's actually quite important to properly identify "on campus" geography under the Clery Act because the next geographic location for which crimes must be reported is public property adjacent to the campus. If an institution cannot accurately describe its on-campus boundaries, it will not be possible to determine the public property within or adjacent to the campus.

Public property within or adjoining the campus is considered sufficiently close to the institution that crimes occurring there must be reported. This is due, in part, to the idea that most of the people in proximity to the campus are likely connected in some way with the activities controlled by the institution. An example of public property within an institution is a public road that bisects the central core of a campus, dividing it into two sections. Another example is a public parking lot within the campus that is owned, operated or maintained by a municipality, or perhaps a stream with a public walking trail along its banks that crosses the campus. Property adjoining the campus around its periphery is another category of public property. Public streets bounding a campus or public parking lots adjacent to the campus property are sites where crimes must be reported in compliance with the Clery Act. A general rule of thumb regarding the geographic limits of public property for which the institution is responsible for reporting crimes is a sidewalk next to the campus, the public street adjacent to the sidewalk, and the sidewalk on the other side of the street. For an urban campus with many buildings scattered across a downtown area, the sidewalk-street-sidewalk geography around each individual building would constitute the public property aspect of the institutional "Clery geography." Crimes occurring on private property bordering a campus are not reported in any circumstances under the Clery Act. Thus, a burglary at a private home adjacent to a campus would not be reported. By contrast, public parks or public waterways bordering the campus or crossing it (as mentioned above) are part of the public property geography under the Clery Act, so crimes occurring there must be reported. Public transit stops (bus stops, bus stations or subway/train stations) adjoining a campus are also part of the public property geography for which crimes must be reported.

Finally, there is a "non-campus property" category of Clery geography. This is perhaps the most difficult to identify and categorize, but it is also very likely the least common for most institutions. Non-campus property and buildings are "owned or controlled by a student organization that is officially recognized by the institution; or any building or property owned or controlled by an institution that is used in direct support of, or in relation to, the institution's educational purposes, is frequently used by students, and is not within the same reasonably contiguous geographic area of the institution."[50] The most obvious examples of this geographic category are sorority and fraternity houses located off the institutional campus, but other examples are buildings affiliated with religious groups (churches, mosques, or similar buildings). At my institution, there is an Institute of Religion owned and operated by the Church of Jesus Christ of Latter-day Saints situated across the street from my university but between the main campus and a university-owned parking lot. This building is used by university students of the LDS faith, and many university students and personnel cross the property every day to the parking lot and campus. Any crimes occurring on this property must be reported in the "non-campus" category. In another example, the Brite Divinity School in Fort Worth, Texas, is an independent institution with a separate board of governance, assets, and employees, but it is affiliated with the divinity academic programs at Texas Christian University. TCU students attend courses at the Brite Divinity School and receive academic credit from TCU toward divinity degrees conferred by the university. Crimes occurring on property associated with the Brite Divinity School must be reported by TCU under the non-campus category. (Interestingly, the Brite Divinity School would also report these crimes as occurring in its "on-campus" category.) One last example of non-campus properties for which crimes must be reported are parks or athletic facilities that may be contracted to host institutional activities of various kinds. During those times that the institution has control of those facilities, any crimes occurring there would require reporting under the "non-campus" category.

These are just a few examples of geographic locations for which crimes must be reported under the Clery Act. I'm certain that you could think of several more and properly assign them to "on campus," "public property," or "non-campus" categories with some thought. Understand, though, that there are many off-campus sites where college students and personnel are victimized that are not reported in campus security reports. Generally speaking, students or others out in the public at large assume the same risks of criminal victimization as any other member of our society, and they are victimized at similar rates. There are no magic shields. College attendance or employment at a college doesn't confer any particular protection in the general society beyond the campus boundaries. And you, my reading friend, already know what the risks of gun violence are in American society. Let's return, then, to the premise of this book, because now the rubber meets the road.

We're engaged in an extraordinary social experiment. Nationwide in our "civil" society, mass shootings in public occur more than once a day.[51] A number of victims equal to the populations of entire cities are killed every year, year after year after year after year. At this moment, it is very likely that there's an active shooter somewhere in America. Within the continental-scale shooting gallery we call the United States of America, we have created tiny islands of unarmed people. They're not sequestered behind walls. They're not held captive in fenced-off reserves. They come and go as they please. The boundaries of their sanctuaries are open. I'm one of the guinea pigs—a human lab rat. It's time to find out how they're doing. Time to pull back the curtain—time for "the big reveal." Time to see the results of this experiment and reflect on those results. It's moment of truth time. Are you ready?

5

The Profile of Collegiate
Homicide in the United States

"The truth will out."
—*William Shakespeare*

Our social experiment is taking shape. I outlined the nature of the experiment for you in chapter 2; then, in chapter 3, I provided you with the context describing the nature and incidence of gun homicides in the United States. In chapter 4, I provided information regarding the source of crime statistics on higher education campuses in the United States: the Jeanne Clery Disclosure of Campus Security Policy and Campus Crime Statistics Act.[1] The Clery Act requires all U.S. institutions of higher education participating in federal student financial aid programs to keep records of certain crimes against persons and certain property crimes committed on and around their campuses. Crime records for a given calendar year must be reported annually on or before 1 October of the next calendar year. For instance, campus crimes for the 2018 calendar year (1 January 2018–31 December 2018) must be reported on or before 1 October 2019. Campus security reports are maintained by authorized campus officers, a task commonly given to campus public safety offices or law enforcement departments. The official records of annual crime statistics are submitted to the U.S. Department of Education, where they are archived and warehoused.

Digital records of annual Clery Act reports are currently available online for the time period of 2001–2016.[2] The Campus Safety and Security Data Analysis Cutting Tool[3] is an interactive data warehouse that is customizable and publicly available (you can access the same data I've used to write this book if you wish) and can be viewed or downloaded at no cost because your tax dollars provide the budget for the U.S. Department of Education and a portion of that budget is used to compile, archive, and make public the data on campus crimes. In short, you already paid for these data, and your government provides you with the means to review the data any time you wish. This is a valuable service to parents across America. As your daughters and sons begin to think about attending college, whether it be a 4-year university or college, a 2-year college or a technical institute, you can review the security status of the campuses under consideration and make your own determination of the relative safety of the campus environment for your soon-to-be college student. Just remember that campus crime reports submitted in compliance with the Clery Act don't represent the total number of crimes on a campus annually, but rather the total number of reported campus crime victims. Nonetheless, this is potentially useful information for parents concerned about the safety and well-being of their children during their college years.

While you may be interested in the security status of a particular campus, I am interested in the totality of campus security across the United States. I don't want to know how many crime victims there are on one campus, but rather how common or uncommon crime is on all campuses. And, true to the experiment I've outlined in previous chapters, I want to test the hypothesis that campus crime is no different from what is the case in society at large. It's important to remember the constraints on this experiment. I'm comparing the incidence of homicides on college campuses to the incidence of homicides in society at large. In particular, I'm interested in the incidence of gun homicides on college campuses and how that compares to gun homicides among the U.S. general public, but I'm creating a profile of all campus homicides as well. I'm focusing on homicides that occur within the boundaries of the college campus—what the Clery Act defines as on-campus homicides. The reason for this focus is because proponents of campus-carry legislation proclaim that our campuses are unsafe. They don't say that the campus and off-campus sites are unsafe. Their focus is placing guns on campus, for the obvious reason that guns are already allowed off campus. And homicides that occur off campus are homicides that occur in society at large—so those crimes are being recorded in FBI crime data[4] and in fatal injuries reported by the CDC.[5] Off-campus homicides are the comparison group for on-campus homicides. To be sure, college students are murdered at off-campus venues. Those murders, however, are included in the murder statistics for society at large, and they are differentiated from homicides that occur on campus for purposes of this experiment.

Another important aspect of this experiment that should be understood (and that differentiates it from many other studies) is that the data being analyzed represent all the data we have available. Many studies of crime depend on surveys—that is, randomized representative samples taken from a much larger population. Results presented here are not survey results extrapolating larger trends from a randomized representative sample. Results contained in this book represent an inventory—the sum total of all homicides on college campuses and in society at large to the extent that we know them. I've endeavored to document each individual homicide reported to the U.S. Department of Education from a college campus during the 21st century.

I want you to understand what the Clery Act data looks like, though. The database of collegiate crimes available from the Department of Education is nothing more than a table of numbers. Data submitted in compliance with the Clery Act by higher education institutions is just a count of crime victims on each campus. There are no details regarding the nature of those crimes. There is no personally identifiable information about the victims or any details about the nature of the crimes they endured. All the data I had to start with from these records was the year in which a homicide occurred and the specific institution's campus where it occurred. However, I was able to uncover additional details of each collegiate homicide in the United States through a simple method.

Using the year and the campus information provided in the Department of Education data, I searched for news reports of each incident from online sources. Basically, I googled the information using search terms like "homicide at Virginia Tech University 2007." That search was sufficient in most cases to reveal one or more news reports of the homicide for which I was searching because homicides on college campuses are rare, newsworthy incidents. Once I found one news article about a homicide, that story often contained further details about the incident that I was able to exploit to find additional stories and (for crimes that happened a number of years ago) even court documents regarding the trial of the murderer. Court documents were particularly useful because they frequently contained a great deal of information from sworn testimony regarding very specific details of each incident—details often omitted from newspaper stories.

From these records, I've been able to compile relatively complete information for 214 of 219 incidents (97.7%). There remain 5 incidents for which I have not found any documentation. It's not certain that those events happened on the college campuses that reported them; that information may have been coded incorrectly in the original reports or entered erroneously into the wrong column of a table. It is also possible that the incident occurred and was initially reported to police but later deemed to be something other than a homicide (for example, a suicide, which is not a criminal offense reportable under the Clery Act). If an incident was originally reported but later determined not to be a homicide, it should have been excluded from the report, but, as I mentioned, mistakes happen. It is curious that there are no news stories about the undocumented incidents, which leads me to think that perhaps they are record-keeping errors. I uncovered several of those in the course of my research for this book. For example, a small community college in Alabama, Enterprise State Community College, reported a homicide in 2011. Finding no records of this event, I called the Enterprise, Alabama, police department and spoke directly to the officer responsible for logging crime data for its FBI reports. She informed me that in this small town, homicide is rare, and there were none during 2011. To recap, I found no public records regarding a homicide at Enterprise State Community College and the person on the local police force responsible for logging crime data (who was already experienced in that position in 2011) checked the records and had none regarding a homicide in 2011. I can only conclude, then, that this episode was misreported in the Clery Act data. This incident and 5 others remain undocumented.

For the 97.7% of incidents I have documented, a detailed profile of collegiate homicide emerges. And that profile is, I think, surprising. Collegiate homicides don't look like you would probably expect. They certainly don't match the description provided by legislators in various states as they outline the necessity for guns on campus laws. My contention, after reviewing all the available data on collegiate homicides, is that these incidents are comprehensible. We can derive understanding about the nature and cause of these incidents by studying the available data, but those data haven't been available until now. What follows in this chapter is the development of a detailed profile of collegiate homicide in the United States. That profile should be used by campus authorities, campus law enforcement departments, and municipal and state police to develop effective methods for policing college campuses and reducing the chances for homicides at college. That is an important contribution of this book, and I hope campus law enforcement and higher education leaders are reading these pages right now. Knowledge is power. The power to reduce college murders—that is something.

So, to sum up, I've corroborated all but a handful of these crimes from published news reports and extracted details of the circumstances for each homicide. In some cases, the level of detail is as precise as knowing the exact time of death and the specific room in a specific building on a college campus. In a few cases, I've been able to identify the specific space in a parking lot where a murder occurred.

Fortuitously, I believe that homicide data are the most completely reported crimes from college campuses. There are several reasons for this belief. Recall that crime reporting in compliance with the Clery Act prioritizes the reporting of crime victims as opposed to criminal victimizations. In addition, there is a hierarchy of crime reporting such that only the most serious crime is reported in most incidents where a single victim may have experienced multiple crimes. Thus, under most circumstances, Clery Act reporting requires that only one crime is reported per victim. Homicides, however, are the most serious criminal incidents in the Clery Act hierarchy, and so homicides will always be reported. Further, homicide can only be perpetrated once against an individual victim. It is, perhaps, the only crime in the database with a strict one victim–one crime correlation. Each count in the database corresponds to exactly one victim and one homicide. So these data are complete (which can't be said for other crimes in the Clery Act database). The facts here are not disputable. They are what we know for every collegiate homicide in the United States from 2001 to 2016. So let's see what we know. Let's review the who, what, when, where, why, and how of collegiate homicides in the United States.

The full complement of data downloaded from the U.S. Department of Education Campus Safety and Security Data Analysis Cutting Tool[6] represents summary tabulations of crime victims from the majority of public and private 4-year universities and colleges, public and private 2-year colleges, and public and private technical institutes across the United States. The data come from reports submitted in compliance with the Clery Act from 2001 to 2016. In total, the database constitutes reports from 8,981 uniquely identified college campuses in the 50 states and the District of Columbia.

Annually, the number of reported collegiate homicides ranged from a low of 8 in 2006 to a high of 45 in 2007; curiously, the year with the lowest homicide count was followed by the year with the highest. The 2007 count was high because 32 individuals were murdered in the third worst mass killing in U.S. history. That incident occurred on the campus of Virginia Tech University on 16 April 2007.[7]

Over the 2001–2016 interval, there were a total of 279 homicides reported across the nation's higher education campuses. Note that this is the record of homicides from all causes (guns, stabbings, beatings, strangulations, and a host of other causes that will be detailed in this chapter) on college campuses—an average of just over 17 per year. This number compares to about 16,300 homicides annually among the general public.[8] Homicides on college campuses are about 1,000 times less frequent than in society at large. That is a remarkably low incidence of victimization.

From 2001 to 2016, there were between 268,796[9] and 281,051 homicides[10] in the United States—more than a quarter-million people murdered throughout the land in 16 years. The difference between the homicide numbers above is derived from slightly different counting of homicide victims as reported by the FBI and the CDC.[11] Homicide data for the FBI are derived from Supplemental Homicide Reports (SHRs) submitted by most local law enforcement jurisdictions as part of their reporting to the national Uniform Crime Reporting system. However, submission of SHR information is strictly voluntary—there is no federal requirement to submit supplemental homicide reports to the FBI. While most law enforcement agencies comply, some do not. The voluntary nature of SHR submissions has recently come to public attention, as police-involved homicides have been found to be widely underreported in FBI annual homicide counts.[12] In addition, FBI homicide counts fall under two broad categories: (1) homicide and non-negligent manslaughter and (2) negligent manslaughter (that is, deaths caused by another person that were not intentional).[13] When the FBI reports homicide numbers and rates for the United States, it is reporting only homicides and non-negligent manslaughter incidents. Negligent manslaughter incidents are reported separately, as are justifiable homicides (that is, homicides committed as a consequence of legal intervention). Justifiable homicide might be due to a police-involved shooting or defensive gun use by an armed civilian to thwart a crime or threat to personal safety. In fact, those incidents are "homicides" (defined as the deliberate taking of another person's life through the application of lethal force), but they are not "criminal homicides." These homicides are functionally permitted under United States law because they were conducted against individuals who were in the act of committing a crime and, in some instances, were necessary to prevent harm to others.

In contrast to the FBI, the CDC compiles homicide statistics as part of its effort to report fatal injuries through the National Vital Statistics System (NVSS).[14] Homicide data are determined from death certificates submitted by medical examiners and coroners, and reporting is mandatory (unlike FBI reports). Further, CDC does not distinguish between homicide, non-negligent manslaughter, and negligent manslaughter, though it does discriminate criminal homicides from "homicides due to legal intervention" (i.e., justifiable homicide).[15] All are reported as homicides in the NVSS reporting scheme, and total homicides may include justifiable homicides, or justifiable homicides may be omitted for some counting procedures. Consequently, CDC homicide counts are commonly somewhat higher than FBI homicides (determined from voluntarily submitted Supplemental Homicide Reports). Regardless of the counting methodology, annual U.S. homicides from 2001 to 2016 represent combat-scale casualties—Killed In Action (KIA), if by "KIA" you actually mean "just trying to live their lives in America." For purposes of comparison in this book, I'm going to use CDC counts of firearm homicides in the United States. Truthfully, I could use the FBI counts, but the calculations don't change in meaningful ways, so I choose to use the more complete counts issued by the CDC throughout the rest of this book. For my purpose in comparing homicides in the general public to homicides on college campuses, I am interested only in the fact that homicides occurred. I am not judging the "purpose" of the homicide (i.e., justifiable or criminal). This approach adheres to the methodology used by the CDC.

For the purposes of the comparisons that follow, I will use total homicides in the United States from 2001 to 2016 (the most recent year available) of 281,051 derived from CDC counts of homicides from all causes during that time period.[16] On college campuses, there were 279 homicides (from all causes) from 2001 to 2016. So, out of 281,051 homicides in America, 279 were on college campuses. That's a mere 0.1% of all homicides in America, meaning that 99.9% of all homicides occur in locations that are not college campuses. Put another way, homicides on college campuses are 1,000 times less frequent than in the general public!

Of those 279 victims of college campuses, 171 were murdered using guns (61.3%). Thus, in our nation where 281,051 people were murdered in 16 years, 171 victims were killed with guns on college campuses. Those 171 collegiate gun-victims constitute just 0.09% of 191,546 gun-homicide victims in America; thus 99.91% of gun homicides occur in locations that are not college campuses. That doesn't look like a public safety issue for colleges to me. Does it look like a public safety issue for colleges to you?

If we compute total campus homicides this century (279) against the total U.S. population during this interval,[17] we get a homicide rate of 0.0057 per 100,000 persons. That calculated homicide rate on college campuses compares to 5.77 homicides per 100,000 in the public at large in America[18]; again, homicides on college campuses are 1,000 times less frequent than homicides in the U.S general population.[19] On college campuses nationwide, 279 victims were murdered in 219 individual incidents on 205 individual college campuses. Out of 8,981 unique campuses reporting annual crime statistics in compliance with the Clery Act, only 205 campuses reported murders over a 16-year interval. In other words, homicides occurred during this century on just 2.3% of college campuses in the United States. The remaining 97.7% of colleges nationally were murder-free up to this point in the 21st century. If you are the parent of a child considering college, or have a child in college right now, or are a person considering becoming a college student, or are currently a college student, or are a legislator in a state considering permitting guns on college campuses, you need to know that. Know that 97.7% of college campuses in the United States did not experience a homicide in 16 years. One more time for emphasis: NO MURDERS ON ALMOST 98% OF U.S. COLLEGE CAMPUSES SINCE 2001!

Supporters of guns-on-campus laws may object to my calculations regarding the homicide incidence rate on college campuses. They will argue that using the U.S. population as the basis for calculating the observed homicide rate from 2001 to 2016 creates an artificially low value. They may argue that I shouldn't inflate the population value by using the entire U.S. population because the entire U.S. population doesn't attend college. While it's true that not everyone attends or is employed at a U.S. college, each of the victims of homicide on each college campus was a member of U.S. society and, therefore, an individual among the entire U.S. population. So the calculation stands. But let's momentarily yield to the argument because I'm a professor and I like a robust academic discussion. I think it's fun to work through various alternative scenarios to see if alternative results (or, in current popular parlance, "alternative facts") present themselves. I also like an argument that I know I'm going to win.

For the sake of argument, let's state that we should determine the homicide rate on college campuses by considering the total number of victims and using only that portion of the U.S. population employed or enrolled in higher education as the population basis for the calculation. The U.S. Department of Education maintains extensive archives of educational statistics for all levels of education in the United States. Much of the data is available online through the data portal of the National Center for Educational Statistics.[20] It turns out this source has historical data documenting employment and enrollment statistics in higher education compiled in tables in the *Digest of Education Statistics*.[21] From 2001 to 2016, it's estimated that higher education employed a total of 58.5 million people.[22] Annually, there are 3–4 million people in the United States employed directly in higher education. That employment statistic reflects all types of employment in higher education: administrators, full-time faculty, part-time faculty, staff, football and basketball coaches, facilities managers, dormitory staff, custodial staff—everyone involved in making our national collegiate system work. During the 2001–2016 interval, U.S. post-secondary institutions enrolled an estimated 310,351,193 students, ranging from 16.3 million in 2001 to 21.6 million in 2010.[23] Adding those values together, higher education in the United States involved at least 368,851,193 people from 2001 to 2016. Within that population, 279 were victims of murder. The computed homicide rate, therefore, is 0.076 per 100,000 persons in higher education. That value is still almost 76 times lower than the observed homicide rate in the U.S. general population. Do supporters of guns-on-campus laws still object to my method of calculation? Probably, but they're wrong. Observed homicide rates on college campuses in the United States are substantially lower than observed homicide rates in the general public, no matter how you want to calculate those rates.

In 10 states, there were no reported murders on any college campus from 2001 to 2016. Congratulations, Alaska, Hawai'i, Minnesota, Montana, Nevada, New Hampshire, North Dakota, Rhode Island, South Dakota, and Vermont!

Utah was among the group of "no homicides on campus" through 2015. Unfortunately, Utah's string of good luck ran out on 29 December 2016. On that day, a woman employed at a medical technology firm operating from offices and laboratories at the University of Utah research park was murdered in the parking lot by her estranged husband, who then took his own life.[24]

Among the group of states above that had no collegiate murders from 2001 to 2016, only Utah permits the carrying of concealed, lethal weapons on campus. And while there were no murders before 2016 on college campuses in these states, that is not to say that there weren't any shootings. I'm talking to you, Utah, where a student with a permit to carry a concealed handgun shot himself in the leg with the concealed handgun he was permitted to carry in 2012.[25] Utah, previously among the zero-homicides-at-college states and the only state in that group that currently permits guns on campuses, was also the only state among the zero-homicides-at-college states to experience campus shootings. Perhaps it is also worth noting that Utah had a single gun murder on a campus in 1993,[26] a decade prior to implementation of its campus-carry law.

In any case, the U.S. higher education system averages fewer than a dozen-and-a-half homicides annually, and observed homicide rates on college campuses are consistently more than 1,000 times lower than in the U.S. general public. Of course, I don't mean to minimize the homicides that do occur on college campuses. I am completely aware that the data I'm using for this book documents 279 murders at colleges during the past 16 years. No one understands more acutely than I do the national tragedy and societal failure those deaths represent. I can't begin to imagine the impact those murders have on the surviving families and friends of the victims. Our society would be quite right to seek positive solutions to the violent impulses that bring murder to college campuses. Indeed, seeking those solutions is a big part of the reason I chose to write this book. But let's also be honest and admit that 17 collegiate murders per year embedded in a society that experiences up to 17,000 murders every year is not a crisis of public safety or college security. The war, it seems, is raging all around our collegiate sanctuaries. About 17 times per year, that civil war leaks through the boundaries of our collegiate sanctuaries and brings death to some of our daughters and sons. I can guarantee, though, that the observed college murder rate state-by-state is vastly lower than even the homicide rate in your state. It's most probably even lower than the homicide rate in your city, and not just by a little bit—by at least an order of magnitude. Prove me wrong.

I've now presented to you the summary of collegiate homicides from 2001 to 2016: 279 homicides nationwide yielding a calculated homicide rate of 0.0057 per 100,000 in the general population. It's interesting to know with certainty how much lower the observed incidence of homicide is on college campuses compared to the general public. That, by itself, ought to be sufficient argument to continue banning guns from college campuses. But it's not. It's not enough to simply add up the total homicides on college campuses since 2001. Doing so would be the laziest possible outcome. Seriously, there's 279 victims in 219 individual incidents. That's not a particularly large number compared to the 17,000 or so homicides in the United States every year. So I took it upon myself to further this analysis—in fact, to go much further than anyone has ever gone into this analysis.

Once I had the total number of homicides in hand, I vowed to track down all the information I could find for each one of the 219 murder incidents on U.S. college campuses. Truthfully, among data sets that I've used for research before, this was a really small inventory. I regularly deal with data sets that hold hundreds of thousands of entries. I'm currently working with one such set on another research project that has more than 12.5 billion individual data entries. It seems 219 is not much of a challenge. So let's see what those 219 incidents might reveal about the true nature of homicides on college campuses. Let's really examine the who, what, when, where, why, and how of collegiate homicides. Let's examine in detail the geography of collegiate homicide. Let's create a full profile of collegiate homicide. Understanding the details of each individual homicide on college campuses in the United States will provide us with greater insight into the phenomenon of collegiate murder. If you understand the phenomenon, you can create strategies to mitigate it. Effective policing and prevention of the most violent crime on college campuses will not only reduce its incidence but also very likely reduce the incidence of other crimes because many homicides occur during the commission of other crimes. This is the loftier objective of this book: providing greater insight and understanding into the nature of murder at college. In this way, law enforcement agencies and institutional authorities will have information that will help them better police the campus and provide for even greater security of their already very secure constituents. Our sanctuaries can become even more peaceful. All that is required is that we try to make them so.

Who are the victims of murder on college campuses? The majority are men (176 or 63.5%). Nationally, men constituted 76.6% of homicide victims.[27] Obviously, then, women were victims of the remaining 37.5% (101) of campus murders and 23.4% of murder victims nationally. Men are victimized more often than women in the general public and on college campuses, though women seem to be slightly more at risk than men among the college cohort. Importantly, though, it should be stated again, very clearly, that murders of either men or women on college campuses are 1,000 times less frequent than in the U.S. general public. However, the reported percentages of men versus women victims can be misleading. The perceived higher proportion of women victims results primarily from the very small number of total murder victims on college campuses compared to all homicides in the general public. It's equally important to remember the absolute scale of the numbers we're discussing here. Male victims of homicide in the general public from 2001 to 2016 totaled 221,287, of whom only 176 were on college campuses; for women, the totals are 59,764 in the general public versus 101 on college campuses. Would you rather take your chances in the general public or on college campuses? I pick college campuses.

All right, let's carry these analyses further. What is the age distribution of college homicide victims? First, let's examine the observed homicide rate among the dominant college age group, 18–24-year-olds, and compare it to the observed homicide rate among the same-aged cohort nationally. It's well known that 18–24-year-olds are the age group most at risk of being victimized by violent crime, including homicide, in the United States.[28] This result is derived, in part, from the social behaviors of this group. Young adults are sociable and congregate in groups frequenting late-night venues such as nightclubs and bars, some of which may be located in seedier parts of urban and suburban centers that have higher crime rates. In addition, young adults engage is recreational drug use that brings them into contact with criminal suppliers, putting their safety at risk. There are other risk factors, but the two I've listed are heavily weighted. The CDC reports homicides among 18–24-year-olds from 2001 to 2016 totaled 68,496.[29] The calculated homicide rate among this age group nationally was 14.20 per 100,000 persons.[30] Among the 279 homicide victims at U.S. colleges during this century, 143 (51.3%) were in the 18–24-year-old age group. The calculated homicide rate among college students in the 18–24-year-old age group as a fraction of that age group in the United States is 0.03 per 100,000 persons: 473 times lower than the observed homicide rate among that age group in the general public. If we compare the homicides of this age group only to that portion of the population enrolled in college (annually about 20 million students and totaling almost 310 million during the last 16 years),[31] the observed murder rate barely nudges upward to 0.046 per 100,000 college students. That's still 309 times lower than in the public at large. Truly, for 18–24-year-olds in America, college campuses are sanctuaries from murderers. Indeed, it's difficult to imagine a more secure and safe sanctuary for our young adults than college campuses nationwide. If you are a parent concerned about the safety and well-being of your college-aged child, your best bet is to send them to college somewhere—anywhere—in the United States.

Do I have data to perform the same calculations demonstrating the extraordinarily low murder rates for other age groups at colleges? I am so glad you asked! Young adults in the 18–24-year-old age group made up only 51.3% of victims. How old were the other 48.7% of campus murder victims?

There were 8 teens younger than 18 years old murdered on college campuses between 2001 and 2016. One was 16 years old; the others were 17 years old. The observed homicide rate among 16- and 17-year-olds in the United States is 6.88 per 100,000 (9,378 since 2001).[32] As a proportion of the U.S. population in that age group, the observed homicide rate of 16–17-year-olds on college campuses during the same interval is 0.006 per 100,000 persons, or more than 1,100 times lower on college campuses. As a proportion of all college students, the murder rate among 16–17-year-olds at college is 0.0026 per 100,000 students: almost 2,700 times lower than among the same age group in the general public. It's very likely that your 16- or 17-year-old would be substantially safer on a college campus than at their high school.

There were 39 murder victims (14.0%) in the age range of 25–34 years from 2001 to 2016. The observed murder rate of that age group on college campuses was 0.0006 per 100,000 as a portion of their representation in the U.S population. As a proportion of total collegiate population, the observed murder rate was 0.01 per 100,000. Note here that I am using the population of college employees and college students because this age group includes victims who were students and college employees. The observed murder frequency of the 25–34-year-old age group on college campuses compares to 11.15 per 100,000 among the general population.[33] Thus, the observed murder rate for 25–34-year-olds on college campuses as a fraction of the general public is more than 18,583 times lower than what is observed among this age group in the general public.

Among 35–44-year-olds, there were 30 homicides at U.S. colleges. The estimated murder rate of that age group is 0.004 per 100,000 as a portion of the U.S. population and 0.008 as a portion of the collegiate population. Elsewhere in America, 35–44-year-olds are murdered at a rate of 7.05 per 100,000. That's about 1,700 times more frequently than on college campuses.

Only 12 individuals aged 45–54 years were murdered on college campuses between 2001 and 2016. That translates to a murder rate of 0.002 per 100,000 as a portion of that age group in the U.S. population, or 0.003 per 100,000 college employees and students. The observed homicide rate for this age group in the general population across America is 4.84 per 100,000 persons.[34] That's roughly 1,600–2,400 times more frequent than on college campuses.

Finally, 19 homicide victims were older than 54 years (the oldest victim was 79 years old). The observed homicide rate for people aged 55–79 years in the United States is 2.71 per 100,000 persons. On college campuses, the observed murder rate was 0.002 per 100,000 as a portion of the U.S. general population, or 0.005 per 100,000 college employees and students. Once again, these numbers are 500–1,300 times lower than in the general public across America. At any age, by any measure, our colleges are sanctuaries from murder and other forms of violent crime victimization, significantly safer than being out in the general public. This is an extraordinary revelation, and we should all marvel at the overall safety and security of our higher education system compared to rates of violent crime victimization elsewhere in society. Rather than introducing lethal concealed weapons into these peaceful, relatively crime-free sanctuaries, we should be seeking to expand the safety and security of college campuses beyond their borders into all aspects of our lives.

What else was I able to glean about the victims from published reports of campus murders? Quite a lot more! To start, 150 victims (53.7%) were students enrolled at the college, and they were victims in 108 (49.3%) of the 219 documented incidents. Students constitute the largest class of victims, naturally, because students constitute the largest population group on college campuses. Notice, however, that students make up less than half the homicide victims on college campuses. Who do you think the other victims are? Faculty? Staff? In fact, the next largest group of murder victims on college campuses was persons unaffiliated with the college. Visitors or others unaffiliated with the campus who became victims of homicide account for 62 (22.2%) of 279 known individuals and were involved in 60 (27.4%) of 219 incidents. Visitors were most commonly victimized at parties at on-campus venues where altercations escalated to homicide. Some victims unaffiliated with the institutions weren't visitors at all but were merely murdered on campus property, or their bodies were dumped on a remote part of campus to be discovered later by bystanders or campus authorities. For example, the only recorded campus homicide in Idaho was a murder-suicide in 2003.[35] Neither person was a student at the institution or affiliated with it in any way. A young man drove his teen girlfriend to the parking lot of a remote campus athletic facility late at night, shot and killed her, and then took his own life. Both victims were discovered by a passing bicyclist. In one instance in California,[36] a woman's body was recovered from a burning vehicle. The resulting investigation determined that she had been murdered by her estranged husband off campus; he subsequently parked the car in a remote campus parking lot and set it on fire to cover up her murder. In another instance, a man was found murdered in the driver's seat of a car that crashed into a street sign along a campus perimeter. It was determined that he had been shot in his car, which eventually rolled onto campus property.[37] Several other instances of homicide were individuals whose bodies were found on campus.[38] It was not clear whether they had been murdered at the sites where they were discovered or whether the bodies were merely placed there after the fact. In a bizarre recent incident in California, a child was murdered by his estranged father in a remote parking lot on a community college campus; then the body was transported to the home and reported to police.[39]

Faculty and staff murders are relatively uncommon aspects of the collegiate homicide phenomenon. Overall, 20 staff personnel (7.2% of victims) and 25 faculty members (8.9%) were among murder victims from 2001 to 2016. However, faculty were rarely targeted by campus murderers and became victims of homicide in only 6.4% of incidents (14 of 219 incidents).

The next largest class of victims is, perhaps, the most shocking and disturbing aspect of the collegiate homicide profile. From 2001 to 2016, there were 10 reported incidents (3.6% of all incidents) of murdered newborns being found on college campuses. In each instance, investigation revealed that these babies were born to students who had hidden their pregnancies from everyone. Upon giving birth in dorm rooms or campus restrooms, at least some of these young women suffocated their children and attempted to dispose of the murdered newborns by various means. In a few instances, it was not determined whether the children were suffocated after birth or were stillborn.

Let us stop right here and ponder this phenomenon for a moment. Approximately every 1.5 years, at a college campus somewhere in America, a young woman is so stigmatized by her sexual activity and ensuing pregnancy that she hides the fact from everyone until a baby is born—up to 9 months later. This phenomenon is a known form of mental illness called neonaticide syndrome. Neonaticide is defined as a mother murdering her newborn within the first 24 hours after birth. Most of these incidents are perpetrated by adolescent mothers.[40] Annually, there are about 250 instances of neonaticide in the United States. Thus, the observed rate of neonaticide annually in this country is about 0.08 per 100,000 population. Every 1.5 years or so, one of those neonaticides occurs on a college campus, which is to say that neonaticide is about 400–500 times less frequent on college campuses than in the general public. The description that follows is taken from a recent review of neonaticide syndrome.[41]

Most of these young women are in their late teens (i.e., college aged) and experience a spectrum of social stigmas. They are commonly unmarried and living with their parents when they aren't away at college, causing them to be somewhat socially isolated, with passive and perhaps immature personalities lacking in a sense of personal responsibility. They may be victims of various forms of abuse, be it psychological, physical, or sexual. The relationship responsible for their pregnancy was probably transitory or fleeting, and the pregnancy was unintended but likely discovered after the relationship ended. The realization of pregnancy elicits many deeply emotional reactions. Chief among these emotions are fear and shame: fear of the pregnancy and eventual birth, fear that the pregnancy will be discovered by friends and family, and fear regarding their inability to properly care for the child developing inside them, being ill equipped to provide daily care, feeding, or parental nurturing for the child or to manage the financial responsibility of child rearing. These combined fears give rise to intense shame. Overwhelmed by the emotional turmoil of their unintended pregnancy and unable to emotionally process the magnitude of their predicament, these young women concoct elaborate plans to hide their condition. Revealing the pregnancy is not a consideration for them. Some develop the delusion that they are not pregnant. At least some of the women among the documented cases of neonaticide on college campuses testified during their trials that they were unable to comprehend the birth event when it happened. They claim to have been completely unaware that they were pregnant. This is real. It actually happens. It happens across our society, and it happens about every other year at a college in the United States. I'm going to wager that those of you who just read this passage had not imagined this form of homicide on college campuses. I hadn't imagined it when I began this research. And it certainly isn't how we imagine murders on college campuses.

So neonaticides account for about 3.6% of all homicides on college campuses. What are the other modes of homicide. Are there any other surprises? Yeah, probably. Mass killings? Yes, there have been mass killings on college campuses.

A mass killing is defined as a single incident in which 4 or more people were killed. Which do you think is more common on college campuses—a mass killing or a neonaticide? As measured by the number of incidents, neonaticides outnumber mass killings from 2001 to 2016 by 3-to-1. The murder records used for this book document 10 neonaticides and 3 mass killings for that time period. Of course, the casualty numbers are greater for mass killings (because they're defined as a minimum of 4 murders per incident), but there have been only 3 mass killings on college campuses since 2001. Three mass killing incidents out of 219 documented incidents—only 1.4% of incidents. In other words, 98.6% of homicide incidents on college campuses were not mass killings. There were 5 triple homicides reported in this century and 7 double homicides—a total of 15 multiple murder incidents (6.8%; 3 mass killings, 12 multiple killings) among 219 reported incidents across the nation. Multiple homicides (i.e., double, triple, or mass killings) accounted for 26.9% of total casualties (75 of 279 victims).

Therefore, multiple homicides and mass killings are significant. They account for slightly more than 25% of homicide victims but make up only 6.8% of all on-campus homicide incidents. They are the embodiment of what risk management professionals refer to as "high-impact, low-probability" events.[42] High-impact, low-probability events (HILPs) are sometimes also referred to as "black swan events," a reference to the sudden, unpredictable appearance of a black swan in a population of white swans. The foundational concept is that some incidents have very high impact but extremely low probabilities of occurrence. An example from recent history is the global economic collapse in 2008. Such events are ones of unprecedented magnitude, as was the 2008 economic downturn and the 2007 mass killing at Virginia Tech. HILPs, owing to their extraordinary improbability, are largely unpredictable. That is not to say, however, that we can't imagine them and prepare as best we can.

Campus homicide data are skewed by the mass killing on the campus of Virginia Tech in 2007. In this incident, 32 individuals, students and faculty, were murdered in the third worst mass killing in U.S. history. It accounts, by itself, for 11.4% of all campus homicides in the 21st century. For nearly a decade, the Virginia Tech mass killing was the worst mass killing perpetrated by a single individual in U.S. history. Now, it's number 3 because in June 2016 the mass killing at Pulse nightclub in Orlando, Florida, surpassed it, and then the mass killing in Las Vegas, Nevada, on 1 October 2017 surpassed Orlando. Nonetheless, Virginia Tech remains a statistical outlier among collegiate homicide incidents.

It is notable that following the events at Virginia Tech, higher education institutions nationwide reviewed what was known about that incident and implemented a broad array of enhanced security measures. It is also notable that there hasn't been a repeat incident of similar magnitude on a college campus since 2007. We cannot predict HILPs—they are extreme events, and there is too much uncertainty surrounding attempts to predict them. Following Virginia Tech, however, higher education institutions nationwide imagined such events, and they implemented strategies for campus security intended to minimize their impacts in the future. Risk management professionals will tell you that's the best strategy to develop; nothing can prevent the next "black swan," but we can prepare for its eventuality and know how to arrest the incident to minimize its impact.

The remaining 204 murder incidents (93.2%) were single homicides. Most of those homicides (as well as several multiple homicides) were not random events with random victims perpetrated by a random assailant. They were not "black swans." Many of the murders committed on college campuses are targeted killings: an individual comes onto the campus seeking a particular person (or persons) and, on finding that person (or persons), kills them. Examining the records of every homicide incident, there is demonstrable evidence that the victims were acquainted with the assailants in at least 62.6% of incidents. There is circumstantial evidence of some prior interaction between victim and assailant in approximately 20 other cases (another 9.1%). So it seems that victims and assailants had some form of acquaintance in up to 72% of known campus murders. Consider this: if you are going to become a victim of homicide on a college campus, it's very likely that you have already met your murderer.

For 142 homicide incidents involving men, the victim was demonstrably acquainted with the assailant in 81 instances. That is, male victims knew their assailant in at least 57% of homicides on college campuses. For women, there were 77 incidents of homicide on college campuses. The female victim knew her assailant in 60 of those 77 incidents (78%). Think about that: nearly 4 out of 5 women murdered on college campuses knew their killer. Furthermore, of the 77 homicide incidents involving women, 47 (61%) were homicides committed as acts of domestic violence by intimate partners. Again, this fact emphasizes that many of these murders were not random events—victims knew their assailants, and there is frequently a documented history of prior abusive behaviors. The violence often escalates over time, culminating in murder. This observation does not challenge sociological theories or abundant evidence from the field of criminal justice and criminal psychology. We have a lot of societal experience with exactly this type of violence, and we have good ideas and best practices to mitigate the escalation to murder, to protect victims from their abusers, and to get help for the abusers so they don't continue to abuse others. We also have abundant evidence of our societal failure to adequately address and treat these issues.

On college campuses, we have perhaps 143 or so murders since 2001 that involved assailants known to the victim(s). That's just over one-half of all collegiate homicides as evidence of our failure to identify and stop murderous acquaintances from targeting their victims. We can do better. But doing better requires understanding the nature and incidence of each event and seeking the underlying clues that reveal a pattern. This book is providing the necessary tools for pattern recognition. Campus security experts will undoubtedly take information provided here and use it to their benefit and the benefit of colleges everywhere to reduce homicide incidents in the future.

What do I know about the murder method for the 219 incidents of collegiate homicide? I know that in 113 incidents (51.6% of incidents with 171 victims), the perpetrator used a gun. Those 113 incidents of gun homicide occurred on 101 college campuses out of 8,981 campuses nationwide. That's just 1.1% of all college campuses in the United States; 98.9% of all college campuses did not experience gun homicides from 2001 to 2016. For those of you preparing to send your daughter or son to college, that should be a reassuring statistic. Your young adults are overwhelmingly likely to be safe during their college experience. Collegiate gun murder statistics compare to 11,000–12,000 gun homicides annually in the general public (191,546 firearm homicides since 2001).[43] Firearm homicides on college campuses account for just 0.09% of all firearm homicides in the United States. Elsewhere in the United States, every day, between 86 and 92 people die from gunfire.[44] Every two days, 172–184 people are killed with guns. On college campuses, 171 people were killed with guns over 16 years—fewer victims than in two days among the American public. Remember our discussion of the "Newtown" and the "Las Vegas" as measures of gun deaths in America? One Newtown is equal to 28 deaths, and one Las Vegas is equal to 58. Every day in the United States, we experience about 3 Newtowns and 1.6 Las Vegases, whereas college campuses nationwide experienced 279 total homicides (about 10 Newtowns and 4.8 Las Vegases) since 2001. Put another way, over the last 16 years there have been 6,841 Newtowns across America, but only 10 on college campuses. Newtowns are more than 684 times more frequent in the public sphere compared to college campuses. Since 2001, America has endured almost 3,302 Las Vegases, but just 4.8 on college campuses. Once again, La Vegases are about 688 times more common in the general public than on college campuses.

No matter how I calculate the numbers or manipulate the statistics, gun violence leading to homicide on college campuses is at least 600–1,000 times less frequent than it is in our armed and very dangerous society. You can't make this up. Facts aren't disputable. Don't try to tell me (and don't let anyone else tell you) that our college campuses nationwide are magnets for murderers. In fact, they are sanctuaries. Know this fact, and know it well. Tell your elected representatives the next time (i.e., this year) they bring forward a bill to permit guns on our campuses. Make them understand how safe college campuses are compared to the society they've enabled with their reckless gun policies. I'm a survivor of an unwitting (or should I say "witless"?) human experiment. I've survived it for 41 years—more than 10 times longer than your college student needs to survive on campus (4 years). The most likely outcome is that your college student will survive just like I did—without ever having a shot fired at them—so long as they attend a college where guns are prohibited. However, if they go to college where guns are permitted, all bets are off.

Every mass murder (i.e., an event with 4 or more homicides) on a college campus was perpetrated with a gun. Collegiate mass killings with guns accounted for 46 victims. All 5 triple murders were perpetrated with a gun, and 6 of 7 double murders were committed with a gun. There are only 3 mass killings reported on college campuses during the past 16 years. In the United States, there's more than one mass shooting every day on average. So it's really no contest to suggest that gun violence on college campuses is overwhelmingly less prevalent than in the U.S. general public. Now, I've generated the data to prove it. Gun homicides on college campuses, like other forms of homicide, are typically 1,000 times lower than in the general public. We can argue about likely causes of this phenomenon, but let me be the first to suggest that it's because colleges generally ban guns. Where there are no guns, there can be no gun violence. My opponents will seize on that last comment and mock it. Just watch. There will be a chorus of guffaws snickering, "But you just told us there were 171 gun deaths on campuses where there's no guns!" My answer is "Just imagine those 113 incidents and their 171 victims without the guns." Go ahead. Think about it all day if you need to. Then get back to me with your answer. Where there are no guns, there can be no gun violence.

The other methods used to commit homicide on college campus were stabbing (38 incidents with 39 victims), strangulation or suffocation (31 incidents with 31 victims), beatings (30 incidents with 30 victims), and 16 other methods with 16 victims. Other methods included drug overdoses administered to others,[45] vehicular homicide,[46] heat stroke,[47] starvation,[48] murder with a crossbow[49] (yes, that's correct—a crossbow), and an embolism suffered during an on-campus SCUBA class that was prosecuted as a non-negligent homicide.[50] Eagle-eyed readers will note that the totals reported here (171, 39, 31, 30, 16) add up to 287 "victims," though I've previously reported only 279. The difference here results because there was more than one reported mode of death for several homicides (for example, stabbing *and* beating, or strangulation *and* beating, or beating *and* suffocation, etc.). Those multiple modes give rise to the overcount.

Where do collegiate homicides occur? Regionally, collegiate homicides were most common in the southeastern United States. Higher education institutions in states of the Old Confederacy (Alabama, Arkansas, Florida, Georgia, Kentucky, Louisiana, Mississippi, North Carolina, South Carolina, Tennessee, and Virginia), as well as West Virginia and Missouri, account for 127 of 279 reported campus murders (45.5%; see Appendix I).[51] In other words, the U.S. South accounts for about half of all collegiate homicides in the United States. It's always the South.[52] Elsewhere, the densely populated northeastern states accounted for 77 collegiate murders (28.0%; see Appendix I), southwestern states accounted for 54 on-campus homicides (18.6%; see Appendix I), and the northwest rounded out the remaining 22 homicides (7.9%; see Appendix I).

Of 219 campus homicide incidents since 2001, I was able to determine the precise location for 214 incidents. Within the campus environment, there is a distinct geography of homicide. The most frequent locations for homicides on college campuses are dormitories and campus apartments—residential spaces occupied primarily by undergraduate and graduate students. Of the 214 incidents for which the specific campus location was known, 83 (38.8%) occurred in residential buildings. At first this might seem shocking, but it makes sense given that the majority of students' time on campus is spent in their residential building. Further, it's in the residential spaces that interpersonal interactions of all kinds play out. Sometimes thousands of students live in close quarters, and in those confined spaces emotions may flare. Altercations and other disagreements develop quite frequently, and they are difficult to escape. Feelings are hurt. Ugly words are spoken. Girlfriends and boyfriends break up. Students suffer a broad spectrum of emotional crises ranging from anxiety to deep depression as a consequence of being on their own for the first time or the stresses of the academic and social life of college. Sexual assaults occur. Simple assaults occur. Petty thefts occur. Dormitory life on college campuses simply isn't easy, and sometimes emotions run amok.

Most college students are somewhat immature. Remember, they are still teenagers for their first two years of college. And 20- or 21-year-olds aren't significantly more mature than 18- and 19-year-olds. As a professor who has interacted with and observed college students for 41 years, I can assure you that is true. They exercise questionable judgment—a lot. They are all struggling in their own ways to navigate their emerging adulthood, and there's often a lot of pressure placed on them to live up to the expectations of others. Mom and Dad want them to do well in their coursework to honor the financial investment being made in them. Professors want them to excel in their coursework to advance their learning. Friends want their undivided attention, and there's lots to participate in while at college—clubs, fraternities and sororities, bands, athletic teams, and intramural sports, to name a few. It's hard to keep up with all that and your studies. In addition, for many students nowadays, there are significant financial burdens associated with college. They have the usual expenses of tuition and fees, books, and supplies, but there's also mobile phone bills and automobile expenses of various kinds. Student loans and accumulating student debt place not only financial but also emotional burdens on students. They fret about finding post-college employment with adequate wages so they can pay back student loans and still meet their daily living expenses. And everything costs money.

As a result of these factors, college residential buildings can become flashpoints where angry moments and other frustrations may end in homicide. Many colleges are the equivalent of modest-sized cities, with similar numbers of residents. And yet the observed homicide rates on those colleges are vastly lower than homicide rates observed in similar sized cities.

In this century, higher education institutions have invested quite heavily in enhanced security for on-campus residences to keep intruders out. There are security cameras and controlled access points requiring students or visitors to check in at desks manned by institutional personnel. There are ID checks. There is controlled entry into dorms using electronic fobs and computer-chipped or magnetic-stripped cards. There are automatically locking doors to external entries, and even automatically locking doors for interior rooms. There is a concerted effort to keep intruders out of campus residence halls, and the security procedures work quite well so long as students don't bypass them. Unfortunately, 18–24-year-olds are social beings. Doors are propped open in anticipation of the arrival of friends, and intruders may enter. Keys are shared, and some enter the building when others are exiting—waiting for that moment when the door is open to all. Sometimes the murderers reside in the dorm and kill their roommates or others living with them. Sometimes they enter at the invitation of others. Rarely, they may break in or gain entry through some devious means. Sometimes they enter the residence hall to deal illegal drugs and kill their prospective customers when the deal goes awry.

Despite the best efforts to keep dormitories and campus apartments secure, murders happen on college campuses. But I want to emphasize once again how truly rare those incidents are. Imagine all the dorms and campus apartment buildings on all the college campuses in the United States. The database I'm using as a source of information for this book currently has 8,981 unique reporting campuses. Most of those campuses have more than one residential facility. To my knowledge, there is no detailed accounting of the total number of on-campus residential facilities in the United States, but some campuses have a dozen or more residence halls. So there are many thousands more dorms and campus apartments than higher education institutions across the country. And in all those facilities nationwide, there were 83 incidents of homicide during the past 16 years in dormitories—an average of just 5 per year. In a nation awash with guns and drowning in gun violence, with 32,000 deaths due to gunfire and 17,000 homicides from all causes every year, the record of safety and security on college campuses is quite extraordinary. Your daughters and sons are safe at college. That's not to say that they are absolutely safe; life in the United States doesn't come with a guarantee of absolute safety. But it's difficult to imagine a safer environment than your child's college campus and their college residential facilities.

The next most dangerous places on campus, as measured by the number of homicides that occurred there, are parking lots. People were murdered in college parking lots in 22.4% of all collegiate homicides. Parking lots on college campuses tend to be located near the campus peripheries. They are easily accessible and often serve as the entryways to campus. Parking lots can cover quite expansive areas; they may be multi-level parking decks. Securing these areas can be challenging. Many of the crimes committed in campus parking lots occur after normal business hours, often late at night when few other people are present. Campus parking lots may be used after normal business hours for regular public parking in downtown areas. Several homicides occurred in campus parking decks used for this purpose—members of the general public were murdered there and had no association or affiliation with the institution beyond using the parking facility after hours like other members of the general public.

Outdoor public spaces ranked third in the hierarchy of campus homicide geography, with 27 incidents (12.6%). Public spaces include sidewalks and streets adjacent to college campuses as well as campus facilities open to the public (such as campus unions, indoor arenas, picnic areas, etc.).

Campus academic buildings (that is, classroom spaces and laboratories) are rather infrequent sites of on-campus homicides, ranking fourth in the hierarchy of campus homicide geography. A total of 17 incidents (7.8%) occurred in academic buildings on college campuses. The 2007 Virginia Tech incident was the most significant to occur in classroom space; 31 of 32 victims were murdered in two classrooms in Norris Hall on the Virginia Tech campus (the 32nd victim was killed in a campus dormitory). The mass shooting on the campus of Umpqua Community College in Oregon in October 2015 was also perpetrated in a single classroom on the campus. There, 9 people were murdered, making it the third worst mass shooting on a college campus in the United States, ranking behind Virginia Tech and the "Texas Tower" mass shooting at the University of Texas in 1966. The only other mass killing on a college campus since 2001 occurred in a lecture hall in the geology building at Northern Illinois University in 2008. There, five people were murdered during an introductory geology class.

Other campus locations where homicides occurred are campus sports and recreation facilities (5.6%), administration buildings (5.1%), medical buildings (i.e., hospitals and mental health clinics—3.7%), and undeveloped campus natural spaces (2.8%). The available evidence for campus homicides indicates quite clearly that the most dangerous campus spaces are residential buildings and parking lots. Together, those two sites account for almost 6 of every 10 campus homicides. Thus, a strategy to reduce even the remote possibility of homicide on college campuses would involve improving the safety and security of dormitories and parking areas, especially parking areas near the periphery of campus or in remote areas. Having identified the campus danger zones, institutional officials should be able to work with campus law enforcement departments and municipal police to make these sites safer than they already are. This is actionable intelligence that can yield immediate improvements in the campus security profile.

Understanding that the majority of homicide incidents on college campuses occur in dormitories and parking lots, I endeavored to look more closely at the geography of collegiate homicide in the United States. I mentioned earlier in this chapter that I was able to determine relatively precise locations for nearly every homicide incident. At a minimum, I know the specific building, or open space on campus, or parking lot, or other location where each incident occurred. In some instances, I know the specific room, or even the specific space in a parking lot, where an incident occurred. These locations were determined from a variety of records—news reports with accompanying photographs, written descriptions of the building or room number, and so forth. You'd be surprised how much geographic information can be derived from multiple records of documented murder incidents. In addition, I have a lot of expertise from my professional training in mapping geographic information onto various platforms and formats. Over the last 30 years or so, I've conducted dozens of surveys of offshore marine areas and constructed maps of lakes and reservoirs from scratch, using only data I collected in the field using a variety of surveying instruments. In short, I'm well qualified to map locations of campus homicides from disparate data of many kinds. And so I had this idea to map every campus homicide using the information I had.

I've mapped homicide locations using a publicly available platform that many of you probably have used before just for fun—Google Earth.[53] Google Earth is an application offered for download by internet giant Google. It utilizes a global database of aerial photography overlaid on a simulated world globe. You can use Google Earth to look at high-resolution aerial imagery of every square foot of the Earth's surface. The people at Google have invested a lot of money in developing this platform as an accurate geographic resource for everyone, and it is quite spectacular. If you've never used it, you should take a look, though most people don't know that you can create your own databases using Google Earth. I've created one that indicates the locations of every college homicide in the Clery Act database, and I've placed markers on my own version of Google Earth showing where on campus these incidents occurred. Here's an example of how I located these incidents.

One of the documented homicides on a college in the United States was the murder of a campus policeman at the Massachusetts Institute of Technology (MIT) in 2013. You might remember this particular incident, though you probably haven't characterized it as a "collegiate homicide." The policeman at MIT was ambushed and killed in his patrol car by the Boston Marathon bombers, Tamerlan and Dzhokhar Tsarnaev. That homicide occurred on the campus of MIT and was reported in compliance with the Clery Act. I was able to locate this particular homicide on the specific area of campus because a Boston newspaper report included a photograph of the crime scene taken from a webcam looking out the window of an adjacent building. In the image there are a number of recognizable landmarks that I was able to find while panning over the MIT campus images on Google Earth.

Once I had the locations of all the college homicides determined on Google Earth, it was also possible to examine how those locations relate to the overall geography of the campuses where they occurred. As I pored over these locations, I looked for some overall pattern to their distribution. What kind of a pattern was I looking for? I didn't know—that's why I was looking for one! But as I examined these locations, it started to become evident that many homicides on college campuses occurred near the peripheral areas of the campus. Only rarely were homicides located near a campus core. So I set about measuring the distance from the location of an on-campus homicide to the nearest campus boundary (Google Earth has a tool that lets you do that). What I discovered from this process is, perhaps, the most important observation about collegiate homicides in this book: The average distance of a homicide to a campus boundary was 119 yards (109 meters). That's about the length of a football field plus both end zones. However, the majority of homicides (61.5%) occurred much closer to the nearest campus boundary; one-third (33.0%) occurred less than half the length of a football field onto the campus property. This indicates that campus homicides represent occasional, short-distance intrusions on campus. Essentially, the violent world beyond the institutional campus occasionally leaks over the campus boundary, bringing its characteristic violence with it. Put another way, intruders who commit homicide on college campuses commit these acts very close to the campus perimeter. Only rarely do these perpetrators penetrate the campus core areas. In a nation drowning in gun violence (or violence in general), this violence occasionally crosses the campus perimeter. In my view, and supported by evidence assembled in writing this book, most campus homicides result from a homicidal society intruding on the campus sanctuary. Most of our campus borders are open and easily crossed. Sometimes murderers cross them. Thus, the problem of homicides on college campuses is really a problem of societal homicides. If we demanded a safer, less violent society, collegiate homicides would decline, too.

Understanding the specific geography of campus homicide and the proximity of most collegiate murders to the campus perimeter is important. A characteristic feature of the overall architecture of most college campuses in the United States is the placement of student residential buildings and parking lots at the campus margins. Residential buildings and parking lots are the locations where almost 60% of collegiate murders occur. That observation matters to institutional law enforcement and administrators if they want to develop strategies to make the campus environment safer. Take a close look at the campus perimeter and understand where access points for intruders exist. Look closely at campus policing methods or available technologies to enhance security around the campus periphery. Those steps might effectively stop the majority of murders that occur on college campuses. Perhaps the campus police station could be located in the vicinity of the residential buildings on campus. That would create an aura of heightened security in the residential area and reduce police response times if there was an incident requiring police response. Campus parking lots can also be made much more secure than they currently are. Perhaps colleges could create more restricted access to parking facilities with RFID chips in campus parking permits or staff parking lots with security personnel, or they could offer greater access to campus-ride and escort services for people going to parking lots after hours, so they aren't going into parking areas alone. I think if colleges examined their campus boundaries with an eye toward enhancing boundary security, there are innumerable solutions that could be enforced. Many would also be quite cost effective and create a much greater sense of safety at our collegiate sanctuaries.

Sadly, homicides are a reality on college campuses in the United States. Yet they are still rare events. In this chapter, we reviewed the information I've gathered regarding every recorded collegiate homicide since 2001. There is a general profile of murder on campus that emerges and can be understood. Annually, there are about 17 murders nationwide on a network of 8,981 higher education institutions. These incidents occur annually on fewer than 0.2% of campuses; more than 99.8% of college campuses are murder-free every year. In this century, 98% of college campuses have been murder-free. Few places in society are as safe from the threat of murder as college campuses. If you're the parent of a child embarking on a college adventure next year, know that your child will be safe—many hundreds of times safer than their peers who don't attend college. You can scroll through the appendix of this book to see a state-by-state listing of the U.S. colleges where murders occurred since 2001. Understand that this list is all of the colleges in the nation where murder occurred. All the others—almost 8,800 of them—were murder-free during the last 16 years.

More than 93% of those homicides are single homicides, and almost two-thirds are targeted killings where the assailant knew the victim. In a nation that experiences 17,000 murders every year, that remains an extraordinary record of safety and security. Murders at college occur 1,000 times less frequently than in the public at large. Gun murders on college campuses have similarly low frequency. That is a remarkable statistic.

Remember our experiment: In a nation awash with guns and drowning in gun violence, society created a nationwide, gun-safe archipelago. We scattered those gun-safe spaces across every state. We put them in urban centers. We put them in rural areas. We put them in suburbs. We put them in affluent communities and in communities wracked with poverty. We put them in communities dominated by white people, and African Americans, and people of Hispanic or Asian descent, and in communities with any other group you can imagine. We put them in crime-ridden inner cities. We put them on sprawling estates. We put them among farm fields, in deserts, near beaches, on lakeshores, and in the mountains. We scattered them throughout the land in all conceivable environments. Then we populated those gun-safe zones with tens of millions of unarmed citizens drawn from the general population. And then what happened? The observed murder rate on gun-safe college campuses was 1,000 times lower than in the armed society surrounding them. Are you paying attention?

6

Historically Black Colleges and Universities Matter

"A mind is a terrible thing to waste."
—slogan of the United Negro College Fund

Homicide as a national phenomenon in the United States has been studied endlessly for decades. Innumerable books exist on the nature and incidence of homicide in America,[1] and I suppose this book is one more in that genre, albeit with a more specific focus than most. Scholarly works on the overall incidence of homicides in the United States have advanced a broad spectrum of social theories to define and understand the societal circumstances leading to violence that results in homicides. A special focus of many studies of homicide in contemporary American culture is the observed very high rates of homicide in the United States during the late 1980s and early 1990s.[2] During this period, homicides and homicide rates were said to have reached epidemic proportions. The term *epidemic* is laden with imagery of pestilence, calamity, and social upheaval.[3] What does this term mean in the context of homicides generally (and gun homicides in particular)? Understanding of the term *epidemic homicide* is important to the context of this book. In epidemiology, a common definition of *epidemic* is a sudden increase in the number of cases of a disease above what is normally expected in that population in that area.[4] In the middle and late 1980s, the rapid rise in homicides and homicide rates nationally certainly fit the definition of epidemic.[5]

Studies of the nature and incidence of homicide across social castes, and within the black American community in particular, are also numerous.[6]

It is not the purpose of this book to explore the multitude of social, cultural, economic, or political factors related to the incidence of homicide across America. Doing so would require many books—and many of those books have already been written while many more remain to be written. Knowledge of the scale of homicides among the African American population in America is relevant, though, in the context of this book. Remember, the premise of this book is comparing the documented homicides in the general public to the documented homicides on college campuses. That experiment can be applied to analysis of homicides within the nation's African American population and on the nation's historically black college and university (HBCU) campuses as well.

Trayvon Martin.[7] Jordan Davis.[8] Michael Brown.[9] Eric Garner.[10] Freddie Gray.[11] John Crawford III.[12] Walter Scott. Philando Castile.[13] These are the names of men seared into the history of the struggle for civil rights in America in the second decade of the 21st century. All of these men were African Americans murdered for contested reasons.[14] Two were killed by armed vigilantes who took the law into their own hands under Florida's "Stand Your Ground" provisions.[15] The others were killed under questionable circumstances by municipal police. All of these men except Philando Castile were unarmed (Castile was legally permitted to carry a sidearm). Their deaths are just a few of many thousands—in fact, war-level casualties—among African American men and women across America every year. From 2001 to 2016, the CDC reported 134,867 homicides among the population of black Americans: 115,137 African American men and 19,730 African American women.[16]

Gun homicides within the African American population in the United States are similarly significant. During the last 16 years of this century, there were 106,072 gun homicides committed against African Americans—excluding those consequent to "legal intervention" (i.e., shootings classified as justifiable homicides).[17] Stop for a moment and review those last few statistics. There were 134,867 African American homicides, of which 106,072 were committed with guns; in other words, nearly 79% of homicides in the African American community were due to gunfire. We too easily pass over these numbers when we see them because we don't easily register the context and meaning of large numbers. I pause and reflect on them largely because I've trained myself to do so as part of my professional life, but I recognize that it's a more difficult task for many readers. But if you take anything from this book, I hope it will be an appreciation that numbers matter. They contain information in compact packages that reveal much about the world in which we live.

From the information above, we can also calculate homicide rates among the African American population. The observed rate of homicide among African Americans in the United States is 19.5 per 100,000 persons,[18] but there are substantial differences in the homicide rates among African American women and men. The observed homicide rate among African American women is 5.65 per 100,000.[19] That is more or less the same as the observed homicide rate of the U.S. general public (5.77 per 100,000 persons).[20] However, the observed homicide rate among African American men is 36.5 per 100,000 persons[21]—6.3 times higher than among the U.S. general public and even higher than the victimization rate observed for *all* African Americans more than 20 years ago (32 per 100,000 persons in 1995).[22] That is a staggering statistic, but more shocking ones await if we care to investigate more deeply.

For gun-related homicides, the murder rate among African Americans is 16.06 per 100,000 persons compared to 3.93 per 100,000 among the general public[23]—4 times higher for African Americans. Interestingly, African American women are victims of gun homicides at a rate of 3.08 per 100,000 persons,[24] about 21.6% lower than the observed rate among the U.S. general public (3.93 per 100,000 persons). However, the firearm homicide rate among African American men is 30.25 per 100,000 persons[25]—almost 8 times higher than the firearm homicide rate among the general public.[26]

The African American population in the United States is the most at risk of being victimized by violent crimes leading to homicide, particularly homicides involving guns. Within this at-risk population, however, individuals in the age group 18–24 years old (the dominant college-aged group) display unimaginably high incidences of homicide—except that we don't imagine them; rather, we observe them year after year after year and do nothing. African Americans aged 18–24 are murdered at rate of 52.95 per 100,000 persons[27]—more than 9 times more frequently than members of the general public and more than 7.5 times more frequently than white young adults in the same age group.[28] African American women aged 18–24 years are murdered at the rate of 10.02 per 100,000 persons,[29] or about 2 times more frequently than members of the general public. African American men in the 18–24-year-old age group, by contrast, are murdered at an astounding, unrelenting rate of 95.62 per 100,000 persons[30]—more than 16.5 times more frequently than the general public and more than 9.5 times more frequently than African American women.

Gun homicides among African American young adults are similarly high. Overall, guns are used to murder 18–24-year-old African Americans at a rate of 48.03 per 100,000 persons[31]—nearly 12 times more frequently than guns kill others in the general public. African American women aged 18–24 years old, however, are murdered with guns at a rate of 7.37 per 100,000,[32] or about 1.9 times as frequently as others in the general public. African American men in this age group are far less fortunate, as they are murdered with guns in the United States at a rate of 88.44 per 100,000 persons[33]—22.5 times more commonly than others in the public and a dozen times more frequently than their female counterparts.

Why the focus here on the dominant college-aged group in the population? Remember, this book is about homicides on college campuses. The dominant age group on college campuses is 18–24-year-old young adults, and the primary victims of collegiate homicides are students. But all colleges are not created equal.

In the United States, there are many systems of higher education. There is not a nationalized system of higher education; every state has its own network of higher education institutions. The control of public education (including higher education) by states is a hallmark of the U.S. education system. With respect to higher education, state control is extraordinarily inefficient but nonetheless results in a remarkably diverse and extensive network of institutional styles and missions that makes the U.S. collegiate education system the envy of the world. There are systems of private institutions, which depend on revenues from tuition, research grants derived from external sources, or gifts and endowments to maintain themselves. There are also systems of public institutions, state-supported colleges and universities that receive funding appropriated by state legislatures for a portion of their operating costs. The remainder of operating expenses for public institutions are, like private institutions, supplied through tuition, research grants derived from external funding sources, and gifts or endowments. No state provides 100% of the funds necessary to operate its higher education systems. During the 21st century, states' financial support of their higher education systems has been continuously declining; since 2008, state appropriations to higher education have declined 20–26% nationwide.[34] The University of Texas at Austin—the flagship institution in Texas and one of the finest universities in the United States—receives only 12% of its operating costs from state-appropriated funds.[35]

There are many component campuses of higher education nationally. Some institutions are 4-year colleges and universities awarding baccalaureate, master's, and doctoral degrees. Other institutions are 2-year colleges awarding associate degrees and enabling students to transfer to 4-year institutions for additional education and training to complete 4-year baccalaureate programs. There are also technical institutes, generally 2-year institutions providing training in skilled professions of all kinds—what were once referred to as vocational-technical colleges.

There is another important system of higher education institutions that deserves mention in this book. It is the nation's network of historically black colleges and universities—known throughout academia as HBCUs. There are 105 institutions nationally identified as HBCUs.[36] The HBCU system comprises 51 private 4-year colleges and universities, 40 public 4-year colleges and universities, 3 private 2-year colleges, and 11 public 2-year colleges.[37] The HBCU collegiate system's similar structure, mimicking the system of higher education serving the majority population, is not accidental. It's a legacy of America's history of segregation. Several of these institutions were established as "Negro colleges" in Pennsylvania and Ohio prior to the Civil War.[38] Their intent was to educate black Americans freed from slavery so they could be functioning, productive members of society in the young Union. As part of Reconstruction in the years following the Civil War, more institutions were established to educate newly freed slaves in the South. In my own state of Arkansas, Branch Normal College (now known as the University of Arkansas at Pine Bluff) was established as a campus of the University of Arkansas. Its primary purpose, like many other black colleges, was to educate former slaves and their children to provide a pool of teachers for segregated public schools in the South.[39] A number of black colleges were established after passage of the second Morrill Act in 1890. In the former Confederacy, this act required each state to establish a separate college for black Americans if they were not permitted to enroll in the institutions admitting white students. Throughout the first half of the 20th century, additional black colleges and universities were established across the Jim Crow South and elsewhere in the United States as a response to the landmark Supreme Court decision *Plessy vs. Ferguson*, which upheld the concept of "separate but equal" facilities for Americans based on their racial identity.

You are likely familiar with the names of several of the foremost HBCUs in America: Howard University, North Carolina A&T, Tuskegee University, Grambling State University, Spelman College, Morehouse College, and so forth. Many others I'm certain you've never heard of (e.g., Tougaloo College, Shaw University, Philander Smith College, etc.), but they are there, teaching many students.

Private and public HBCUs participate in federal financial aid programs just as "majority" universities do. As such, HBCUs are also required to submit annual crime reports in compliance with the Clery Act.[40] Data documenting crime victims within the HBCU network of colleges are archived with those from all other higher education institutions on the U.S. Department of Education website, Campus Safety and Security Data Analysis Cutting Tool.[41] The crime data for HBCUs are comingled with those of other institutions organized by state. Identifying crimes occurring specifically at HBCUs requires knowledge of which institutions they are. For this book, I was able to identify HBCUs from several publications.[42]

Examining their crime statistics, America's HBCUs seem to be disproportionately represented in campus homicide data used for this book.

Whereas institutions in the national network of HBCUs make up just 1.2% of the institutions in the Clery Act database, homicides at HBCUs account for 11.5% of victims and 14.6% of homicide incidents. There were 32 homicides (29 were black people) reported in 32 incidents from 24 HBCUs from 2001 to 2016. That's a homicide incident at 22.9% of HBCU campuses during the last 16 years compared to just 2% of all other higher education institutions during the same interval. That difference—a 10-fold higher proportion of campuses reporting homicides—seems significant. At least one homicide has occurred at almost a quarter of HBCUs in the United States. This creates a clear perception that the nation's HBCUs have a serious safety and security issue, a perception that has been noted by academic researchers.[43] Outwardly, it seems that the simple observation that homicides occurred at nearly 23% of HBCU campuses is sufficient proof of their security and safety issues. However, is the perception that our nation's HBCUs are more prone to homicides correct? How might we analyze the phenomenon of homicide at HBCUs? What factors might contribute to the higher observed frequency of homicide on black college campuses?

We can examine the observed number of homicides at HBCUs in the same way that we've already examined them for all the nation's colleges. Consider that there were 32 homicides among HBCUs during the last 16 years, which computes to two murders per year within the HBCU network nationwide. That's a small fraction (just 12.5%) of the 17 homicides occurring on college campuses nationally during an average year. Among the population of college students and employees in the United States (from the previous chapter, we learned this was 344,464,917 people from 2001 to 2016), these 32 homicides convert to an observed homicide rate of 0.009 per 100,000 people. That's 8 times lower than the calculated homicide rate for all higher education institutions—essentially, 32 homicides on HBCU campuses versus 247 on all other campuses nationwide. The 32 homicides within the national HBCU network are fewer than the 34 homicides recorded at a single majority institution, Virginia Tech, during the same interval. Of course, 32 of those homicides at Virginia Tech occurred during the same incident (the third worst mass killing in U.S. history), so critics will complain that this is an unfair comparison. I will counter that, to date, there has never been a mass killing at an HBCU. Ever. In the entire history of HBCUs dating back to the establishment of the first such institution, Cheney University, in 1837.

The preceding statements illustrate a profound difficulty in reporting crime statistics. Those statistics are subject to broad, subjective interpretations and must be understood in some context. But context is controlled by those reciting the narrative. Is it fair to single out an individual institution that was unfortunate enough to be the locus of a horrific mass murder as a comparator to other institutions? Perhaps or perhaps not, depending on your perspective. It might also be said that no shopping mall in America has ever been the locus of a mass shooting on the scale of the incident at Virginia Tech in 2007. But let us return to the foundational premise of this book that campuses of higher education nationwide are vastly less dangerous than other sectors of our society and that the observed homicide rate on college campuses is 1,000 times lower than in the U.S. public. The statistics reported above are objectively correct, and while it may seem that HBCUs are overrepresented in homicide data, one should take care in reporting that belief directly because there are many ways to interpret this situation. Perspective, always. In the following pages, I will demonstrate that HBCUs are far safer than the society beyond their borders for members of the African American public. That, to me, seems a fair comparison and consistent with other comparisons in this book.

We may begin by calculating the homicide rate for HBCUs using the total number of students enrolled at HBCUs from 2001 to 2016. Enrollment data for HBCUs are maintained by the U.S. Department of Education. Those records are available for inspection and download from the National Center for Education Statistics Integrated Post-Secondary Education Data System (IPEDS)[44] as a table in the *Digest of Educational Statistics*.[45] It's estimated that total employment and enrollment in HBCUs from 2001 to 2016 was about 5.5 million people.[46] During that time, 32 individuals on HBCU campuses were murdered. Thus, as a proportion of the total population of students, staff, and faculty at HBCUs, the observed rate of homicide at HBCUs is 0.58 per 100,000 persons, or 36 times lower than among African Americans and 10 times lower than in the U.S. public at large. No matter how I choose to calculate it, observed homicides at HBCUs are substantially lower than in America's general public, and even more substantially lower than among the African American population nationwide. There is more to say about this, though.

Among the 32 murder victims at HBCUs, 7 were women. Thus, among the HBCU population, women were victimized at a rate of 0.13 per 100,000 persons. That homicide rate compares to rates of 5.72 per 100,000 persons among African American women in the general public (about 44 times higher than among the HBCU population). If we calculate the observed homicides of women at HBCUs with the U.S. population during 2001–2016 as the basis, their rate is 0.00014 per 100,000 persons. That's more than 41,200 times lower than the observed homicide rate for the American public (5.77 per 100,000 persons[47])! Empirically, about 1 woman is killed on an HBCU campus every other year compared to more than 1,200 African American women every year in the general public—1 victim every other year versus more than 3 every day elsewhere in America. That is a stunning statistic for a member of the population that is most at risk for homicide in the United States and speaks directly to the concept of college campuses as sanctuaries from the most violent crimes in our society. If you are a woman, HBCU campuses are extraordinary sanctuaries from murderers.

While the safety of women on HBCU campuses is comparatively extraordinary, it's utterly astounding for African American men. Among the U.S. population, African American men are the single demographic most at risk of being victimized by violent crimes resulting in homicide. Within the nation's HBCU network, there were 25 African American men murdered from 2001 to 2016. That translates to an observed homicide rate of 0.45 per 100,000 persons among the HBCU population, but only 0.0005 per 100,000 among the U.S. national population. The observed homicide rate for African American men in the United States is 36.5 per 100,000 persons. The observed murder rate of African American men on the streets and towns of America is 73,000 times higher than on our black colleges and universities. In the United States, 115,137 black men have been murdered since 2001. Only 25 of those were on the campuses of black colleges and universities; that is 1.5 per year versus more than 7,000 per year (one African American man murdered every 75 minutes every day during the last 16 years).

The murder victims at HBCUs ranged in age from 17 to 60 years old. Of those victims, 27 were between the ages of 18 and 24 years old. That computes to an observed homicide rate of 0.49 per 100,000 persons among the HBCU population nationwide. Recall that the observed murder rate for African American young adults (18–24 years old) in the United States is 52.95 per 100,000 persons, or about 108 times higher than what is observed among the HBCU population. Using the U.S. population as the basis for this calculation, the observed homicide rate among 18–24-year-olds on HBCU campuses was 0.0005 per 100,000 persons. That is more than 105,000 times lower than observed murder rate of 18–24-year-old African Americans in the U.S. general population! Put another way, if 18–24-year-old African Americans at HBCUs were murdered at the same rate that they are murdered in society at large, we would expect total homicides at HBCUs to number around 3,000 students since 2001. Instead, only 27 homicides were observed within that age group. HBCUs are anything but magnets for murderers.

Of the homicide victims between 18 and 24 years old, 22 were men. Applying the methodology above to calculate the observed murder rate of these men, I derived a value of 0.4 per 100,000 members of the HBCU population, or 0.0004 per 100,000 members of the U.S. population. Recall that the observed homicide rate for African American men aged 18–24 in the United States is 95.62 per 100,000 persons. That homicide rate is 239,000 times higher than what is observed on HBCU campuses nationwide! Again, if 18–24-year-old African American men on HBCU campuses were murdered at the same rate they are murdered across U.S. society, we would expect at least 5,000 homicides of male HBCU students nationwide. Instead, since 2001, we have observed 22. If you are an African American man in the dominant college age group, your very best bet to avoid becoming a victim of homicide is to enroll at a college!

Aside from the calculations above demonstrating the remarkable disparity of homicide rates for African American young adults on HBCU campuses (very low) and in U.S. society during the 21st century (very high), what more did I glean from news articles and other sources regarding reported homicides at HBCUs? What else do I know about the homicide victims? Once again, I want to emphasize that there have been only 32 African American victims of murder at HBCUs since 2001, compared to 134,867 in the U.S. general population during the same interval. Just as with homicides on other campuses in the United States, I endeavored to locate more detailed reports on each incident to determine whether there were patterns in the data and whether those patterns differed from those observed for other collegiate homicides or homicides in the general public. I was able to find additional information for all 32 homicides occurring at HBCUs.

For the 32 homicide incidents for which I have additional information, I was able to determine that 24 of the victims (75%) were students enrolled at the respective institutions at the time of their murder. As with homicides at non–HBCU institutions, students make up the largest group of murder victims. That seems reasonable given that students constitute the largest population of individuals on college campuses. An additional 6 HBCU murder victims (18.8%) appear to have been persons unaffiliated with the institution—people who happened to be on campus for one reason or another and were killed. This is also consistent with the observed pattern of homicide at non–HBCU campuses— the next largest group of victims after students were people unaffiliated with the campus. Finally, there were 2 staff employees among murder victims on HBCU campuses. Interestingly, there were no faculty members murdered on HBCU campuses or instances of neonaticide during the 2001–2016 interval, both categories with measurable frequencies at other institutions nationally.

As mentioned previously, to date there has never been a mass killing or even a multiple homicide (i.e., double or triple murder) on an HBCU campus. All the reported incidents are single homicides, despite the fact that guns figure more prominently in the recorded homicide incidents at HBCUs compared to other institutions. Of the 32 confirmed homicide incidents, 24 (75%) were committed with firearms (compared to 53.4% of incidents on non–HBCU campuses). Of the remaining HBCU murders, 4 were stabbings. One of the stabbings was adjudicated during trial as self-defense, and the murder charges against the perpetrator were dismissed.[48] The remaining known murder modes included beating (3) and strangulation (2).

The associations of murder victims with their assailants are less certain for HBCU murders than for many other cases. From news reports and other documents, it is confirmed that victims knew their assailants in just 18 (56.3%) of the 32 reported homicides. That compares to victims knowing their assailants in approximately 70% of murders at other institutions nationally. In 11 instances of homicide at HBCUs (34.4%), the victim was murdered consequent to an altercation that escalated to homicide. In 4 instances, victims were killed during the commission of armed robberies. Two instances involved murder of women by men who were employed at the institutions. Two victims appear to have been targeted in gang assassinations, and one victim died when she was struck by a stray bullet fired from a location remote from her position on the campus.

How does the geography of homicide at HBCUs compare to that at other institutions? How far from a campus boundary do these incidents occur? On average, homicides on HBCU campuses occur within 138 yards (126 meters) of a campus boundary. Just as with homicides at other colleges and universities all over America, the homicides at HBCUs occur within a football field length or so of the campus perimeter, representing short incursions of violent crime over the campus perimeter. Essentially, the violence of U.S. society at large occasionally seeps through the campus border. This is no different from what is observed at other campuses across America.

The most common sites for campus homicide at HBCUs are also residential facilities. Of the 32 reported murders at HBCUs, 16 (50.0%) occurred at residential facilities, either dormitories or campus apartment buildings or apartments managed off campus for the institution by private contractors. This is a somewhat higher incidence than is observed nationwide. Nationally, about 38.8% of homicides occur at campus residential facilities, though residential facilities are still the primary locus for campus homicides. Again, this makes sense, since students residing on campus spend most of their out-of-class time in their residences and this is the most likely location for conflicts to arise. The next most common sites for campus murders at HBCUs are public spaces on or adjacent to the campus. A total of 9 homicides (28.1%) occurred outdoors in public spaces on HBCU campuses. A number of these homicides were coincident with parties involving large numbers of people, including many people unaffiliated with the campus. It is not clear whether these parties were sanctioned by the institutions, but altercations among participants associated with these festivities escalated to murder. Academic buildings were the sites of 3 homicides (9.4%) at HBCUs, the same proportion observed at majority institutions. Finally, parking lots (2 homicides) and athletic-recreation facilities (1 homicide) completed the locations of reported murders at HBCUs.

In general, the site proportions are similar to those reported for homicides at majority institutions nationwide. However, HBCUs report a substantially larger proportion of murders in public spaces compared to other institutions. At least some of these results may be related to the urban setting of a number of HBCUs and the inherently higher crime rates associated with urban areas and public spaces bordering the campus. In addition, the coincidence of homicides with large social gatherings on campus property contributed to a number of murders at HBCUs. This phenomenon is less prevalent at non–HBCU campuses, perhaps because many of these large gatherings often take place at off-campus locations (e.g. fraternity-sorority houses or rented properties). That may represent a significant difference in the culture and life of students at HBCUs compared to other institutions.

On average, homicides at HBCUs occur within 138 yards (126 meters) of a campus boundary. That's similar to, though slightly greater than, the average distance onto campus at other types of institutions (119 yards/109 meters). Nonetheless, the incidents that occur at HBCUs are almost all located near the campus periphery, where residential, parking, and sports or recreation facilities are present. This geography, it seems, is quite important. The same general pattern of violent crime is associated with the campus perimeter nationally, as described in the previous chapter. As such, it is important for institutional administrators and institutional law enforcement departments to examine the security status of the campus boundary. Knowing that the peripheral area extending onto campus approximately the length of a football field is the "red zone" (i.e., the area most prone to violent interactions leading to homicide) is a valuable part of understanding how to make our very safe collegiate sanctuaries even more secure going forward.

The observed higher incidence of homicide at HBCU residential sites is likewise of interest in understanding campus security and safety. This high incidence of murder should be examined by institutional authorities to determine the root causes of violence on their campuses. On the outside looking in, however, there appears to be a pattern emerging that may be impacting the security of HBCU residential facilities.

In the 21st century, many HBCUs are privatizing residential facilities as they struggle with financial exigencies related to chronic underfunding and declining enrollments. It seems fair to ask whether security of privatized dormitories and apartments is being compromised in efforts to control costs. A detailed examination of that issue is beyond the scope of this book but worthy of greater investigation in the future.

In addition to diminishing sources of revenue from state and federal appropriations, shrinking donor contributions, and declining research allocations, enrollments and graduation rates at HBCUs have been decreasing.[49] Many private HBCUs struggle to attract students, and state-sponsored HBCUs are deemed increasingly irrelevant as larger state institutions are no longer segregated and black students opt to enroll in those institutions. In the 21st century, it is anticipated that the majority of HBCUs will close.[50] So we might ask whether the observed homicide rates at HBCUs might ultimately solve themselves as HBCUs close their doors.

One way to examine that question is to examine the incidence of homicides involving African American victims on campuses of majority institutions—that is, institutions that are not HBCUs—as a proportion of all campus homicides on those campuses. So, let's do that.

In total, 89 black people were murdered on all college campuses from 2001 to 2016. This accounts for nearly one-third (31.9%) of all homicide victims on college campuses across the nation. Of those 89 homicides, 32 African Americans were murdered on HBCU campuses and 57 on campuses of majority-serving institutions. So 57 of 247 homicides on majority campuses were black people (23.1%). Nationwide, black people constitute about 15% of total collegiate enrollments.[51] Thus, as a proportion of total homicides, black people are disproportionately represented (32% of 279 victims) compared to their representation in higher education settings (15%). Even excluding homicides associated with HBCUs, the proportion of black homicide victims on majority institutions (22.9%) exceeds their representation on campus by a significant amount—50% greater than their representation in nationwide enrollments. Despite their disproportionate representation as victims of homicide on college campuses, however, nationally black people are victims of homicide in 47.7% of homicide incidents in society at large. So even majority campuses are substantially safer than the general public for black students, staff, or faculty.

As we did with HBCUs, let's compare the observed homicides of black people on majority college campuses to homicides observed among black people in the U.S. general public. There were 57 black individuals murdered on majority campuses from 2001 to 2016 compared to 134,867 black murder victims in the United States during the same period.[52] Black homicides on majority college campuses therefore constitute just 0.04% of homicides among the U.S. black population.

In total, there were 35 gun homicides committed against black people on the nation's non–HBCU campuses (61.4% of majority-campus homicides of black people) from 2001 to 2016. In the U.S. general public during the same time period, 106,072 black people were gunned down. Thus, gun homicides on majority college campuses constitute just 0.03% of all gun murders in the black community.

Are you wondering what the observed murder rate (i.e., murders per 100,000 persons) was for black people on majority college campuses? I was just wondering that, too, so here it is. To estimate the murder rate of black people on majority college campuses in the United States, we will use as the population base the total number of people enrolled or employed in U.S. higher education. I reported this population estimate in chapter 5 from the National Center for Educational Statistics' *Digest of Education Statistics*. From 2001 to 2016, this estimate was 344,462,917 people.[53] The calculated murder rate using that base population is 0.017 per 100,000 persons. The observed murder rate of African Americans in the United States is 20.4 per 100,000 persons.[54] On majority college campuses, the observed murder rate during the 2001–2016 interval was 1,200 times lower than in the U.S. general public. If we were to calculate the murder rate against the baseline U.S. population during this interval,[55] the calculated rate falls to 0.001 per 100,000 persons, and 20,400 times lower than in the general public—once more indicating a 1,000 times lower homicide rate on college campuses than in the general public!

I previously mentioned profoundly different murder rates among black women and black men in the general public and on HBCU campuses. Do those differences also persist on campuses of majority colleges? I'll wager that they do, but let's calculate them to see. Does anyone want to bet I'm wrong at this point?

The observed homicide rate among African American women was 5.75 per 100,000 in the general public.[56] At HBCUs, the observed homicide rate for black women was 0.13 per 100,000 (using the total HBCU population as baseline) or 0.00015 per 100,000 (using the U.S. population as baseline). On majority campuses, 17 black women were murdered from 2001 to 2016. The calculated murder rate, using the total majority-institution population, as the base is 0.005 per 100,000 (1,150 times lower than in the general public) or, using the total U.S. population as the baseline, 0.0004 per 100,000 (14,375 times lower than in the general public)!

For African American men, the observed U.S. homicide rate was 36.4

per 100,000 persons.[57] At HBCUs, the observed homicide rate for black men was 0.44 per 100,000 (using the total HBCU population as baseline) or 0.0005 per 100,000 (using the U.S. population as baseline). On majority college campuses, 40 black men were murdered from 2001 to 2016. Using the total majority-institution population as baseline, the calculated murder rate for black men is 0.01 per 100,000 persons—twice the rate of black women on majority campuses. As with homicides on college campuses, where two-thirds of victims are men, black men are victims in about two-thirds of homicide incidents involving black people on majority campuses. Using the U.S. population as the baseline, the calculated murder rate for black men on majority college campuses is 0.0009 per 100,000—again, about twice the rate of black women! However, this rate for black men is 40,400 times lower than what is observed in the U.S. general public![58] Absolutely astonishing!

Among the dominant college age group (18–24-year-olds), the observed murder rates among black people on majority colleges are equally remarkable for their low incidence. I previously reported that the overall murder rate for African Americans aged 18–24 years was 52.95 per 100,000 persons.[59] On HBCU campuses, this incidence declined to just 0.44 per 100,000 (using the HBCU population as baseline) or 0.0005 per 100,000 (using the U.S. population as baseline). Of the 57 black homicide victims on majority campuses, 30 (52.6%) were in the 18–24-year-old age group. The observed murder rate of this demographic group was calculated to be 0.008 per 100,000 (using the total collegiate population as baseline) or 0.0006 per 100,000 (using the U.S. population as the base). Thus, the calculated homicide rates for 18–24-year-old black people on majority college campuses are 6,600–96,250 times lower than in the U.S. general public![60]

For black men in the 18–24-year-old age group (the most at risk of being victimized by homicide in the United States), the observed murder rate in society at large is 94.83 per 100,000 population.[61] On HBCU campuses, the observed murder rate of this group was only 0.35 per 100,000 (using the HBCU population as base) or 0.0004 per 100,000 (using the total U.S. population as base). Of the 57 total black homicides on majority-serving campuses, 25 were black men aged 18–24 years. Taken as a proportion of the majority-institution population, the computed murder rate for 18–24-year-old black men was 0.007 per 100,000 persons—more than 13,500 times lower than in society at large. Taken as a proportion of the total U.S. general public, the computed murder rate is 0.0005 per 100,000—almost 190,000 times less frequent than in society at large!

I could go on and on with these comparisons, but they would continue to show the same thing. Despite the several dozen murders of black people on college campuses during this century, the overall incidence of homicide among black people is thousands to many tens of thousands of times lower than in the U.S. general public. If you are a black person (or any other person of color, or a white person for that matter) and you wish to minimize the chances that you'll be victimized by violent crimes and murder, your best bet is to enroll in a post-secondary institution! And it doesn't matter whether you enroll in a majority-serving institution or in a historically black college or university. You are equally safe at any college and far safer on a college campus than almost anywhere else in the general public.

Admitting that homicides occasionally occur on college campuses, the incidence of homicide for black people is almost nonexistent compared to the peril they encounter in U.S. society at large. This is the same result we demonstrated for the general college population in the previous chapter. Say it with me again: college campuses in the United States are not magnets for murders—they are sanctuaries from them. I don't care who you are.

7

The Guns of August

"...no man has a right to be wrong in his facts."
—Bernard Baruch

Every year, beginning in mid–August and extending through the Labor Day holiday, there is a magnificent migration. It is even more predictable than the swallows returning to Mission San Juan Capistrano. From all across America they come, migrating to our college campuses from every conceivable hometown across the nation. Many are arriving on campus for the very first time. Many are the first in their families to attend college. Many others are returning for their second, third, fourth, fifth, and, yes, sometimes sixth year on our campuses. They may come to be part of our graduate schools, where master's and doctoral degrees are conferred. Some may attend medical school or law school. Some are among the ranks of the faculty and other employees in higher education. I'm speaking, of course, about guns on campus. More properly, I'm speaking about people who are permitted to carry guns on college campuses, because, as my NRA-sponsored opponents will quickly point out, guns don't attend college—people carrying guns attend college.

Increasingly, year after year, more and more college campuses are being forced to permit individuals to carry concealed, lethal weapons everywhere on their campuses.[1] No one really wants people carrying guns on college campuses—well, no one with any sense of responsibility wants guns on college campuses. So, responding to the complete absence of demands to permit people to carry guns on college campuses, state legislatures are forcing guns onto campuses by fiat. This is done over the explicit requests of large numbers of Americans to keep campuses "gun-safe." Incredible. Elected representatives in state after state have rejected the recommendations of institutional governing boards (boards of trustees and boards of regents), many of whom are constitutionally authorized to make policies for higher education institutions in their states. These elected representatives have rejected the recommendations of virtually all university administrators,[2] faculty,[3] campus police,[4] state and municipal law enforcement, civic groups, and ordinary citizens to keep campuses "gun-safe." Quite literally, no large group has requested that guns be permitted on college campuses. Nonetheless, starting in the 21st century, there has been a focused, long-term, persistent and pernicious effort to force guns onto college campuses of almost every state in this country. In many states, the annual or biennial session of the state legislature is guaranteed to bring forward a bill (or several) forcing guns onto college campuses.

At the beginning of this century, concealed handguns were not permitted at any college in the United States.[5] Colorado State University made an individual decision to permit guns on its campus in 2003 when the Colorado legislature passed its statewide general concealed carry law.[6] It was said that crime on the CSU campus fell dramatically from 2002 to 2003, when campus concealed carry was implemented.[7] However, data from the U.S. Department of Education[8] shows that total reported crimes on the CSU campus in 2002 were 70, whereas total reported crimes in 2003 were 74. That is an increase, not a decline, in total reported crimes. It is true that reported sexual assaults declined from 20 in 2002 to 8 in 2003, and gun rights activists claimed (without evidence) that this decline resulted from permitting guns on campus.[9] Responding to that claim, CSU police chief Wendy Rich Goldschmidt said that she was unaware of any incidents of attempted sexual assault being thwarted by someone with a gun on the CSU campus.[10] But time marches on, and reported sexual assaults on the armed campus of CSU returned to an average of 20 every year from 2013 to 2015—the same as before the institution permitted guns on campus.[11] Since peaking at 74 in 2003, total crimes on the Colorado State University campus have declined to about 50 per year. So, as a proportion of reported crimes, sexual assaults have increased from 11% in 2003 to 40% in 2015. Even as overall crimes on campus are declining, the number of reported incidents of sexual assault has remained 20 per year. So what is the efficacy of permitting guns on campus at Colorado State University? The answer to that question isn't as obvious as guns-on-campus proponents would have you believe. I will offer this conclusion, though: There were 20 sexual assaults reported in the year before guns were permitted on campus (2002) and an average of 20 sexual assaults per year reported over four subsequent years with guns on campus (2013–2015). It doesn't appear that the absence or presence of guns has any impact on the reporting of sexual assaults at Colorado State University.

In 2004, Utah became the first state to force guns onto every public college campus.[12] But the mass shooting at Virginia Tech in 2007 started an avalanche of so-called campus-carry bills in state legislatures, driven by NRA lobbyists in every state. Since 2007, guns-on-campus legislation has been introduced in 39 states, including 6 states that have not experienced a homicide on any college campus during this century (hello, Alaska, Minnesota, Montana, Nevada, New Hampshire, and South Dakota!). For those 6 states where no homicides have occurred on any college campus during this century, ask yourself, "What is the public safety crisis on college campuses requiring legislation to permit guns there?" What is the justification for arming campuses when there doesn't appear to be a tangible threat to safety? I think the obvious answer is that there is no justification for it—at least from a public safety perspective—but laws to permit "campus carry" have been introduced in those six states 14 times since 2007! The push to place guns in the hands of everyone on a college campus is strictly ideological. Nothing more. Arguments that arming college campuses makes everyone safer are not supported by observed incidents, as we shall see in this chapter.

Did the 2004 implementation of a guns-on-campus law prevent shootings on Utah public institutions of higher education? Well, there weren't any shootings on Utah public institutions of higher education from 2004 to 2012. However, there weren't any prior to enactment of the law from 1994 to 2004, either. In 2012, a student licensed to carry a concealed handgun shot himself in the leg with the pistol he was licensed to carry at Weber State University in Ogden, Utah.[13] Fortunately, the student's injury was not fatal, and no one else was wounded during that incident. Sadly, such luck ran out in Utah on 29 December 2016, when a murder-suicide occurred on the research campus of the University of Utah in Salt Lake City.[14]

Up until 2016, Utah had been held up by the NRA and the national gun lobby as a state where the guns-on-campus policy was working splendidly because there had been no shootings. However, a negligent shooting and a murder-suicide should raise some questions regarding the efficacy of this law. I suppose some gun lobby shill somewhere will argue that we can never know how many shootings were thwarted by those carrying guns around on Utah campuses during all those years. Roll your eyes now. I suppose they might also argue that one wounded person and one murdered person is a tolerable threshold of campus shootings that the rest of us must accept to permit everyone else to carry guns on every campus statewide every day. You may roll your eyes again!

Has Utah's guns-on-campus law reduced overall crime on Utah college campuses? No. Crimes on Utah college campuses have remained the same before and after implementation of campus-carry legislation.[15] So there is no tangible benefit to campus safety by permitting guns on college campuses there.

In 2011, Wisconsin and Mississippi enacted laws that permitted guns to be carried on college campuses in varying ways. In Wisconsin, Senate Bill 93[16] was enacted and permitted the carrying of concealed handguns on college campuses, but it also included a provision for individual college campuses to prohibit carrying guns inside institutional buildings.[17] Evidently, to this day no campus in Wisconsin currently permits handguns to be carried into any campus buildings. You see, no one associated with higher education wants guns on college campuses. In every state where guns-on-campus laws have been enacted, if there is a provision to exempt an institution or portions of an institution for any reason, those exemptions are applied—without fail. Still, legislatures force these laws onto an unwelcoming constituency. Did the permission to carry guns on the *grounds* of Wisconsin colleges prevent murders there? Since implementation in 2011, there have been two homicides on Wisconsin college campuses—one in 2012[18] and one in 2015.[19] One of those incidents occurred in a campus dormitory and did not involve guns, and the other was a gun homicide on the grounds of a Wisconsin college. So, no, Wisconsin campus carry has not deterred homicide on Wisconsin college campuses. Did anyone really believe it would?

The Mississippi guns-on-campus law is similar to the one in Wisconsin in that individual institutions have some latitude to prohibit concealed handguns in some buildings or during certain events, even if a person holds an enhanced concealed-carry permit. (Enhanced permits in Mississippi are obtained by passing an additional training course focused on gun handling and gun safety.[20]) Have there been any murders on Mississippi college campuses since enhanced concealed carry was enacted in 2011? Yes. There was one in 2012[21] and one in 2015,[22] both involving handguns. Did enhanced concealed carry of handguns on Mississippi college campuses prevent these two murders? No. Are Mississippi college campuses safer because citizens may be permitted to carry concealed handguns there? No. By what measure, then, can one declare the implementation of guns-on-campus law in Mississippi a success?

In 2012, Colorado institutions were forced to permit the carrying of concealed handguns on public college campuses pursuant to a decision by the Colorado Supreme Court.[23] While Colorado State University had a long history of permitting guns to be carried on its campus (detailed above), no other institution in the state permitted the practice. The Colorado Supreme Court decision was a bitter defeat, but Colorado institutions complied with the court's decision.[24] The policy was implemented at the beginning of the fall semester in 2012. Seventy-seven days later, a staff member who was licensed to carry a concealed weapon negligently discharged her gun in an office at the CU-Denver School of Dental Medicine.[25] The gun-carrying employee and a co-worker were injured in that incident. Evidently, the employee was showing her concealed weapon to co-workers when she caused it to discharge. You can't make this up! Did I mention that she was also summarily fired?[26]

In 2013, Kansas and Arkansas both enacted versions of guns-on-campus laws. In Kansas, the law did not specifically target public university campuses, instead permitting concealed handguns to be carried in any public building (that is, state or municipal building) statewide.[27] This category included the Kansas state capitol building, courthouses, public hospitals (such as the medical center of the University of Kansas, though, in 2017, the Kansas legislature passed a supplemental bill exempting public hospitals), all buildings on public university and college campuses, and the personal residences of college and university presidents in Kansas.[28]

The Kansas statute (which originated as KS HB 2052 in 2013) included a 4-year moratorium on implementation for many public buildings (including colleges, universities) to allow institutions to consider implementing an exemption to the law. How was an exemption to be obtained? Any public building with "adequate security measures" could apply for an exemption and prohibit concealed handguns so long as those security measures were in place. While this may appear to be a reasonable concession in the bill for those buildings that legitimately wished to prohibit lethal weapons on their premises, it was practically impossible to implement. "Adequate security measures" were defined in the bill as development of a written security plan for each building and "the use of electronic equipment and personnel at public entrances to detect and restrict the carrying of any weapons into the state or municipal building, including, but not limited to, metal detectors, metal detector wands or any other equipment used for similar purposes to ensure that weapons are not permitted to be carried into such building by members of the public."[29] So a public building could earn an exemption from this law by placing a staffed metal detector at every entrance. This method might be practicable for a county courthouse, where there may be only one front and one back entrance, but try to imagine that setup at a college or university or public hospital. I occupy a building at a university that has 10 entrances. Many other buildings on my campus have equally complex floorplans. There is no conceivable way for the university to purchase a metal detector and the associated trained staff necessary to operate those devices for every entrance to every building on the campus. And that's true for every campus in the nation. So the "exemption" in Kansas was really designed to be not an exemption at all because there was no practical way for any public institution to meet the requirement.

In addition to permitting concealed handguns on every public institution of higher education in Kansas, another act of the Kansas legislature in

2015 allowed anyone in the state to carry their concealed weapon without a permit.[30] No concealed handgun licenses are required in Kansas because, evidently, it's still the frontier. In Kansas, you can purchase a gun at a gun show or through a private transaction without a background check, receive no training whatsoever, and carry your gun into a public space—including your daughter's or son's college classroom. No questions asked.

The 4-year moratorium on HB 2052 ended on 1 July 2017. You can now carry a lethal weapon on a college campus in Kansas without a permit. In the frontier days of Kansas, they didn't even allow that in Dodge City.[31] How will this experiment work out for Kansas? Ask me in a few years. I have compiled all the "before" data for this book, and I'm prepared to gather the "after" data year-by-year from 1 July 2017. Tick-tock, tick-tock. Never mind. The waiting is over. On 14 July 2017, just two weeks after guns were permitted on every public higher education institution, someone forgot their gun in a restroom on the campus of Wichita State University.[32] Then it happened again on the campus of the University of Kansas in September 2017![33] Tick-tock, JAY-HAWK!

Arkansas also passed a guns-on-campus bill in 2013, Act 226.[34] You may recall that the sponsor of this bill in the Arkansas General Assembly was my neighbor. It was essentially the same bill he had proposed in the 2011 legislative session that died in committee. How did it pass in 2013? Here's how. The statewide opposition was much better organized this time around, and the bill was on its way to another committee death. My neighbor saved it with a late concession by agreeing to an amendment. The law, as enacted, would permit faculty and staff at all public colleges, universities, and technical institutes statewide to carry concealed, lethal weapons on campus so long as they had an Arkansas concealed handgun license issued by the Arkansas state police. However, the amended bill authorized the governing boards of higher education institutions to hold an annual vote to opt out of the law. If the boards of trustees of the state's public higher education institutions voted by simple majorities to opt out of Act 226, the institution could continue to prohibit everyone from carrying handguns or other lethal weapons on campus. Let that sink in. In 2013, Arkansas Act 226 forced state colleges to permit licensed faculty and staff to carry concealed handguns on every campus statewide—that is, unless the boards of trustees of each institution voted each year to reject the law. Then they could continue to prohibit guns on campus, as had been the historical preference. Do you get it? My neighbor passed legislation that was the law of the land unless folks voted to ignore it every year.

You may be wondering how that worked out in Arkansas. I can report that it worked great! In 2013, 2014, 2015, and 2016, over four consecutive annual voting cycles, every higher education institution in Arkansas—52 private and public institutions overall—voted to opt out of Act 226 and continued to prohibit guns on campus. And in 2013, 2014, 2015, and 2016, there wasn't a single homicide on any college campus in Arkansas. Coincidence?

The opt-out provision in Act 226 became an annual humiliation for my neighbor. Every spring, the governing boards of Arkansas higher education institutions would begin meeting, and, one by one, they would vote to ignore Act 226 and continue prohibiting guns on their respective campuses. It was a beautiful thing to watch as local newspapers and television stations would report the results and every year the outcome statewide was the same. Unanimous rejection of guns on all 52 campuses. Of course, this was unacceptable to my neighbor, despite widespread support for prohibiting guns from just about every constituency in the state. Really, truly humiliating for a legislator whose signature legislation was this one that everyone voted to ignore every year. So, in 2017, bolstered by supermajorities in both houses of the general assembly and a sympathetic governor who doubled as an agent of the NRA,[35] he ran his guns-on-campus bill again. This time, he removed the provision permitting institutions to opt out of the law, and he expanded provisions for carrying concealed handguns into every public space in the state as well as private businesses, including bars. Of course, this bill passed on party-line votes in both houses and was signed into law by the ever-accommodating governor. As I write this, guns are now present on every public college and university campus of Arkansas. As with other states, I've already documented the "before" data—now I'm gathering the "after" data. In a few years, it will be possible to document the impacts of guns on campuses statewide. I expect that the immediate result (based on prior history in other states) will be campus shootings. This just in—the wait is over. On 25 October 2017, a University of Arkansas student committed suicide on property owned by the University of Arkansas. While details of the suicide are sketchy, she obtained the gun from another student.[36]

In 2014, a very public and highly contentious bill to permit guns on college campuses in Idaho was newsworthy throughout the winter and spring.[37] College presidents, faculty, students, local police, campus police, and the general public opposed the proposed bill to permit anyone with an enhanced concealed-carry permit to bring handguns onto Idaho colleges. (As in Mississippi, an enhanced concealed-carry permit in Idaho is acquired by completing a modest training course on gun safety and gun handling.) Despite widespread public opposition to this bill, it moved easily through both houses of the Idaho state legislature and was signed into law by Governor Butch Otter on 12 March 2014. The law became effective on July 1 that same year.

During the first week of classes in the fall semester of 2014, a professor with an enhanced Idaho license to carry a concealed handgun shot himself in the foot with the handgun he was licensed to carry in his pants pocket.[38] His gun went off in a chemistry lab-classroom occupied by 19 students on the campus of Idaho State University. So much for his enhanced training in handgun safety and handgun handling in Idaho. How would you feel if your child had been a student in that classroom on that day? How fortunate was every student in the classroom that the bullet entered the professor's foot and didn't fragment or ricochet off the floor and go zooming around the classroom? And, Idaho, how's that campus carry policy going? Did it prevent a shooting on an Idaho college campus? No. It caused one.

Next up in the collegiate Wild West show was Texas in 2015. It's somewhat surprising that Texas waited until 2015 to pass a guns-on-campus law. Perhaps there was some reluctance in the Lone Star State because its flagship campus, the University of Texas at Austin, was the site of the nation's first mass shooting in 1966: the infamous Texas Tower shooting, perpetrated by an ex-Marine sharpshooter who climbed the stairs of the landmark tower on the central campus and opened fire on unsuspecting people below; he killed 14 and wounded 29 in the first and worst mass shooting in U.S. history up to that time.[39] The 2015 Texas guns-on-campus bill (SB 11) led to a contentious, statewide battle with legislators and the usual broad constituency opposed to guns on campus. The chancellor of the University of Texas system, Admiral William H. McRaven, came out with strong statements opposing the legislation.[40] This was significant because Admiral McRaven was a military hero. In 2011, he commanded U.S. Special Operations Command and was responsible for orchestrating the clandestine military raid that killed international terrorist Osama bin Laden. If he opposed guns on college campuses, who would dare pass that bill? The Texas legislature, that's who.

After months of debate and protests at the Texas state capitol building, the legislature passed the bill near midnight, mere minutes before adjourning the session. The law granted 4-year institutions a little more than a year's time to prepare the concealed-carry policies under the law, and 2-year institutions were given until 1 August 2017 to implement the law. Each individual campus was mandated to propose "sensitive areas" on the campus where guns would still be prohibited. But the law cautioned that these "sensitive areas" could not include classrooms or dormitories outright and could not, in total, amount to "wholesale" prohibition of guns across campus. With appropriate justification, places like chemistry labs (with dangerous, flammable, or explosive chemicals) could be exempted. Daycare centers, some medical facilities, and other sites might also be excluded, but each campus had to prepare a detailed, itemized list and submit that list for review and approval by the leg-islature. It was incumbent on institutions to pick and choose their exclusion zones with care and deliberation. Private institutions were granted the priv-ilege of opting out of the law, and every private institution except one took advantage of that privilege.[41] However, all public institutions had to comply.

The law was implemented statewide on 1 August 2016—the 50th anniver-sary of the Texas Tower shootings. That was a purposeful joke perpetrated on the people of Texas by their legislature. Hilarious, no?

So, have guns on campus in Texas prevented murders? No. In April 2016, a young woman was murdered on the University of Texas campus by a home-less 17-year-old.[42] In 2017, a murder-suicide involving a gun occurred at a Dallas–Fort Worth area community college, North Lake College. Eagle-eyed proponents of guns-on-campus policies will note that both incidents occurred months before concealed carry was "permitted" on the campuses. So, they will say, those incidents cannot be tallied against the newly enacted campus-carry law. Okay, let's remind concealed-carry proponents that carrying con-cealed handguns on the *grounds* of Texas colleges (not inside buildings) has been legal since 1995.[43] Let's also recall the stabbing murder incident on 1 May 2017 on the University of Texas at Austin campus, nearly a year after the Texas guns-on-campus law was enacted.[44] Did guns on campus deter this killer? No. Did a citizen armed with a concealed handgun aid in stopping the incident and apprehending the perpetrator? No.[45]

Once again, carrying concealed handguns on college campuses doesn't seem to deter murders on those campuses. On 10 October 2017, barely 14 months after implementation of the guns-on-campus policy at Texas public higher education institutions, an armed student murdered a Texas Tech Uni-versity policeman with the concealed handgun he was carrying—in the cam-pus police station.[46] Again, you cannot make this up. Wherever guns are permitted, gun violence will follow.

The gun violence incidents perpetrated by those who shot themselves or others with the guns they were licensed to carry on college campuses that per-mit concealed handguns illustrates quite clearly the dilemma we all confront when we permit virtually anyone to carry guns in public places. Licensing people to carry concealed handguns doesn't make them responsible or capable gun handlers. Poorly trained "good guys with guns" toting their weapons in public places and on college campuses are a public safety menace. The imme-diate consequence of permitting guns on campus in Colorado[47] and Idaho[48] was enabling shootings on college campuses. In Utah, it took 8 years, but the shootings occurred eventually.[49] At Umpqua Community College in Roseburg, Oregon, permitting guns on campus did not deter a mass killer in 2015.[50]

In some instances, the people who carry guns are incompetent. In other instances, "good guys with guns," who had no prior criminal records, premeditated murders. The law armed them, and they used their weapons.[51] The Violence Policy Center attempts to track killers known to possess concealed handgun licenses.[52] It has also attempted to document mass shootings committed by those with concealed handgun licenses.[53] The organization has verified many hundreds of homicides and 31 mass shootings committed by licensed concealed handgun permittees, but it's a daunting, sometimes impossible task. In many states, records of who was issued a concealed handgun license are not available to the public—yet another example of purposeful ignorance perpetrated by state legislatures that interferes with our capacity to grasp the nature of gun violence across our society. News reports of homicides rarely report on whether the murderer had a concealed handgun license because—you guessed it—reporters cannot access state records of who has a concealed handgun license. So our understanding of how many concealed carriers commit violent crimes leading to homicide is quite incomplete. Almost certainly, crimes committed by concealed handgun licensees are grossly underdocumented due to state laws banning public access to these records.

Do you see how insidious the gun culture gripping our nation is? Concealed handgun license records are sequestered from public scrutiny, so we're not permitted to know when a crime is committed by a concealed handgun licensee. The NRA and their allies crow that licensed concealed handgun carriers almost never commit crimes—they are *all* good guys with guns, all the time. The truth is that they don't know, they don't want to know, and they don't want you to know. It's the perfect public policy formulation of hear no evil, see no evil, speak no evil—to the detriment of us all. In failing to make necessary connections between gun ownership, concealed handgun licensing, and gun violence, we fail to develop effective public policy to significantly reduce gun violence. Voilà!

In 2017, Tennessee[54] and Georgia[55] colleges joined the ranks of armed campuses. Gun mishaps are sure to follow. Tick-tock, tick,-tock. The waiting is already over in Georgia, which permitted concealed handguns on college campuses on 1 July 2017. On 24 July 2017, a student at Kennesaw State University had his gun taken from him during—wait for it—an armed robbery on campus![56] Read that again. A student carrying a handgun for his personal protection was accosted by two armed robbers who took his wallet and his gun!

Excepting those states that implemented campus carry in 2017 (Arkansas, Georgia, Kansas, Tennessee), there has been a shooting on a college campus in every state that permits guns. In several states (Colorado and Idaho), the immediate impact of implementing guns-on-campus policies was enabling a person licensed to carry a gun to shoot themselves with the gun they were licensed to carry! The empirical probability that a state permitting guns on its college campuses will experience a campus shooting is 1.00—that is, it is 100% certain a gun will discharge on a campus where guns are permitted. Odd how that works, isn't it? Thus, if you live in a state that has recently implemented a guns-on-campus law, watch your statewide newsfeeds carefully. There's going to be a shooting on a college campus. No one can predict which campus will be affected or who the shooter will be, but there will be at least one shooting. It is certain. Stand by, Arkansas, Georgia, Kansas, and Tennessee.

Currently, there are about 300 institutions nationally that permit concealed handguns on their campuses. Virtually all of those campuses permit guns only because the state legislature forced them to do so by legislative fiat—no one in the affected constituencies asked for guns on their campuses or suggested to the state legislatures that guns might be a good idea to maintain campus safety. The data used for this book reports homicides for nearly 9,000 institutions. Thus, guns are currently permitted at just 3.3% of college campuses in the United States, but that number is growing substantially every year as individual states pass guns-on-campus laws and mandate concealed handguns at every public institution of higher education in their state. In 2017 alone, at least 173 institutions were added, more than doubling the number of campuses in America that permitted concealed handguns.

Why is this happening nationwide? Why have 40 state legislatures made an annual issue of permitting guns on college campuses? Is there a common justification for this nonsense?

Commonly, bills introduced to state legislatures focus on the guns-on-campus issue as one of public safety rather than an expansion of gun rights. The common argument puts forward a narrative centered on the most horrific events—mass shootings—but wildly overestimates the probability of these incidents on college campuses. In short, state legislators pander to the fear that these incidents are not only possible but highly probable at their states' college campuses. During the past 8 years, I have listened to or read transcripts of legislators in most of the statehouses in the United States reciting their own versions of "crazy killers" entering college auditoria packed with students and opening fire. To hear them tell it, those incidents are happening with greater and greater frequency, and there is an immediate need to arm civilians as a mass deterrent force on every college campus.

So let's revisit the original premise of this book and see whether these claims are valid. Do you remember what this book is attempting to report?

Think back to the design of the grand social experiment that this book documents. In a nation awash with guns and drowning in gun violence, our society established a nationwide archipelago of gun-safe college campuses where, for the most part, guns are completely prohibited. Gun-safe colleges have been the norm in the United States since the time that colleges were established. The founding fathers who wrote the Second Amendment even prohibited guns at the university they founded—the University of Virginia![57] And guns remain banned there to this day. So this experiment has been running for many decades, and the results are all around us if we care to look for them. Of particular interest are results of the most recent century (since 2001) because we have readily available data from almost all higher education institutions regarding the frequency of homicides, thanks to the provisions of the Clery Act. What was the experimental hypothesis? Recall that we seek to determine that the incidence of homicide on gun-safe college campuses was no different from the incidence of homicides in the public at large. That is to say, homicides on college campuses were at least as frequent as among the general public, possibly even more frequent because, after all, everyone on a college campus is a defenseless rube waiting for armed criminals to slaughter them. That's the premise of our experiment. And what was discovered from this experiment? In fact, we've discovered quite a lot.

College campuses in the United States are among the safest sanctuaries from violent crimes leading to homicide. During this century, from 2001 to 2016, the U.S. Department of Education reported only 279 homicides on nearly 9,000 campuses nationwide. This against a background of 281,051 homicides in the U.S. general public during the same interval.[58] Homicides on college campuses are 1,000 times less frequent than in society at large. As was documented in chapters 5 and 6, those homicides generally involve murderers making short-distance incursions onto the college campus—approximately the length of a football field. The most-at-risk locations are campus residential facilities and parking lots. The majority of campus homicides are targeted killings—more than 92% are single homicides and are commonly committed by an individual who crossed the campus perimeter seeking another specific individual. Almost three-quarters of campus homicides are perpetrated by an assailant known to the victim (72%); women are most frequently targeted by intimate partners or acquaintances. People of color and men are disproportionately represented among victims; women are most frequently targeted by intimate partners or acquaintances (yes, I'm repeating that for emphasis). Most incidents of homicide on campus are acts of domestic violence or consequences of altercations that escalate to murder. Just over half of campus homicide incidents are committed using guns (53.4%).

Mass shootings and mass murders are extremely rare on college campuses, despite broad public perceptions to the contrary. How often has a crazy killer entered a classroom and committed mass murder on college campuses in this century? Although the third-worst mass killing in U.S. history occurred on the campus of Virginia Tech University in 2007, there are only 2 other mass killings—defined as a single incident in which 4 or more persons were killed—in a college classroom on college campuses during the 2001–2016 interval. Those mass killings, in chronological order, were Virginia Tech (2007),[59] Northern Illinois University (2008),[60] and Umpqua Community College (2015).[61] Compare that to the many dozens of mass killings in the United States *every year*.

Since 2013, the Gun Violence Archive and Mass Shooting Tracker have crowd-sourced information on mass shootings across America. These data-gathering operations use slightly different definitions for mass shootings. Both define a mass shooting as any incident during which 4 or more people are shot, but Mass Shooting Tracker counts the shooter if that person is killed or wounded during the incident, whereas the Gun Violence Archive does not count the shooter. Nonetheless, both data-gathering organizations reported an average of one mass shooting per day in the United States during the last 4 years. An average of one mass shooting every day in America's general public versus an average of 1 mass shooting every 5 years on our nation's colleges—more than 365 mass shootings per year in America versus 3 mass shootings in the last 16 years on college campuses. Far from attracting murderers, college are in fact sanctuaries from them.

Homicides on college campuses are rare, averaging 17 per year compared to 17,000 in U.S. society at large. Homicides on college campuses are 1,000 times less frequent than in the general public. These are facts. Unassailable facts. Facts that should matter in the forced and unnecessary debate about permitting guns on college campuses. Those gun-safe archipelagos that we established decades ago, college campuses, are among the safest places in our society. If you want to avoid becoming a victim of homicide, your best bet is to enroll in college and live on campus. Hands down.

Nonetheless, during this century there has been (and continues to be) a persistent, focused, and aggressive effort by gun advocacy organizations (notably the National Rifle Association, National Shooting Sports Federation, and Gun Owners of America) to lobby for and pass legislation in every state that will permit the carrying of concealed handguns on college campuses. In state after state, year after year, you can expect legislators to introduce bills permitting guns on college campuses. Frequently, there are nationally coordinated efforts to run guns-on-campus or campus-carry bills in multiple state legislatures simultaneously. Proponents of these bills claim they are necessary because college campuses are "magnets for murderers." It is said that your children are in grave peril on college campuses. According to this argument, there is someone in your state, right now, formulating meticulous plans to enter a crowded lecture hall with a fearsome semi-automatic assault weapon affixed with a high-capacity ammunition clip or drum magazine and open fire. It is claimed that these presumed assailants will choose a university because it is a gun-free zone—they're coming to slaughter everyone, and they're coming soon, because they know everyone is defenseless. So everyone should be armed. Faculty, staff, and students at universities should carry equivalent firepower under their shirts, inside their bras, in their pants pockets or their backpacks or briefcases or purses every day because those guns will be needed sooner or later. Never mind that college campuses aren't gun-free zones. Virtually all college and universities now have armed, professional police departments or contract with municipal police (armed with guns) to patrol their campuses. Never mind that the observed frequency of murder on college campuses is 1,000 times lower than in the general public. College employees, students, parents of students, and citizens of states are told, repeatedly, that "unarmed" college campuses are places of great peril. These claims are lies. Lies that should wither in the heat of truth (i.e., facts) presented in this book. College campuses are sanctuaries from murderers. I will say that as often as it takes for the truth to come out.

I've been on a college campus somewhere in the United States virtually every working day since 1977—41 years as either a student or employee in higher education, across 5 different states—and I've never been shot.

Do I deny the probability that someone might commit the next mass shooting or mass killing on a college campus in the United States? Do I deny that someone might come onto a campus in search of another individual and murder them with a gun or another lethal weapon? I do not. I am a scientist, and I deal in facts. I am aware of the probability of those incidents—perhaps more aware than most people—because I've been studying the nature and incidence of collegiate homicides for several years now. I know that there have been 3 mass killings in college classrooms since 2001—an average of one mass killing on a college campus every five years. I freely admit and have attempted to document for this book every homicide on every college campus in the United States during the 21st century. That's currently 279 homicides. And I know there will be additional homicides next year and in years to follow. However, I am a scientist, and I also understand probability. We live in a probabilistic world. Let's think through the probability of a being shot on a college campus in the United States.

In the early 1960s, an astronomer, Frank Drake, developed an elegant formula to estimate the potential number of intelligent, technological civilizations in the universe.[62] The Drake Equation wasn't intended to establish with certainty how many communicating civilizations actually existed; instead, it was an intellectual exercise to determine a reasonable estimate based on what was known of the universe at that time. In truth, it was a heuristic device that set about simply attempting to determine the necessary parameters for determining how many advanced civilizations might exist. It was intended to initiate a scientific discussion of the probabilities of discovering extraterrestrial intelligence.

In a similar way, I think we can set out to attempt a simple estimate of the probability of a campus homicide, and, by extension, being murdered with a gun, based on what we know about the incidence of campus and societal homicides described throughout this book. Will this equation be an accurate estimate of that probability? That is not my intent at this point. My intent in walking you through this exercise is to illustrate the variety of factors you should consider when you attempt to estimate the probability of a campus shooting at your college (or whichever college your children may choose). This is an attempt to initiate a discussion. I have no doubt that colleagues of mine in natural sciences and social sciences and mathematics will enjoy examining this equation and offering constructive critiques. I am also convinced that there will be harsh criticism from those who promote guns-on-campus legislation. Some of their criticism may be valid; a lot of it will be hyperbolic balderdash. But at least they'll be engaged in the conversation! And, to be fair, their balderdash will be unmasked quite easily if there are enough academics involved in vetting this equation!

So we're going to set out to do some math. Don't be apprehensive. It's easy math, and we'll walk through each step in detail. Don't you want to know what the probability of a campus shooting might be? Sure you do! Be forewarned that the numbers we're going to use will be very crude, because we don't have accurate counts of some of the parameters that I think we need to determine the "actual" answer to the question "What is the probability of a shooting homicide on a college campus?" But we're not seeking an "actual" answer here—we want an estimate, and for now that estimate (hopefully) will be the correct order of magnitude. That's the best we can do right now. It's a starting point for more detailed investigation and research into what the probability might actually be. It's the beginning of a conversation.

In order to make this estimate, we will need to make some assumptions. The assumptions I make will be a source of contention, but if I don't make some assumptions at the outset, we really can't make any progress on this calculation. I'm going to begin with an assumption that there's a murderer somewhere in the United States who wants to enter a college campus classroom and kill someone. That is, that killer wants to commit a random homicide of a single person. We'll start there. When we're done, we might go back and change that to multiple killers or multiple victims if we want to, just to see how the equation might be changed by altering those parameters. In fact, if we have a good equation, we should be able to examine many different scenarios to determine how probabilities change under those varying scenarios. A good model is useful for running many scenarios and examining how outcomes vary.

Let's begin by estimating the probability of being murdered in the United States. Annually, about 17,000 people are murdered in this country. I've already reported that this observed murder frequency translates to a murder rate of about 5.77 people per 100,000 population. But what is the probability of a particular person being murdered? The U.S. Centers for Disease Control and Prevention suggested in 2010 that this probability was 1 in 18,989.[63] In 2015, this probability was 1 in 18,694.[64] From 2001 to 2016, the probability averaged 1 in 17,405.[65] How is this probability determined? It's not at all mysterious. In fact, it's a very simple estimate. To determine this probability, you just divide the number of homicides each year by the U.S. population. Let's estimate using round numbers. Annually, there are about 17,000 homicides in the United States. The U.S. population is about 322,000,000. The probability of being murdered in the United States? It's just 17,000 ÷ 322,000,000 = 0.000053. This is equivalent to 1 in 18,941—just about the same as the values derived above. And those are pretty small odds. What else has a probability of about 1 in 19,000? This is the same probability that the favored team (that is, the higher-seeded team) wins all 64 first-round games in the NCAA men's basketball tournament.[66] How often does that happen? If you make a bracket every year like tens of millions of Americans, you know the answer. I don't think it has ever happened, and it is unlikely that it ever will. How unlikely? One chance in nineteen thousand unlikely.

The estimate above has some implicit assumptions that should be mentioned. By dividing the observed number of homicides each year by the U.S. population, we're assuming that every person in the United States has an equal chance of being murdered. Strictly speaking, this is not true. Further, we're assuming that homicides occur at random across America. Homicides, in general, are not random events, and the victims aren't selected randomly—most of the time. Nonetheless, we frequently use the assumption of randomness to estimate probabilities of many events. And we will make this assumption on subsequent calculations because this makes it possible to derive an estimate. Not only do we assume that each person in the following estimates has an equal chance of being murdered, but we also assume that the parameters we're using are independent of each other—that is, the parameters we're going to specify in the estimates below are not influenced by one another's outcomes. That is also a common assumption in establishing probabilities for sequential events, as it keeps the mathematics simple. To determine the probability of any sequence of events when the events are random and independent, all you need to do is determine the probability of each event, and then multiply the probabilities together.[67]

Look, I just loaded the outcome of this probability estimate with empirical data regarding homicides in America. The probability of being murdered in the United States is about 1 in 19,000. That is a very unlikely event. Most people will never be murdered. Just as most people will never be killed by a tornado, even among those who experience a tornado. Yet that probability is substantially greater than in most developed nations. For example, across much of the European Union, homicide rates are 5 times lower than in the United States.[68] Think of that. Across the EU, the probability of someone being murdered is about 1 in 95,000. However, even with a probability of being murdered in the United States of 1 in 19,000, I can tell you right now that, based on this value, the end calculation of this exercise is going to be a ridiculously small probability. Think about it. Even if the probability of every other variable we consider is 1—that is, the probability of every other variable is equal to "certainty"—the end calculation is going to be 1 in 19,000. That's an exceedingly unlikely occurrence. So we could quit here and declare that you aren't likely to be murdered on a college campus in America. We could argue that we already know collegiate murders are 1,000 times less frequent than in the general public, so we might conclude that the probability of being murdered on a college campus is about 1 in 19 million—a thousand times less probable than in the general public—or we could derive an estimate if we simply divide the annual number of collegiate homicides by the total population of college students and employees; 17 homicides per year divided by about 30,000,000 people on college campuses yields a probability of being murdered equal to $17 \div 30,000,000 = 0.00000057$, or about 1 in 1.8 million. So we could stop right here. But let's not stop. Let's concoct a Frank Drake–like estimate of the probability of being murdered in a college classroom and test whether that theoretical equation comports with reality.

Let's attempt to derive an estimate of the probability that a person in the United States may be found at a college campus. How many people in America are college students? Annually, there are about 25 million students enrolled in U.S. colleges.[69] The probability that a person in the United States is enrolled in college is 25,000,000 ÷ 322,000,000 = 0.078, or about 7.8% (1 of every 13 people in America). What is the probability that someone will be murdered in America *and* will also be a student enrolled in college? Since these are independent conditions, the probability can be estimated using the multiplication rule—it's simply the probability of someone being murdered times the probability of someone being a college student. Thus, (17,000 ÷ 322,000,000) × (25,000,000 ÷ 322,000,000) = 0.000053 × 0.078 = 0.0000041, or 1 in 243,902. Those are very long odds. What else had odds of about 1 in 244,000? That's the same chance that an 80-foot wide (24 meters across) asteroid named 2012 BY1 will strike Earth in the middle of this century![70] I will predict now, with confidence, that this asteroid will not strike Earth. And your daughter or son will not be murdered on a college campus. But the probability of being murdered on a college campus is substantially less than the above tally.

The next parameter we need to consider is the probability that someone is murdered in America *and* that person is a college student *and* they are murdered on a college campus. We just estimated the probability of the first two parameters at 1 in 243,902. But what are the odds that this person is also killed on a college campus? Let's assume that the collegiate population has equal access to any of 9,000 or so institutions of higher education in the United States. In this scenario, geography is not a barrier to access in any way. Nor is tuition a barrier to entry into any college in the United States, or the enrollment capacity of any institution. We're just going to assume the collegiate population is evenly distributed across our 9,000 campuses. If we assume that any person in the U.S. collegiate population has an equal chance of being at any individual campus, the probability of them being on any individual campus in the United States is simply 1 ÷ 9,000 = 0.00011, or approximately 1 in 10,000. What other events in life have probabilities of about 1 in 10,000? Being struck by lightning during your lifetime.[71]

Since we are allowing that the collegiate population is evenly spread among our 9,000 higher education institutions, that parameter is independent of the previous two parameters, so the probability that someone is murdered in the United States *and* that person is a college student *and* that person is murdered on a college campus is just the multiplied product of those three parameters. Thus, (17,000 ÷ 322,000,000) × (25,000,000 ÷ 322,000,000) × (1 ÷ 9,000) = 0.00000000046, or 1 in 2,173,913,043. A probability of 1 in 2.2 billion. A person is almost 10 times more likely to win the Powerball lottery![72] We are really done here, because this is functionally a probability of zero. Don't believe me? Round the estimated probability above to eight decimal places—0.00000000. See? Zero! But let's continue anyway to see how much more outrageous the probabilities might become.

In addition to the probability of being a murder victim in the United States (probability = 0.000053) *and* being a college student (0.078) *and* being on a college campus (0.00011), what is the probability of the murder occurring in a college classroom? Assuming the killer chooses a classroom randomly, what is the probability that the killer arrives on a college campus *and* arrives at a particular classroom? Since we're treating all conditions as independent and random choices in this scenario, the probability of arriving on campus and arriving at a classroom is simply the probability of a college student in the United States being murdered on a college (0.00000000046) times the probability of being in a classroom. To determine the probability of being in a classroom, we need to know how many classrooms exist on a typical college campus. We don't have a tabulation of that number anywhere that I am aware of, but, nationwide, the total number of classrooms on college campuses is very large. If we assume that a typical college has 250 classrooms and there are 9,000 colleges in the nation, that's 2.25 million classrooms! If we assume that all classrooms have an equal chance of being the murder scene, the probability of a college student being murdered in a classroom is 0.00000000046 × (1 ÷ 250) = 0.0000000000018, or approximately 1 in 555 billion!

However, the odds that an individual student might be killed in a classroom are still quite a lot less than 1 in 555 billion. There are other parameters that must be considered. First, the murder must occur in the classroom during a time when the classroom is in use and occupied. When might that be? Again, if we assume that the murderer arrives randomly at any of the times a classroom is in use, we can estimate that probability.

Most college classrooms are available during regular working hours, plus, perhaps, a few additional hours during weekdays. Weekend classes at universities are rather rare, in part because there are other activities ongoing at colleges on weekends—activities like football or other major sports events. Weekends are a time for colleges to generate supplemental revenue beyond tuition, academic fees, state appropriations, grants and gifts. Collegiate athletics mean big money, even for small colleges. Thus, college classrooms are generally available Monday through Friday. The chance that the murderer arrives on one of these weekdays is 5/7 = 0.71. The estimated probability, then, of being a murder victim in the United States (probability = 0.000053) *and* being a college student (0.078) *and* being on a college campus (0.00011) *and* in a classroom (0.004) during a weekday (0.71) is 0.0000000000013, or 1 in 769 billion!

In addition to arriving on a weekday, the murder must be committed during a time of day when the classroom is open for instruction. In general, college classrooms are open from about 7:30 a.m. to 7:30 p.m. on any given weekday. That equates to 12 hours of availability during a 24-hour day. So, the estimated probability a murderer arrives during an hour in which the classroom in is use is 12 ÷ 24 = 0.5. Therefore, the estimated probability of being a murder victim in the United States (17,000 ÷ 322,000,000) *and* being a college student (25,000,000 ÷ 322,000,000) *and* being on a college campus (1 ÷ 9,000) *and* being in a classroom (1 ÷ 250) during a weekday (5 ÷ 7) between 7:30 a.m. and 7:30 p.m. (12 ÷ 24) is 0.000000000000646, or 1 in 1.55 trillion.

What we have attempted to estimate so far is the probability of a person being murdered in the United States who is a college student on a college campus in a classroom on a weekday during the hours that a class might be conducted. I think we need a couple more parameters and our estimate will be done. Most college classes have a duration of about one hour. During a 12-hour day, an individual student might be present in a particular classroom during one of those hours. So the estimated probability that a student will be in the classroom during a particular hour during the 12-hour day is 1 ÷ 12 = 0.083. Multiplying this number by our previous result yields a value of 0.000000000000054, or about 1 chance in 18.7 trillion that a student will be in a particular classroom during a class session between 7:30 a.m. and 7:30 p.m. on a weekday at a college in the United States.

Finally, we need to consider that if a person is murdered in the United States *and* is a college student at a randomly chosen college *and* in a randomly chosen classroom on a randomly chosen weekday at a randomly chosen time when the classroom is in use *and* a randomly chosen time when a student is present in the classroom, what is the likelihood that *this* student will be murdered? That depends, in part, on how many others are in the classroom. Let's assume it's a typical college class size of 50 and all students have an equal chance of being murdered. The probability of a student being killed is 1 ÷ 50 = 0.02. So, finally, our estimate of the probability of a particular college student being murdered at a time they are in class *and* at a time the classroom is available for class *and* on a weekday *and* in a particular classroom *and* at a particular college in the United States is (17,000 ÷ 322,000,000) × (25,000,000 ÷ 322,000,000) × (1 ÷ 9,000) × (1 ÷ 250) × (5 ÷ 7) × (12 ÷ 24) × (1 ÷ 12) × (1 ÷ 50) = 0.0000000000000026. This is 1 in 1.1 quadrillion (1.1 × 10^{-15})! I cannot imagine any event with such a low probability. No one can. The probability that a vending machine could fall on you and crush you is 1 in 112 million.[73] Nonetheless, that utterly improbable circumstance is almost 10 million times more likely than a killer arriving in a college classroom.

These are outlandish probabilities. "Completely unrealistic!" my critics will howl, and I agree. I told you when we started the estimate above that it was rigged from the first term in the equation. Every term has a rather small probability, and multiplying those small probabilities together yields an astoundingly small probability. There will be much discussion and finger-pointing regarding the incorrect aspects of the above formulation. I invite that. Consider the formulation above the "collegiate homicide Drake equation." If I formulate it like the Drake equation, it looks something like this:

$$f_m \times f_s \times P_u \times P_c \times f_d \times f_h \times f_a \times f_e = \text{probability of a particular student}$$
being murdered where

f_m = fraction of people in the United States murdered annually (17,000 ÷ 322,000,000 = 0.000053)

f_s = fraction of people in the United States who are college students (25,000,000 ÷ 322,000,000 = 0.078)

P_u = probability of individual being on the campus of a particular college (estimated as 1 ÷ 9,000 = 0.00011)

P_c = probability of a student being in a particular classroom (estimated as 1 ÷ 250 = 0.004)

f_d = fraction of days per week a classroom is available for classes (5 ÷ 7 = 0.71)

f_h = fraction of hours per day a classroom in available for classes (12÷ 24 = 0.5)

f_a = fraction of hours per day a particular student might be in a particular classroom (1 ÷ 12 = 0.083)

f_e = fraction of enrolled students in a particular class that a particular student attends (estimated as 1 ÷ 50 = 0.02)

I'd like to see a serious conversation in our society to determine more accurately the probability of a single student being murdered in a college classroom. Very likely it is not as small as I've just presented, but it's going to be very, very small indeed. And that is the point I wish to make. Our gun-safe colleges are extraordinarily safe. The probability of any particular person, such as you or your daughter or son, being murdered in a college classroom is incredibly small. Did I mention that I've been on a college campus almost every working day for 41 years? If we assume that I've managed 270 days per year over that span, that's a total of 11,070 days on college campuses. The probabilities above bear out how I've managed to survive unarmed *and* unharmed!

The probability of a college student being murdered on college campus is minuscule. If you spend 4 years on a college campus (or 5 years, or 6 years, or 41 years like me), it is most unlikely that you will be murdered. End of story? Of course not. The extraordinary probabilities presented above are based on many assumptions, some of which are not tenable. So let the discussion and refinement of these risk estimates take place. However, regardless of how well refined the associated individual probabilities become, I am convinced that the odds of being murdered on gun-safe college campuses will be found to be minuscule. Thus, for individuals, this probability is so unlikely that it will not happen in their lifetimes. (My critics are already yelping that this is wrong and they can prove it.)

Most people in the general public don't fully appreciate the nature of probabilities. I feel confident that some reading these passages will already have asked themselves, "If the probability of murder on a college campus is 1 in 1.08 quadrillion, how can there be 17 murders per year?"

Answering this question speaks to the nature of the probability of rare *and* independent events—not to mention the statistics of truly large numbers.[74] The probability of a college student being murdered on campus of 1 in 1.1 quadrillion is the probability of any individual student being murdered on any given hour that a classroom is open during a weekday in any given classroom on any given college campus in the United States *and* assuming those parameters are independent of one another *and* that murders occur at random. And because the parameters used to derive that probability are independent, that's the probability for every student, every day, on every college campus, but still assuming that murders occur at random (i.e., every student has an equal chance of being murdered). That's a lot of specific conditions to be met, and it's highly unlikely that *all* of those conditions will be met, so the resulting probability estimate becomes improbably small. Still, the improbable murder of students is realized on college campuses about 17 times every year. How is this possible?

The frequent realization of probabilistically rare events is described in the 2014 book by statistician D.J. Hand, *The Improbability Principle: Why Coincidences, Miracles, and Rare Events Happen Every Day.*[75] The realization of rare events depends on the accumulation of opportunities for the event to occur given that events occur due to random chance. In the case of the probability described here, 1 in 1.1 quadrillion, its realization depends on the same accumulation of opportunities. What we have described ad nauseam (sorry!) has such a small probability because we've formulated an approximation using a very large number of variables, each of which has a small probability. Nonetheless, such a small probability can be realized if a sufficiently large number of "student college hours" accumulates *or* if murders aren't random events.

How many student college hours are there in a typical year? We estimated above that a typical college classroom is available to conduct classes 12 hours per day. We also estimated that a typical college has 250 classrooms. Thus, there are 3,000 classroom hours per day on a typical college campus. Multiply that by 9,000 colleges nationwide, and you have 27,000,000 classroom hours per day across the United States! The typical academic year runs 160 days (two sixteen-week semesters, 5 days per week), so multiply that value by 27,000,000 classroom hours, which comes to 4,320,000,000—4.32 billion classroom hours per academic year. Finally, multiply 4.32 billion classroom hours by 25 million students: $4{,}320{,}000{,}000 \times 25{,}000{,}000 = 108{,}000{,}000{,}000{,}000{,}000$, or 108 quadrillion student classroom hours! Annually in the United States, we estimate 108 quadrillion student classroom hours offered across the nation. What a staggeringly large number! Who knew?

If the probability of a collegiate murder is 1 for every 1.08 quadrillion student classroom hours in a nation where 108 quadrillion student classroom hours are offered every year, we should expect about 100 murders annually (simply divide 108 quadrillion by 1.08 quadrillion). In the United States, we average 17 homicides on college campuses every year. Predict about 100 collegiate murders annually; realize 17 on-campus homicides. It would seem that our college campuses nationwide are outperforming our crude statistical prediction for collegiate homicides. That is to say, the observed frequency of homicides (17 or so per year) is substantially less than one would predict if collegiate homicides were completely random events and all the parameters we've used above are independent of each other.

Truthfully, I don't really have much faith in the above formulation beyond the first two terms in the equation. The rest of the formulation is entirely speculative and, in all likelihood, incorrect. So let's back up to the foundational parameters in this estimate. The probability of being murdered in the United States is, indeed, $17{,}000 \div 322{,}000{,}000$, or about 1 in 19,000.[76] The probability of being a college student is, indeed, $25{,}000{,}000 \div 322{,}000{,}000$, or about 1 in 13.[77] Those two parameters are truly independent of each other. Thus, the probability of someone being murdered *and* a college student is about 1 in 244,000. Those odds are also the estimated probability of a known Earth-crossing asteroid hitting the Earth in 2050.[78]

Granted, we have made many assumptions to arrive at these estimates— I've already admitted to that. And we've assumed all the parameters are independent. We know this is not strictly the case, but, still, it seems that with some additional discussion and refinement, we might develop a realistic probabilistic model based on what we know regarding collegiate homicides.

For example, we know students are more commonly murdered in dormitories as opposed to classrooms. How many dorm rooms exist on a college campus and what fraction of students reside in those dorms and how many hours per day are they present in their dorms? If we substitute dorm rooms for classrooms in our estimate, we know most colleges have more than 200 dorm rooms, so there will be greater numbers of dorm spaces than classrooms. However, not all students live in dorms. We need to know the fraction of 25 million students nationwide residing in dorms. We also need to estimate the number of hours per day students are present in their dorms or dorm rooms—that number is probably about the same as the 12 hours per day we estimated for classroom availability. (Think about it: students are generally in their dorms 8 hours nightly, plus at least 4 additional hours per day eating meals and socializing.) If we start evaluating numbers for the parameters above, we're going to come to values similar to those already presented. And we'll still be estimating a stunningly small chance of homicide against an enormously large number of opportunities for it to occur—our improbable event becomes likely to occur less than a dozen and a half times annually. It's the realization of the Improbability Principle![79]

The foregoing discussion will likely generate a great deal of debate and critique, and that is my purpose. I know many of my colleagues won't agree with this evaluation or like it. I've presented the case above not to declare that these are the actual probabilities of being murdered on a college campus in the United States but to illustrate that determining the probability of such an event, while challenging, is possible. I invite folks to prove me wrong and, in so doing, to develop a better approximation.

Among the incorrect assumptions in previous calculations is the assumption that all parameters are independent of one another and that the probabilities associated with each parameter are random among the population. While it seems evident that the probability of being murdered in the United States and the probability of being a college student are unrelated, independent variables, the phenomenon of collegiate homicide is definitely not random. Many are targeted killings of specific individuals perpetrated by killers who are known to the victims. Those who become murderers on college campuses don't become killers at random; every person in society at large is not equally likely to become a killer. There are many factors that contribute to violent tendencies among individuals. Nor is the geography of college murders random; I demonstrated previously that the average distance of a collegiate homicide from a college boundary is about the length of a football field plus its end zones. Dormitories and parking lots are much more common sites of homicide than classrooms. Men are more likely to be victims than women. All of these factors are not random, though they are useful in understanding the phenomenon of homicide on college campuses. Developing more realistic probabilities to evaluate the chances that a particular individual might be murdered at college is possible if we take these facts into consideration.

Collegiate homicides aren't random. That's good news. If collegiate homicides aren't random, then they are understandable and, possibly, predictable. With appropriate research into the nature and incidence of collegiate homicides, society should be able to develop a profile of the phenomenon. We should be able to determine the appropriate weighting of factors contributing to the profile of a collegiate murder incident. We should be able to create a profile of the collegiate murderer. We should be able to develop effective countermeasures to limit the occurrence of collegiate homicides.

One element that could reduce collegiate homicides by more than half? Making sure that guns don't cross the college perimeter. To appease my critics who say "guns don't kill people; people with guns kill people," we must make sure that people with guns don't cross the campus threshold. Overall, we already do a masterful job of achieving that objective. Out of 108 quadrillion student classroom hours annually, we fail to prevent gun homicides only 10 times per year. We succeed in keeping killers with guns away from our college campuses in 99.99999999999999% of student classroom hours every year. That's an extraordinary record of safety and security.

It's hard to argue that we can make our college campuses much safer in a nation awash with guns and drowning in gun violence. However, I think this goal is feasible. First, we need to develop a comprehensive understanding of the nature and incidence of homicide on college campuses. That was a primary goal of this book. The data presented in these pages represent an important start to that process, but there is much more we can do to develop a more comprehensive profile of collegiate homicides and how to prevent them. All that is required is the will to do so. Do we have that will? Every person on a college campus is someone's daughter or son. It seems to me that the least we can do is preserve our collegiate sanctuaries for each of them. Even better, we can expand those sanctuaries across all sectors of our society. Why am I the dreamer?

8

Speak Truth to Power

"We don't have to live like this!"
—Richard Martinez, father of a gun
violence victim

America has dug itself a hole. Or maybe it's a grave. A large, deep grave that we fill with 32,000 victims of gun violence every year. Year after year. We've been at it for decades. We seem unable or unwilling to stop it. By "we," I mean primarily our elected officials at the national and state levels. Their actions and inactions oppose the desires of most of the American public.

Our legislators' debate over adding more guns to our society begs an important question: How many guns does it take to keep us safe? Gun rights advocates and the legislators who bow to them keep advocating for more and more guns. That advocacy seems to suggest that they believe there is some magic threshold of gun possession above which gun violence is thwarted. If we just had the magic number of guns, all acts of gun violence would be deterred. So what is that magic number of guns? Evidently, in the minds of gun rights advocates, the 380–400 million guns currently in the private stockpiles of United States citizens have not yet achieved that threshold. How many more guns will it take to keep us safe? It's a legitimate question to ask, but I think it's a trick question. What is the magic number of guns beyond which all future acts of gun violence are deterred? If you're thinking, "That must be a very large number of guns," you are incorrect because you aren't conceiving the problem of gun violence correctly. Do you want to know how many guns are required to prevent all future acts of gun violence? The answer is *zero*. Think about it: where there are no guns, there can be no gun violence. It's a simple answer. The simplest answer, in fact. And there is empirical evidence that it's true.

In 1996, there was a mass killing in Port Arthur, Tasmania. The assailant used a semi-automatic AR-15 rifle to kill 35 people and wound 23 more. Following the massacre, the Australian government enacted severe restrictions on gun ownership, banned semi-automatic weapons like the AR-15, established a national gun registry, and instituted a 28-day waiting period on all gun purchases. A mandatory government gun buy-back was implemented that expended $350 million and netted 643,000 guns. There hasn't been a mass shooting in Australia since 28 April 1996. Where there are no semi-automatic assault rifles, there are no mass killings committed with semi-automatic assault rifles. Or, more simply, where there are no guns, there is no gun violence. How many guns does it take to deter all future acts of gun violence? Zero guns. That is the answer you seek.

By very large majorities, the American public wants some restrictions on our gun-owning culture. Repeated public polling of gun owners and non–gun owners demonstrates widespread support for universal background checks on gun purchases. The most recent Pew report indicates 77% of gun owners and 87% of non–gun owners want universal background checks for every gun purchase.[1]

With respect to who should *not* be permitted to purchase guns, 89% of both gun owners and non–gun owners believe people with mental illnesses should be prevented from purchasing guns.[2] Gun owners and non–gun owners (82% and 84%, respectively) agree that people on terrorist or other criminal watch lists should also be prohibited from purchasing guns.[3] Of course, a significant issue with both of these concerns is that guns are freely available in the United States. People may purchase guns and develop mental illnesses after they are already in possession of lethal weapons. Likewise, individuals may already possess firearms when they turn to radical ideologies. At least some states are addressing issues related to the onset of mental disorders by passing or considering legislation to remove weapons from individuals at the request of family members or concerned authorities—so-called gun violence restraining orders (GVROs)[4] or extreme risk protection orders (ERPOs).[5]

The general public shares a good deal of common ground surrounding commonsense regulations on gun ownership and public carrying of guns. We can honor constitutional privileges while developing reasonable safeguards to ensure public safety. Most Americans understand that no constitutionally protected privileges are absolute. There are reasonable restrictions on speech, assembly, and even the practice of religion (for example, no one in the United States is permitted to practice a religion requiring human sacrifices). And the U.S. general public is somewhat accepting of reasonable regulations on gun ownership and the right to bear arms.

The previous chapters recounted statistics on gun violence and homicide in America and provided insight into the nature and incidence of homicide on college campuses across the nation. Our institutions of higher education are not completely immune from homicide, as I've documented. Yet there are far fewer murders on college campuses than in society at large—1,000 times fewer murders every year. I have demonstrated that colleges are anything but magnets for murders. Rather than eliminate these sanctuaries, we should be looking to them to determine how we might expand their overall safety and security to include the rest of our society. Everyone deserves to be secure every day in our nation. We all deserve sanctuary, and the government has the constitutionally authorized task of "promot[ing] the general welfare" and "ensur[ing] domestic tranquility." What do colleges do that creates an environment where homicides are rare occurrences? One thing they have traditionally done is ban guns outright. I'll say it again: where there are no guns, there can be no gun violence.

Unfortunately, in state after state, legislatures are rolling back provisions to maintain sanctuary on our college campuses and elsewhere in society. In the 21st century, dozens of states have passed hundreds of laws lessening or eliminating restrictions on guns in many public spaces. State legislatures are making repeated attempts to pass laws permitting guns on college campuses—even in states that haven't recorded a single homicide on any college campus since 2001! State legislatures are busy enabling the worst of society to carry guns without permits. They even invented a term for this practice to make it sound acceptable: "constitutional carry." As if the U.S. Constitution authorizes citizens to saunter around town fully armed at all times. It does not. In fact, it is reasonable to question whether the Constitution authorizes individual citizens at all.

The Second Amendment references "the right of The People to keep and bear arms." "The People" is an aggregate population, not an individual. When the Constitution mentions "The People," it refers to the body politic, not to you or me individually. The Second Amendment doesn't declare "the right of you, individually, to keep and bear arms." Furthermore, the Second Amendment, first and foremost, asserts, "A well-regulated militia being necessary to the security of a free State…." One might rewrite this statement to read "the security of a free State necessarily requires a well-regulated militia." In that context, the Second Amendment begins to look like a right reserved to the states to raise an armed security force rather than a right reserved to you and me as private citizens. So maybe it is. At least, that's how it was interpreted by the Supreme Court of the United States throughout most of U.S. history.[6]

The legal concept that the Second Amendment guarantees the right for an individual to keep and bear arms is the 21st-century revelation of the "constitutional originalist," Supreme Court Justice Antonin Scalia. Justice Scalia wrote the majority opinion for the Supreme Court in its 2008 decision in *District of Columbia vs. Heller.*[7] The *Heller* decision is a landmark case in U.S. law. The majority opinion penned by Justice Scalia overturned nearly two centuries of Supreme Court rulings on the Second Amendment that indicated the amendment itself was a right reserved to states to raise an armed military force.[8] However, despite the *Heller* ruling that individuals had the right to maintain lethal weapons for their personal self-defense in their domiciles, Justice Scalia was careful to articulate that this ruling was limited strictly to that purpose. He even went so far as to insist:

> Of course the right was not unlimited, just as the First Amendment's right of free speech was not…. Thus, we do not read the Second Amendment to protect the right of citizens to carry arms for *any* sort of confrontation, just as we do not read the First Amendment to protect the right of citizens to speak for *any* purpose.[9]

These are powerful and unambiguous words from one of the most conservative Supreme Court justices in U.S. history: "Of course the right [to keep and bear arms] was not unlimited, just as the First Amendment's right of free speech was not." As if to ensure that no one would misconstrue his intentions, Justice Scalia expounded on the majority opinion that the right to keep and bear arms has boundaries:

> Like most rights, the right secured by the Second Amendment is not unlimited. From Blackstone through the 19th-century cases, commentators and courts routinely explained that the right was not a right to keep and carry any weapon whatsoever in any manner whatsoever and for whatever purpose…. For example, the majority of the 19th-century courts to consider the question held that prohibitions on carrying concealed weapons were lawful under the Second Amendment or state analogues…. Although we do not undertake an exhaustive historical analysis today of the full scope of the Second Amendment, nothing in our opinion should be taken to cast doubt on longstanding prohibitions on the possession of firearms by felons and the mentally ill, or laws forbidding the carrying of firearms in sensitive places such as schools and government buildings, or laws imposing conditions and qualifications on the commercial sale of arms.[10]

Justice Scalia announced in no uncertain terms that the majority of the court stood not only with the "right to keep and bear arms" but also with the "well-regulated" aspect. No one has an unlimited right to carry a lethal weapon anywhere they want in our society. I didn't say so; the Supreme Court of the United States said so. In the case of *District of Columbia vs. Heller*, the Supreme Court sides with the majority of "The People" (i.e., the aggregate, not the individuals). In other words, the Supreme Court recognizes commonsense restrictions on gun ownership and the carrying of guns in society at large.

Among the privileged sanctuaries that traditionally excluded guns were schools—all schools: preschools, kindergartens, elementary schools, middle schools, junior high schools, high schools, technical institutes, community colleges, 4-year colleges and universities. Public and private schools. All the schools. With respect to post-secondary education institutions, the prohibition of guns on campus has worked well. As stated before, homicides on those campuses are 1,000 times lower than in the general public. I've stated it before, but I'll do so again: I'm in my 41st year on a college campus, and I've never be shot at. I've never even had a gun pointed at me. Because all the colleges I've attended or worked at prohibited people from carrying guns on campus. Of course, the campus police were always armed. And that was good enough for everyone's safety.

I'm not naïve. I understand that there are a small number of families across America who have not had my experience. They had a loved one murdered on a college campus. Some of those loved ones were murdered with guns. Some are survivors of campus shootings. I am friends with some of those families of victims and with some of the survivors. Of course, I understand their loss. As a professor who interacts with those families' daughters and sons—their very hopes and dreams—every working day, I am acutely aware of the tragedy that collegiate homicides represent. So much future promise snuffed out with every incident. I feel the loss of those beautiful, young, hopeful, ambitious, eager, happy, smiling, innocent lives at the transition of childhood and adulthood. It makes my heart heavy. My own children are two of those people right now. I would be lost if one of them were taken from me. I will not claim to know the pain of such a loss. But I do realize the long-term effect on our nation. Who knows whether we may lose a brilliant doctor who would cure a debilitating disease? Who knows whether we may lose the visionary artist who would show us the world in ways we don't see? Who knows whether we may lose the social worker whose grace and compassion might end hunger, or poverty, or abuse … at least for a few? Have we already lost the historian or political scientist who could bring clarity to our political discourse or the economist who could bring certainty to financial affairs? I understand what we lose when we lose 17 human beings on a college campus every year. My mind boggles at the thought that we lose an additional 17,000 across America every year. So much lost human potential. We can do better. "We don't have to live like this!"

We should also be aware that arguments about guns on campus reducing campus crime are lies. Lies told by paid liars. Let's look at the available record of campus gun crimes in our nation—the same records we've discussed *ad nauseum* throughout this book. Guns are now permitted in various ways on college campuses in almost half the states.[11] In some states, guns are permitted only in locked cars in campus parking lots. Other states permit concealed handguns to be carried by anyone with a state-issued license. One state, Kansas, permits the carrying of concealed handguns on college campuses without a permit or any specific training whatsoever. As with everything else in this book, there are data that relate directly to the reported crimes and other incidents committed by people carrying guns on these campuses. So let's examine the incidence of reported crimes and gun-related incidents on college campuses with guns and those without to determine whether there is a "deterrent effect"—that is, a suppression of crime—on campuses that permit guns versus campuses the ban them altogether.

Currently, there are 8 states that allow persons with state-issued concealed handgun licenses to carry guns on their campuses: Utah, Colorado, Idaho, Texas, Tennessee, Georgia, Kansas, and Arkansas. Of those 8 states, Utah has the longest statewide experience with guns on campus, having permitted guns on its colleges since 2004. How many crimes were reported on Utah college campuses in the years before guns were permitted on campus (2001, 2002, 2003, and 2004)? There were 223 total crimes reported in 2001, 221 total crimes in 2002, 199 total crimes in 2003, and 252 total crimes in 2004. Averaged over those 4 years, Utah colleges reported 223.75 ± 21.7 crimes annually. After 2004, campus carry was fully implemented statewide in Utah. Did campus carry reduce reported crimes at Utah colleges? From 2005 to 2016 (the most recent year of reporting), Utah colleges averaged 217.1 ± 59.2 crimes annually. Prior to the guns arriving on campus, 224 crimes per year; afterward, 217 crimes per year. The plus-or-minus values following the reported averages are called standard deviations (statistical measures of the variability from year to year in reported crimes). What we can conclude from these measures, however, is that the average annual number of crimes in Utah is a statistical tie. Guns on campus have not increased or decreased reported crimes on Utah college campuses. So there is no observable "deterrent effect" from the presence of guns on campus. Furthermore, data since the 2004 implementation of Utah's guns-on-campus law indicate that no individual crime has ever been stopped by someone carrying a gun on a Utah campus. However, there have been at least 3 campus shootings in Utah since campus carry was enacted (in 2012,[12] 2016,[13] and 2017[14]). How many shootings occurred on Utah colleges prior to the implementation of campus carry? So far as I can determine, there was one—in 1993.[15] Has the presence of guns on Utah campuses made them safer? No.

Colorado State University was the first institution in the United States to permit guns on campus in 2003. The remainder of public colleges and universities in Colorado were ordered to implement campus carry by the Colorado Supreme Court in 2012.[16] Has the presence of guns on Colorado college campuses decreased or increased crime rates? At Colorado colleges and universities, total reported crimes have been decreasing since 2004. The most precipitous decline in campus crimes occurred from 2004 to 2008, and then the rate leveled off somewhat, though it continued declining until 2012. Since implementation of campus carry statewide in 2012, total reported campus crimes have remained fairly consistent, averaging 435 per year. Did guns on Colorado colleges reduce overall crime incidence? No. Total campus crimes were declining quite nicely from 2004 to 2012. The 2012 implementation of the guns-on-campus policy seems to have arrested declining crime rates. On top of that, in 2012[17] and again in 2014,[18] there were incidents involving guns at the University of Colorado Anschutz Medical Campus in Denver. Did the presence of people carrying guns there make anyone safer? Evidently not. The very best thing that one might be able to say about having guns on Colorado campuses is that crime rates have not increased dramatically as a consequence—so far. But the presence of guns on campus in Colorado did enable shootings to occur. That's a fact.

In Idaho, guns were permitted on every state college campus in 2014. During the first week of the 2014 fall semester, a professor shot himself in the foot with the gun he was licensed to carry. Did I mention that he was irresponsibly carrying the gun in his pants pocket in a classroom with 19 students when he negligently shot himself? It has never been publicly reported how the gun in his pocket was discharged, but gun-safety experts and firearms instructors will tell you, unanimously, that putting a gun in your pocket is the wrong way to carry a concealed handgun.

Next up in the campus-carry Wild West Show was Texas, where concealed handguns were authorized on 4-year college campuses on 1 August 2016—the 50th anniversary of the infamous Texas Tower mass shooting in 1966. In truth, guns were permitted on the public outdoor spaces of every Texas college starting in 1995, but the 2016 implementation permitted guns to be carried into campus interior spaces of public 4-year institutions. Barely 6 weeks after authorizing broad concealed handgun privileges at Texas public universities, a student with a concealed handgun license negligently discharged a gun in a dorm room at Tarleton State University.[19] Ridiculously, that negligent discharge occurred in a campus dormitory named Integrity Hall. In May 2017, a murder-suicide occurred at North Lake College,[20] a community college in the Dallas–Fort Worth metropolitan area. Gun fetishists will argue that guns were not permitted at Texas 2-year colleges until 1 August 2017, but they ignore the 1995 Texas law permitting guns on outdoor public spaces. And, let's be truthful, that nuance doesn't matter to the victims. On top of that, in October 2017, a student murdered a campus police officer on the campus of Texas Tech University.[21]

In the remaining states where guns are now permitted wholesale on campuses (Kansas, Georgia, Tennessee, and Arkansas), the implementation is too recent for crime statistics to be available. However, in Kansas, guns have been left in restrooms by individuals who were carrying them.[22] It should be noted again that Kansas doesn't require a permit or training to carry a gun.[23] It shows, Kansas.

At Kennesaw State University in Georgia, students have been victims of armed robberies on campus since guns were authorized on college campuses in 2017.[24] In one instance, a student was robbed of the gun he was carrying.[25] Do you want to know how many armed robberies occurred at Kennesaw State University before guns were permitted there? From 2001 to 2016, there were 5. In 2017, after guns were permitted to "make the campus safer," there were 2. Have guns made Kennesaw State University safer? No.

In Arkansas, guns were authorized by the General Assembly in 2017. In October of that year, a 17-year-old undergraduate student committed suicide with a gun she obtained from another student.[26] A month later, at John Brown University (a private Christian institution that prohibits lethal weapons), a student was arrested with guns and bomb-making materials in his dorm room.[27]

It seems quite obvious that introducing guns into the collegiate environment leads to incidents with those guns. Wherever guns appear on college campuses, gun violence follows. There's a simple equation to describe that phenomenon: Guns + Colleges = Gun Violence at Colleges. See? Simple! And, as has been demonstrated in this book, it's so unnecessary to have guns on college campuses. Colleges are among the safest refugia from crime in our society. Why would we permit anyone to erode the safety and security of our nation's higher education institutions?

Bills permitting guns on college campuses were once a rarity. In 2003, Colorado State University relented as a response to concealed-carry law that was passed by the Colorado legislature, making it the first college in the United States to permit concealed handguns on its campus. No other Colorado higher education institution permitted guns on their campuses for the next 9 years. It took a decision by the Colorado Supreme Court to overrule the University of Colorado Board of Regents in a suit that was brought to the courts by an Astroturf gun rights organization called Students for Concealed Carry.

In 2004, the quirky state of Utah enacted guns-on-campus legislation requiring public higher education institutions to allow anyone with a concealed handgun license to carry guns on all campus locations. That law was enacted in response to nothing whatsoever. No one requested it. No one wanted it. There wasn't a horrific act of gun violence on any college campus anywhere in Utah or elsewhere in the United States. The legislators passed it anyway, even though the only documented shooting on a college campus in Utah had occurred 11 years earlier. In 1993, a student at Weber State University brought a gun to a disciplinary hearing and opened fire.[28] He wounded three people at the hearing, including a campus police officer who returned fire and killed the assailant.

So, for the first decade of the 21st century, only Utah and Colorado State University permitted concealed handguns on their college campuses. That would all start to change after the 2007 mass shooting at Virginia Tech University.

Following the mass shooting at Virginia Tech, campus-carry bills became regular submissions during legislative sessions. Dozens of campus-carry bills have been introduced in almost every state since 2007. They are widely opposed in the states where they have been introduced, but they are re-introduced over and over and over until they finally pass—even though no one but the NRA wants them.

In my own state, Arkansas, the issue of arming college campuses appeared for the first time in 2009, prior to the 2010 elections. My next-door neighbor, who was running for a seat in the Arkansas General Assembly, made guns-on-campus legislation his platform for election. Here's an example of how guns-on-campus laws get passed in state after state, taken from the experience I lived from 2009 to 2017.

As in many other states during the 2010 election, the Tea Party made significant gains in the Arkansas General Assembly. I was aware of this development because my neighbor, an ultra-conservative, Tea Party–backed Republican, was elected as my state representative, unseating a well-liked incumbent Democrat by 93 votes on a promise that he would pass legislation permitting those with concealed handgun licenses to carry their weapons on my university's campus and all others statewide. Yes, I said he was my neighbor. Such is America, where a single property line separates the residences of a left-embracing university professor and a Tea Party–embraced politician.

My dear neighbor and rookie state representative kept his campaign promise and introduced a bill permitting persons possessing valid Arkansas concealed handgun licenses (ACHLs) to carry those weapons on any college or university campus statewide. That bill promptly died in committee when an overwhelming majority voted against it. For a freshman state representative, this was a legislative defeat so humiliating that in ordinary times it would never come to the committee again, never mind reaching the floor of the state House of Representatives or state Senate for a vote. However, we do not live in ordinary times. That fact was overlooked by many in 2010 but driven home in the elections of 2012 and 2014, when Tea Party–backed political hacks, aided by unlimited campaign contributions from undisclosed sources, drove many state legislatures into the control of conservative zealots nationwide. In my own state, the Arkansas General Assembly witnessed the election of Republican majorities in both the state Senate and the state House of Representatives for the first time since Reconstruction.

As a consequence of congressional redistricting and computer-aided gerrymandering after 2010, my neighbor was elected to a second term in the state House of Representatives in 2012, this time by a very clear majority of several thousand gerrymandered votes. Once again, he vowed to introduce a bill to permit the carrying of concealed, lethal weapons on college and university campuses statewide. Given the Republican majorities in both houses of the Arkansas General Assembly and their extremist agenda, this time his bill (HB 1243) appeared to be on the fast track to approval and implementation. Then, on 14 December 2012, the unspeakable atrocity at Sandy Hook Elementary School occurred—just weeks before the General Assembly was to convene in January. It was time to take a stand.

I began this book by disclosing that I am not a social scientist or an expert in public health, or even an expert on the origins and causes of gun violence in our society. A sociologist colleague at the University of Arkansas asked me why I was doing this. "Because you are not" was my simple response.

My colleagues and I had much to do. HB 1243—"TO ALLOW TRAINED AND LICENSED STAFF AND FACULTY TO CARRY A CONCEALED HANDGUN ON A UNIVERSITY, COLLEGE, OR COMMUNITY COLLEGE CAMPUS UNDER CERTAIN CIRCUMSTANCES"—was being fast-tracked through a committee stacked with Second Amendment absolutists and was guaranteed to get a floor vote in the state House of Representatives, where it would almost certainly pass on a party-line vote; then it would go to the Senate, where another majority awaited. Several colleagues and I convened on 28 January 2013 to determine how we might best address this badly conceived and ill-timed bill, to provide our university administrators with information they could use to counter the child-like (yet catchy) arguments being made in support of this law in the wake of Sandy Hook (such as "the only thing that stops a bad guy with a gun is a good guy with a gun"), to determine how we might best mobilize public opposition to this law, and to determine how we might divide the workload among ourselves to focus on our particular strengths. As I mentioned previously, I became "the data guy" based on my background in physical sciences and my familiarity with publicly available databases.

Since the advent of the internet, I have incorporated publicly available databases into every course I teach. As a faculty member at the University of Arkansas since 1996, I earned the reputation among students in my courses of being a "data hound," sniffing out interesting public data from many sources that I use to illustrate basic concepts related to my course content and to familiarize students with data gathering, data analysis, and data interpretation methods—all skillsets that are valuable in the 21st century workforce. I gather data from academic institutions, government research laboratories, federal and state government agencies, the U.S. Census Bureau, the United Nations, the European Union … if there are data to be had, I am likely to have used them in my courses. You've seen that skillset at work in this book.

So I began seeking data—hard numbers on gun violence in the United States and, more important, hard numbers on gun violence at U.S. colleges and universities. I knew I would find an abundance of both in publicly available databases online. I have advised my students for more than two decades that we live is a world literally swimming in data of all kinds, and those data can be mined, reviewed, and contextualized to address most of the issues that interest us. I have at times even suggested, tongue in cheek, to my advanced classes that humankind should declare a moratorium on all data collection until the backlog of data in hand has been thoroughly analyzed, synthesized, and duly interpreted because in those data there remain much to be learned and, perhaps, answers to some of our pressing societal issues— but no one knows because no one has looked at the data! The catchphrase of the 1990s science-fiction television series *The X-Files* was "the truth is out there." And so, I believe, it is—in the form of data we gather all the time. Thus I had no doubt that I would find an abundance of data on gun violence in our society and on our college campuses that would be informative regarding the question of whether we should overturn longstanding tradition and permit lethal weapons on our university and college campuses.

It doesn't take long in the 21st century to gather very large quantities of data from internet sources. Go ahead and "use the Google" sometime to see how much actual information you can find relevant to gun violence by typing in the search words "United States gun violence data." There are summary reports from many organizations dedicated to reducing gun crimes such as the Violence Policy Center, the Brady Campaign to Prevent Gun Violence, the Harvard School of Public Health, and the Johns Hopkins University Center for Gun Policy Research. The Sydney School of Public Health at the University of Sydney (Australia) maintains a very useful website with international firearms statistics called GunPolicy.org. There are also statistics on all manner of crimes available online from the U.S. Federal Bureau of Investigation (FBI) through the Uniform Crime Reporting (UCR) Program; these data can be queried and downloaded for every year from 1960 to 2016 (note that for many publicly available data sets there is commonly a lag time of 1–2 years, so the most recent year reported or available in the online database is 1 or 2 years behind the calendar date). For college crime statistics, there are summary reports from the FBI and, most important, from the U.S. Department of Education. The Department of Education is the repository for information on college crimes reported in compliance with the Jeanne Clery Disclosure of Campus Security Policy and Campus Crime Statistics Act. Data from annual Clery Act reports can be accessed publicly from a website known as the Campus Safety and Security Data Analysis Cutting Tool (maintained by the Department of Education).

In addition to sources of primary data like the UCR program and Campus Safety and Security Data Analysis Cutting Tool, there are numerous sources of synthesized data. There are articles published in peer-reviewed academic journals documenting a vast array of gun violence statistics from novel scenarios. Unfortunately, most members of the general public do not have access to academic journals because they aren't members of the academic and professional organizations that sponsor those journals, they don't have subscriptions to those journals, and they don't have access to those journal resources through an academic library system. Access to information like this is one of the necessary perks of my profession as a university professor. Much of the cutting-edge knowledge of our academic disciplines is first reported in academic journals, and a significant responsibility of my job is keeping up with those advances.

Other sources of synthesized information can be found in academic volumes and popular books written by academics and other authors. Indeed, in reviewing the literature on gun violence in America, it doesn't take long to encounter many of these books and the data they contain. However, not all books are created equal, and one needs to discern which data sources are credible and which are not. This is more of a challenge with popular books than with academic books or journal articles because all academic journal articles and most academic books are peer-reviewed, whereas popular books are not. Dubious claims or contrarian data are scrutinized by authoritative reviews in the academic world and can be rejected outright during the review process. By contrast, in the world of popular publishing, you can often make any claim whatsoever and get it published if you have the right publisher and target the right audience.

My role with my colleagues was to serve as not only the "data finder" but also the "data filter." It would be important as we began compiling mountains of data on gun violence to actively scrutinize the data for accuracy and attribution to appropriate data sources. This is a particular skill developed in the academic profession, and so we were all cognizant of the rules of engagement in this regard. We would only cite data for which we could provide valid, substantiable sources or that were derived from appropriately vetted academic journals and books. My personal preferences in this regard are archives and repositories for data submitted in compliance with federal and state laws. These data are usually quality-checked, as there are penalties levied on the submitters when mistakes are made. So I spent a lot of time searching and re-searching data sources from government agencies, and those searches provided troves of data useful to our arguments to keep lethal weapons off college campuses, but very often those data needed to be compiled into brief, yet meaningful summaries. That was something that played to our strengths, since we synthesize complex data into brief, yet meaningful summaries for our college courses all the time. Data and facts would drive our challenge to this bill, but we had to acquire, analyze, and synthesize those data very fast because our opposition was poised to ram HB 1243 through the Arkansas House of Representatives and Senate in less than two weeks.

On Monday, 4 February 2013, I met with my colleagues after business hours to map out a strategy, but first I had to locate some data, any data, that would help us make an argument, so it was "off to the internet" for me to find out where the truth was lurking.

I was starting cold with this data search, though I do have colleagues who know more than I do, and I reached out to several to ask where I might begin this task. Going online, I googled "U.S. crime statistics" and found the most obvious source: the FBI's online compendium of crime data from the Uniform Crime Reporting (UCR) Program, the "granddaddy" of U.S. crime databases. As I perused these data for the first time, I tried to gain a sense of the magnitude of crimes across the United States and within each state, focusing especially on my current home state, Arkansas. The UCR database is a fine repository extending back in time several decades, and certainly offered much of the baseline data we needed to begin our arguments in favor of preserving gun-safe college campuses, but we needed information specifically documenting college crimes across the United States and in each state. I searched the UCR database for "college and university crimes," and it returned several summary tables of college crimes documenting crimes against persons and crimes against property on the nation's college campuses, but the data were quite general—actually, too general for the context of interest to us. However, this was a start.

Sometime during the day, as I was searching databases, downloading relevant files, ingesting that information into spreadsheets, and developing a strategy for research on the topic of gun violence on college campuses, one of my collaborators sent me a text message: There would be a legislative forum in our town on Friday, 8 February 2013, from 4:00 to 5:00 p.m. in the assembly room of the Chamber of Commerce building. The sponsors of the campus gun bill were going to be there, so we needed to be there, too.

Legislative forums in our town are biweekly meetings hosted by the Chamber of Commerce when the Arkansas General Assembly is in session. They serve as an opportunity for state legislators to meet with the electorate to listen to their concerns and to share information from the state assembly about recent legislative activities. Ordinarily, these forums are very genteel affairs attended by fewer than a dozen people, mostly the local political junkies or folks who desire to share with their elected representatives their most recent concern about dogs loose in the neighborhood or the loudly partying college students down the street or the recent accomplishments of the high school pom-pom squad or the poor condition of the sidewalks in town or the need for a stoplight at that busy intersection or any of a number of mundane issues that are the foundations of local politics all across America. In the case of the meeting on 8 February, who was going to be there? The sponsor of the campus gun bill and several of his co-sponsors as well as several other representatives from northwest Arkansas.

So, late in the afternoon of Monday, 4 February 2013, we learned that the upcoming legislative forum would bring the representatives proposing HB 1243 (also known as the "faculty-staff concealed carry bill") to our university town. We vowed to make certain they faced the people who would be directly affected by their bill so we could make them aware of our concerns. We had three days to prepare for this event. Three days to mobilize as many citizens as we could muster to speak against this foolish bill and to document a strong, fact-based argument (using data) to demonstrate why this bill was unnecessary and a danger to the sanctity of higher education in Arkansas. It seemed a tall order for three faculty members engaged in teaching hundreds of students in multiple courses that spring semester, but we had no choice. We could make our case on Friday or forfeit the opportunity altogether. There would not be a second opportunity, and this bill would pass. Three days to change our world, or it would be changed for us and sanctuary would be doomed. No pressure.

My literary colleague posted an online petition and started gathering signatures. My colleague in political communications commenced communicating. Here I learned of another colleague who was working with us who had many political contacts across Arkansas and was using those contacts to mine for information about HB 1243: Where was it in the legislative process?

Which committee was going to hear it? Who was on that committee? How many Republicans? How many Democrats? Who were they? What districts did they represent? What colleges or universities were in their districts? Where did they stand? Was the information reliable? Who in the General Assembly was talking about the bill off the record? What were other colleges and universities saying about HB 1243? Where did law enforcement stand on HB 1243? Did any police departments support this bill? A veritable flood of human intelligence (using the parlance of the military industrial complex), and all of it interesting to me (who were these people and how did they all know each other?), but I had to focus on data and numbers. How was that going? The online petition was inching toward 2,500 signatures. Got any good data yet? Working on it! What information have you got for us? Working on it!

Meanwhile, the clock was ticking toward Friday, 8 February 2013, and a "showdown," as it were, at the Chamber of Commerce–sponsored legislative forum. As I compiled data, my colleagues organized the opposition. On Wednesday, 6 February, our "communications officer" put out a call to supporters who signed our online petition opposing HB 1243:

Friends:

You've signed the petition to prohibit concealed carry on Arkansas college and university campuses. Now tell legislators in person how you feel at two events THIS WEEKEND in Northwest Arkansas:

Friday, February 8 at 4 p.m.: Representative from District 84 (sponsor of HB 1243 to permit concealed carry on colleges and universities in Arkansas) at the Fayetteville Chamber of Commerce at 123 W. Mountain St Fayetteville, AR 72701/(479) 521–1710. The Facebook Event Page for the Fayetteville forum can be found here:
https://www.facebook.com/events/212962905510414/

Saturday, February 9 at 9 a.m.: Representatives from Benton County who sit on the state legislature's crucial Education Committee will hear community feedback at NWACC's Shewmaker Center at 1000 SE Eagle Way, Bentonville, AR 72712/(479) 936–5145

The Facebook Event Page for the Bentonville forum can be found here:
https://www.facebook.com/messages/conversation-id.405757179515661

Also, please join the Arkansans Against Guns on Campus Facebook page: https://www.facebook.com/ArkansansAgainstGunsOnCampus?fref=ts

And follow us on Twitter at @UAAgainstCarry

Thanks so much for your support.

So the call to action went out, and we hoped we would fill the modest assembly room at the Chamber of Commerce building with the sensible townsfolk and those likely to be affected by passage of this bill—namely, our faculty colleagues and students at the university. Even so, we needed to work quickly to organize a coherent message regarding the nature of any law permitting guns on campus and why we believed it was wholly unnecessary. Despite our common experiences that gun violence on our nation's college campuses was exceedingly rare, our anecdotal accounts were not the evidence-laden arguments we wanted to promote for this venue. So I worked away on the data I could find from publicly available sources. Thank goodness for digital technology, digital data archives, and Microsoft Excel!

On Wednesday, 6 February, preparations were underway to mobilize our colleagues to attend and speak out against HB 1243, the faculty concealed carry bill, at the community legislative forum in Fayetteville, Arkansas, on Friday. I was busy teaching my classes and preparing my personal statements for the forum, rehearsing them in my head so the words would flow freely when needed on Friday. And then the data floodgates opened. Boom! I had finally found the data warehouse of college crimes that would provide the evidence-based narrative I and my colleagues needed to defend our sanctuary from the legislative barbarians.

As mentioned earlier, the U.S. Department of Education maintains an online repository of data reporting crimes for every institution of higher education that accepts federal support for student financial aid. Data in this repository is reported annually by institutions in compliance with the Jeanne Clery Disclosure of Campus Security Policy and Campus Crime Statistics Act[29] (also known as the Clery Act). I discussed the origin and purpose of the Clery Act, as well as details of the types of crimes reported and the various college venues for which crimes must be reported, in chapter 4. For now, recall that virtually every institution of higher education in the United States—private and public 4-year universities or colleges, private and public 2-year colleges, and private and public technical institutes—must track and report crimes against persons and crimes against property committed on their campuses, and each institution must make those reports publicly available by 1 October every year. Online, data reported in compliance with the Clery Act since 2001 can be found at the Campus Safety and Security Data Analysis Cutting Tool.[30]

Given the small window in which to gather information before the local legislative forum just two days away, I decided to focus exclusively on the available data for Arkansas. Off I went to locate and download the data we needed. A few keystrokes and less than 10 minutes later, I had a data file uploaded in a spreadsheet showing every reported crime for every institution of higher education in Arkansas for the time period 2001–2011 (remember, there is typically a two-year lag in data availability for public databases like this). First impressions? I had no idea there were so many post-secondary institutions in Arkansas! Beyond that, I was impressed overall with the extraordinarily low number of reported crimes on campuses statewide. Many campuses reported "0" for all crimes against persons and all property crimes in multiple years. Entire years with zero reported crimes on campus. How much safer can our campuses statewide be than zero crimes? They're not gun-free colleges—they're crime-free colleges! Extraordinary! And what was the justification for pushing a bill to permit people to carry concealed, lethal weapons on campuses with no crime?

Poring through the data as quickly as I could, I took note of the homicide tally on Arkansas college campuses between 2001 and 2011. There were three: two on the campus of the University of Central Arkansas in 2008 and one at the Arkansas State University main campus in Jonesboro, Arkansas in 2010. I had a vague recollection about the incident at UCA—two students killed outside a dormitory on campus on a Sunday night in October 2008.[31] The other reported incident at Arkansas State University I did not recall. Off to the internet to see what news reports there were on it! This particular case was as perplexing as it was disturbing—a young man murdered while he slept in his off-campus apartment managed by Arkansas State University.[32] No motive. No suspect(s). No leads. Well, I resolved to come back to that incident at some point in the future and try to find additional information that might shed light on the specific circumstances. At the moment, it was Wednesday afternoon, and I needed to summarize information for the legislative forum in less than two days. I took the number, noted it, and started finding more data for comparisons that we wanted to make at the public forum.

I set myself the task of creating a brief data sheet to illustrate the relative safety and security of Arkansas college campuses compared to the U.S. general public. Using data on documented firearms homicides obtained from the FBI's UCR system as well as the known population of the United States from 2001 to 2011, I came up with the following items to share at the Fayetteville legislative forum and formatted them into this fact sheet to share with legislators and public in attendance:

NATIONWIDE STATISTICS:

U.S. Murder and Non-Negligent Manslaughter rate (2001–2010) averaged 5.5 people per 100,000 in population.[33]

U.S. College and University Murder and Non-Negligent Manslaughter rate (2001–2010) averaged 0.007 per 100,000 population[34]

The observed U.S. College and University Murder and Non-Negligent Manslaughter rate (2001–2010) is **785 times LOWER** than that for the public-at-large in the United States if college students are considered as part of the Public-At-Large.

The observed Murder and Non-Negligent Manslaughter rate at Arkansas colleges and universities over the same time interval is 0.000097 per 100,000 population (effectively 1 in 1 billion).

The observed Arkansas College and University Murder and Non-Negligent Manslaughter rate is **56,700 times LOWER** that for the public-at-large in the United States and **72 times LOWER** than that at U.S. Colleges and Universities.

Colleges and Universities in the United States are among the SAFEST refuges from murder and non-negligent manslaughter, and Arkansas colleges and universities are among the SAFEST in the United States!

The take-home message is this: If you are a person who desires to minimize your chances of being a victim of murder or non-negligent manslaughter, your best bet is to attend an Arkansas college or university!

DATA SOURCES:

United States Department of Justice Uniform Crime Reporting System http://bjs.ojp.usdoj.gov/ucrdata/Search/Crime/Crime.cfm

United States Department of Education, Office of Post-Secondary Education, Campus Safety and Security Data Analysis Cutting Tool: http://ope.ed.gov/security/index.aspx

Based on college and university enrollment data from National Center for Education Statistics: http://nces.ed.gov/datalab/tableslibrary/home.aspx

I shared this fact sheet with my colleagues, who were as impressed by the low numbers as I was. Many activities that we engage in every day have vastly greater frequencies than the empirical frequency of gun violence on Arkansas college campuses. In fact, to put the "1 in 1 billion" frequency in perspective, any individual in the United States is five to six times more likely to win the Powerball lottery; of course, none of us really expects to win the Powerball lottery during our lifetimes even though some actually do, and the observed frequency of gun homicides on Arkansas colleges is five to six times less than "virtually never" even though a campus murder occurs rarely. I was quite certain these would be difficult statistics for our legislators to defend, and I was even more certain they didn't know about them, but I was committed to making them and everyone else at the forum aware. With one day before the opportunity to face the legislative sponsors of the "faculty carry" bill, I felt for the first time that we had a very good chance to knock this bill down and defeat it.

Friday was a busy day at the University of Arkansas. My classes there typically meet Monday, Wednesday, and Friday, and I had a full slate planned as well as the legislative forum at the Chamber of Commerce assembly room that afternoon. I had copies of my fact sheet printed from home and ready to hand out to the legislators in attendance and those members of the public who showed up. The forum was scheduled to begin at 4:00 p.m. All set to go, so now off to teach for the day. My morning classes went as planned and were uneventful, my early afternoon class was fine—nothing seemed extraordinary about the day until I returned to my office around 2:00 p.m. and I discovered the "system was blinking red"! Multiple messages on my voicemail, text messages with that little red exclamation point indicating urgency, personal messages on social media, and notes in my mailbox from people who had called my departmental office and left call-back messages with our administrative assistant. What could possibly be going on? Was the forum cancelled? It all seemed too urgent for something as mundane as a cancellation.

I picked up my phone to listen to the first voicemail message as I simultaneously thumbed through the handwritten call-back paper slips given to me by our departmental assistant. The voice on the phone message belonged to a colleague who had been strategizing with us about the campus-carry bill: "Didja hear what happened at the KUAF building?" KUAF is our university radio affiliate of National Public Radio (NPR). And the next words on the phone message were "A student was shot!" As I was sitting in front of my computer, it was off to Google to search the newsfeed. Honestly, my next thought as I typed "KUAF shooting" in the Google box was "You can't make this up." The monitor screen flickered, and there was a string of reports:

Man accidentally shoots self at KUAF radio station in downtown Fayetteville[35]
Student accidentally shoots himself on UA campus[36]
Legal or not, gun goes off on UA campus[37]
Student wounded accidentally by gunshot[38]

and this favorite from a Southeastern Conference sports chat board:

Dummy shoots himself at KUAF[39]

As I read the reports in succession, I just kept saying to myself, "You can't make this up! You can't make this up! You can't make this up!" and, really, you just can't! On the same day that I and many concerned citizens were going to sit down face-to-face with our elected representatives to voice our concerns about permitting concealed handguns on university campuses, a student employed through our work-study program had actually shot himself with a gun he was carrying illegally in his backpack at his workplace, the campus affiliate of NPR radio. Two hours from now, members of the Arkansas General Assembly were going to look me in the eye and tell me they were sponsoring a bill to permit concealed lethal weapons on university and college campuses statewide because they wanted everyone to be "safer." I actually wanted to hear them say that. In the aftermath of a negligent shooting on the campus. Today. I decided I should go a little early to make sure I got a seat near the front. And don't forget the fact sheets. I made a mental note to personally place one in the hands of each legislator in attendance.

I called my colleagues to confirm that they were still going (of course they were!) and what time they thought they'd head downtown. We also spoke briefly about our strategy to address the legislators. We agreed, given the current situation, that we would focus on the public safety aspect of this issue. We weren't going to get mired in a pseudo-debate over the merits of the right to bear arms or the constitutionality of permitting lethal weapons on college campuses. This discussion was going to be about the real danger posed by permitting individuals to carry guns among us and the empirical frequency of negligent discharges like the one that occurred at 12:30 p.m. Central Standard Time at our own campus facility. What possible argument could be made in favor of carrying concealed handguns in view of the day's excitement at the KUAF studio?

For the next hour and a half or so, I tried to get as much information about the KUAF shooting as I could. As I discovered, a little after noon, a student carrying a loaded revolver in his backpack was showing it to another student in the break room at the radio station. Why? No explanation for that. Mysteriously (according to the victim who was also the perpetrator), it discharged and severely wounded his left hand. What his left hand was doing in front of the muzzle of a loaded pistol may also never be known. This was not a tiny pistol, either. A five-shot revolver manufactured by Taurus International Manufacturing, Inc., this particular model chambered either .45 caliber bullets or .410 shotgun shells. It comes in a matte stainless-steel finish, and, according to the company advertising, it's called "The Judge" because of the number of judges who carry it into their courtrooms for their personal protection. I am not making that up. Per the company website, "The 'Taurus Judge' is one decision-maker that lays down the law." Supposedly, it's "ideal for short distances—where most altercations occur."[40] And our woeful student was carrying this mini-cannon around in his backpack.

We'd learn a day or so after the KUAF incident that the student was no kid. He was a navy veteran in his 30s who'd completed his service and come back for a college degree. Why he thought he needed this heavy-duty firepower at the university affiliate of NPR has never been explained. But this is precisely the type of irresponsible gun handling that campus-carry laws engender, as has already been discussed.

The hour of the legislative forum was approaching, and it was time to head downtown to the Chamber of Commerce building to make our case. When I arrived, there was already a pretty good turnout—my colleagues had been busy recruiting the townsfolk via social media and through the email list compiled from the online petition to stop HB 1243, the "faculty/staff campus-carry bill." I saw several friends from town and my colleagues from the university who were prepared to speak up with me during the forum. No sign yet of the legislators, but it was a little early. There was a rumor circulating among the audience that the campus-carry bill's sponsor, my next-door neighbor and state representative, wasn't going to make it because he had been delayed at the campus of the University of Central Arkansas, where he'd been holding a public forum on his bill. What a convenient excuse to avoid answering any questions from his constituents, in the college town he represented, about the idea to permit people to carry concealed lethal weapons on a campus where a student had shot himself just a few hours earlier.

Within a few minutes, the crowd swelled to proportions that could no longer be accommodated by the Chamber of Commerce assembly room. Every seat was quickly occupied, and those standing crowded together as closely as they could to admit as many people as possible. Even so, they were overflowing out onto the sidewalk and into the street. I don't know what the room capacity was, but we were surely over it. Good thing the fire marshal wasn't there.

The executive director of the Chamber of Commerce appeared with the legislators in tow and directed them to take their seats on the dais at the front of the assembly room—three Democrats opposed to HB 1243 on the left, two state Senate Republican co-sponsors of the campus-carry bill on the right, and an empty seat for the missing-in-action sponsor of HB 1243, who was supposedly engaged in thoughtful conversation in a community 160 miles away with people who were not his constituents and who could not cast votes for or against him. In fact, he did not make it back to Fayetteville in time to meet with the townsfolk, but he did appear live on camera during the 6:00 news in front of the KUAF building to comment on the shooting incident. So, recapping, he was not able to get to town in time for the 4:00 p.m. legislative forum to answer questions from his constituents, but he was there in time to politicize the crime scene during the news broadcast two hours later.

As the forum was about to open, one of the Republican co-sponsors of HB 1243 sheepishly observed, "There's a lot of people here. Y'all must be mad about somethin', because we only get a crowd like this when people are mad about somethin'," ending with a toothy grin and receiving a smattering of nervous chuckles from the audience. I thought to myself, "You have no idea."

The forum began with introductions from the Chamber of Commerce executive director and quickly moved to discussion of HB 1243, the campus concealed-carry bill. The two Republicans were co-sponsors of the bill in the Arkansas Senate, so much of the discussion was aimed at them and comments they made in an effort to justify the bill's origin and purpose. Questions and comments from the assembled constituents were unanimously opposed to HB 1243. Not one person spoke favorably about concealed carry on our university campuses. A number of faculty expressed great concern regarding the potential presence of lethal weapons in their classrooms; someone mentioned the difficulty for law enforcement arriving at the scene of an active shooting with multiple guns present: How would they know who was the bad guy or the good guy? How was a police officer to assess this situation? What was the probability of increased casualties due to cross-fire between a perpetrator and poorly trained individuals carrying concealed weapons? For that matter, what training was required for someone to be permitted to carry a concealed handgun and respond to an active shooter incident? All of these were good questions for the legislative sponsors of the bill.

Members of the public asked about their daughters and sons attending a university or college where the person sitting next to their kid might be carrying a weapon. That was a common misconception: while the bill my neighbor had proposed in 2010 included concealed carry for students old enough to qualify for an Arkansas concealed handgun license (ACHL), the bill under consideration in 2013 was restricted to faculty and staff with ACHLs (my neighbor had learned that the idea of arming college students was the fatal flaw in his previous bill, and so he removed that provision in this round). One of the Democratic legislators offered that he referred to the bill as the "shoot faculty first" bill—implying that an active shooter would assume any faculty member was armed and make them the first victim of their mayhem. Several people in the audience attempted to engage the Republican senators on the merits of the proposed campus-carry bill with respect to the Second Amendment guarantee to keep and bear arms. At this point, one of the senators spoke up and very clearly articulated that the bill was not being sponsored as an effort to fortify Second Amendment privileges. He explained very eloquently that, for him, the bill was entirely an issue of ensuring safety on our state's college campuses. My colleagues and I turned to each other, somewhat amazed that the senator had just given us the perfect setup for our strategy to focus discussion on public safety. I looked at my colleague from communications and whispered, "Now?" She nodded in agreement.

I raised my hand and was recognized by the Chamber of Commerce director, who was serving as moderator. I stood and introduced myself, stating that I was a professor at the university and I was opposed to permitting concealed lethal weapons on campus. I thanked the senator for framing the issue as one of public safety and suggested this was a topic on which we could all agree—that our college campuses should be as safe as we can make them. I then turned to my fact sheet and offered to share what was already known about the safety and security of our state's college campuses derived from publicly available data. I read through each item on the fact sheet slowly and deliberately so the facts would sink in. As I looked at the audience, I saw many nodding in agreement. This was playing quite well. I noted that the observed murder rate on Arkansas college campuses, if taken as part of the general population of the United States, was 0.000097 per 100,000, pausing briefly on each zero so people listening could absorb what a small number this was—almost 57,000 times lower than the observed murder rate among the U.S. general population. I ended with this statement: "For anyone who wants to minimize the chance of being victimized by gun violence, enrolling in an Arkansas university or college is their best bet." The Democratic legislators were smiling. I also caught a smile from the chief legislative liaison of the university, who was attending the forum to listen to the discussion.

The Republican senator who had commented on the size of the audience at the outset of the forum tried to recover from the statistical truth of our state's campus security by suggesting to the crowd that the three lives lost to campus homicides during the prior decade or so were three lives too many. On the one hand, I completely agreed with this sentiment. On the other hand, I completely rejected the notion that arming faculty and staff would alter those statistics. The audience didn't fall for his crocodile tears and let him know it, so I didn't have to respond except to repeat that the observed frequency of homicide on Arkansas college campuses was 57,000 times less than for the U.S. public at large.

The political battle over the bill went back and forth throughout the 2013 legislative session. In the end, we had the bill bottled up in committee, and it appeared that we had the votes to kill it again. This led the bill's sponsor (my neighbor) to propose a compromise: he would amend the bill to permit the governing boards of higher education institutions to vote each year to opt out of the law and continue prohibiting lethal weapons on campus. Higher education (and, in particular, the University of Arkansas system) relented and agreed to the compromise, and the bill passed. For the next 4 years (2013–2016), higher education institutions statewide unanimously voted to opt out of the law. Guns and other lethal weapons continued to be prohibited on college campuses throughout Arkansas. The annual, well-publicized votes of each institution to reject guns on campus became an annual embarrassment for my neighbor—52 campuses strong voted year after year to reject his singular legislative accomplishment.

Of course, that annual comeuppance didn't sit well with his fragile psyche, so he re-introduced his bill without the opt-out amendment in the 2015 legislative session. That action was widely derided as a spiteful and unjustified personal vendetta against higher education. The proposed law removing the opt-out clause died again in committee. Fifty-two higher education institutions statewide promptly voted to ignore the law and continued to prohibit lethal weapons of all kinds from entering the sanctuaries that were their campuses.

Sadly, the Arkansas drift toward authoritarianism continued into the 2016 elections, and Arkansas Republicans gained supermajorities in both houses of the general assembly. They also had a compliant governor willing to sign much of their nonsense into law. Emboldened as never before, my neighbor once again introduced his bill to permit guns on college campuses, stripping the opt-out provision and, for the first time, extending permission to carry concealed handguns to college students. That maneuver was widely opposed as a step too far, and the battle for the sanctity of the collegiate experience in Arkansas was on again—for the eighth consecutive year and the fourth consecutive legislative session. This year, however, the NRA showed up—literally—with NRA staffers hanging around the Arkansas capitol building every day of the legislative session to glower from the galleries overlooking each legislative chamber. There is no telling what threats they were making face-to-face with legislators after hours.

Even with the massive intimidation campaign mounted against legislators by the national office of the NRA, the bill struggled to find sufficient support from the two supermajorities. At one point in the session, the bill narrowly avoided failure by one vote on the floor of the state Senate. After that near calamity for the NRA in one of the most NRA-friendly legislatures in the United States, they got serious. They seized the bill from my neighbor's cold, legislatively ineffective hands and forced a number of procedural gimmicks to get their bill to the floor of both houses for votes. Not satisfied with placing guns on college campuses, the NRA goons strong-armed amendments permitting guns in every public place in Arkansas, including churches and bars. And, oh yeah, for good measure, they made sure guns were permitted everywhere on college campuses. And by everywhere, I mean they made sure that you could bring concealed handguns to college sports events. That primarily meant big-time college football with the University of Arkansas Razorbacks. Every Saturday from September through December, there would be 76,000 rabid (sometimes drunk) fans in the stands—now permitted to carry guns. The NRA, almost literally at gunpoint, rammed votes through both houses of the legislature, and, with the Number-Two-In-Charge at the NRA, Chris Cox, glaring over his shoulder, the governor signed the bill into law with his cheesy grin.

As the NRA was slapping itself on the back for forcing another state to comply with its agenda of domestic terror, and as the governor was clutching at his heart and wiping his brow (probably thankful that the NRA thugs hadn't sent him floating face-down in the Arkansas River), the governor's phone rang. I don't know what was said in that phone conversation, but I fantasize that the conversation was something like this:

"Hi," said the voice on the other end. "This is the SEC."

"The SEC?" the governor asked. No. *The* SEC. The Southeastern Conference. The mightiest and most powerful athletic conference in all of collegiate sports (and, in the opinion of some, mightier and more powerful than the NCAA, its "governing" body). Dedicated SEC fans will insist they are even mightier and more powerful than Major League Baseball, the NFL, and the NBA combined. Not joking.

The Southeastern Conference had found out that guns were going to be permitted at sports events at the University of Arkansas—the only SEC member institution in the state. You know what they said to the governor? I don't either, but evidently it was something like "The SEC won't be playing any sports balls in Arkansas."[41] So powerful and influential is the SEC that its governing organization, the NCAA, didn't say anything. The NCAA just let the SEC do the talking. "Yeah. What they said."

The brouhaha over guns at Arkansas Razorback sports events raised the possibility that the governor might be making that face-down float in the Arkansas River at the hands of the SEC and Arkansas Razorback fans. This was now a "situation." The U.S. military services have a robust nomenclature for similar situations. The one military term I can print to describe this situation comes in the form of an acronym: FUBAR. Google it or just ask a vet. I've said it before, but I'll say it again: You can't make this up. The sheer stupidity of permitting people (especially drunk people) to carry concealed handguns into an SEC football game boggles the mind. And football fans knew it. The SEC knew it. The NCAA knew it. The national sports-o-sphere knew it.[42] However, my next-door neighbor and the governor didn't know it, bless their hearts. So, do you want to know what my neighbor proposed as a fix for this mess? SNIPERS![43] I am not making that up. In order to counter individuals with concealed weapons licenses carrying their guns into sports events, my neighbor-the-legislator proposed that collegiate sports events should deploy teams of snipers.

Faced with the prospect of losing literally hundreds of millions of dollars in revenue from intercollegiate athletics statewide, the governor urged (that is, he got on his knees and begged) the Arkansas General Assembly to quickly amend a different bill so they could fix the problems in the bill he had just signed into law. Once again, dear readers, this is what we call "fancy legislatin'"! The governor was literally begging the Arkansas General Assembly to exempt intercollegiate athletics and prohibit guns at those venues—and do it quickly because the General Assembly was about to adjourn until 2019.

FUBAR barely begins to describe the chaos that had descended on one of the poorest states in the nation. Incredibly (well, not really), the NRA opposed banning guns from athletic events and was busy strong-arming legislators to keep the bill as it was signed by the governor.[44]

In the end, Big College Football—SEC football—beat the NRA. The bill was amended to permit collegiate athletic events to prohibit guns, albeit with one provision: Every state institution of higher education was required to submit a detailed security plan for every sports event to the Arkansas state police for review. The state police were then required to review the plan and approve or disapprove it. If approved, guns could be banned from sports events—but only collegiate sports events on the college campus. High school sports events at collegiate sports facilities would still be required to permit individuals to carry concealed handguns under the law. Of course, the amended law did not provide any financial resources to higher education to cover the costs of persons who would be charged with writing the detailed security plans for every sports event on every college campus in the state. It also did not provide any financial resources to the Arkansas state police for the manpower that would be required to review, approve/disapprove, and archive all those detailed security plans. It didn't even provide funds for a filing cabinet to store those plans, much less the security to ensure that some "bad guy with a gun" could not gain access to the plans and use them to plan an attack on a collegiate sports event. But those are just details. Details omitted from the amended bill that was supposed to fix the problems with the bill the governor had signed into law without reading. FUBAR.

The tale above is a true story of how we get gun laws passed in the 21st century. No one asked for this law. No one (aside from the NRA) wanted it. Indeed, broad constituencies opposed it. The legislature passed it anyway. This happens in state after state nationwide. It's even happening in the federal government. What you are witnessing is the triumph of an ideology over all other concerns. Reflect on that phenomenon for a moment. Recall how the Clery Act came into existence. Once upon a time in America, barely 30 years ago, a vibrant college freshman was murdered in her dorm room at a private liberal arts college. Her grieving parents thought there should have been a law that informed parents of the security status of America's college campuses. These two people went to Washington, D.C., to discuss this idea with their congressional representative and convinced him that such a law would have merit. He then worked with them to pass that law. It took a number of years, and the state of Pennsylvania passed a similar law first, but that simple idea—to document crimes on college campuses and report annually on the security status of each campus in the United States—was a law that was passed to meet a societal need. It was a law that materially improved our society. Once upon a time in America, you or I or the parents of a murdered college co-ed could speak to an elected representative and get a law passed if there was a need for it. Elected representatives listened to constituent needs. Once upon a time in America. Can you imagine that happening now?

In 2013, on the heels of the atrocity at Sandy Hook Elementary School, dozens of parents of murdered first graders went to Washington, D.C., to appeal to elected officials to pass laws that would help prevent a repeat atrocity in the future. Thousands of Americans rallied on the grounds of the U.S. Capitol. Tens of thousands of Americans rallied across the country. Hundreds of thousands of Americans joined gun violence prevention groups on social media platforms nationwide. Their elected representatives did nothing. Nothing. NOTHING!

In truth, it's unfair to say our elected representatives did nothing. More accurately, I should state that after witnessing 20 first graders and 6 of their teachers slaughtered by a gun that fired 155 rounds in 5 minutes, they did nothing to avert the next mass killing. So, as a nation, we endured Orlando, and San Bernardino, and Las Vegas, and Parkland, and, on average, a mass shooting somewhere in America every day. Our Congress and our state legislatures have worked very hard to relax as many gun regulations as they could—literally hundreds of gun bills became laws after Sandy Hook. Laws that significantly curtailed reasonable regulation of guns across society. Laws that enable more people to carry greater firepower into more places. None of us are safer. We are all at risk. Your elected officials are hard at work, every day, dismantling sanctuaries from gun violence. Have you had enough yet? They don't think you have.

So what should we all do? Do what I did. I became an activist on 28 January 2013. If you don't want to become an activist, at least become active. I was forced to shake off my complacency and take a stand. I had to learn many things about which I had no prior knowledge—or at least no prior useful knowledge. I met huge numbers of activists in the gun violence prevention community. Some of those people were already activists themselves when I was blithely drifting through college in the 1970s dreaming of becoming an environmentalist. Those people are still activists. Because that's how long it takes. And they haven't reached their objective yet. There remains much to do.

I'm 59 years old. I joined a union for the first time in my life last year— in a right-to-work state. People asked me what I thought the union would do for me. I answered that it was not what the union would do for me; it's what I could do with a union. I've stood on the street corner in front of our courthouse with hundreds of others—with signs—regularly. I could have gone home and watched TV, but I joined other people instead. And I'm not a "joiner." I reached out to and worked with gun violence prevention organizations. I crowd-sourced funding to print "Carrying a Handgun Is Prohibited" signs for local businesses. I organized a local campaign to persuade these businesses to post "Carrying a Handgun Is Prohibited" signs at their establishments. I actually walked into the Chamber of Commerce and asked the people there to help me distribute those signs to their member businesses. And I'm doing it again this week. I'm going to remind the Chamber of Commerce director that I take this issue seriously. I want those "guns prohibited" signs distributed to any business that wants them. I'm not going to demand that every business post them. That's their business—literally and figuratively. But I want businesses to know they can post those signs if they want to, and they can get the signs for free at the Chamber of Commerce.

I will advocate that major businesses in our area help with community gun buy-backs to get guns off the streets and out of people's homes. I will advocate for safe gun storage and distribute free gun locks to anyone who wants them. I will organize community vigils for victims of gun violence. I'll ask my mayor to issue proclamations to memorialize those gun violence victims. (And he will do it.) I'll work with local and national gun violence prevention organizations in whatever capacity I can. The life I save could very well be my own or that of someone very close to me. I wrote this book to spread the word that our college campuses are not magnets for murderers— they are sanctuaries from them. I'm reaching out to my campus police department to let them know that I recognize the fantastic work they do in keeping my campus safe and secure. I'm reaching out to campus police departments at institutions near me and offering to share my data and the story they tell. I'm reaching out to campus police departments nationwide to share results of my research on the nature and incidence of homicide at U.S. colleges. The police chief at my institution invited me to make a presentation to the regional conference of his professional organization: the International Association of Campus Law Enforcement Administrators (IACLEA).[45] I'm hoping they'll invite me to present at their international conference, too!

I'll keep going. I'll keep trying to inform others. I'll work toward the day when reason once again triumphs over ideology. I won't be silenced, and I won't shut up. But I want to tell you something: I'm 59 years old. I've attended college every working day in some capacity since I was 18 years old. All my collegiate sanctuaries prohibited the carrying of lethal weapons on their campuses during those 41 years. Right now, guns are permitted in my collegiate sanctuary for the first time.

For the first time in 41 years, I don't want to go to college.

Appendix (by State)

Table 1. Annual Homicides on College Campuses by State, 2001–2016

State	'01	'02	'03	'04	'05	'06	'07	'08	'09	'10	'11	'12	'13	'14	'15	'16	Total
Alabama	1	0	1	0	0	0	0	0	0	4	2	1	0	0	0	0	9
Alaska	0	0	0	0	0	0	0	0	0	0	0	0	0	0	0	0	0
Arizona	0	4	0	0	0	0	1	0	0	0	1	0	0	0	1	0	7
Arkansas	0	0	1	0	0	0	0	2	0	1	0	0	0	0	0	0	4
California	2	0	1	1	0	1	1	0	2	3	3	0	4	1	3	4	26
Colorado	1	1	0	0	0	0	0	0	0	0	0	0	0	0	0	0	2
Connecticut	0	0	0	0	0	0	0	0	3	0	0	0	0	0	0	0	3
Delaware	0	0	0	0	0	1	1	0	0	0	0	0	0	0	0	0	2
Florida	0	0	1	3	2	1	1	0	1	1	1	1	0	0	0	0	12
Georgia	0	0	0	0	0	0	0	0	2	0	0	1	3	0	3	0	9
Hawaii	0	0	0	0	0	0	0	0	0	0	0	0	0	0	0	0	0
Idaho	0	0	1	0	0	0	0	0	0	0	0	0	0	0	0	0	1
Illinois	0	1	0	0	0	0	0	5	0	0	2	0	1	2	0	2	13
Indiana	2	0	0	1	0	0	0	1	0	0	0	1	0	2	0	1	8
Iowa	0	0	0	1	0	0	0	0	0	0	0	0	0	0	0	0	1
Kansas	0	0	0	0	0	0	0	0	0	0	0	0	1	0	1	0	2
Kentucky	1	0	1	0	0	0	0	2	0	0	1	0	2	0	0	0	7
Louisiana	1	1	0	1	0	1	2	2	0	0	0	0	0	0	0	0	8
Maine	0	0	0	0	0	0	0	1	0	0	0	0	0	0	0	0	1
Maryland	0	0	0	1	1	0	0	0	0	1	1	0	0	0	0	1	5
Massachusetts	0	1	0	0	0	0	0	0	3	1	0	0	2	0	0	0	7
Michigan	1	0	0	1	1	1	0	0	1	1	0	0	0	1	0	1	8
Minnesota	0	0	0	0	0	0	0	0	0	0	0	0	0	0	0	0	0
Mississippi	0	0	0	2	0	0	0	0	0	0	0	1	1	0	1	0	5
Missouri	0	0	0	1	1	0	0	1	0	0	0	0	0	0	0	0	3
Montana	0	0	0	0	0	0	0	0	0	0	0	0	0	0	0	0	0

Table 1. Annual Homicides on College Campuses by State 157

Table 1. Annual Homicides on College Campuses by State

State	'01	'02	'03	'04	'05	'06	'07	'08	'09	'10	'11	'12	'13	'14	'15	'16	Total
Nebraska	0	0	0	0	0	0	0	0	0	0	0	0	0	1	0	0	1
Nevada	0	0	0	0	0	0	0	0	0	0	0	0	0	0	0	0	0
New Hampshire	0	0	0	0	0	0	0	0	0	0	0	0	0	0	0	0	0
New Jersey	0	2	0	0	0	0	1	0	0	0	1	1	0	0	0	0	5
New Mexico	0	0	0	0	0	0	0	0	0	0	0	0	0	1	0	0	1
New York	0	2	1	0	1	0	1	1	1	1	0	0	0	0	0	1	9
North Carolina	1	0	0	2	0	0	1	0	1	0	0	0	2	1	2	0	10
North Dakota	0	0	0	0	0	0	0	0	0	0	0	0	0	0	0	0	0
Ohio	0	1	2	0	1	0	1	0	1	1	0	0	1	0	1	0	9
Oklahoma	0	0	0	0	0	0	0	0	0	0	0	0	1	1	1	0	3
Oregon	1	0	0	0	0	1	0	0	0	0	0	0	0	0	9	0	11
Pennsylvania	1	1	0	0	1	0	1	0	0	0	1	0	0	0	1	0	6
Rhode Island	0	0	0	0	0	0	0	0	0	0	0	0	0	0	0	0	0
South Carolina	1	0	0	0	1	0	0	0	1	0	1	0	0	1	1	0	6
South Dakota	0	0	0	0	0	0	0	0	0	0	0	0	0	0	0	0	0
Tennessee	0	1	0	1	1	0	1	0	1	0	0	0	0	1	1	0	7
Texas	1	0	0	0	0	0	0	0	1	0	1	1	1	1	2	6	14
Utah	0	0	0	0	0	0	0	0	0	0	0	0	0	0	0	1	1
Vermont	0	0	0	0	0	0	0	0	0	0	0	0	0	0	0	0	0
Virginia	0	3	1	1	1	1	33	0	1	1	1	0	1	0	0	0	44
Washington	1	0	0	0	0	0	0	0	2	0	0	0	0	0	0	0	3
Washington, D.C.	1	0	0	0	0	0	0	0	0	0	0	0	0	0	0	0	1
West Virginia	0	0	0	0	0	2	0	0	0	0	0	0	0	0	0	0	2
Wisconsin	0	0	0	0	0	0	0	0	0	0	0	1	0	0	1	0	2
Wyoming	0	0	0	0	0	0	0	0	0	0	0	1	0	0	0	0	1
Total	17	20	9	16	11	8	45	13	18	15	15	11	24	10	29	18	279

Table 2. Source Information (URLs)
for Collegiate Homicides in the United States, 2001–2016

Alabama

Troy University (2001)

http://media.ca11.uscourts.gov/opinions/unpub/files/200415055.pdf
http://www.troymessenger.com/2001/09/20/grand-jury-to-hear-evidence/
https://www.leagle.com/decision/20041608333fsupp2d127511479
https://www.wtvy.com/home/headlines/1176306.html
http://www.troymessenger.com/2008/12/29/man-charged-with-murder/

Miles College (2003)

http://www.jstor.org/stable/4133713
http://legacy.decaturdaily.com/decaturdaily/news/050213/murder.shtml
http://www.kcchronicle.com/2005/04/10/man-sentenced-to-35-years-for-students-death/aqrp5s7/archive-115248437964.txt
http://www.tuscaloosanews.com/article/20050213/news/502130359

University of Alabama (2007)

http://www.tuscaloosanews.com/article/20080728/NEWS/970031537
http://blog.al.com/live/2007/04/fairhope_man_dies_in_college_s.html

University of Alabama at Birmingham (2010)

http://blog.al.com/spotnews/2010/10/man_charged_with_killing_child.html
http://blog.al.com/spotnews/2012/04/judge_declares_mistrial_in_cap.html
http://blog.al.com/spotnews/2011/04/birmingham_man_pleads_guilty_r.html

University of Alabama at Huntsville (2010)

http://en.wikipedia.org/wiki/2010_University_of_Alabama_in_Huntsville_shooting

Enterprise State Community College, Alabama (2011)

Unconfirmed incident; URL unavailable

Southern Union State Community College (2011)

http://www.wbtv.com/story/14397278/possibleshooter-at/
http://www.wbtv.com/story/14398568/2011/04/06/opelika-police-seeking-fatal-shooting-suspect
http://www.oanow.com/news/crime_courts/plain-and-simple-i-lost-it-thomas-franklinmay-iii/article_1a57431c-b6011–7e3-a2de-0071a43b370.html
http://www.oanow.com/news/crime_courts/thomas-franklin-may-iii-found-guilty-of-capital-murder-in/article_d1f823ee-b461–11e3–8753–0017a43b2370.html
http://www.oanow.com/news/crime_courts/southern-union-shooter-thomas-may-sentenced-to-life-in-prison/article_bfbc9908-e12f-11e3-b6fe-001a4bcf6878.html
http://www.oanow.com/news/crime_courts/may-s-mental-health-discussed-during-southern-union-shooting-case/article_26e4cb02-b3c0–11e3-a0db-001a4bcf6878.html

University of South Alabama (2011)

http://blog.al.com/live/2011/07/apparent_homicide_of_universit.html
http://blog.al.com/live/2013/02/brandon_ajizadeh_trial_begins.html
http://blog.al.com/live/2011/08/usa_stabbing_brandon_ajizadeh.html
http://blog.al.com/live/2011/07/james_dean_south_alabama_murder.html
http://blog.al.com/live/2013/02/jury_takes_20_minutes_to_convi.html
http://www.universityherald.com/articles/3015/20130327/former-university-south-alabama-student-sentenced-life-stabbing.htm

Gadsden State Community College (2012)

http://blog.al.com/spotnews/2012/11/murder_investigation_underway.html
http://abc3340.com/archive/man-faces-murder-charge-in-college-killing
http://www.al.com/news/anniston-gadsden/index.ssf/2015/02/cherokee_county_man_pleads_gui.html
https://www.weisradio.com/vinnie-leroy-keaton-sentenced-to-life-without-possibility-of-parole/
http://www.weisradio.com/exclusivejury-select

Table 2. Source Information for Collegiate Homicides   159

ed-in-capital-murder-trial-of-vinnie-leroy-keaton/

Alaska

University of Alaska Fairbanks (2001)
Unconfirmed incident; URL unavailable

Arizona

Arizona State University (2002)

http://www.eastvalleytribune.com/local/tempe/article_16e579f9-f9fd-5f70-b78d-b6becfe56c9a.html
http://tucsoncitizen.com/morgue2/2001/08/22/118292-lawyer-surrenders-in-hit-run-death/
http://www.eastvalleytribune.com/news/article_58de7529-582b-525a-9c09-e29e4f440cb8.html
http://asuwebdevilarchive.jmc.asu.edu/issues/2002/10/29/campusnews/309080
http://archive.azcentral.com/arizonarepublic/arizonaliving/articles/20111102fathers-forgiveness-brings-out-best-in-another-after-tragedy.html

University of Arizona (2002)

http://articles.latimes.com/2002/oct/29/nation/na-shoot29
https://www.nytimes.com/2002/10/29/us/student-kills-3-instructors-and-himself-at-u-of-arizona.html
http://murderpedia.org/male.F/f/flores-robert-stewart.htm

University of Arizona (2007)

http://tucson.com/news/ua-student-convicted-in-killing-of-dorm-roommate/article_da765ffc-192d-5816-a3de-6c5e8e432876.html
http://murderpedia.org/female.H/h/harrison-galareka.html
http://tucsoncitizen.com/morgue/2008/09/13/96560-woman-describes-dorm-stabbing-scene/

University of Arizona (2011)

http://www.tucsonnewsnow.com/story/16491197/u-of-a-area-murder-investigation-still-ongoing/
http://tucson.com/news/blogs/police-beat/trial-in-post-game-killing-gets-started/article_920488ee-b280-5aea-8f0e-33640ddef75c.html
http://tucson.com/news/blogs/courthouse/man-

found-guilty-for-killing-after-ua-football-game/article_c2ce8bbd-230a-5f6a-be03-6576f30a4d3c.html
http://tucson.com/news/local/crime/accused-shooter-in-ua-murder-found-guilty/article_b808ce06-1c91-5089-8f6e-4c7361ffdc77.html
http://tucson.com/news/local/crime/car-jacking-murder-draws-life-sentence/article_3b1fe8c8-309d-5e3e-8d39-9448939c1301.html
http://cases.justia.com/arizona/court-of-appeals-division-two-unpublished/2014-2-ca-cr-2013-0508.pdf?ts=1411516883

Northern Arizona University (2015)

https://www.nytimes.com/2015/10/10/us/northern-arizona-university-flagstaff-shooting.html?_r=0
http://abcnews.go.com/US/deadly-shooting-reported-northern-arizona-universitys-flag staff-campus/story?id=34363113
http://www.azcentral.com/story/news/local/arizona-investigations/2016/03/23/what-happened-flagstaff-nau-shooting/80811934/
http://www.nbcnews.com/news/us-news/murder-assault-charges-filed-deadly-northern-arizona-university-shooting-n444901
http://azdailysun.com/news/local/crime-and-courts/steven-jones-shooting-case-set-for-trial/article_7b920f82-c3dc-5687-8ccc-1b1331709f0e.html

Arkansas

University of Central Arkansas (2008)

https://en.wikipedia.org/wiki/University_of_Central_Arkansas_shootings
http://katv.com/archive/kelsey-perry-sentenced-for-killing-2-uca-students

Arkansas State University, Main Campus (2010)

http://www.kait8.com/story/15371309/asu-asking-for-assistance-in-open-murder-investigation?clienttype=printable
http://www.helena-arkansas.com/article/20150420/NEWS/150429944
http://www.brownshomeforfuneralsinc.com/obituary/5017272

Arkansas Baptist College (2012)

http://katv.com/archive/murder-across-from-arkansas-baptist-college-rattles-campus
https://baptistnews.com/article/arkansas-cbf-mourns-students-murder/#.Wrg4V4jwa00

http://www.arkansas-catholic.org/news/article/3198

https://www.change.org/p/arkansas-governor-mayor-chief-of-police-of-the-city-of-little-rock-find-justice-for-derek-olivier-implement-a-new-anti-violence-program/u/4661995

California

Don Bosco Technical Institute (2001)

http://homicide.latimes.com/post/huong-heng-lim-peak/

East Los Angeles College (2001)

http://articles.latimes.com/2001/mar/08/local/me-35064

http://www.courts.ca.gov/opinions/revnppub/B168750.PDF

City of Hope Graduate School of Biological Science (2002)

https://www.firerescue1.com/fire-news/107026-calif-firefighter-and-wife-killed-in-city-of-hope-shooting/

http://articles.latimes.com/2006/jun/15/local/me-cityofhope15

http://www.topix.com/forum/city/compton-ca/TNP1KJ0VGLTLFURT7

http://www.sbsun.com/general-news/20060615/shooting-called-murder-suicide

City College of San Francisco (2003)

http://www.sfgate.com/bayarea/article/SAN-FRANCISCO-Ex-sheriff-s-deputy-s-son-2597077.php

http://www.sfgate.com/crime/article/Man-arrested-in-buddy-s-shooting-He-feared-2553252.php

Advance Beauty College, California (2004)

Unconfirmed incident; URL unavailable

California State University, Monterey Bay (2007)

https://www.campussafetymagazine.com/news/csu-monterey-bay-student-accused-of-murdering-husband/

https://otterrealm.wordpress.com/2008/02/26/domestic-violence-leads-to-first-murder-in-csumb-history/

http://www.mercurynews.com/2007/12/26/cal-state-monterey-bay-student-accused-of-stabbing-husband-to-death/

https://tinyurl.com/y9r8xnjy

California State University, Sacramento (2009)

http://www.sandiegouniontribune.com/sdut-murder-assault-charges-for-sac-state-student-2009nov06-story.html

https://www.mercurynews.com/education/ci_13618568

http://eastsacramento.abc10.com/content/sac-state-cops-witnesses-describe-final-violent-moments-dorm-suite

https://www.mercurynews.com/2012/05/16/sacramento-man-gets-18-years-for-killing-college-roommate-from-santa-clara/

http://www.legacy.com/obituaries/sacbee/obituary.aspx?pid=135147413

https://www.mercurynews.com/2009/10/22/student-from-santa-clara-beaten-to-death-in-his-sac-state-dorm/

http://northiowatoday.com/2012/04/13/man-who-fatally-beat-dorm-roommate-is-sentenced/

University of California, Irvine (2009)

http://latimesblogs.latimes.com/lanow/2009/09/graduate-student-held-in-shooting-death-of-exwife-at-uc-irvine.html

http://latimesblogs.latimes.com/lanow/2009/09/uci-graduate-student-pleads-xxxx-to-shooting-death-of-exwife.html

http://www.ocregister.com/articles/benedict-634975-murphy-son.html

California State University, Bakersfield (2010)

http://www.cbsnews.com/news/bianca-jackson-murdered-gunfire-at-cal-state-bakersfield-halloween-party-kills-student/

http://bakersfieldnow.com/news/local/murder-of-teen-at-csub-still-unsolved

http://www.kget.com/news/who-killed-bianca-jackson/857307332

San Diego City College (2010)

http://latimesblogs.latimes.com/lanow/2012/02/estranged-husband-arrested-in-murder-of-san-diego-city-college-student.html

https://www.nbcsandiego.com/news/local/Armando-Perez-Pleads-Guilty-in-Murder-of-Diana-Gonzalez-City-College-283724081.html

https://www.nbcsandiego.com/news/local/I-Just-Became-a-Monster-Armando-Perez-City-College-Stabbing-Killing-444726643.html

Table 2. Source Information for Collegiate Homicides   161

https://www.nbcsandiego.com/news/local/Body-
Found-in-City-College-Restroom-1050800
24.html
http://www.nbcsandiego.com/news/local/Arm
ando-Perez-Withdraws-Plea-in-San-Diego-
City-College-Students-Killing-288840891.
html

University of California, San Diego (2010)

http://www.lajollalight.com/sdljl-ucsd-burning-
car-estranged-husband-arrested-on-2010nov
08-story.html
http://www.lajollalight.com/news/2011/nov/18/m
an-pleads-guilty-in-death-of-his-wife-in-
burning/
http://www.10news.com/news/man-who-
strangled-wife-burned-body-in-car-sentenced

Coast Career Institute (2011)

http://latimesblogs.latimes.com/lanow/2011/02/
suspect-briefly-left-security-guard-class-before-
he-returned-and-immediately-opened-fire.
html
http://www.cbsnews.com/news/coast-career-
institute-teacher-roberto-herrera-shot-by-
student-in-los-angeles-say-cops/
http://www.dailymail.co.uk/news/article-1360
255/LA-student-Law-Thien-Huynh-shoots-
teacher-dead-walks-cigarette.html
http://losangeles.cbslocal.com/2011/02/23/stud
ent-kills-his-teacher-in-los-angeles-classroom/
http://www.sandiegouniontribune.com/sdut-
student-charged-in-la-trade-school-teacher-
slaying-2011feb25-story.html

San Jose State University (2011)

http://www.californiabeat.org/2011/05/12/shoot
ing-victims-from-sjsu-murder-suicide-named-
two-were-students
http://www.californiabeat.org/2011/05/10/break
ing-2-killed-1-wounded-in-san-jose-state-
shooting
http://www.mercurynews.com/2011/05/12/sjsu-
shooting-three-who-died-are-identified/

Santa Monica College (2013)

http://en.wikipedia.org/wiki/2013_Santa_
Monica_shooting

University of California, Berkeley (2013)

http://www.dailycal.org/2013/09/23/uc-berkeley-
sophomore-maliq-nixon-dies-19/
http://www.dailycal.org/2013/11/12/parents-
demand-improved-mental-health-services-
sons-suicide/

Los Angeles Valley College (2014)

http://www.nbclosangeles.com/news/local/
shooting-valley-college-valley-glen-24200
1321.html
http://articles.latimes.com/2014/jan/26/local/
la-me-ln-2-arrested-shooting-valley-college-
20140126
http://articles.latimes.com/2014/jan/26/local/la-
me-ln-2-arrested-shooting-valley-college-201
40126
http://homicide.latimes.com/post/two-men-
sentenced-life-prison-drug-robbery-killing-
2014/
http://losangeles.cbslocal.com/2015/09/25/2-
men-sentenced-to-life-in-prison-for-fatally-
shooting-robbery-victim-in-college-parking-
lot/

Life Chiropractic College West (2015)

http://www.fugitive.com/2015/02/13/body-found-
at-hayward-life-chiropractic-college-west-
police-investigating-as-homicide/
http://abc7news.com/news/hayward-police-
investigating-fatality-at-chiropractic-college-
as-homicide/516047/
http://patch.com/california/unioncity/man-
arrested-suspicion-murder-death-during-
burglary-life-chiropractic-college-west
http://www.nbcbayarea.com/news/Man-Arrested-
After-Break-In-Crash-at-Hayward-Chiro
practic-College-292443831.html

Sacramento City College (2015)

http://www.theblaze.com/news/2015/09/03/
police-three-shot-one-fatally-near-sacramento-
city-college-gunman-sought/
http://www.sacbee.com/news/local/crime/
article52588265.html
https://www.sacbee.com/news/local/crime/ar-
ticle132096144.html

Ventura College (2015)

https://www.vcccd.edu/departments/police/
crime-prevention-information/crime-log/
january-2015
http://losangeles.cbslocal.com/2015/01/02/boy-
1-found-stabbed-to-death-in-ventura/
http://ktla.com/2015/01/02/baby-boy-1-fatally-
stabbed-father-also-injured-in-ventura-
home/
http://www.latimes.com/local/lanow/la-me-ln-
ventura-man-jailed-in-sons-slaying-20150105-
story.html
http://www.timesheraldonline.com/article/ZZ/
20150226/NEWS/150227795

http://archive.vcstar.com/news/local/ventura/ventura-man-pleads-guilty-to-stabbing-kid napping-his-son-296a624c-2e3b-509e-e053–0100007fd480–365504821.html
http://archive.vcstar.com/news/local/ventura/ventura-man-sentenced-to-life-in-prison-for-killing-baby-son-2c257cd6–7ebc-7965-e053–0100007fd371–369466522.html

Sonoma State University (2016)

http://abc7news.com/news/teen-found-dead-on-sonoma-state-campus-had-multiple-stab-wounds/1591972/
http://www.latimes.com/local/lanow/la-me-ln-sonoma-state-slaying-20161108-story.html
http://kron4.com/2016/11/05/sheriff-deputies-murder-victim-found-at-sonoma-state-was-stabbed/
http://www.sonomastatestar.com/news/2017/11/14/one-year-later-kirk-kimberlys-death-remains-unsolved

University of California, Los Angeles (2016)

https://www.cnn.com/2016/06/01/us/ucla-shooting-report/index.html
https://en.wikipedia.org/wiki/2016_UCLA_shooting
https://www.washingtonpost.com/news/grade-point/wp/2016/06/02/ucla-shooting-suspect-and-victim-a-professor-identifed-in-murder-suicide/?utm_term=.f9d16ab585bf
https://www.washingtonpost.com/news/grade-point/wp/2016/06/01/ucla-on-lockdown-after-reports-of-shooting/?utm_term=.2716a247e270
http://www.latimes.com/local/lanow/la-me-ln-ucla-shooting-20160601-snap-story.html
https://www.usatoday.com/story/news/2016/06/01/police-check-reports-shooter-ucla/85245782/

University of California, San Francisco (2016)

https://www.sfgate.com/crime/article/Police-woman-killed-by-companion-near-UCSF-6761296.php
http://sfist.com/2016/01/19/woman_slain_at_ucsf_was_victim_of_d.php
http://www.sfexaminer.com/ucsf-homicide-suspect-charged-murder-domestic-violence/
https://www.mercurynews.com/2016/01/15/san-francisco-woman-killed-in-fight-with-companion-on-ucsf-campus/

University of Southern California (2016)

http://www.laweekly.com/news/usc-professor-fatally-stabbed-on-campus-7678628

https://www.dailynews.com/2016/12/03/student-who-allegedly-killed-usc-professor-identified-by-police/
https://www.dailynews.com/2016/12/06/usc-graduate-student-charged-in-campus-stabbing-death-of-professor/
https://www.nbclosangeles.com/news/local/USC-Graduate-Student-Charged-With-Murder-in-Fatal-Stabbing-of-Professor-4050277 55.html
https://www.morningnewsusa.com/david-jonathan-brown-facts-usc-student-stabbed-professor-death-23127766.html
https://dailytrojan.com/2018/01/31/judge-rules-student-insane-professors-murder/

Colorado

Community College of Aurora (2001)

http://www.thefreelibrary.com/Police+probe+apparent+murder-suicide+at+Colo.+College.-a080634061

Colorado College (2002)

https://www.colorado.gov/apps/coldcase/case detail.html?id=387
http://www.kktv.com/home/headlines/697567.html
http://catalystnewspaper.com/news/cold-case-murder-outside-of-colorado-colleges-arm-strong-hall/
http://gazette.com/the-cold-case-files-murder-on-ccs-doorstep-2002/article/59978
http://blogs.denverpost.com/coldcases/2014/04/05/pueblo/8222/

Connecticut

University of Connecticut (2009)

https://www.courant.com/sports/uconn-football/jasper-howard/hc-unconnmain1019.artoct19-story.html
http://www.nytimes.com/2009/10/28/sports/ncaa football/28uconn.html
http://espn.go.com/college-football/news/story?id=4598158
http://espn.go.com/ncf/news/story?id=6257549
https://en.wikipedia.org/wiki/Jasper_Howard

Wesleyan University (2009)

https://www.nytimes.com/2009/05/08/nyregion/08wesleyan.html
http://www.nytimes.com/2009/05/09/nyregion/09wesleyan.html?pagewanted=all

http://www.nytimes.com/2011/12/17/nyregion/
in-wesleyan-students-killing-not-guilty-by-
reason-of-insanity.html
http://www.courant.com/news/connecticut/hc-
wesleyan-fatal-shooting-stories-storygallery.
html

Yale University (2009)

http://en.wikipedia.org/wiki/Murder_of_Annie_
Le
http://murderpedia.org/male.C/c/clark-ray
mond.htm

Delaware

Delaware State University (2007)

http://www.washingtonpost.com/wp-dyn/con
tent/article/2007/09/21/AR2007092102224.
html
http://en.wikipedia.org/wiki/Delaware_State_
University_shooting
http://www.nytimes.com/2007/09/21/us/21cnd-
dover.html
http://www.nj.com/news/index.ssf/2009/05/del_
attorney_general_will_not.html

Wilmington University (2011)

http://www.doverpost.com/article/20111024/
NEWS/310249997
http://www.wboc.com/story/15790386/dover-
man-murdered
http://www.newarkpostonline.com/news/local/
article_631b7322-98f4-5bc7-b21e-caa1ee0b
295f.html

District of Columbia

Gallaudet University (2001)

http://content.time.com/time/magazine/article/
0,9171,130940,00.html
http://deafness.about.com/cs/archivedarticles/a/
gallyarrest.htm
http://articles.latimes.com/2001/feb/27/news/
mn-30744
http://caselaw.findlaw.com/dc-court-of-appeals/
1147115.html
http://articles.chicagotribune.com/2002-07-11/
news/0207110303_1_gallaudet-university-life-
terms-sign-language-interpreter

Florida

Broward College (2002)

https://www.upressonline.com/2002/01/shoot
ing-hits-close-by/

http://www2.ljworld.com/news/2002/jan/19/mur
dersuicide_suspected_in/?print
http://articles.sun-sentinel.com/2002-01-19/
news/0201190217_1_shootings-shots-student

Eckerd College (2002)

http://www.sptimes.com/2002/03/26/South
Pinellas/Eckerd_College_mainte.shtml

Daytona State College (2003)

http://daytonastate.edu/marketing/files/news/
Daytona%20State%20safety%20drill%20We%
20have%20to%20be%20ready.pdf
http://articles.orlandosentinel.com/2003-10-24/
news/0310240306_1_daytona-beach-police-
torres-beach-community-college

Florida Institute of Technology (2004)

http://articles.orlandosentinel.com/2004-05-
07/news/0405070206_1_security-guard-
melbourne-florida-institute
http://articles.orlandosentinel.com/2004-10-23/
news/0410230266_1_mike-mccain-melbourne-
careless-driving
http://privateofficerbreakingnews.blogspot.com/2
009/05/retrial-of-security-guard-murder.html
http://www.iaclea.org/visitors/memberservices/
awards/valor/winner05.cfm

Santa Fe College (2004)

http://www.workplaceviolence911.com/sites/
workplaceviolence911.com/files/20041104_1.
htm
http://www.gainesville.com/article/20070725/
LOCAL/707250333
http://www.gainesville.com/article/20070726/
local/707260317

University of Florida (2004)

http://www.gainesville.com/article/20060605/
LOCAL/206050313
http://www.crime-research.org/news/20.02.
2004/vedam_praveen/
http://www.ocala.com/article/LK/20050121/
News/604220966/OS/
https://news.google.com/newspapers?nid=1320
&dat=20050313&id=G8BPAAAAIBAJ&sjid=
kQYEAAAAIBAJ&pg=6962,3070660&hl=
en

Edward Waters College (2005)

http://www.news4jax.com/news/EWC-Student-
Who-Wrote-About-Safety-Concerns-Shot-
Dead/-/475880/1938734/-/13651qsz/-/index.
html
http://articles.chicagotribune.com/2004-12-18/

news/0412180145_1_edward-waters-college-charged-student

http://articles.chicagotribune.com/2006-07-20/news/0607200277_1_johnathan-glenn-edward-waters-college-sake

https://www.news4jax.com/news/jury-finds-man-guilty-of-murdering-ewc-student

Miami Dade College, Florida (2005)

Unconfirmed incident; URL unavailable

University of South Florida, Main Campus (2006)

http://www.forgottenvictims.com/Ronald%20Stem.htm

http://www.tbo.com/news/guilty-plea-to-murder-stuns-court-170962

http://www.sptimes.com/2006/04/05/Hillsborough/Two_charged_in_fatal_.shtml

Florida State College at Jacksonville (2007)

http://z10.invisionfree.com/usedtobedoe/ar/t31377.htm

Northwest Florida State College (2009)

http://www.wjhg.com/home/headlines/43357237.html

http://www.tbo.com/news/marshals-shoot-slaying-suspect-94901

http://www.theledger.com/news/20120328/man-gets-death-in-fatal-shooting

http://caselaw.findlaw.com/fl-supreme-court/1653332.html

http://www.wjhg.com/home/headlines/Man_Gets_Death_Sentence_in_2009_DFS_Murder_144282915.html

http://sheriff-okaloosa.org/wp-content/pdfs/newsreleases/2009/NR04122009.htm

Florida International University (2010)

http://articles.sun-sentinel.com/2010-03-26/news/fl-fiu-football-player-stabbing-20100326_1_florida-international-university-students-fiu-athletic-director-stabbing

http://www.local10.com/news/local/miami/jury-finds-quentin-wyche-guilty-in-stabbing-death-of-fiu-football-player_20151127041441158

http://www.nbcmiami.com/news/local/Quentin-Wyche-Sentenced-to-More-Than-20-Years-in-Prison-in-2010-Stabbing-of-Florida-International-University-Football-Player-233363381.html

Georgia

Clark Atlanta University (2009)

http://www.cau.edu/CMFiles/docs/CAU%20RESPONDS%20TO%20ARREST%20IN%20SPELMAN%20STUDENT%20MURDER.pdf

http://talk.collegeconfidential.com/college-search-selection/774967-spelman-college-student-murdered-clark-atlanta-university-tragedy-atlanta.html

http://thegrio.com/2009/11/06/clark-atlanta-university-sued-after-girl-is-shot-on-campus/

http://www.ajc.com/news/news/local/spelman-trial-benton-gets-life-plus-25-years-in-mu/nQcjc/

North Georgia Technical College (2009)

http://www.accessnorthga.com/detail.php?n=216539

http://framedfathers.proboards.com/thread/1552/wife-shoots-husband-blairsville

Valdosta State University (2012)

http://www.valdosta.edu/about/news/releases/2012/11/vsu-police-update.php

http://www.wctv.tv/home/headlines/Testimony-Continues-in-Murder-Trial-of-Darien-Meheux-240354401.html

Columbus State University (2013)

http://police.columbusstate.edu/crime_alert.php#crime2

http://www.wtvm.com/story/24283585/one-person-dead-after-shooting-in-downtown-columbus

http://www.ledger-enquirer.com/news/local/article29316580.html

http://www.ledger-enquirer.com/news/local/crime/article29316499.html

http://meredith.worldnow.com/story/24283585/one-person-dead-after-shooting-in-downtown-columbus

Georgia Perimeter College (2013)

https://gbi.georgia.gov/press-releases/2013-06-11/body-found-georgia-perimeter-college-clarkston-campus-identified-alpha

https://www.wsbtv.com/news/local/body-found-georgia-perimeter-college/243029684

https://www.wsbtv.com/news/local/gbi-2-arrested-death-man-found-gpc-campus/243103138

http://www.crossroadsnews.com/news/two-held-in-slaying-of-man-at-gpc/article_29a2b47a-f556-54e4-badd-499e9f80c774.html

Table 2. Source Information for Collegiate Homicides 165

Savannah State University (2013)

https://usgunviolence.wordpress.com/2013/09/
21/killed-donald-bernard-lewis-savannah-
ga/
http://www.onlineathens.com/article/20130922/
NEWS/309229952
http://www.savannahnow.com/crime/2016–02-
16/mother-slain-savannah-state-university-
student-pleads-help-solving-homicide

Clayton State University (2015)

http://www.usatoday.com/story/news/crime/
2015/11/09/police-investigating-shooting-
near-clayton-state-univ-campus/75497798/
https://gbi.georgia.gov/press-releases/2015–12-
15/witness-sought-shooting-death-clayton-
state-university
http://www.ajc.com/news/crime—law/man-
shot-clayton-state-apartment-complex-dies-
suspect-still-sought/1AeSp29Ah5JdFSM9
hKjaYJ/
http://www.news-daily.com/news/hampton-
woman-arrested-for-murder-of-man-on-
clayton-state/article_6621c549-baaa-50e8-
a935-c897c9892ca3.html
http://www.effinghamherald.net/archives/10287/

Fort Valley State University (2015)

http://www.ajc.com/news/local/fort-valley-state-
senior-from-powder-springs-killed-wreck/
IaFdwlo71vyfTInBsVKnoM/
http://www.macon.com/news/local/community/
houston-peach/article34012221.html
http://www.macon.com/news/local/commu-
nity/houston-peach/article34801380.html

Savannah State University (2015)

http://www.cnn.com/2015/08/28/us/georgia-
savannah-state-university-shooting/
http://insider.foxnews.com/2015/08/28/savannah-
state-university-student-christopher-starks-
killed-manhunt-underway
https://www.ajc.com/news/crime—law/dekalb-
football-standout-fatally-shot-savannah-state/
oif3qSyyyVSkjUsRjFWgsM/
http://www.11alive.com/news/crime/one-year-
later-no-arrests-in-christopher-starks-
death/309744104
http://www.11alive.com/news/local/savannah-
state-university-wrongful-death-lawsuit/
228418017

Hawaii (None)

Idaho

Boise State University (2003)

http://scholarworks.boisestate.edu/cgi/view
content.cgi?article=2322&context=student_
newspapers
http://scholarworks.boisestate.edu/cgi/viewcon-
tent.cgi?article=2323&context=student_news-
papers

Illinois

Illinois Institute of Technology (2002)

https://data.cityofchicago.org/Public-Safety/
Crimes-2002/g9qy-h66j?q=murder

Benedictine University (2004)

http://articles.chicagotribune.com/2004–01-22/
news/0401220128_1_apartment-building-
first-homicide-chicago-man
http://articles.chicagotribune.com/2004–01-23/
news/0401230029_1_miller-home-invasion-
apartment

Northern Illinois University (2008)

http://en.wikipedia.org/wiki/Northern_Illinois_
University_shooting

Dominican University (2011)

http://thedominicanstar.wordpress.com/2011/
07/14/shooting-near-priory-campus/
http://southtownstar.suntimes.com/news/
6516091–418/blue-island-man-son-charged-
in-murder-plot.html
http://chicago.cbslocal.com/2011/07/14/3-men-
charged-in-womans-murder-near-dominican-
university/
http://www.austinweeklynews.com/News/Arti
cles/5–15-2014/Father-and-son-found-guilty-
of-Chervon-Alexander's-murder/
http://www.austinweeklynews.com/News/Arti
cles/8–7-2014/95-years-in-ambush-murder-of-
Chervon-Alexander/

University of Illinois at Chicago (2011)

http://articles.chicagotribune.com/2011–11-27/
news/chi-man-charged-with-shooting-
estranged-wife-at-uic-held-without-bail-2011
1127_1_prosecutors-parking-area-shooting
http://chicago.cbslocal.com/tag/uic-medical-
center/feed/
http://chicago.cbslocal.com/2011/11/27/no-bond-
for-man-charged-with-murder-at-uic-hospital/

http://www.huffingtonpost.com/2011/11/27/earl-roberts-charged-with_n_1115189.html

Chicago State University (2013)

http://abc7chicago.com/archive/8960204/

http://articles.chicagotribune.com/2014–01-17/news/chi-family-of-teen-killed-after-basket ball-game-sues-chicago-state-cps-20140116_1_chicago-state-university-cps-officials-basketball game

http://www.chicagotribune.com/news/chi-2-charged-slaying-tyrone-lawson-teen-kille-001-photo.html

Illinois Valley Community College (2015)

http://www.pjstar.com/article/20150622/NEWS/150629828

http://www.newstrib.com/news/local_news/murder-in-the-parking-lot-man-shot-killed-with-arrow/article_31a634aa-82ab-5b6f-8628–467a9ddfc943.html

https://www.pjstar.com/article/20150621/news/150629874

http://www.newstrib.com/free/plea-coming-for-accomplice-in-the-bow-and-arrow/article_31193344-adf8–11e6–8e1e-1724aecb1b be.html

http://www.newstrib.com/news/local_news/french-changed-story-in-ivcc-killing-but-claims-self-defense-article_ad9aaf96-5407-5e4b-a4be-93abfaf78cd4.html

https://www.mywebtimes.com/articles/n/2016/08/05/07069ef1a8b75296a04b4efa28c13126/index.xml

Illinois Institute of Technology (2016)

https://www.dnainfo.com/chicago/20160128/bronzeville/top-iit-student-beaten-death-by-fellow-student

https://chicago.suntimes.com/news/no-bond-for-iit-student-charged-with-beating-class mate-to-death/

https://abc7chicago.com/news/man-charged-in-iit-students-beating-death/1181064/

http://www.chicagotribune.com/news/local/brea king/ct-iit-student-killing-charges-20160130-story.html

http://chicago.homicidewatch.org/category/suspects/carlos-wilson/index.html

University of Illinois at Urbana–Champaign (2016)

http://www.chicagotribune.com/news/local/

breaking/ct-illinois-student-dorm-baby-death-20160413-story.html

http://www.news-gazette.com/news/local/2016–04-12/updated-ui-student-charged-murder-infants-death.html

http://www.news-gazette.com/news/local/2016–06-02/judge-allows-woman-charged-murder-leave-state.html

http://www.chicagotribune.com/suburbs/daily-southtown/news/ct-sta-lindsay-johnson-plea-st-0409–20170407-story.html

---

Indiana

Purdue University, Main Campus (2001)

http://www.purdue.edu/uns/html3month/2001/010803.Bennett.deaths.html

https://news.uns.purdue.edu/html3month/2001/010813.Yin.murder.html

http://www.theindychannel.com/news/purdue-murder-suspect-to-face-judge-Tuesday

http://azdailysun.com/ex-purdue-student-gets-life-sentence-for-killing-sisters/article_a522895b-900d-5f8–1696c-e77b3f62e5af.html

http://www.purdueexponent.org/campus/article_513bd737–458f-593a-bb3a-8d3bb0b1 b1fd.html

http://www.wthr.com/story/2302240/double-murderer-found-dead-in-cell

Butler University (2004)

https://www.wthr.com/article/butler-police-officer-killed-police-kill-suspect

https://www.odmp.org/officer/17454-police-officer-james-l-davis-jr

Indiana University–Purdue University Fort Wayne (2008)

http://www.campussafetymagazine.com/article/indiana-student-stabbed-in-dorm-by-room mates-mother

http://articles.southbendtribune.com/2008–04-21/news/26849734_1_gabriel-martinez-court-documents-exchange-program

http://www.abqjournal.com/21428/abqnewsseek er/updated-at-1210pm-nmsu-students-killer-gets-60-years.html

Indiana State University (2012)

http://www.huffingtonpost.com/2012/08/27/william-mallory-isu-shooting-indiana_n_1832905.html

http://www.in.gov/judiciary/opinions/pdf/09091402jgb.pdf

http://www.tribstar.com/news/local_news/mallory-guilty-on-six-counts/article_500506e1-6a4b-5e47-81f4-ca668c155508.html

Indiana University–Purdue University Indianapolis (2014)

https://protect.iu.edu/doc/police-safety/asr/asr-iupui-2015.pdf
http://www.wthr.com/story/20332035/body-found-at-white-river-state-park
http://www.wlky.com/news/man-charged-with-wifes-death-on-walking-trail/27221072
https://nixle.com/alert/5241918/

Purdue University, Main Campus (2014)

http://www.purdueexponent.org/city_state/article_e43cfe73-0518-55e8-a861-631a5e57188a.html
http://fox59.com/2014/09/19/cousins-to-learn-fate-today-will-public-learn-motive-behind-purdue-campus-shooting/
http://www.jconline.com/story/news/crime/2014/10/29/cody-cousins-found-dead/18114495/

Manchester University (2016)

https://www.wthr.com/article/manchester-univ-student-arrested-for-murder-for-newborn-sons-death
http://www.nydailynews.com/news/crime/ind-woman-baby-died-birth-college-dorm-arrested-article-1.2622386
https://www.southbendtribune.com/news/publicsafety/ex-manchester-student-charged-with-murder-weighed-abortion/article_2a165fd2-850d-53d3-8d3e-5e0af10f2344.html
http://wsbt.com/news/local/court-docs-elkhart-woman-googled-at-home-abortion-before-death-of-son
https://www.usnews.com/news/best-states/indiana/articles/2017-07-13/trial-delayed-over-newborns-death-in-college-dorm-bathtub

Iowa

Maharishi University of Management (2004)

http://en.wikipedia.org/wiki/Maharishi_University_of_Management_stabbing
http://www.religionnewsblog.com/6283/investigators-work-murder-case-at-maharishi-university
http://www.theguardian.com/world/2004/may/02/usa.theobserver

http://www.culteducation.com/group/1195-transcendental-meditation-movement/20498-mum-murder-trial-set-to-begin-tuesday.html
http://culteducation.com/group/1195-transcendental-meditation-movement/20500-ex-maharishi-student-not-guilty-of-murder-by-insanity.html

Kansas

Kansas State University (2013)

http://www.k-state.edu/today/announcement.php?id=11340&category=news&referredBy=todayRSSFeed
http://www.wibwnewsnow.com/police-investigate-student-death-k-state/
http://www.wibw.com/home/headlines/K-State-Police-Investigate-Student-Death-232810761.html
http://1350kman.com/arrest-in-k-state-students-death/
http://www.littleapplepost.com/2015/01/12/defendant-makes-plea-deal-in-ksu-student-death/
http://www.kstatecollegian.com/2015/02/15/suspect-in-overdose-investigation-sentenced/

Wichita State University (2015)

http://www.kansas.com/news/local/crime/article30488382.html
http://ksn.com/2015/08/10/victim-identified-two-arrested-in-shooting-at-wichita-state-university/
http://www.kansas.com/news/local/crime/article41700759.html
https://www.hayspost.com/2016/03/19/woman-enters-plea-deal-in-shooting-death-on-wichita-state-campus/
https://www.kansas.com/news/local/crime/article30610167.html
http://www.kansas.com/news/local/crime/article54674225.html
http://www.kansas.com/news/local/crime/article61114347.html

Kentucky

Murray State University (2001)

http://enquirer.com/editions/2001/04/05/loc_murder_charge_in2.html
http://www.freerepublic.com/focus/f-news/831874/posts
http://162.114.92.72/COA/2003-CA-000847.pdf
http://murrayledger.com/drug-charge-changed-

for-angelita-turner/article_3145683e-1c9a-57
cc-bb0e-7ba0a5b0c278.html

Western Kentucky
University (2003)

http://www.cnn.com/2003/US/South/05/11/
dorm.fire/
http://wkuherald.com/news/article_3b36a046-
b428–11e2-af05–001a4bcf6878.html
https://www.bgdailynews.com/former-autry-
roommate-court-ordered-to-testify/article_
8affe57a-1432-57ff/b131-763ba8dc6f91.html
http://www.14news.com/Global/story.asp?s=
3076673&clienttype=printable
http://www.wave3.com/story/3090660/good
rum-takes-stand-in-his-defense-in-western-
murder-case
http://www2.ljworld.com/news/2005/mar/22/
defendant_acquitted_in/
http://www.wbko.com/news/headlines/665021.
html
http://mugshots.com/US-Counties/Kentucky/
Warren-County-KY/Stephen-Lee-Soules.454
8306.html

ITT Technical
Institute–Lexington (2011)

http://www.kentucky.com/news/local/crime/
article44088243.html
http://www.wkyt.com/home/headlines/Man_
shot_and_killed_outside_Lexington_bar_11
9173689.html

Hazard Community
and Technical College (2013)

http://www.kentucky.com/2013/01/15/2477560/
at-least-3-injured-in-shooting.html
http://www.wkyt.com/home/headlines/Police-
Two-dead-in-shooting-at-Hazard-Commu-
nity-Technical-College-187033371.html
https://www.cbsnews.com/news/kentucky-
college-shooting-two-killed-in-domestic-
dispute-at-community-college-police-say/
http://www.wkyt.com/home/headlines/Perry-
County-man-sentenced-for-triple-murder-
262035431.html

Lindsey Wilson
College (2013)

https://www.wlky.com/article/body-found-in-
truck-on-college-campus-identified/3439
230
http://accvonline.com/body-identified-as-
jamison-stephens-lwc-student-from-russell-
springs/

Louisiana

Grambling State University (2001)

http://www.leagle.com/decision/20041226874
So2d352_11125/STATE%20v.%20SPIVEY
https://www.docketalarm.com/cases/Louisiana_
Western_District_Court/3—12-cv-02226/
Spivey_v._David_Wade_Correctional_Center/
17/

Southern University
and A&M College (2002)

http://www.la-fcca.org/Opinions/Pub2007/
2007–11/2007CA0189Nov2007.Not.13.pdf
http://www.hbcusports.com/forums/threads/
killing-at-southern-under-investigation.6894/
https://cases.justia.com/louisiana/first-circuit-
court-of-appeal/2007ca0189–1.pdf?ts=139
6122960

University of Louisiana
at Lafayette (2004)

http://www.kplctv.com/story/1872635/ny-police-
arrest-ull-murder-suspect?clienttype=printable
http://www.la3circuit.org/opinions/2007/05/053
007/07–0058np.pdf
http://www.findagrave.com/cgi-bin/fg.cgi?page=
gr&GRid=8875951

University of New Orleans (2006)

https://www.websleuths.com/forums/show
thread.php?201345-LA-Patrick-Turner-42-
UNO-student-New-Orleans-30-Oct-2006
http://www.wafb.com/story/5638873/strangled-
uno-student-identified-death-may-have-been-
sexually-motivated

Louisiana State University (2007)

http://www.wafb.com/global/story.asp?s=749
6248
http://www.cnn.com/2007/US/12/14/lsu.slaying/
http://www.nytimes.com/2007/12/15/us/15lsu.
html?_r=0
https://www.ktbs.com/news/guilty-plea-years-
in-lsu-grad-students-deaths/article_444
dd752-dc31–5ad4–95a4-e5a2f59be460.html
http://www.wafb.com/story/23626847/closing-
arguments-in-trial-for-lsu-grad-student-mur
ders

Capital Area Technical
College–Baton Rouge Campus (2008)

http://www.wafb.com/story/7842633/3-dead-
in-ltc-shooting
http://www.ktbs.com/story/22335671/woman-
kills-two-people-then-herself-at-baton-
rouge-vo-tech

Table 2. Source Information for Collegiate Homicides   169

http://www.lsureveille.com/baton-rouge-college-shooter-showed-signs-of-paranoia/article_fdef5f47-1055-5062-8ed7-7e20af245a96.html

Maine

Mercy Hospital School of Radiologic Technology (2008)

http://thebollard.com/2009/01/04/after-four-months-hospital-guards-murder-still-a-mystery/

http://www.portlandmaine.gov/Document Center/View/2246

https://refugeeresettlementwatch.wordpress.com/2009/04/28/portland-maine-sudanese-refugee-pulls-out-gun-and-is-killed-by-police/

http://bangordailynews.com/2008/09/07/news/state/maine-hospital-guard-shot-dead-during-break/

http://www.pressherald.com/2011/07/07/police-hope-cash-draws-new-leads-in-slaying_2011-07-07/

http://bangordailynews.com/2008/09/14/news/300-attend-hospital-guardrsquos-funeral/

Maryland

University of Maryland, Baltimore County (2004)

http://articles.baltimoresun.com/2004-06-30/news/0406300454_1_umbc-baltimore-county-man-and-woman

https://www.aacu.org/publications-research/periodicals/jessica-effect-valuing-cultural-and-familial-connections-broaden

http://articles.baltimoresun.com/2004-07-01/news/0407010026_1_umbc-graduate-students-campus-police

Stevenson University (2005)

http://www.washingtonpost.com/wp-dyn/content/article/2005/11/30/AR2005113002059.html

http://articles.baltimoresun.com/2005-12-01/news/0512010122_1_julie-college-infant-riley

http://articles.baltimoresun.com/2005-12-03/news/0512030259_1_riley-pretrial-services-prince-george

http://articles.baltimoresun.com/2007-03-16/news/0703160200_1_riley-garbage-bag-storm-drain

Johns Hopkins University (2010)

http://articles.baltimoresun.com/2010-07-26/news/bs-ci-md-homicides-stabbing-2-20100726_1_robbery-arrested-charged

http://baltimore.cbslocal.com/2011/11/07/sec-ond-person-sentenced-in-johns-hopkins-researcher-death/

http://articles.baltimoresun.com/2011-10-21/news/bs-md-ci-wagner-sentenced-20111021_1_pitcairn-family-john-alexander-wagner-lavelva-merritt

Bowie State University (2011)

http://articles.baltimoresun.com/2011-09-16/news/bs-md-bowie-stabbing-20110916_1_roommates-campus-police-students

http://hbcubuzz.com/alexis-d-simpson-arrested-by-maryland-state-police-in-relation-to-bowie-state-stabbing/

http://www.nbcwashington.com/news/local/Jury-Deciding-Case-Of-Fatal-Bowie-State-Stabbing-179564591.html

Morgan State University (2016)

https://www.baltimoresun.com/news/maryland/baltimore-city/bs-md-ci-morgan-state-stabbing-20160202-story.html

https://foxbaltimore.com/news/local/baltimore-police-make-arrest-in-death-of-morgan-state-student

Massachusetts

University of Massachusetts Amherst (2002)

http://dailycollegian.com/2004/03/31/jennifer-paluseo-faces-12-years-in-prison-today/

http://dailycollegian.com/2004/02/26/former-umass-student-pleads-guilty-to-manslaughter/

Harvard University (2009)

http://www.nydailynews.com/news/crime/harlem-man-arrested-murder-harvard-son-retired-nypd-article-1.410465

http://www.huffingtonpost.com/2009/05/18/harvard-shooting-victim-c_n_204946.html

http://www.thecrimson.com/article/2011/9/30/brittany-smith-harvard-shooting-sentenced/

http://www.thecrimson.com/article/2011/4/22/murder-copney-firstdegree-jury-murder-guilty-harvard-shooting/

https://www.bostonglobe.com/metro/2012/05/23/mother-justin-cosby-who-was-fatally-shot-harvard-dorm-room-files-suit-against-college/yL7PFzSaXtglLmxhzjx0MK/story.html

https://newsone.com/1611245/ex-harvard-student-admits-to-being-drug-dealer-in-murder-trial/

Massachusetts General Hospital Dietetic Internship (2009)

http://www.boston.com/news/local/massachu

setts/articles/2009/10/28/doctor_stabbed_
attacker_killed_at_massachusetts_general_
hospital/
http://www.boston.com/news/local/massachu
setts/articles/2009/11/10/mgh_doctor_returns_
home_after_stabbing/
http://homenewshere.com/article_349185f6–
3025–5ca2–835b-18eadd063e27.html
http://www.nicholsfuneralhome.com/obituaries/
carciero-jay.html#comments

Regis College (2010)

http://www.telegram.com/article/20100924/
news/100929751
http://boston.cbslocal.com/2010/09/30/arrest-
made-in-regis-college-murder/
http://www.wickedlocal.com/article/20101001/
News/310019842
http://patch.com/massachusetts/weston/judge-
upholds-murder-charge-in-regis-college-
killing
http://thebrandeishoot.com/articles/12304
https://www.youtube.com/watch?v=uXLq9oO9
8O8

Massachusetts Institute of Technology (2013)

http://boston.cbslocal.com/2013/04/23/miller-
tsarnaev-brothers-killed-mit-officer-because-
they-needed-a-gun/
https://en.wikipedia.org/wiki/Massachusetts_In-
stitute_of_Technology_Police_Department
https://news.mit.edu/2015/sean-collier-memo-
rial-unveiled-0429

University of Massachusetts Medical School Worcester (2013)

http://www.telegram.com/article/20131108/
NEWS/311089869&Template=printart
http://www.telegram.com/article/20140319/NE
WS/303199894
http://www.telegram.com/article/20131108/
NEWS/311089718
http://www.masslive.com/news/worcester/index.
ssf/2016/04/defense_claims_patient_who_kil.
html
http://www.masslive.com/news/worcester/index.
ssf/2016/05/aldo_dunphe_found_guilty_of_
mu.html
http://www.telegram.com/article/20160505/
NEWS/160509483

Michigan

Davenport University, Michigan (2001)

Unconfirmed incident; URL unavailable

Western Michigan University (2004)

http://groups.yahoo.com/group/NatNews/
message/33863
http://www.wmich.edu/wmu/news/2004/0405/
0304-x242.html
http://www.amazon.com/review/R21CXUI5FN
QXXA/ref=cm_cr_pr_viewpnt#R21CXUI5
FNQXXA
http://publicdocs.courts.mi.gov:81/opinions/
Final/COA/20070515_C266509_48_266509.
OPN.PDF
http://bailbondcity.com/michigan/midoc-
inmate-PERRY/244528

Lansing Community College (2005)

http://vnnforum.com/showthread.php?t=29421
https://statenews.com/multimedia/29115f9e-
05a3-4dc0-8bd1-932cb96b1cf1
http://lansingcitypulse.com/article-15243-Sum-
mer-of-terror-10-years-later.html
http://truthinjustice.org/mccollum.htm
https://www.law.umich.edu/special/exonera-
tion/Pages/casedetail.aspx?caseid=3421
http://murderpedia.org/male.M/m/macon-
matthew.htm

Eastern Michigan University (2006)

http://en.wikipedia.org/wiki/Murder_of_Laura_
Dickinson
http://www.michigandaily.com/content/taylor-
found-guilty-emu-death
http://articles.latimes.com/2007/jun/19/nation/n
a-murder19
http://blog.mlive.com/annarbornews/2008/05/
orange_taylor_apologizes_to_fa.html

Henry Ford Community College (2009)

http://www.mlive.com/news/index.ssf/2009/04/
person_with_gun_reported_at_mi.html
https://www.theoaklandpress.com/news/dead-
in-shooting-at-dearborn-college/article_b8af
2d38-61f8-5437-b90e-e72c37f03216.html
https://www.michigandaily.com/content/2009–
04-10/2-killed-dearborn-mich-community-
college-shooting
http://archive.li/E93p
http://www.whataboutourdaughters.com/waod/
2009/4/14/youtube-facebook-murder-black-
woman-slaughtered-by-crazed-fe.html

Baker College of Jackson (2010)

http://www.mlive.com/news/jackson/index.ssf/
2010/11/amanda_ball_pleads_guilty_to_m.html
http://www.mlive.com/news/jackson/index.ssf/2
010/05/family_of_heroin_overdose_vict.html

Table 2. Source Information for Collegiate Homicides   171

http://www.mlive.com/news/jackson/index.ssf/
2016/01/hold_a_purpose_in_life_mike_hi.
html
http://www.mlive.com/news/jackson/index.ssf/
2010/12/jackson_judge_sentences_19-yea.
html
http://www.mlive.com/news/jackson/index.ssf/
2012/06/court_of_appeals_orders_resent.
html
http://www.mlive.com/news/jackson/index.ssf/
2013/02/following_court_of_appeals_dec.html

Delta College (2014)

http://www.mlive.com/news/saginaw/index.ssf/
2015/10/saginaw_man_dies_year_after_as.
html
http://www.mlive.com/news/saginaw/index.ssf/2
016/08/man_pleads_to_manslaughter_in.
html
http://www.mlive.com/news/saginaw/index.ssf/
2016/09/man_gets_15_years_for_beating.html

Grand Rapids Community College (2016)

http://www.mlive.com/news/grand-rapids/
index.ssf/2016/05/woman_stabbed_assaulted_
in_ran.html
http://www.mlive.com/news/grand-rapids/
index.ssf/2016/05/homicide_victim_last_per-
son_wh.html#incart_2box_news_grand-rapids
http://www.mlive.com/news/grand-rapids/index.
ssf/2017/01/teen_accused_of_killing_woman.
html
http://woodtv.com/2017/07/19/guilty-verdict-
in-murder-near-grcc-parking-ramp/
http://www.mlive.com/news/grand-rapids/
index.ssf/2017/08/man_sentenced_for_
killing_home.html

Minnesota (None)

Mississippi

Alcorn State University (2001)

http://www.natchezdemocrat.com/2001/10/09/
asu-student-killed-while-helping-girl/
https://www.seattlepi.com/sports/article/
College-Football-Alcorn-State-player-shot-
to-1068240.php
http://caselaw.findlaw.com/ms-court-of-appeals/
1446377.html

Coahoma Community College (2004)

http://caselaw.findlaw.com/ms-supreme-court/
1523067.html

http://www.pressregister.com/article_1283a5f9–
5122–5e3b-89ec-2887ec009209.html

Holmes Community College (2004)

http://www.ecases.us/case/miss/865444/montrell-
jordan-v-state-of-mississippi

Mississippi State University (2012)

https://www.cnn.com/2012/03/27/justice/missi
ssippi-college-shooting/index.html
http://wreg.com/2012/03/25/fatal-shooting-at-
mississippi-state-university/
http://www.cbsnews.com/news/3rd-suspect-
arrested-in-miss-state-students-shooting-death/
http://www.clarionledger.com/story/news/2015/
03/19/man-accused-in-12-death-of-madison-
msu-student-enters-plea/25015221/
http://www.cdispatch.com/news/article.asp?aid=
40839
http://www.foxnews.com/us/2012/03/26/2-missi
ssippi-college-students-killed-in-separate-shoot
ings-over-weekend.html#ixzz1qCo9dFjD

Delta State University (2015)

http://www.cnn.com/2015/09/14/us/mississippi-
delta-state/
https://www.washingtonpost.com/news/grade-
point/wp/2015/09/15/history-professor-shot-
and-killed-at-delta-state-university-known-as-
mentor/?utm_term=.d3469bdc7d45
https://www.theguardian.com/us-news/2015/
sep/14/campus-shooting-mississippi-delta-state
http://www.clarionledger.com/story/news/2015/
09/14/active-shooter-delta-state-university-
campus/72254712/

Missouri

University of Missouri–Columbia (2005)

http://www.hannibal.net/article/20130131/NEWS/
130139722
http://mizzouweekly.missouri.edu/archive/2013/
34–17/murder-solved/index.php
http://www.stevequayle.com/index.php?s=165
https://mizzoumag.missouri.edu/2013/01/mupd-
solves-professors-murder/
http://www.columbiaheartbeat.com/index.php/
crime/444–0130132
http://www.columbiatribune.com/news/crime/k
iller-identified-in-murder-of-mu-professor/
article_e3048cae-6ade-11e2–98b2–001a4bcf
6878.html

Lester E. Cox Medical Center–School of Medical Technology (2008)

http://crimesceneinvestigations.blogspot.com/2009/10/verdict-watch-jury-deliberating-boldens.html

http://www.odmp.org/officer/19505-officer-monte-ruby

https://www.campussafetymagazine.com/news/missouri-patient-accused-of-murdering-security-officer-charged-with-murder/

https://law.justia.com/cases/missouri/court-of-appeals/2013/wd75563.html

Cox College (2013)

http://www.bransontrilakesnews.com/news_free/article_06cd1c88–5c64–11e3-b5b8–0019bb2963f4.html

https://www.news-leader.com/story/news/2013/12/16/cox-south-hospital-shooting-details-cloudy/1581124/

https://www.news-leader.com/story/news/2013/12/16/cox-south-hospital-shooting-details-cloudy/1581124/

http://www.news-leader.com/story/news/local/ozarks/2014/03/29/report-comes-fatal-shooting-wounding-inside-cox/7068125/

http://bransontrilakesnews.com/news_free/article_1949d354-b9ea-11e3-a479–001a4bcf887a.html

Montana (None)

Nebraska

Creighton University (2014)

http://www.ketv.com/news/teen-very-critical-after-fight-last-week/25956704

http://www.omaha.com/news/metro/two-omaha-teens-charged-in-fatal-fight/article_4e68bc8f-cbbf-5121–9c9d-2013b55e68fa.html

http://www.omaha.com/news/crime/two-omaha-teens-sentenced-to-probation-for-fight-that-fatally/article_b94943ac-0851–11e4-ae9d-0017a43b2370.html

http://www.wowt.com/home/headlines/Sixteen-Year-Old-Boy-Extremely-Critical-After-Assault-259119821.html

http://www.omaha.com/news/crime/two-omaha-teens-sentenced-to-probation-for-fight-that-fatally/article_b94943ac-0851–11e4-ae9d-0017a43b2370.html

Nevada (None)

New Hampshire (None)

New Jersey

Fairleigh Dickinson University, Metropolitan Campus (2002)

https://www.nytimes.com/2002/04/16/nyregion/student-killed-in-dorm-room-her-ex-boyfriend-is-charged.html

https://archive.hudsonreporter.com/2002/04/19/young-love-gone-wrong-former-st-aloysius-hoop-star-charged-with-strangling-jc-ex-girlfriend-2/

http://www.newjerseyhills.com/year-old-pleads-guilty-in-student-s-death-to-serve/article_93ad86b0-fe06–59ef-b36d-281396db65ec.html

http://archive.hudsonreporter.com/2001/01/05/athlete-of-the-week-179/

Gibbs College, New Jersey (2002)

Unconfirmed incident; URL unavailable

Rowan University (2007)

http://www.nj.com/news/index.ssf/2007/10/rowan.html

https://www.nbcphiladelphia.com/news/local/Rowan-University-Donnie-Farrell-Murder-Beating-Death-New-Jersey—336671721.html

http://www.philly.com/philly/news/new_jersey/rowan-student-murder-unsolved-10-years-after-despite-100000-reward-20171030.html

Rutgers University–Newark, New Jersey (2011)

Unconfirmed incident; URL unavailable

Hudson County Community College (2012)

http://www.nj.com/hudson/index.ssf/2012/03/hudson_county_community_colleg_18.html

http://www.nj.com/hudson/index.ssf/2012/03/body_found_in_journal_square_v.html

http://www.wiredjc.com/index.php/topic,6419.msg47220.html?PHPSESSID=dpu08lrshmv-jgo3sg7qsupvgf4#msg47220

http://www.nj.com/jjournal-news/index.ssf/2012/11/jersey_city_men_hit_with_multi.html

http://www.nj.com/hudson/index.ssf/2012/04/accomplice_17_arrested_in_murd.html

http://www.nj.com/jjournal-news/index.ssf/2012/11/jersey_city_men_hit_with_multi.html

http://www.nj.com/hudson/index.ssf/2012/08/man_charged_with_murder_as_17-.html

Table 2. Source Information for Collegiate Homicides   173

New Mexico

Southwestern Indian Polytechnic Institute (2010)

http://www.krqe.com/news/mother-whose-daughter-died-speaks-out-to-prevent-hot-car-deaths/1019688265
https://www.abqjournal.com/news/metro/25233749metro07-25-10.htm
http://www.koat.com/Mother-Charged-In-Death-Of-Child-Left-In-Car/6137938

Eastern New Mexico University–Roswell (2014)

https://www.koat.com/article/man-found-dead-in-enmu-dorm-room-identified/5055745
http://www.rdrnews.com/archive/?p=101340
http://www.washingtontimes.com/news/2014/apr/8/state-police-investigating-death-at-enmu-roswell/

New York

SUNY College at Buffalo (2003)

http://buffalonews.com/2003/03/22/death-of-abandoned-baby-is-a-sad-but-familiar-story/
http://buffalonews.com/2003/10/04/with-guilty-plea-harsh-punishment-for-student-who-killed-newborn/
http://freerepublic.com/focus/f-news/1012868/posts

Cayuga County Community College (2005)

http://auburnpub.com/news/local/cell-phone-fight-ends-in-fatal-stabbing/article_7a51c955-8e92-5c01-8489-58e601f946a3.html
http://auburnpub.com/news/teen-dating-violence-increasing/article_7b1fa789-4e70-5497-b356-2c73fe178290.html
http://article.wn.com/view-travelagents/2005/09/10/Auburn_Teen_Sentenced_for_Girl friends_Murder_z/

New York University (2007)

http://www.nysun.com/new-york/ex-boyfriend-is-charged-in-nyu-murder-case/60171/
https://www.nytimes.com/2010/04/08/nyregion/08nyu.html
http://nypost.com/2010/04/29/tears-and-rage/
http://www.nytimes.com/2010/04/29/nyregion/29nyu.html

http://www.nytimes.com/2010/04/08/nyregion/08nyu.html?action=click&contentCollection=N.Y.%20%2F%20Region&module=RelatedCoverage&region=EndOfArticle&pgtype=article
http://query.nytimes.com/gst/fullpage.html?res=9A04E3D91738F93BA3575BC0A9619C8B63&sec=&spon=&scp=2&sq=Michael%20A.%20Cordero&st=cse

SUNY College of Technology at Delhi (2008)

http://thedailystar.com/local/x546378977/Trial-for-stabbing-in-Delhi-begins/print
http://www.thedailystar.com/archives/plea-made-in-stabbing-trial/article_c2d29b85-208a-57da-943b-08a0fda4dac1.html
http://www.thedailystar.com/news/local_news/stabbed-suny-delhi-student-tyshawn-bierria-dies/article_bacfe0f9-794d-5250-a275-d38f83510473.html
https://cwrite.wordpress.com/2008/05/08/friend-of-murdered-student-tyshawn-bierria-speaks-out-on-black-on-black-violence/

SUNY at Binghamton (2009)

http://www.nytimes.com/2009/12/07/nyregion/07binghamton.html?_r=0
https://en.wikipedia.org/wiki/Richard_T._Antoun

Manhattanville College (2010)

http://www.huffingtonpost.com/2010/02/23/manhattanville-college-mu_n_473023.html
http://www.nytimes.com/2010/02/25/nyregion/25student.html?ref=manhattanvillecollege
https://patch.com/new-york/harrison/stacey-pagli-sentenced-to-20-years-for-daughters-death

University of Rochester (2011)

http://www.rochesterfirst.com/news/latest-headlines/woman-at-heart-of-murder-trial-testifies/192652786
https://www.rochester.edu/pr/Review/V74N1/pdf/0309_yellowjackets.pdf
http://www.rochesterfirst.com/news/u-of-r-report-on-on-campus-deadly-stabbing/194306676
http://www.whec.com/whecimages/repository/cs/files/judge-demarco-ruling.pdf
http://www.rochesterfirst.com/news/latest-headlines/murder-trial-of-daren-venable-winding-down/193790411

http://www.rochester.edu/pr/Review/V73N4/pdf/0802_bordeaux.pdf
http://www.rochester.edu/news/bordeaux/

SUNY College at Brockport (2012)

http://www.cbsnews.com/news/alexandra-kogut-murder-boyfriend-charged-in-beating-death-of-suny-brockport-college-student/
http://www.nydailynews.com/news/crime/alexandra-kogut-boyfriend-admits-beating-death-article-1.1186521
http://www.huffingtonpost.com/news/alexandra-kogut/
http://www.uticaod.com/article/20140515/News/140519492
http://www.democratandchronicle.com/story/news/2014/08/05/whittemore-sentenced-savage-beating-death-gf/13614259/
https://www.mirror.co.uk/news/real-life-stories/i-killed-girlfriend-just-snapped-4975558
http://www.inquisitr.com/2223828/alexander-kogut-clayton-whittemore-dateline-nbc-to-focus-on-dorm-room-college-coed-beating-at-brockton-state-college/

Cornell University (2016)

https://www.cnn.com/2016/08/28/us/cornell-ithaca-college-students-stabbed/index.html
http://cornellsun.com/2016/11/07/ithaca-man-charged-with-murder-of-anthony-nazaire/
https://ithacavoice.com/2016/11/ithaca-man-nagee-green-arraigned-cornell-murder-charge/
http://cornellsun.com/2017/09/28/ithaca-man-found-guilty-for-murder-on-cornells-campus/
http://www.ithacajournal.com/story/news/2017/11/06/freeville-man-convicted-murder-stabbing-sentenced-20-years-prison/835452001/?from=new-cookie
https://ithacavoice.com/2017/09/cornell-homicide-jury-finds-accused-man-guilty-murder-re-trial/

North Carolina

Elizabeth City State University (2001)

http://www.witn.com/home/headlines/6104221.html
http://pilotonline.com/news/local/crime/man-gets-life-in-prison-for-killing-of-elizabeth-city/article_377fae34-217c-558e-9d32-bc11be018715.html

Catawba College (2002)

http://www.ucc.org/shooting-at-catawba-college

http://poststar.com/sports/college/catawba-athletes-killed-in-shooting/article_d963ea94-5b1c-5b04-b2c7-bc50ea074b22.html
http://azdailysun.com/college-football-player-killed-in-shooting-hurt/article_45b0403e-0540-555c-b2ec-d8092f7c3172.html
https://cases.justia.com/north-carolina/court-of-appeals/05-85-5.pdf?ts=1323905087

North Carolina State University at Raleigh (2002)

http://www.dailytarheel.com/article/2002/10/murdersuicide_shocks_n.c._state
http://www.wral.com/news/local/story/103082/
http://www.wral.com/news/local/story/107573/
https://news.google.com/newspapers?nid=1454&dat=20021017&id=nRIzAAAAIBAJ&sjid=sSYEAAAAIBAJ&pg=3045,486040&hl=en

University of North Carolina at Chapel Hill (2004)

http://www.wral.com/news/local/story/114201/
http://www.wral.com/news/local/story/114166/
https://alumni.unc.edu/news/two-dead-in-apparent-murder-suicide/

University of North Carolina at Wilmington (2005)

http://abcnews.go.com/Primetime/storynew?id=1320331
http://www.wral.com/news/local/story/114534/
http://www.wect.com/story/2702314/curtis-dixon-faulkner-not-original-intended-victim
http://www.starnewsonline.com/article/20041209/BREAKING/41209015

Mid-Atlantic Christian University (2010)

http://www.truecrimereport.com/2010/10/jonathan_schipper_murdered_at/
https://www.cbsnews.com/news/jonathan-schipper-murder-nc-bible-college-student-killed-in-dorm/
http://www.13newsnow.com/story/news/2014/09/03/14549988/
http://www.pilotonline.com/news/local/crime/murder-trial-begins-for-n-c-christian-school-student/article_9b7eba0a-3778-5402-b837-d371a0d0fbc0.html
https://www.rockymounttelegram.com/news/ncwire/man-sentenced-life-campus-slaying-2119107
http://www.dailyadvance.com/News/2013/07/23/Amyx-guilty-of-murder-sentenced-to-life.html
http://cases.justia.com/north-carolina/court-of-appeals/2014-14-383.pdf?ts=1420046703

Table 2. Source Information for Collegiate Homicides   175

http://www.wcti12.com/news/911-tape-offers-
new-insight-into-macu-shooting/14770812
http://pilotonline.com/news/local/crime/for
mer-police-officer-guilty-in-fatal-n-c-dorm-
shooting/article_cf356ffa-d877-5c1c-b45f-4d
517103516f.html

Wingate University (2013)

http://www.wxii12.com/news/local-news/north-
carolina/nc-campus-on-lockdown-after-near
by-shooting/23296482
https://usgunviolence.wordpress.com/2013/12/04/
double-murder-killed-juan-carlos-garcia-
wingate-nc/
http://myfox8.com/2013/12/04/wingate-univer
sity-on-lockdown-2-dead-1-injured-in-shoot
ing-near-campus/
https://slammerpics.com/all-mugshots/sheerer-
daniel-steven/
http://www.wcti12.com/news/2-arrested-in-
shooting-near-n-c-university/15128632

Wayne Community College (2015)

http://myfox8.com/2015/04/13/shooting-reported-
at-wayne-county-community-college/
http://www.wral.com/man-wanted-in-wayne-
community-college-shooting-arrested-in-
florida/14584498/
http://abc11.com/news/goldsboro-killing-sus
pect-makes-shocking-allegations-in-court/
657913/
http://www.wral.com/suspect-in-wayne-commu
nity-college-shooting-removed-from-court
room/14587369/
http://goldsborodailynews.com/blog/2015/04/
30/new-court-date-set-for-confessed-killer-
kenneth-stancil/
http://goldsborodailynews.com/blog/2015/07/
23/stancil-gets-new-court-date-after-second-
wayne-district-court-continuance/
http://abc11.com/news/wayne-community-
college-shooter-gets-life-without-parole/
1945600/

**Winston-Salem
State University (2015)**

http://www.wxii12.com/article/student-killed-
student-injured-in-shooting-on-winston-
salem-state-university-campus/2061345
http://www.charlotteobserver.com/news/local/cr
ime/article42133578.html
http://www.nydailynews.com/news/national/
student-arrested-winston-salem-school-
shooting-article-1.2421797
http://www.foxnews.com/us/2015/11/02/ex-stu
dent-charged-with-killing-student-on-win
ston-salem-state-university.html

http://www.journalnow.com/news/crime/argu
ment-over-liquor-cellphone-charger-spurred-
fatal-shooting-of-wssu/article_19e1bf30–
1064–59eb-8299–5f7a2c078a43.html
http://www.twcnews.com/nc/triad/news/2015/
11/4/man-accused-of-killing-wssu-student-
appears-in-court.html

North Dakota

**United Tribes Technical
College (2008)**

http://bismarcktribune.com/news/local/buckley-
wants-trial-in-baby-death/article_dd35c863-
b6db-5ef2–9bed-20c29e28b118.html
http://bismarcktribune.com/news/local/crime-
and-courts/manslaughter-trial-begins/article_
8c005b3e-bd9b-11de-9baa-001cc4c002e0.html
http://bismarcktribune.com/news/local/crime-
and-courts/buckley-gets-years-in-death-of-
daughter/article_f0bbe416–0513–11df-bb20–
001cc4c03286.html
http://bismarcktribune.com/news/local/crime-
and-courts/north-dakota-supreme-court-
upholds-stevie-buckley-s-manslaughter-convic
tion/article_16d66b70–0d52–11e0-ac99–001cc
4c03286.html
http://www.ndcourts.gov/Court/Briefs/201000
33.atb.htm

Ohio

Muskingum University (2002)

http://www.zanesvilletimesrecorder.com/story/
news/local/2015/04/23/dead-baby-found-
muskingum-university/26235529/
https://www.washingtonpost.com/news/morn
ing-mix/wp/2016/06/28/no-more-baby-sor
ority-sister-gets-life-term-for-tossing-new
born-into-trash-to-die/?utm_term=.37e759
ea2ea2
http://www.tulsaworld.com/archives/student-
arrested-in-death-of-newborn/article_60db
35f7–3aa3–5c68–8928-d8e1462d5324.html
http://www.dispatch.com/content/stories/local/
2016/07/10/young-women-who-killed-new
borns-got-very-different-sentences.html

**Case Western Reserve
University (2003)**

http://en.wikipedia.org/wiki/Biswanath_Halder
http://murderpedia.org/male.H/h/halder-
biswanath.htm

Central State University (2003)

https://img.newspapers.com/img/thumbnail/10

3777096/400/400/0_0_3582_6635.jpg?cs=604
800
https://www.ourmidland.com/news/article/
Ohio-Student-Charged-in-Death-of-Friend-
7109353.php

Baldwin-Wallace College (2005)

https://www.news-herald.com/news/man-
facing-murder-charge/article_bc69b5d4-
bef4-5c72-86d6-48162354801d.html
http://www.news-herald.com/article/HR/200
60428/NEWS/304289983
http://www.cleveland19.com/story/2891267/for-
mer-student-sentenced-in-fraternity-broth-
ers-death
http://www.wclt.com/news/wclt/wclt15841.html
http://www.snyderfuneralhomes.com/obituary/
brent-robert-jones/

Ohio University, Main Campus (2009)

http://www.youtube.com/watch?v=9iU73MUg
674
http://blog.cleveland.com/metro/2009/04/
student_hurt_falling_from_4th.html
http://www.thenewscenter.tv/home/headlines/
44017332.html
http://www.athensnews.com/news/campus/
former-ou-student-takes-plea-in-psilocybin-
death-given-days/article_26432fba-bed2-
5078-90b2-55e851529c22.html
http://www.zimbio.com/The+Searched/articles/
970/Eric+Hansen+Ohio+University+student+
falls
http://www.athensnews.com/news/campus/judge-
rejects-ex-student-s-plea-to-exit-jail-early/arti
cle_7b404583-1f0f-5e8d-9f13-87c4fbc8b6c9.
html

Ohio State University, Main Campus (2010)

http://blog.cleveland.com/metro/2010/03/osu_
gunman_dies_after_shooting.html
http://www.dispatch.com/content/stories/local/2
010/03/09/1-killed-in-triple-shooting-on-osu-
campus.html
http://www.cnn.com/2010/CRIME/03/09/ohio.
state.shooting/
http://www.legacy.com/obituaries/dispatch/
obituary.aspx?n=larry-wallington&pid=1406
30105
http://www.dispatch.com/content/stories/local/
2010/03/10/janitors-desperation-turns-deadly
at-osu.html
http://www.10tv.com/article/1-year-after-ohio-
state-shooting-family-moving-forward

http://thelantern.com/2010/03/campus-shoot
ing-supervisors-described-shooter-as-hostile/
http://thelantern.com/2010/03/updated-osu-
janitor-kills-a-supervisor-wounds-another-
then-shoots-and-kills-himself/

University of Toledo (2012)

https://www.toledoblade.com/Police-Fire/2012/
12/21/Fight-on-University-of-Toledo-campus-
ends-with-1-dead-1-seriously-hurt-knife-re
covered.html
http://nbc24.com/news/local/univ-of-toledo-
stresses-fatal-stabbing-was-isolated-incident
http://www.toledoblade.com/Courts/2013/08/14/
Grand-jury-does-not-indict-student-in-fatal-
stabbing-Copy.html

Muskingum University (2015)

http://www.dailymail.co.uk/news/article-3058
387/Dead-infant-Ohio-university-campus-
born-alive.html
http://www.dispatch.com/content/stories/local/
2015/07/23/Mom-charged-in-baby-death.
html
http://www.cantonrep.com/article/20160511/
news/305119988
http://www.dispatch.com/content/stories/local/
2016/05/13/Muskingum-University-baby-
death-trial.html
http://www.dispatch.com/content/stories/local/
2016/06/27/Ex-Muskingum-University-stu
dent-murder-sentence.html

Oklahoma

Spartan College of Aeronautics and Technology (2013)

http://www.fox23.com/news/news/breaking-
news/victim-released-from-hospital-in-spart
an-apt-shoot/nddfM/
http://www.newson6.com/story/21311600/tulsa-
police-search-for-motive-in-shooting-of-
spartan-aeronautics-students
http://www.tulsaworld.com/news/former-spar
tan-student-pleads-guilty-to-murder-in-
shooting-that/article_d5ee3811-2a2b-5c44-b
6bb-111b0cbd74ee.html
http://www.morelaw.com/verdicts/case.asp?s=
OK&d=63861
http://www.tulsaworld.com/news/courts/man-
sentenced-to-life-terms-in-student-shootings/
article_7056e58b-92b8-5aed-9be8-8adc03035
ef3.html

University of Tulsa (2014)

http://www.tulsaworld.com/newshomepage3/
university-of-tulsa-student-charged-with-

Table 2. Source Information for Collegiate Homicides   177

child-abuse-murder-in/article_584888f8–
9f64–518c-9582-d1b90dea0c00.html
http://www.tulsaworld.com/news/crimewatch/
former-tu-student-accused-of-child-abuse-
murder-is-denied/article_1bd18701-e490–
558a-8414-dfec7fa92029.html
http://www.tulsaworld.com/news/courts/trial-
set-for-former-tu-student-charged-with-mur
der-in/article_c94aea0a-c914–5a2b-9af6-a84
15b3c4a50.html

Oregon

University of Portland (2001)

http://www.wweek.com/portland/article-980-
the_murder_at_mehling_hall.html
http://www.catholicsentinel.org/main.asp?Sect
ionID=2&SubSectionID=35&ArticleID=75
55
http://www.portlandmercury.com/portland/
death-a-threat-of-silence/Content?oid=25505
https://groups.google.com/forum/#!topic/alt.
true-crime/b2kxh4O0c_Q
http://www.shouze.com/display-cases.asp?art
ID=13
http://www.oregonlive.com/news/index.ssf/2009/
05/court_rejects_turkish_mans_app.html

Umpqua Community College (2015)

https://en.wikipedia.org/wiki/Umpqua_Comm
unity_College_shooting
https://www.nytimes.com/2015/10/02/us/oregon-
shooting-umpqua-community-college.html?_
r=0
http://www.oregonlive.com/pacific-northwest-
news/index.ssf/2015/10/horror_in_roseburg_
10_minutes.html
https://www.washingtonpost.com/news/morning-
mix/wp/2015/10/02/oregon-shooter-said-to-
have-singled-out-christians-for-killing-in-hor
rific-act-of-cowardice/
http://www.nydailynews.com/news/national/
shooting-oregon-umpqua-community-college-
article-1.2381711

Central Oregon Community College (2016)

http://www.bakercityherald.com/newsroom
stafflist/5471438–151/family-sues-cocc-in-kay
lee-sawyer-murder
https://www.cnn.com/2016/07/27/us/oregon-
murder-carjacking-shooting/index.html
http://www.koin.com/news/missing-persons/
bend-woman-23-vanishes-with-cellphone-
no-car/960392535

http://www.oregonlive.com/pacific-northwest-
news/index.ssf/2016/08/suspect_in_bend_wo
mans_slaying.html
https://www.campussafetymagazine.com/univer
sity/central-oregon-community-college-safety-
officer/

Pennsylvania

Indiana University of Pennsylvania, Main Campus (2001)

http://triblive.com/x/pittsburghtrib/news/region
al/s_61428.html#axzz3w2luINpr
http://triblive.com/x/pittsburghtrib/news/region
al/s_61679.html#axzz3w2luINpr
https://www.gpo.gov/fdsys/pkg/USCOURTS-
pawd-2_07-cv-00465/pdf/USCOURTS-pawd-
2_07-cv-00465–0.pdf
http://old.post-gazette.com/regionstate/200
10618iupstabbingsreg6p6.asp
http://triblive.com/x/pittsburghtrib/news/region
al/s_89874.html

Clarion University of Pennsylvania (2002)

http://www.deseretnews.com/article/944486/Coll
ege-student-charged-with-killing-newborn-
son.html?pg=all
http://old.post-gazette.com/localnews/20030506
clarion0506p5.asp
https://archive.org/stream/CLARION_CALL_
2002–2003_v88/CLARION_CALL_2002–
2003_v88_djvu.txt
http://old.post-gazette.com/localnews/20030
506clarion0506p5.asp
http://www.apnewsarchive.com/2003/College-
Student-Sentenced-for-Baby-Death/id-221def
1456efd9cafe35678c903bd696
https://sites.google.com/a/umail.iu.edu/tau-
beta-sigma-rho-chapter/karen-mako

University of Pennsylvania (2005)

http://www.thecrimson.com/article/2005/1/7/
upenn-student-accused-of-murder-an/
http://www.upenn.edu/gazette/0305/0305gaz11.
html
http://www.thedp.com/article/2006/09/student_
murder_trial_exboyfriend_tells_tale_of_ob
session
http://www.pravdareport.com/news/society/08–
11-2007/100532-love_triangle-0/
http://www.wboc.com/story/8436778/russian-
student-pleads-no-contest-in-love-triangle-
slaying

Drexel University (2006)

http://www.klinespecter.com/sites/www.kline
specter.com/files/Palmer-Case-1.pdf
http://www.klinespecter.com/sites/www.kline
specter.com/files/Palmer-Case-2.pdf
http://www.klinespecter.com/sites/www.kline
specter.com/files/Palmer-Case-3.pdf
https://www.jvra.com/verdict_trak/article.aspx?
id=143256

Mercyhurst College (2007)

http://sports.espn.go.com/ncaa/news/story?id=
3026172
http://www.washingtonpost.com/wp-dyn/con
tent/article/2007/09/18/AR2007091801750.html
http://www.theoaklandpress.com/article/OP/
20081121/NEWS/311219922
http://merciad.mercyhurst.edu/1870/news/former-
mercyhurst-volleyball-player-receives-three-
six-years-prison/

Millersville University
of Pennsylvania (2015)

https://www.millersville.edu/chep/karlie-hall.
php
http://lancasteronline.com/news/local/man-
charged-in-millersville-university-woman-s-
death-to-stand/article_7dcae0f2-dc80-11e4-
bc64-57b645540720.html
http://lancasteronline.com/complete-coverage-
murder-of-millersville-university-freshman-
karlie-hall/collection_a3ca6cf6-5424-11e6-
a725-47902d0623f6.html
http://lancasteronline.com/news/local/police-
describe-bloody-scene-frantic-behavior-in-
millersville-university-dorm/article_449d5
e2c-07e0-11e6-a87c-1b2935ed9080.html
http://lancasteronline.com/news/local/no-
winners-gregorio-orrostieta-found-guilty-of-
rd-degree-murder/article_d8f11f2e-109f-11e6-
9983-6f5008453ff3.html
http://www.dailylocal.com/article/DL/20160727/
NEWS/160729834
http://lancasteronline.com/news/local/family-
of-karlie-hall-files-suit-against-millersville-
university-others/article_5e0d6b92-e339-11
e6-a121-03b6dba03690.html

Rhode Island (None)

South Carolina

South Carolina
State University (2000)

https://thetandd.com/news/info-about-murder-
sought-robbery-suspect-wanted/article_607
16f06-40d9-580c-968b-03547d0ee5be.html
https://www.questia.com/magazine/1g1-71760814/
student-deaths-shake-up-college-campuses
http://thetandd.com/news/opinion/slain-student-
must-not-be-forgotten/article_f792600b-24
d1-5923-9f50-37af7eb455b2.html

Benedict College (2001)

http://diverseeducation.com/article/1178/#
http://caselaw.findlaw.com/sc-court-of-appeals/
1204512.html
http://www.wistv.com/story/686128/charged-
benedict-murder-trigger-man-briefly-in-ny
pd-custody-in-sept
http://www.wistv.com/story/686490/sentencing-
for-2-brothers-found-guilty-of-killing-bene
dict-student

Charleston Southern
University (2005)

http://community.hsbaseballweb.com/topic/char
leston-southern-student-dies-after-beating
http://www.wistv.com/story/5813506/former-
charleston-southern-university-student-pleads-
guilty-in-beating-death
http://usatoday30.usatoday.com/sports/college/
baseball/2005-11-09-pitcher-killed_x.htm
http://www.wral.com/news/local/story/1091226/

South Carolina
State University (2011)

http://www.sled.state.sc.us/CISystem/Images/
NewsPress/SNP0614.pdf
http://www.wistv.com/Global/story.asp?S=144
91962
http://hbcubuzz.com/jonathan-bailey-south-car
olina-state-student-shot-killed-family-asks-
why-buzzkiller/
http://www.wlox.com/story/14494990/sc-state-
students-funeral-set-no-suspects-in-campus-
murder
http://collegefootball.ap.org/article/suspect-
charged-murder-sc-campus-shooting
http://thetandd.com/news/third-arrest-made-
in-fatal-s-c-state-shooting/article_7c79136a-
81d3-11e0-beb8-001cc4c002e0.html
http://wach.com/news/local/sc-teen-gets-35-
years-for-deadly-shooting-on-sc-state-campus?
id=789735
http://www.wyff4.com/article/student-killed-
1-suspect-arrested-in-scsu-shooting/7007254
http://thetandd.com/news/guilty-of-murder-
young-gets-years-in-prison-for-senseless/
article_ce62f4b6-e834-11e1-8c35-001a4bcf
887a.html

Table 2. Source Information for Collegiate Homicides   179

http://thetandd.com/julian-young-convicted-of-murder/image_33d0e2e0-e835–11e1-b722–001a4bcf887a.html

Coastal Carolina University (2013)

http://www.huffingtonpost.com/2013/02/27/coastal-carolina-shooting_n_2770909.html

http://www.myhorrynews.com/news/crime/article_62106c80–5074–11e4-b6b6–0017a43b2370.html

http://www.islandpacket.com/news/state/south-carolina/article33610314.html

http://www.myrtlebeachonline.com/news/local/crime/article16686119.html

http://www.wmbfnews.com/story/21390783/ccu-shooting-latest3

South Carolina State University (2014)

http://www.usatoday.com/story/news/nation/2014/01/24/south-carolina-school-shooting/4831069/

http://www.cnn.com/2014/01/25/us/sc-state-shooting/

http://thetandd.com/news/man-guilty-of-killing-scsu-student/article_49494783-a5a5–54d9–9e15–931a51a3ca6a.html

http://abcnews4.com/archive/police-investigate-shooting-on-sc-state-campus

http://www.thestate.com/news/local/crime/article13941902.html

http://www.espn.com/college-football/story/_/id/10349249/south-carolina-state-bulldogs-player-brandon-robinson-shot-killed-dorm

University of South Carolina Columbia (2015)

http://www.usatoday.com/story/news/nation/2015/02/05/university-of-south-carolina-shooting/22928851/

http://www.thestate.com/news/local/crime/article13947398.html

http://www.cnn.com/2015/02/05/us/south-carolina-shooting/

http://www.foxnews.com/us/2015/02/07/shooting-reported-at-university-south-carolina.html

South Dakota (None)

Tennessee

University of Tennessee (2002)

http://www.utdailybeacon.com/news/article_e10f5443-b242–54a9-a9cf-f346085cd465.html

http://www.advocate.com/news/2003/03/25/virginia-man-pleads-guilty-killing-activist-8126

http://www.glapn.org/sodomylaws/usa/virginia/vanews113.htm

http://www.advocate.com/news/2003/10/21/tennessee-man-who-strangled-gay-activist-back-court-10233

Tennessee State University (2005)

http://www.campussafetymagazine.com/article/delivery-man-shot-killed-at-tennessee-state/public

https://www.courtlistener.com/opinion/1050934/state-of-tennessee-v-ronnie-cortez-akins/

http://www.tsc.state.tn.us/sites/default/files/OPINIONS/tcca/PDF/094/State%20vs%20Ronnie%20Cortez%20Akins.pdf

University of Memphis (2007)

http://www.cnn.com/2007/US/10/01/student.shooting/

http://www.cnn.com/2007/US/10/08/memphis.university.shooting/index.html?eref=time_us

http://espn.go.com/college-football/news/story?id=3055586

http://www.wmcactionnews5.com/story/7191987/new-documents-show-connections-in-bradford-murder?clienttype=printable

http://www.dailyhelmsman.com/archives/trezevant-found-guilty-of-bradford-murder-handed-life-prison-sentence/article_fc4145cd-066e-591c-88b3–11b325a0547e.html

http://www.cbsnews.com/news/devin-jefferson-guilty-of-murdering-u-of-memphis-football-player-taylor-bradford/

http://www.wmcactionnews5.com/story/1393975/bradford-triggerman-convicted-of-first-degree-murder

http://www.tncourts.gov/sites/default/files/trezevantvictoropn.pdf

Tennessee State University (2009)

https://www.timesfreepress.com/news/local/story/2009/dec/11/tennessee-co-worker-slain-tsu-research-assistant-i/246329/

http://www.legacy.com/obituaries/name/nathaniel-adefope-obituary?pid=132918487

https://law.justia.com/cases/tennessee/court-of-criminal-appeals/2015/m2014–01374-cca-r3-pc.html

https://cases.justia.com/tennessee/court-of-criminal-appeals/2015-m2014-01374-cca-r3-pc.pdf?ts=1429132691

Lane College (2012)

https://nixle.com/alert/4911484/
http://privateofficerbreakingnews.blogspot.com/2013/08/jackson-man-pleades-guilty-to-lane.html
http://www.wbbjtv.com/2013/08/09/father-of-murder-victim-speaks-after-sentencing/

Union University (2012)

http://wreg.com/2014/11/03/man-indicted-for-union-university-murder/
https://baptistnews.com/article/former-union-university-student-pleads-guilty-to-murder/#.Wrmiqojwa00
http://www.cardinalandcream.info/tag/olivia-greenlee/
http://www.cardinalandcream.info/2014/senior-music-major-found-dead-outside-luther-hall-today/
http://www.cardinalandcream.info/2014/fiance-arrested-charged-in-connection-with-green-lees-death/
http://www.cardinalandcream.info/2014/new-president-writes-open-letter-to-union-community/
http://www.cardinalandcream.info/2014/pittman-case-send-to-grand-jury-in-october/
http://www.cardinalandcream.info/2014/grand-jury-indicts-pittman-for-first-degree-murder-tampering-with-evidence/
http://www.cardinalandcream.info/2014/charlie-pittman/
http://www.cardinalandcream.info/2015/pittman-pleads-guilty-to-second-degree-murder/
http://www.cardinalandcream.info/2015/pittman-withdraws-guilty-plea/
http://www.cardinalandcream.info/2015/pittman-withdraws-motion-for-new-trial/

Tennessee State University (2015)

http://www.tennessean.com/story/news/crime/2016/08/23/two-people-custody-2015-tsu-campus-shooting/89211076/
https://www.cnn.com/2015/10/24/us/tennessee-state-university-campus-shooting/index.html
https://www.theguardian.com/us-news/2015/oct/23/tennessee-state-university-three-shot-in-nashville
http://fox17.com/news/local/how-tsu-security-measures-have-changed-since-cameron-selmon-murder
https://www.tennessean.com/story/news/crime/2016/08/31/duo-pleads-not-guilty-fatal-tsu-shooting/89648174/

Texas

University of Texas at Austin (2001)

http://articles.latimes.com/2001/nov/16/local/me-4897
http://articles.sun-sentinel.com/2001-11-17/news/0111160885_1_charles-whitman-david-gunby-kidney

Texas Southern University (2004)

http://diverseeducation.com/article/6764/
http://www.houstonpress.com/news/books-bullets-and-guns-6550280
https://www.questia.com/magazine/1G1-156651758/trouble-at-texas-southern-the-campus-murder-of-a
http://www.chron.com/news/houston-texas/article/Man-charged-in-shooting-death-of-TSU-student-1991084.php
http://www.chron.com/news/houston-texas/article/Gunman-found-guilty-in-TSU-slaying-1923087.php
http://cases.justia.com/texas/first-court-of-appeals/01-11-00515-cr.pdf?ts=1396150340

Texas School of Business–East (2007)

http://www.topix.com/forum/blogs/TC4EKE9V9UL5HR8L0

Fortis Institute, Texas (2009)

Unconfirmed incident; URL unavailable

University of Texas Southwestern Medical Center (2013)

http://www.nbcdfw.com/news/local/Police-Identify-UT-Southwestern-Murder-Victim-186149682.html
http://www.dallasnews.com/news/crime/headlines/20130109-dallas-woman-killed-soon-after-police-told-her-they-would-arrest-husband.ece
http://crimeblog.dallasnews.com/2013/01/police-arrest-suspect-name-victim-in-shooting-at-ut-southwestern-parking-garage.html/
http://www.nbcdfw.com/news/local/Husband-Gets-50-Years-For-Killing-Wife-in-UTSW-Parking-Garage-230667041.html
http://dfw.cbslocal.com/2013/11/05/family-50-years-for-killer-life-sentence-for-us/

Texas Christian University (2014)

https://unfinishedlivesblog.com/2014/02/10/gay-

Table 2. Source Information for Collegiate Homicides 181

panic-murder-at-tcu-raises-unanswered-ques
tions/
https://www.tcu360.com/story/19351hidago-char
ged-murder/
http://www.star-telegram.com/news/local/com
munity/fort-worth/article34663581.html
http://www.nbcdfw.com/news/local/Investiga
tion-Continues-Into-TCU-Students-Stewart-
Trese-Death-243721781.html
http://dfw.cbslocal.com/2014/02/06/man-con
fesses-to-killing-tcu-student-claims-self-
defense/

Texas Southern University (2015)

http://www.fox26houston.com/news/31550724-
story
http://www.cnn.com/2015/10/09/us/texas-south
ern-shooting/
http://www.cbsnews.com/news/houston-man-
22-charged-in-texas-southern-university-
shooting/
http://kfoxtv.com/news/local/man-arrested-in-
connection-to-texas-southern-university-
shooting
http://www.click2houston.com/news/man-ac
cused-of-shooting-killing-tsu-student-makes-
first-court-appearance_20151123155631721
http://www.yourconroenews.com/news/article/
State-briefs-Houston-man-charged-with-
murder-in-9502920.php
http://www.chron.com/houston/article/2-
reportedly-shot-near-TSU-6561321.php

**Texas Southern
University (2015)**

https://watchtheyard.com/colleges/shooting-at-
texas-southern-university-leaves-one-injur
ed-and-one-in-critical-condition/
http://www.houstonpress.com/news/texas-south
ern-university-has-seen-four-shootings-in-
six-weeks-7841343
http://www.nbcdfw.com/news/local/Man-Dies-
Shot-in-Dispute-at-Texas-Southern-University-
Parking-Lot-323732171.html
http://www.click2houston.com/news/charges-
upgraded-against-tsu-sophomore-after-shoot
ing-victim-dies

El Centro College (2016)

http://graphics.wsj.com/how-a-gunman-killed-
five-dallas-police-officers/
https://heavy.com/news/2016/07/dallas-police-
shooting-locations-map-timeline-micah-john
son-texas-black-lives-matter-murder-death/
https://commons.wikimedia.org/wiki/File:2016_
shooting_of_Dallas_police_officers_map.
jpg

https://www.dallasnews.com/news/dallas-
ambush/2016/07/11/footsteps-killer
https://www.nbcdfw.com/news/local/Protests-
in-Dallas-Over-Alton-Sterling-Death-38578
4431.html
https://en.wikipedia.org/wiki/2016_shooting_of_
Dallas_police_officers

**University of Texas
at Austin (2016)**

http://www.rafu.com/2016/04/university-of-
texas-student-murdered-suspect-arrested/
https://www.nbcdfw.com/news/local/Body-
Found-on-UT-Campus-Identified-as-Fresh-
man-Theater-Dance-Student-374922691.html
https://www.nbcdfw.com/news/local/Austin-
Police-Take-Over-Probe-of-Body-Found-on-
UT-Campus-374797971.html
https://www.mystatesman.com/interactives/news/
haruka-weiser-murder-timeline/
http://cbsaustin.com/news/local/pre-trial-hear
ing-for-suspect-in-murder-of-ut-student-har
uka-weiser-happening-thursday
http://ktla.com/2016/04/08/suspect-held-in-death-
of-university-of-texas-freshman-haruka-weiser/
http://college.usatoday.com/2016/04/13/murder
ed-ut-austin-student-was-sexually-assaulted-
strangled/
http://kxan.com/2016/06/10/meechaiel-criner-
indicted-for-capital-murder-of-ut-student/
http://www.dailytexanonline.com/2018/02/12/trial-
to-begin-june-9-meechaiel-criner-appears-in-
court-for-status-hearing-in-haruka

Utah

University of Utah (2016)

http://kutv.com/news/local/1-dead-at-shooting-
at-university-of-utah-campus
https://www.cbsnews.com/news/university-of-
utah-murder-suicide-married-couple-shot-
dead-in-in-parking-lot/
https://www.deseretnews.com/article/865670
203/Family-Woman-killed-in-murder-suicide-
at-U-was-targeted-because-she-wanted-
divorce.html

Vermont (None)

Virginia

**Appalachian School
of Law (2002)**

http://en.wikipedia.org/wiki/Appalachian_
School_of_Law_shooting

http://www.nytimes.com/2002/01/17/us/3-slain-at-law-school-student-is-held.html

Norfolk State University (2003)

http://hamptonroads.com/node/216881
http://stthomassource.com/content/news/local-news/2004/03/04/man-charged-st-thomas-students-death
http://pilotonline.com/news/local/crime/man-to-serve-two-life-terms-for-abduction-murder-of/article_99e02104–810b-576a-8713-c6958cbece55.html

Virginia Commonwealth University (2004)

http://www.rapnews.net/0–202-259384–00.html
http://www.styleweekly.com/richmond/vcu-cops-seize-guns-near-campus/Content?oid=1366398
http://www.commonwealthtimes.org/2006/10/02/violent-crime-drops-in-2005/
http://www.richmond.com/news/local/city-of-richmond/article_44ae9502–96dd-5f61-a694–526c8645c40a.html

Virginia Commonwealth University (2005)

http://en.wikipedia.org/wiki/Murder_of_Taylor_Behl
http://www.washingtonpost.com/wp-dyn/content/article/2006/08/09/AR2006080901486.html
http://www.richmond.com/news/virginia/article_3ff69dc9–43ce-577f-86c3-c076357a20f7.html

Virginia Wesleyan College (2006)

http://hamptonroads.com/node/167221
http://hamptonroads.com/node/261491
http://www.pilotonline.com/news/local/crime/years-later-no-justice-for-slain-vwc-security-guard/article_f31ed166-fcc4–5e6d-8e1d-c1451fdf2f03.html
http://pilotonline.com/news/local/crime/security-officer-found-dead-on-virginia-wesleyan-campus/article_bd574d6d-938e-554b-be62–4758426865b4.html
http://crimesolvers.com/crime/walter-zakrzewski
http://pilotonline.com/news/local/crime/police-investigate-leads-in-death-of-wesleyan-security-guard/article_22a7cd13-f500–5e73–98c2–533282669963.html

Norfolk State University (2007)

http://articles.dailypress.com/2007–04-02/news/0704020071_1_williams-norfolk-state-university-stabbed

http://www.pilotonline.com/news/local/crime/friend-says-nsu-stabbing-victim-came-to-his-aid-after/article_b4d48eca-0c1d-53c6-ae69–206238f311a3.html
http://www.pilotonline.com/news/local/crime/case-of-fatal-stabbing-at-nsu-will-go-before-grand/article_75adf43b-bd6f-5bed-9173-f23432e30d4b.html
http://www.pilotonline.com/news/local/crime/suspect-denied-bail-in-nsu-stabbing-death/article_54c3e373-aaca-59e8-b035-c671ecde6cb7.html
http://www.pilotonline.com/news/nsu-student-accused-in-stabbing-freed-on-bond/article_cacaa178-a99d-5be5–8570-fb9f9f46f307.html
http://www.pilotonline.com/news/local/crime/man-pleads-guilty-in-fellow-norfolk-state-student-s-death/article_958b69bb-dc38–58c9–9354-d11017589af9.html
http://articles.dailypress.com/2008–08-06/news/0808050150_1_crime-briefs-two-girls-state-police
http://pilotonline.com/news/local/crime/man-gets-years-for-fatally-stabbing-fellow-nsu-student/article_23be54ac-c478–5433-af10–5a3d9a27a99e.html

Virginia Polytechnic Institute and State University (2007)

https://en.wikipedia.org/wiki/Virginia_Tech_massacre
https://governor.virginia.gov/media/3772/full-report.pdf

Virginia Commonwealth University (2008)

https://groups.google.com/forum/#!topic/alt.true-crime/j3A5Wqdzcx8
http://www.commonwealthtimes.org/2008/03/31/vcu-community-reacts-to-tyler-binsteds-death/
http://www.nbc12.com/story/9361880/life-sentence-for-shooter-in-vcu-student-murder-case?clienttype=printable
http://www.whsv.com/home/headlines/22735129.html
http://www.whsv.com/home/headlines/28053469.html
http://www.breezejmu.org/woman-gets-life-for-murder/article_1187183c-f98e-5315–8182–151c508ef036.html
http://wric.com/2009/01/16/teen-sentenced-in-vcu-students-death/
http://www.richmond.com/news/article_dbca3f81-a8de-5873–8d40–3acad1a936f0.html
http://www.nbc12.com/story/9361880/life-sentence-for-shooter-in-vcu-student-murder-case?clienttype=printable

Liberty University (2009)

http://studentaid.ed.gov/sites/default/files/1194_001.pdf

http://www.newsplex.com/home/headlines/78135977.html

http://www.newsadvance.com/news/local/clues-sought-in-cassandra-morton-s-death/article_5cd59792-8c32-5c35-ab11-924e06468aa1.html

http://wtvr.com/2014/09/30/jesse-matthew-cassandra-morton-investigation/

Virginia Polytechnic Institute and State University (2009)

http://www.foxnews.com/story/2009/01/23/virginia-tech-student-decapitated-with-kitchen-knife-by-attacker-knew.html

http://www.vtnews.vt.edu/articles/2009/01/2009-38.html

http://www.cnn.com/2009/CRIME/12/21/virginia.tech.death/index.html

http://www.nytimes.com/2009/01/23/us/23brfs-KILLINGATVIR_BRF.html?_r=0

http://www.washingtonpost.com/wp-dyn/content/article/2009/01/22/AR2009012200943.html

http://www.roanoke.com/news/tech-knife-murder-nets-life-term-for-haiyang-zhu/article_ea91bb24-89f2-5fdd-9c02-93037200865f.html

http://www.collegiatetimes.com/news/new_river_valley/zhu-sentenced-to-life-in-prison/article_1f28daca-f295-5a1d-8763-b8584d0eac89.html

Virginia Polytechnic Institute and State University (2011)

http://www.nytimes.com/2011/12/09/us/violence-revisits-virginia-tech-after-two-are-killed-in-shooting.html?_r=0

http://www.reuters.com/article/2011/12/10/us-virginiatech-idUSTRE7B71XL20111210

https://www.vtnews.vt.edu/articles/2011/12/120811-unirel-crousememoriam.html

http://www.cnn.com/2011/12/09/justice/virginia-tech-incident/

http://www.legacy.com/Obituaries.asp?Page=LifeStory&PersonId=155013611

Virginia State University (2013)

http://wtvr.com/2013/11/22/arrest-made-in-fatal-shooting-of-vsu-student/

http://www.richmond.com/news/local/crime/fatal-shooting-at-virginia-state-university-off-campus-apartments/article_03ed9216-535b-11e3-b4b6-0019bb30f31a.html

http://www.richmond.com/news/local/crime/vsu-student-shot-at-party-wasn-t-the-intended-victim/article_03ed9216-535b-11e3-b4b6-0019bb30f31a.html

http://www.richmond.com/news/virginia/article_6bb88594-3133-5b2a-b271-3750ed674222.html

http://www.chesterfieldobserver.com/news/2014-08-13/News/Chester_man_pleads_guilty_to_killing_VSU_student.html

http://wtvr.com/2014/08/07/bryan-williams-vsu-murder/

Washington

Pacific Lutheran University (2001)

http://community.seattletimes.nwsource.com/archive/?date=20010518&slug=plu18m

http://www.seattlepi.com/local/article/PLU-shooter-s-suicide-note-released-1055338.php

University of Washington Seattle (2007)

https://www.seattletimes.com/seattle-news/months-of-stalking-end-with-2-dead-at-uw/

https://www.seattlepi.com/local/opinion/article/The-UW-failed-Rebecca-Griego-1236107.php

http://www.radicalwomen.org/rebecca_griego.shtml

http://www.historylink.org/index.cfm?DisplayPage=output.cfm&file_id=10236

http://www.seattletimes.com/seattle-news/uw-killer-was-a-man-of-many-tales-friends-say/

Central Washington University (2013)

http://www.nbcrightnow.com/story/24810713/man-arrested-in-connection-with-july-2013-murder-at-cwu

http://www.dailyrecordnews.com/members/murder-suspect-held-on-m-bail-authorities-believe-death-was/article_9e3685d2-a0ed-11e3-a0dc-0019bb2963f4.html

http://www.khq.com/story/22926149/investigators-collect-evidence-in-cwu-stabbing-investigation

http://www.ci.ellensburg.wa.us/DocumentCenter/View/4337

http://www.khq.com/story/24810713/man-arrested-in-connection-with-july-2013-murder-at-cwu

West Virginia

Shepherd University (2006)

https://ssristories.org/father-kills-his-two-sons-at-college-then-kills-self/

http://www.inthepanhandle.com/paparazzi/

2006/09/shepherd_university_murder_sui.
html

http://www.washingtonpost.com/wp-dyn/con
tent/article/2006/09/02/AR2006090201223.
html

http://www.foxnews.com/story/2006/09/03/3-
dead-in-apparent-murder-suicide-at-w-virgin
ia-university.html

Wisconsin

University of Wisconsin–
Milwaukee (2012)

http://www.wisn.com/article/man-dies-in-uw-
milwaukee-dorm-room-student-arrested/631
2635

http://fox6now.com/2013/08/19/uwm-student-
charged-in-connection-with-heroin-over
dose-death/

http://www.jsonline.com/news/crime/man-gets-
40-yers-for-selling-heroin-tied-to-2-deaths-
b99444466z1–291895881.html

University of Wisconsin–
Green Bay (2015)

http://www.wisn.com/article/fatal-shooting-
reported-near-uw-green-bay-campus/6327107

http://www.greenbaypressgazette.com/story/
news/local/2015/07/15/suspect-custody-mur
der-near-uwgb/30188085/

http://www.nbc15.com/home/headlines/Appar
ent-homicide-victim-identified-in-Green-
Bay-306644551.html

http://fox11online.com/news/local/green-bay/
sims-sentenced-to-life-in-prison-for-torres-
smith-murder

Wyoming

Casper College (2012)

http://usnews.nbcnews.com/_news/2012/11/30/
15574250-bow-and-arrow-type-attack-leaves-
3-dead-in-casper-wyo-including-2-in-college-
classroom-officials-say

http://www.k2tv.com/news.php?id=2385

http://www.nydailynews.com/news/national/
killer-bow-arrow-kill-father-article-1.1211499

Table 3. Mode of Collegiate Homicide   185

Table 3. Mode of Collegiate Homicide
in the United States, 2001–2016

	Institution	Gun	Stabbing	Strangled	Suffocate	Beating	Other
Alabama							
2001	Troy University			X			X
2003	Miles College	X					
2007	University of Alabama						X
2010	University of Alabama at Birmingham				X		
2010	University of Alabama at Huntsville	X					
2011	Southern Union State Community College	X					
2011	University of South Alabama		X				
2012	Gadsden State Community College			X		X	
Alaska (none to report)							
Arizona							
2002	Arizona State University						X
2002	University of Arizona	X					
2007	University of Arizona		X				
2011	University of Arizona	X					
2015	Northern Arizona University	X					
Arkansas							
2008	University of Central Arkansas	X					
2010	Arkansas State University, Main Campus	X					
2012	Arkansas Baptist College	X					
California							
2001	Don Bosco Technical Institute	X					
2001	East Los Angeles College	X					

	Institution	Gun	Stabbing	Strangled	Suffocate	Beating	Other
(California, *cont.*)							
2003	City College of San Francisco	X					
2004	Advance Beauty College						
2006	City of Hope Graduate School of Biological Science	X					
2007	California State University, Monterey Bay		X				
2009	California State University, Sacramento					X	
2009	University of California, Irvine	X					
2010	California State University, Bakersfield	X					
2010	San Diego City College		X				
2010	University of California, San Diego			X			
2011	Coast Career Institute	X					
2011	San Jose State University	X					
2013	Santa Monica College	X					
2013	University of California, Berkeley					X	
2014	Los Angeles Valley College	X					
2015	Life Chiropractic College West					X	
2015	Sacramento City College	X					
2015	Ventura College		X				
2016	Sonoma State University		X				
2016	University of California, Los Angeles	X					
2016	University of California, San Francisco		X				
2016	University of Southern California		X				
Colorado							
2001	Community College of Aurora	X					
2002	Colorado College		X				
Connecticut							
2009	University of Connecticut		X				

Table 3. Mode of Collegiate Homicide   187

	Institution	Gun	Stabbing	Strangled	Suffocate	Beating	Other
(Connecticut, *cont.*)							
2009	Wesleyan University	X					
2009	Yale University			X			
Delaware							
2007	Delaware State University	X					
2011	Wilmington University		X				
Florida							
2002	Broward College	X					
2002	Eckerd College	X					
2003	Daytona State College	X					
2004	Florida Institute of Technology	X					
2004	Santa Fe College		X				
2004	University of Florida		X				
2005	Edward Waters College	X					
2005	Miami Dade College						
2006	University of South Florida, Main Campus	X					
2007	Florida State College at Jacksonville					X	
2009	Northwest Florida State College	X					
2010	Florida International University		X				
Georgia							
2009	Clark Atlanta University	X					
2009	North Georgia Technical College	X					
2012	Valdosta State University				X		
2013	Columbus State University	X					
2013	Georgia Perimeter College			X			
2013	Savannah State University	X					
2015	Clayton State University	X					

	Institution	*Gun*	*Stabbing*	*Strangled*	*Suffocate*	*Beating*	*Other*
(Georgia, *cont.***)**							
2015	Fort Valley State University						X
2015	Savannah State University	X					
Hawaii **(none to report)**							
Idaho							
2003	Boise State University	X					
Illinois							
2002	Illinois Institute of Technology						
2004	Benedictine University	X					
2008	Northern Illinois University	X					
2011	Dominican University	X					
2011	University of Illinois at Chicago	X					
2013	Chicago State University	X					
2015	Illinois Valley Community College	X					X
2016	Illinois Institute of Technology					X	
2016	University of Illinois at Urbana–Champaign				X		
Indiana							
2001	Purdue University, Main Campus		X			X	
2004	Butler University	X					
2008	Indiana University–Purdue University Fort Wayne		X				
2012	Indiana State University	X					
2014	Indiana University–Purdue University Indianapolis	X					
2014	Purdue University, Main Campus	X					
2016	Manchester University				X		
Iowa							
2004	Maharishi University of Management		X				

Table 3. Mode of Collegiate Homicide   189

	Institution	Gun	Stabbing	Strangled	Suffocate	Beating	Other
Kansas							
2013	Kansas State University						X
2015	Wichita State University	X					
Kentucky							
2001	Murray State University					X	X
2003	Western Kentucky University				X		
2011	ITT Technical Institute–Lexington	X					
2013	Hazard Community and Technical College	X					
2013	Lindsey Wilson College						X
Louisiana							
2001	Grambling State University	X					
2002	Southern University and A&M College	X					
2004	University of Louisiana at Lafayette		X				
2006	University of New Orleans			X			
2007	Louisiana State University	X					
2008	Capital Area Technical College–Baton Rouge Campus	X					
Maine							
2008	Mercy Hospital School of Radiologic Technology	X					
Maryland							
2004	University of Maryland, Baltimore County	X					
2005	Stevenson University				X	X	
2010	Johns Hopkins University		X				
2011	Bowie State University		X				
2016	Morgan State University		X				
Massachusetts							
2002	University of Massachusetts Amherst				X		

	Institution	Gun	Stabbing	Strangled	Suffocate	Beating	Other
(Massachusetts, *cont.***)**							
2009	Harvard University	X					
2009	Massachusetts General Hospital Dietetic Internship	X					
2009	MGH Institute of Health Professions	X					
2010	Regis College		X				
2013	Massachusetts Institute of Technology	X					
2013	University of Massachusetts Medical School Worcester				X	X	
Michigan							
2001	Davenport University						
2004	Western Michigan University						X
2005	Lansing Community College			X			
2006	Eastern Michigan University			X			
2009	Henry Ford Community College	X					
2010	Baker College of Jackson						X
2014	Delta College					X	
2016	Grand Rapids Community College		X				
Minnesota (none to report)							
Mississippi							
2001	Alcorn State University	X					
2004	Coahoma Community College	X					
2004	Holmes Community College	X					
2012	Mississippi State University	X					
2015	Delta State University	X					
Missouri							
2005	University of Missouri–Columbia		X				
2008	Lester E. Cox Medical Center–School of Medical Technology					X	

Table 3. Mode of Collegiate Homicide 191

Institution	Gun	Stabbing	Strangled	Suffocate	Beating	Other
Missouri						
2013 Cox College	X					
Montana (none to report)						
Nebraska						
2014 Creighton University					X	
Nevada (none to report)						
New Hampshire (none to report)						
New Jersey						
2002 Fairleigh Dickinson University, Metropolitan Campus			X			
2002 Gibbs College						
2007 Rowan University					X	
2011 Rutgers University–Newark	X					
2012 Hudson County Community College	X					
New Mexico						
2010 Southwestern Indian Polytechnic Institute						X
2014 Eastern New Mexico University–Roswell	X					
New York						
2003 SUNY College at Buffalo				X		
2005 Cayuga County Community College		X				
2007 New York University			X			
2008 SUNY College of Technology at Delhi		X				
2009 SUNY at Binghamton		X				
2010 Manhattanville College			X			
2011 University of Rochester		X				
2012 SUNY College at Brockport					X	
2016 Cornell University		X				

	Institution	*Gun*	*Stabbing*	*Strangled*	*Suffocate*	*Beating*	*Other*
North Carolina							
2001	Elizabeth City State University	X					
2002	Catawba College	X					
2002	North Carolina State University at Raleigh	X					
2004	University of North Carolina at Chapel Hill	X					
2004	University of North Carolina at Wilmington			X		X	
2010	Mid-Atlantic Christian University	X					
2013	Wingate University	X					
2015	Wayne Community College	X					
2015	Winston-Salem State University	X					
North Dakota							
2008	United Tribes Technical College						
Ohio							
2002	Muskingum University				X		
2003	Case Western Reserve University	X					
2003	Central State University					X	
2005	Baldwin-Wallace College					X	
2009	Ohio University, Main Campus						X
2010	Ohio State University, Main Campus	X					
2012	University of Toledo		X				
2015	Muskingum University				X		
Oklahoma							
2013	Spartan College of Aeronautics and Technology	X					
2014	University of Tulsa					X	
Oregon							
2001	University of Portland			X			

Table 3. Mode of Collegiate Homicide 193

	Institution	Gun	Stabbing	Strangled	Suffocate	Beating	Other
(Oregon, *cont.*)							
2015	Umpqua Community College	X					
2016	Central Oregon Community College			X		X	
Pennsylvania							
2001	Indiana University of Pennsylvania, Main Campus		X				
2002	Clarion University of Pennsylvania				X		
2005	University of Pennsylvania					X	
2006	Drexel University	X					
2007	Mercyhurst College				X		
2015	Millersville University of Pennsylvania			X		X	
Rhode Island (none to report)							
South Carolina							
2001	Benedict College	X					
2000	South Carolina State University	X					
2005	Charleston Southern University					X	
2011	South Carolina State University	X					
2013	Coastal Carolina University	X					
2014	South Carolina State University	X					
2015	University of South Carolina Columbia	X					
South Dakota (none to report)							
Tennessee							
2002	University of Tennessee			X			
2005	Tennessee State University	X					
2007	University of Memphis	X					
2009	Tennessee State University		X			X	
2012	Lane College	X					
2014	Union University	X					

	Institution	*Gun*	*Stabbing*	*Strangled*	*Suffocate*	*Beating*	*Other*
(Tennessee, cont.)							
2015	Tennessee State University	X					
Texas							
2001	University of Texas at Austin	X					
2004	Texas Southern University	X					
2007	Texas School of Business–East					X	
2009	Fortis Institute	X					
2013	University of Texas Southwestern Medical Center	X					
2014	Texas Christian University		X				
2015	Texas Southern University	X					
2015	Texas Southern University	X					
2016	El Centro College	X					X
2016	University of Texas at Austin			X			
Utah							
2016	University of Utah	X					
Vermont (none to report)							
Virginia							
2002	Appalachian School of Law	X					
2003	Norfolk State University			X			
2004	Virginia Commonwealth University	X					
2005	Virginia Commonwealth University			X			
2006	Virginia Wesleyan College		X				
2007	Norfolk State University		X				
2007	Virginia Polytechnic Institute and State University	X					
2008	Virginia Commonwealth University	X					X
2009	Liberty University					X	

Table 3. Mode of Collegiate Homicide 195

	Institution	Gun	Stabbing	Strangled	Suffocate	Beating	Other
(Virginia, *cont.***)**							
2009	Virginia Polytechnic Institute and State University		X				
2011	Virginia Polytechnic Institute and State University	X					
2013	Virginia State University	X					
Washington (state)							
2001	Pacific Lutheran University	X					
2007	University of Washington Seattle	X					
2013	Central Washington University		X				
Washington, D.C.							
2001	Gallaudet University		X				
West Virginia							
2006	Shepherd University	X					X
Wisconsin							
2012	University of Wisconsin–Milwaukee						X
2015	University of Wisconsin–Green Bay	X					
Wyoming							
2012	Casper College						X

Table 4. Victims of Collegiate Homicide
On-Campus, 2001–2016

	Institution	M	F	Victim Age(s)	Faculty/Staff/ Student, etc.
Alabama					
2001	Troy University		1	17	Student
2003	Miles College	1		19	Student
2007	University of Alabama	1		21	Student
2010	University of Alabama at Birmingham	1		3	Child
2010	University of Alabama at Huntsville	2	1	52(M), 52(M), 50(F)	Faculty
2011	Southern Union State Community College		1	63	Campus visitor
2011	University of South Alabama	1		19	Campus visitor
2012	Gadsden State Community College		1	32	Staff
Alaska (none to report)					
Arizona					
2002	Arizona State University		1	18	Student
2002	University of Arizona		3	50(F), 44(F), 45(F)	Faculty
2007	University of Arizona		1	18	Student
2011	University of Arizona	1		38	Campus visitor
2015	Northern Arizona University	1		20	Student
Arkansas					
2008	University of Central Arkansas	2		18, 19	Students
2010	Arkansas State University, Main Campus	1		24	Student
2012	Arkansas Baptist College	1		19	Student
California					
2001	Don Bosco Technical Institute	1		54	Unknown
2001	East Los Angeles College	1		20	Student
2003	City College of San Francisco	1		24	Unaffiliated with campus
2004	Advance Beauty College				Unknown

Table 4. Victims of Collegiate Homicide On-Campus 197

	Institution	M	F	Victim Age(s)	Faculty/Staff/ Student, etc.
(California, *cont.*)					
2006	City of Hope Graduate School of Biological Science		1	33	Unaffiliated with campus
2007	California State University, Monterey Bay	1		40	Husband of student
2009	California State University, Sacramento	1		23	Student
2009	University of California, Irvine		1	30	Unaffiliated with campus
2010	California State University, Bakersfield		1	18	Unaffiliated with campus
2010	San Diego City College		1	19	Student
2010	University of California, San Diego		1	38	Unaffiliated with campus
2011	Coast Career Institute	1		44	Instructor
2011	San Jose State University	1	1	26(F), 26(M)	Students
2013	Santa Monica College	4	1	55(M), 24(M), 68(M), 26(F), 68(M)	Student, public
2013	University of California, Berkeley	1		19	Student
2014	Los Angeles Valley College	1		31	Unaffiliated with campus
2015	Life Chiropractic College West	1		42	Unaffiliated with campus
2015	Sacramento City College	1		25	Unaffiliated with campus
2015	Ventura College	1		1	Unaffiliated with campus
2016	Sonoma State University	1		18	Unaffiliated with campus
2016	University of California, Los Angeles	1		39	Faculty
2016	University of California, San Francisco		1	60	Unaffiliated with campus
2016	University of Southern California	1		53	Faculty
Colorado					
2001	Community College of Aurora		1	29	Student

	Institution	M	F	Victim Age(s)	Faculty/Staff/ Student, etc.
(Colorado, *cont.*)					
2002	Colorado College		1	42	Staff
Connecticut					
2009	University of Connecticut	1		20	Student
2009	Wesleyan University		1	21	Student
2009	Yale University		1	24	Student
Delaware					
2007	Delaware State University		1	17	Unaffiliated with campus
2011	Wilmington University	1		47	Unaffiliated with campus
Florida					
2002	Broward College		1	20	Student
2002	Eckerd College		1	44	Staff
2003	Daytona State College		1	29	Student
2004	Florida Institute of Technology	1		62	Staff
2004	Santa Fe College		1	35	Staff
2004	University of Florida	1		24	Student
2005	Edward Waters College	1		18	Student
2005	Miami Dade College				Unknown
2006	University of South Florida, Main Campus	1		57	Student
2007	Florida State College at Jacksonville			30–49	Unaffiliated with campus
2009	Northwest Florida State College	1		38	Unaffiliated with campus
2010	Florida International University	1		22	Student
Georgia					
2009	Clark Atlanta University		1	19	Student
2009	North Georgia Technical College	1		UNK	Unaffiliated with campus
2012	Valdosta State University		1	17	Student

Table 4. Victims of Collegiate Homicide On-Campus   199

		M	*F*	*Victim Age(s)*	*Faculty/Staff/ Student, etc.*
	Institution				
(Georgia, *cont.***)**					
2013	Columbus State University	1		23	Unaffiliated with campus
2013	Georgia Perimeter College	1		23	Unaffiliated with campus
2013	Savannah State University	1		20	Unaffiliated with campus
2015	Clayton State University	1		23	Unaffiliated with campus
2015	Fort Valley State University		1	21	Student
2015	Savannah State University	1		22	Student
Hawaii (none to report)					
Idaho					
2003	Boise State University		1	17	Unaffiliated with campus
Illinois					
2002	Illinois Institute of Technology				Unknown
2004	Benedictine University	1		19	Campus visitor
2008	Northern Illinois University	1	4	20(F), 32(F), 19(F), 20(M), 20(F)	Students
2011	Dominican University		1	29	Unaffiliated with campus
2011	University of Illinois at Chicago		1	48	Staff
2013	Chicago State University	1		17	Unaffiliated with campus
2015	Illinois Valley Community College	1		38	Unaffiliated with campus
2016	Illinois Institute of Technology	1		36	Student
2016	University of Illinois at Urbana–Champaign	1		0	Newborn
Indiana					
2001	Purdue University, Main Campus		2	31, 29	Student, campus visitor

	Institution	M	F	Victim Age(s)	Faculty/Staff/ Student, etc.
(Indiana, *cont.*)					
2004	Butler University	1		31	Staff
2008	Indiana University–Purdue University Fort Wayne		1	22	Student
2012	Indiana State University	1		24	Unaffiliated with campus
2014	Indiana University–Purdue University Indianapolis		1	51	Unaffiliated with campus
2014	Purdue University, Main Campus	1		21	Student
2016	Manchester University	1		0	Newborn
Iowa					
2004	Maharishi University of Management	1		19	Student
Kansas					
2013	Kansas State University	1		18	Student
2015	Wichita State University	1		23	Student
Kentucky					
2001	Murray State University		1	0	Newborn
2003	Western Kentucky University		1	18	Student
2011	ITT Technical Institute–Lexington	1		32	Unaffiliated with campus
2013	Hazard Community and Technical College	1	2	53(M), 20(F), 12(F)	Unaffiliated with campus
2013	Lindsey Wilson College	1		24	Student
Louisiana					
2001	Grambling State University	1		unknown	Student
2002	Southern University and A&M College	1		19	Student
2004	University of Louisiana at Lafayette		1	24	Student
2006	University of New Orleans	1		42	Student
2007	Louisiana State University	2		33, 31	Student, campus visitor
2008	Capital Area Technical College–Baton Rouge Campus		2	26, 21	Student

Table 4. Victims of Collegiate Homicide On-Campus   201

	Institution	M	F	Victim Age(s)	Faculty/Staff/ Student, etc.
Maine					
2008	Mercy Hospital School of Radiologic Technology	1		27	Staff
Maryland					
2004	University of Maryland, Baltimore County		1	27	Student
2005	Stevenson University		1	0	Newborn
2010	Johns Hopkins University	1		23	Student
2011	Bowie State University		1	18	Student
2016	Morgan State University	1		20	Student
Massachusetts					
2002	University of Massachusetts Amherst	1		0	Newborn
2009	Harvard University	1		21	Unaffiliated with campus
2009	Massachusetts General Hospital Dietetic Internship	1		37	Psychiatric patient
2009	MGH Institute of Health Professions	1		37	Psychiatric patient
2010	Regis College	1		18	Unaffiliated with campus
2013	Massachusetts Institute of Technology	1		27	Staff
2013	University of Massachusetts Medical School Worcester	1		31	Psychiatric patient
Michigan					
2001	Davenport University				Unaffiliated with campus
2004	Western Michigan University		1	37	Faculty
2005	Lansing Community College		1	60	Student
2006	Eastern Michigan University		1	22	Student
2009	Henry Ford Community College		1	20	Unaffiliated with campus
2010	Baker College of Jackson	1		24	Unaffiliated with campus

	Institution	M	F	Victim Age(s)	Faculty/Staff/ Student, etc.
(Michigan, *cont.*)					
2014	Delta College	1		61	Unaffiliated with campus
2016	Grand Rapids Community College		1	34	
Minnesota (none to report)					
Mississippi					
2001	Alcorn State University	1		20	Student
2004	Coahoma Community College	1		21	Student
2004	Holmes Community College	1		18	Student
2012	Mississippi State University	1		21	Student
2015	Delta State University	1		39	Faculty
Missouri					
2005	University of Missouri–Columbia	1		72	Faculty
2008	Lester E. Cox Medical Center–School of Medical Technology	1		62	Staff
2013	Cox College	1		79	Patient
Montana (none to report)					
Nebraska					
2014	Creighton University	1		16	Unaffiliated with campus
Nevada (none to report)					
New Hampshire (none to report)					
New Jersey					
2002	Fairleigh Dickinson University, Metropolitan Campus		1	18	Student
2002	Gibbs College				
2007	Rowan University	1		19	Student
2011	Rutgers University–Newark	1		22	Student
2012	Hudson County Community College	1		24	Unaffiliated with campus
New Mexico					
2010	Southwestern Indian Polytechnic Institute	1		2	Child

Table 4. Victims of Collegiate Homicide On-Campus   203

	Institution	M	F	Victim Age(s)	Faculty/Staff/ Student, etc.
(New Mexico, *cont.***)**					
2014	Eastern New Mexico University–Roswell	1		22	Unaffiliated with campus
New York					
2003	SUNY College at Buffalo		1	0	Newborn
2005	Cayuga County Community College		1	17	Student
2007	New York University		1	20	Student
2008	SUNY College of Technology at Delhi	1		22	Student
2009	SUNY at Binghamton	1		77	Faculty
2010	Manhattanville College		1	18	Student
2011 2012	University of Rochester SUNY College at Brockport	1	1	20 18	Student Student
2016	Cornell University	1		19	Unaffiliated with campus
North Carolina					
2001	Elizabeth City State University	1		21	Student
2002	Catawba College	1		21	Student
2002	North Carolina State University at Raleigh		1	31	Student
2004	University of North Carolina at Chapel Hill		1	37	Staff
2004	University of North Carolina at Wilmington		1	18	Student
2010	Mid-Atlantic Christian University	1		25	Student
2013	Wingate University	2		19, 18	Unaffiliated with campus
2015	Wayne Community College	1		44	Staff
2015	Winston-Salem State University	1		19	Student
North Dakota					
2008	United Tribes Technical College		1	0.5	Infant
Ohio					
2002	Muskingum University	1		0	Newborn
2003	Case Western Reserve University	1		30	Student

	Institution	M	F	Victim Age(s)	Faculty/Staff/ Student, etc.
(Ohio, *cont.*)					
2003	Central State University	1		18	Student
2005	Baldwin-Wallace College	1		21	Student
2009	Ohio University, Main Campus	1		20	Student
2010	Ohio State University, Main Campus	1		48	Staff
2012	University of Toledo	1		20	Student
2015	Muskingum University		1	0	Newborn
Oklahoma					
2013	Spartan College of Aeronautics and Technology	1		18	Student
2014	University of Tulsa	1		0	Newborn
Oregon					
2001	University of Portland		1	21	Student
2015	Umpqua Community College	5	4	19(F), 18(M), 59(F), 18(M), 33(M), 67(M), 44(F), 20(M), 18(F)	8 students, 1 faculty
2016	Central Oregon Community College		1	23	Student
Pennsylvania					
2001	Indiana University of Pennsylvania, Main Campus	1		21	Student
2002	Clarion University of Pennsylvania	1		0	Newborn
2005	University of Pennsylvania		1	24	Student
2006	Drexel University	1		18	Staff
2007	Mercyhurst College		1	0	Newborn
2015	Millersville University of Pennsylvania		1	18	Student
Rhode Island (none to report)					
South Carolina					
2001	Benedict College	1		20	Student
2005	Charleston Southern University	1		18	Student
2011	South Carolina State University	1		22	Student

Table 4. Victims of Collegiate Homicide On-Campus   205

	Institution	M	F	Victim Age(s)	Faculty/Staff/ Student, etc.
(South Carolina, *cont.***)**					
2013	Coastal Carolina University	1		19	Student
2014	South Carolina State University	1		20	Student
2015	University of South Carolina Columbia	1		45	Faculty
South Dakota (none to report)					
Tennessee					
2002	University of Tennessee	1		36	Unaffiliated with campus
2005	Tennessee State University	1		37	Unaffiliated with campus
2007	University of Memphis	1		21	Student
2009	Tennessee State University	1		60	Staff
2012	Lane College	1		21	Unaffiliated with campus
2014	Union University		1	21	Student
2015	Tennessee State University	1		19	Unaffiliated with campus
Texas					
2001	University of Texas at Austin	1		58	Student
2004	Texas Southern University		1	20	Student
2007	Texas School of Business–East	1		Unknown	Unaffiliated with campus
2009	Fortis Institute				
2013	University of Texas Southwestern Medical Center		1	40	Staff
2014	Texas Christian University	1		23	Student
2015	Texas Southern University	1		18	Student
2015	Texas Southern University	1		24	Unaffiliated with campus
2016	El Centro College	5		48, 43, 55, 40, 32	Unaffiliated with campus
2016	University of Texas at Austin		1	18	Student

	Institution	M	F	Victim Age(s)	Faculty/Staff/ Student, etc.
Utah					
2016	University of Utah		1	23	Staff
Vermont	**(none to report)**				
Virginia					
2002	Appalachian School of Law	2	1	42(M), 41(M), 33(F)	2 faculty, 1 student
2003	Norfolk State University		1	22	Student
2004	Virginia Commonwealth University	1		21	Student
2005	Virginia Commonwealth University		1	17	Student
2006	Virginia Wesleyan College	1		57	Staff
2007	Norfolk State University	1		18	Student
2007	Virginia Polytechnic Institute and State University	1		20	Student
2007	Virginia Polytechnic Institute and State University	17	14	35, 49, 45, 76, 53, 20, 25, 18, 21, 24, 19, 27, 18, 19, 20, 22, 20, 34, 20, 22, 26, 26, 18, 23, 23, 19, 18, 32, 20, 22, 20	26 Students, 5 faculty
2008	Virginia Commonwealth University	1		19	Student
2009	Liberty University		1	23	Unaffiliated with campus
2009	Virginia Polytechnic Institute and State University		1	22	Student
2011	Virginia Polytechnic Institute and State University	1		39	Staff
2013	Virginia State University	1		22	Student
Washington (state)					
2001	Pacific Lutheran University	1		40	Faculty
2007	University of Washington Seattle		1	26	Staff
2013	Central Washington University	1		23	Unaffiliated with campus
Washington, D.C.					
2001	Gallaudet University	1		19	Student

Table 4. Victims of Collegiate Homicide On-Campus   207

	Institution	M	F	Victim Age(s)	Faculty/Staff/ Student, etc.
West Virginia					
2006	Shepherd University	2		26, 24	Students
Wisconsin					
2012	University of Wisconsin–Milwaukee	1		56	Visitor to campus
2015	University of Wisconsin–Green Bay		1	39	Unaffiliated with campus
Wyoming					
2012	Casper College	1		56	Faculty

Chapter Notes

Chapter 1

1. Anonymous. 2016. Cuyahoga River fire. Ohio History Connection, Ohio History Central, Cleveland State University. Accessed online 28 March 2018. http://www.ohiohistorycentral. org/w/Cuyahoga_River_Fire

2. Earth Day Network. 2016. The history of Earth Day. Accessed online 28 March 2018. http://www.earthday.org/about/the-history-of-earth-day/

3. Kent State 1970. 2016. Online archive and repository of information, source documents, and history of the 1970 student uprising and Ohio National Guard shootings at Kent State University. Accessed online 28 March 2018. https://www.kent.edu/may-4-1970

4. Carson, R. 1962. *Silent Spring.* Boston, MA: Houghton Mifflin.

5. Sexton, J. 2004. The university as sanctuary. Reflections of President John Sexton, New York University (November). Accessed online 28 March 2018. https://www.nyu.edu/about/ leadership-university-administration/office-of-the-president-emeritus/communications/the-university-as-sanctuary.html

6. Lendinara, P. 1991. The world of Anglo-Saxon learning. In E.M. Godden & M. Lapidge (Eds.), *The Cambridge Companion to Old English Literature* (pp. 264–281). Cambridge, UK: Cambridge University Press.

7. Sexton, J. 2004. The university as sanctuary. Reflections of President John Sexton, New York University (November). Accessed online 28 March 2018. https://www.nyu.edu/about/ leadership-university-administration/office-of-the-president-emeritus/communications/the-university-as-sanctuary.html

8. Sexton, J. 2004. The university as sanctuary. Reflections of President John Sexton, New York University (November). Accessed online 28 March 2018. https://www.nyu.edu/about/ leadership-university-administration/office-of-the-president-emeritus/communications/the-university-as-sanctuary.html

Chapter 2

1. Campaign to Keep Guns Off Campus. 2018. Accessed online 28 March 2018. http://keepgunsoffcampus.org/state-battles/; Hurley, D.J. 2015. Countering the push to put guns on campus. *Public Purpose* (Spring), 14–15. Accessed online 28 March 2018. http://www.aascu.org/MAP/ PublicPurpose/2015/Spring/CounteringGuns/

2. Price, J.H., et al. 2014. University presidents' perceptions and practice regarding the carrying of concealed handguns on college campuses. *Journal of American College Health, 62*(7), 461–469; College Presidents for Gun Safety. 2012. Open letter to President Obama. Accessed online 28 March 2018. http://collegepresidentsforgun safety.org/

3. International Association of College Law Enforcement Administrators. 2008. Position statement on concealed carrying of firearms proposals on college campuses. Accessed online 28 March 2018. https://www.okhighered.org/cam pus-safety/resources/CBP-guns-iaclea-statement. pdf; Thompson, A., et al. 2009. Reducing firearm-related violence on college campuses— Police chiefs' perceptions and practices. *Journal of American College Health, 58*(3), 247–254. Accessed online 28 March 2018. https://www. tandfonline.com/doi/pdf/10.1080/07448 480903295367?needAccess=true

4. Bennett, K., Kraft, J., & Grubb, D. 2011. University faculty attitudes toward guns on campus. *Journal of Criminal Justice Education, 23*(3), 336–355. Accessed online 28 March 2018. https:// www.researchgate.net/publication/239790628_ University_Faculty_Attitudes_Toward_Guns_ on_Campus; Thompson, A., et al. 2013. Faculty

perceptions and practices regarding carrying concealed handguns on university campuses. *Journal of Community Health, 38*(2), 366–373; Dahl, P., Bonham, G., Jr., & Reddington, P. 2016. Community college faculty: Attitudes toward guns on campus. *Community College Journal of Research and Practice, 40*(8), 706–717. Accessed online 28 March 2018. https://www.researchgate. net/publication/294874873_Community_ College_Faculty_Attitudes_Toward_Guns_on_ Campus; Price, J.H., et al. 2016. Presidents of historically black colleges and universities perceptions and practices regarding carrying of concealed handguns on their campuses. *College Student Journal, 50*(1), 135–144.

5. Cavanaugh, M.R., et al. 2012. Student attitudes toward concealed handguns on campus at 2 universities. *American Journal of Public Health, 102*(12), 2245–2247. Accessed online 28 March 2018. http://www.hhs.iup.edu/rlct/SAFE806HPf 13/MR%20Cavanaugh%20guns%20student %20attitudes%202012.pdf; Thompson, A., et al. 2013. Student perceptions and practices regarding carrying concealed handguns on university campuses. *Journal of American College Health, 61*(5), 243–253.

6. Grayson, P., & Meilman, P. 2013. Guns and student safety. *Journal of College Student Psychotherapy, 27*(3), 175–176.

7. Hemenway, D., Azrael, D., & Miller, M. 2001. National attitudes concerning gun carrying in the United States. *Injury Prevention, 7*(4), 282–285; Skorton, D., & Altschuler, G. 2013. Do we really need more guns on campus? *Forbes*, 21 February. Accessed online 28 March 2018. http:// www.forbes.com/sites/collegeprose/2013/02/21/ guns-on-campus/#518adeb264c4

8. Hancock, P. 2016. University leaders share personal concerns about guns on campus. *Lawrence Journal-World*, 14 September. Accessed online 28 March 2018. http://www2.ljworld.com/ news/2016/sep/14/university-chiefs-share-personal-concerns-about-pe/

9. Idaho Senate Bill 1254. 2014. Legislature of the State of Idaho, 62nd Session, 2nd Regular Session. Accessed online 28 March 2018. https: //legislature.idaho.gov/wp-content/uploads/ses-sioninfo/2014/legislation/S1254.pdf; Mackey, M. 2014. Why you shouldn't send your child to an Idaho college. *Fiscal Times*, 9 March. Accessed online 28 March 2018. http://www.thefiscal times.com/Articles/2014/03/09/Why-You-Shouldn-t-Send-Your-Child-Idaho-College; Russell, B.Z. 2014. Idaho college leaders oppose guns-on-campus bill, but lawmakers press on anyway. *Idaho Statesman*, 3 February. Accessed online 28 March 2018. http://www.spokesman.

com/stories/2014/feb/03/idaho-college-leaders-oppose-guns-campus-bill-lawm/

10. Zuckerman, S. 2014. Idaho professor accidentally shoots himself in the foot in chemistry class. *Reuters*, 3 September. Accessed online 28 March 2018. http://www.reuters.com/article/us-usa-guncontrol-idaho-idUSKBN0GY2E620140 904; Schwarz, H. 2014. Idaho professor shoots himself in foot two months after state legalizes guns on campuses. *Washington Post*, 5 September. Accessed online 28 March 2018. https://www. washingtonpost.com/blogs/govbeat/wp/2014/09/ 05/idaho-professor-shoots-himself-in-foot-two-months-after-state-legalizes-guns-on-campuses/

11. Benning, T. 2015. Group opposed to "campus carry" says its polling shows most Texans do too. *Dallas Morning News*, 17 March. Accessed online 28 March 2018. http://www.dallas news.com/news/politics/2015/03/17/group-opposed-to-campus-carry-says-its-polling-shows-most-texans-do-too

12. Vertuno, J. 2016. Texas private colleges oppose guns on campus. *Christian Science Monitor*, 21 February. Accessed online 28 March 2018. http://www.csmonitor.com/USA/Society/ 2016/0221/Texas-private-colleges-oppose-guns-on-campus; CBS DFW. 2015. Students & professors sound off on "campus carry" gun bill. 18 March. Accessed online 28 March 2018. http:// dfw.cbslocal.com/2015/03/18/students-profess ors-sound-off-on-campus-carry-gun-bill/; Loyd, R. 2015. Survey: Majority of UTSA students polled oppose guns on campus. KSAT TV, 24 December. Accessed online 28 March 2018. http://www.ksat.com/news/survey-majority-of-utsa-students-polled-oppose-guns-on-campus; McCann, M. 2015. Campus carry pushback heats up: More than 800 UT professors oppose guns on campus. *Austin Chronicle*, 30 October. Accessed online 28 March 2018. http://www. austinchronicle.com/news/2015-10-30/campus-carry-pushback-heats-up/; Goard, A. 2015. Hundreds sign petition opposing campus carry at Texas Tech. *Everything Lubbock*, 19 October. Accessed online 28 March 2018. http://www. everythinglubbock.com/news/kamc-news/ hundreds-sign-petition-opposing-campus-carry-at-texas-tech; Gonzalez, M.C. 2015. UTEP students rally against campus carry law. *El Paso Times*, 19 October. Accessed online 28 March 2018. http://www.elpasotimes.com/story/news/ politics/2015/10/19/utep-students-rally-against-campus-carry-law/74229956/

13. Abadi, M. 2016. An officer who helped end one of the worst school shootings in US history has a problem with Texas' new gun law. *Business Insider*, 1 August. Accessed online 28

March 2018. http://www.businessinsider.com/ramiro-martinez-opposes-texas-campus-carry-law-2016–8; KXAN. 2015. Chief Acevedo stands by statements on campus carry bill. 13 February. Accessed online 28 March 2018. http://kxan.com/2015/02/13/chief-acevedo-stands-by-statements-on-campus-carry-bill/

14. University of California. 2016. Understanding science. University of California Museum of Paleontology, 3 January 2016. Accessed online 28 March 2018. https://undsci.berkeley.edu/

Chapter 3

1. Krouse, W.J. 2012. Gun control legislation. Congressional Research Service Report RL32842, Washington, DC, p. 8. Accessed online 28 March 2018. http://www.fas.org/sgp/crs/misc/RL32842.pdf

2. GunPolicy.org. 2018. United States—Gun facts, figures and the law. School of Public Health at the University of Sydney, Australia. Accessed online 28 March 2018. http://www.gunpolicy.org/firearms/region/united-states

3. World Bank. 2018. Population growth (% annual) for the United States. Accessed online 28 March 2018. http://data.worldbank.org/indicator/SP.POP.GROW?locations=U.S.

4. American Fact Finder. 2018. United States Census Bureau, Population Division, Annual Estimates of the Resident Population: April 1, 2010 to July 1, 2015. Accessed online 28 March 2018. http://factfinder.census.gov/faces/tableservices/jsf/pages/productview.xhtml?src=bkmk

5. Bureau of Alcohol, Tobacco, and Firearms. 2018. Permanent Brady permit chart. Office of Enforcement Programs and Services, Bureau of Alcohol, Tobacco, and Firearms, U.S. Department of Justice. Accessed online 28 March 2018. https://www.atf.gov/rules-and-regulations/permanent-brady-permit-chart

6. Federal Bureau of Investigation. 2016. Online version of the National Instant Criminal Background Check System (NICS) Operations Report for the 2016 calendar year. Accessed online 28 March 2018. https://www.fbi.gov/file-repository/2016-nics-operations-report-final-5-3-2017.pdf

7. Federal Bureau of Investigation. 2016. Online version of the National Instant Criminal Background Check System (NICS) Operations Report for the 2016 calendar year. Accessed online 28 March 2018. https://www.fbi.gov/file-repository/2016-nics-operations-report-final-5-3-2017.pdf

8. Anonymous. 2012. Remarks from the NRA press conference on Sandy Hook school shooting, delivered on Dec. 21, 2012 (Transcript). *Washington Post*, 21 December. Accessed online 28 March 2018. https://www.washingtonpost.com/politics/remarks-from-the-nra-press-conference-on-sandy-hook-school-shooting-delivered-on-dec-21–2012-transcript/2012/12/21/bd1841fe-4b88–11e2-a6a6-aabac85e8036_story.html

9. Federal Bureau of Investigation. 2014. Online version of the National Instant Criminal Background Check System (NICS) Operations Report for the 2014 calendar year. Accessed online 28 March 2018. https://www.fbi.gov/file-repository/2014-nics-ops-report-050115.pdf

10. Bureau of Alcohol, Tobacco, and Firearms. 2015. Report on firearms commerce in the U.S. Accessed online 28 March 2018. https://www.atf.gov/about/docs/report/2015-report-firearms-commerce-us/download

11. Karp, A. 2012. Estimating law enforcement firearms. *Small Arms Survey Research Notes* (24)(December). Accessed online 28 March 2018. http://www.smallarmssurvey.org/fileadmin/docs/H-Research_Notes/SAS-Research-Note-24.pdf

12. Bureau of Alcohol, Tobacco, and Firearms. 2015. Report on firearms commerce in the U.S. Accessed online 28 March 2018. https://www.atf.gov/about/docs/report/2015-report-firearms-commerce-us/download

13. Karp, A. 2007. Completing the count: Civilian firearms. In *Small Arms Survey 2007: Guns and the City* (pp. 38–71). Cambridge, UK: Cambridge University Press. Accessed online 28 March 2018. http://www.smallarmssurvey.org/fileadmin/docs/A-Yearbook/2007/en/full/Small-Arms-Survey-2007-Chapter-02-EN.pdf

14. GunPolicy.org. 2018. United States—Gun facts, figures and the law. School of Public Health at the University of Sydney, Australia. Accessed online 28 March 2018. http://www.gunpolicy.org/firearms/region/united-states

15. Bureau of Alcohol, Tobacco, and Firearms. 2015. Report on firearms commerce in the U.S. Accessed online 28 March 2018. https://www.atf.gov/about/docs/report/2015-report-firearms-commerce-us/download

16. Ingraham, C. 2015. There are now more guns than people in the United States. *Washington Post*, 5 October. Accessed online 28 March 2018. https://www.washingtonpost.com/news/wonk/wp/2015/10/05/guns-in-the-united-states-one-for-every-man-woman-and-child-and-then-some/

17. Steffen, J., & Hernandez, E. 2015. Four dead in Colorado Springs officer-involved shooting. *Denver Post*, 31 October. Accessed on-

line 28 March 2018. http://www.denverpost. com/2015/10/31/four-dead-in-colorado-springs-officer-involved-shooting/

18. Achenbach, J., et al. 2016. Five Dallas police officers were killed by a lone attacker, authorities say. *Washington Post*, 8 July. Accessed online 28 March 2018. https://www.washingtonpost.com/news/morning-mix/wp/2016/07/08/like-a-little-war-snipers-shoot-11-police-officers-during-dallas-protest-march-killing-five/

19. Giffords Law Center to Prevent Gun Violence. 2018. Gun violence statistics. Accessed online 28 March 2018. http://lawcenter.giffords.org/category/gun-studies-statistics/gun-violence-statistics/

20. Mayors Against Illegal Guns. 2013. Analysis of recent mass shootings. Accessed online 28 March 2018. http://libcloud.s3.amazonaws.com/9/56/4/1242/1/analysis-of-recent-mass-shootings.pdf

21. Brady Campaign to Prevent Gun Violence. 2018. Gun death and injury statistics sheet: 3-year average. Accessed online 28 March 2018. http://www.bradycampaign.org/sites/default/files/GunDeathandInjuryStatSheet3YearAverageFI-NAL.pdf

22. Love, J. 2012. Reading fast and slow. *The American Scholar* (Spring). Accessed online 28 March 2018. http://theamericanscholar.org/reading-fast-and-slow/#.UiyX9dKshdI

23. Lennard, N. 2013. Newtown massacre: 155 bullets in five minutes. *Salon*, 28 March. Accessed online 28 March 2018. https://www.salon.com/2013/03/28/newtown_massacre_155_bullets_in_five_minutes/

24. Kirk, C., & Kois, D. 2013. How many people have been killed by guns since Newtown? *Slate*, 16 September. Accessed online 28 March 2018. http://www.slate.com/articles/news_and_politics/crime/2012/12/gun_death_tally_every_american_gun_death_since_newtown_sandy_hook_shooting.html

25. Centers for Disease Control and Prevention. 2018. National Center for Injury and Violence Prevention and Control Web-based Injury Statistics Query and Reporting System (WISQARS). Accessed online 28 March 2018. http://www.cdc.gov/injury/wisqars/index.html

26. Edwards-Levy, A. 2015. 40 percent of Americans know someone who was killed with a gun. *Huffington Post*, 8 October. Accessed online 28 March 2018. http://www.huffingtonpost.com/entry/americans-know-gun-violence-victims_us_56169834e4b0e66ad4c6bd2b

27. Brady Campaign to Prevent Gun Violence. 2018. Gun death and injury statistics sheet: 3-year average. Accessed online 28 March

2018. http://www.bradycampaign.org/sites/default/files/GunDeathandInjuryStatSheet3YearAverageFINAL.pdf

28. Firearm and Injury Center at Penn. 2011. Firearm Injury in the U.S. (Resource Book Online). University of Pennsylvania Health System, Philadelphia, Pennsylvania. Accessed online 28 March 2018. http://www.uphs.upenn.edu/ficap/resourcebook/pdf/monograph.pdf

29. GunPolicy.org. 2018. United States—Gun facts, figures and the law. School of Public Health at the University of Sydney, Australia. Accessed online 28 March 2018. http://www.gunpolicy.org/firearms/region/united-states

30. GunPolicy.org. 2018. United States—Gun facts, figures and the law. School of Public Health at the University of Sydney, Australia. Accessed online 28 March 2018. http://www.gunpolicy.org/firearms/region/united-states

31. Gun Violence Archive. 2018. Accessed online 28 March 2018. http://www.gunviolencearchive.org/

32. Centers for Disease Control and Prevention. 2018. National Center for Injury and Violence Prevention and Control Web-based Injury Statistics Query and Reporting System (WISQARS). Accessed online 28 March 2018. http://www.cdc.gov/injury/wisqars/index.html

33. GunPolicy.org. 2018. United States—Gun facts, figures and the law. School of Public Health at the University of Sydney, Australia. Accessed online 28 March 2018. http://www.gunpolicy.org/firearms/region/united-states

34. GunPolicy.org. 2018. United States—Gun facts, figures and the law. School of Public Health at the University of Sydney, Australia. Accessed online 28 March 2018. http://www.gunpolicy.org/firearms/region/united-states

35. GunPolicy.org. 2018. United States—Gun facts, figures and the law. School of Public Health at the University of Sydney, Australia. Accessed online 28 March 2018. http://www.gunpolicy.org/firearms/region/united-states

36. Anonymous. 2013. Gun violence: A public health issue. *Harvard Magazine*, 9 January. Accessed online 28 March 2018. http://harvardmagazine.com/2013/01/gun-violence-and-public-health; Mozaffarian, D., Hemenway, D., & Ludwig, D.S. 2013. Curbing gun violence: Lessons from public health successes. *Journal of the American Medical Association, 309*(6), 551–552.

37. Centers for Disease Control and Prevention. 2018. National Center for Injury and Violence Prevention and Control Web-based Injury Statistics Query and Reporting System (WISQARS). Accessed online 28 March 2018. http://www.cdc.gov/injury/wisqars/index.html

38. Anonymous. 1997. Rates of homicide, suicide, and firearm-related death among children—26 industrialized countries. *Centers for Disease Control and Prevention Morbidity and Mortality Weekly Report, 46*(5)(7 February), 101–105. Accessed online 28 March 2018. http://www.cdc.gov/mmwr/preview/mmwrhtml/00046149.htm

39. Anonymous. 2012. Protect children not guns 2012. Children's Defense Fund online report. Accessed online 28 March 2018. https://www.childrensdefense.org/wp-content/uploads/2018/08/protect-children-not-guns-2012.pdf

40. Centers for Disease Control and Prevention. 2018. National Center for Injury and Violence Prevention and Control Web-based Injury Statistics Query and Reporting System (WISQARS). Accessed online 28 March 2018. http://www.cdc.gov/injury/wisqars/index.html

41. Centers for Disease Control and Prevention. 2018. National Center for Injury and Violence Prevention and Control Web-based Injury Statistics Query and Reporting System (WISQARS). Accessed online 28 March 2018. http://www.cdc.gov/injury/wisqars/index.html

42. Centers for Disease Control and Prevention. 2018. National Center for Injury and Violence Prevention and Control Web-based Injury Statistics Query and Reporting System (WISQARS). Accessed online 28 March 2018. http://www.cdc.gov/injury/wisqars/index.html

43. Centers for Disease Control and Prevention. 2018. National Center for Injury and Violence Prevention and Control Web-based Injury Statistics Query and Reporting System (WISQARS). Accessed online 28 March 2018. http://www.cdc.gov/injury/wisqars/index.html

44. Centers for Disease Control and Prevention. 2018. National Center for Injury and Violence Prevention and Control Web-based Injury Statistics Query and Reporting System (WISQARS). Accessed online 28 March 2018. http://www.cdc.gov/injury/wisqars/index.html

45. Krug, E.G., et al. (Eds.). 2002. World report on violence and health. Geneva, World Health Organization. Accessed online 28 March 2018. http://www.who.int/violence_injury_prevention/violence/world_report/en/full_en.pdf

46. Hemenway, D., & Miller, M. 2000. Firearm availability and homicide rates across 26 high income countries. *Journal of Trauma, 49*, 985–88.

47. Centers for Disease Control and Prevention. 2018. National Center for Injury and Violence Prevention and Control Web-based Injury Statistics Query and Reporting System (WISQARS). Accessed online 28 March 2018. http://www.cdc.gov/injury/wisqars/index.html

48. Centers for Disease Control and Prevention. 2018. National Center for Injury and Violence Prevention and Control Web-based Injury Statistics Query and Reporting System (WISQARS). Accessed online 28 March 2018. http://www.cdc.gov/injury/wisqars/index.html

49. Centers for Disease Control and Prevention. 2018. National Center for Injury and Violence Prevention and Control Web-based Injury Statistics Query and Reporting System (WISQARS). Accessed online 28 March 2018. http://www.cdc.gov/injury/wisqars/index.html

50. Centers for Disease Control and Prevention. 2018. National Center for Injury and Violence Prevention and Control Web-based Injury Statistics Query and Reporting System (WISQARS). Accessed online 28 March 2018. http://www.cdc.gov/injury/wisqars/index.html

51. Centers for Disease Control and Prevention. 2018. National Center for Injury and Violence Prevention and Control Web-based Injury Statistics Query and Reporting System (WISQARS). Accessed online 28 March 2018. http://www.cdc.gov/injury/wisqars/index.html

52. Centers for Disease Control and Prevention. 2018. National Center for Injury and Violence Prevention and Control Web-based Injury Statistics Query and Reporting System (WISQARS). Accessed online 28 March 2018. http://www.cdc.gov/injury/wisqars/index.html

53. Green, M.S., et al. 2002. When is an epidemic an epidemic? *Israeli Medical Association Journal, 4*, 3–6.

54. Centers for Disease Control and Prevention. 2018. National Center for Injury and Violence Prevention and Control Web-based Injury Statistics Query and Reporting System (WISQARS). Accessed online 28 March 2018. http://www.cdc.gov/injury/wisqars/index.html

55. Centers for Disease Control and Prevention. 2018. National Center for Injury and Violence Prevention and Control Web-based Injury Statistics Query and Reporting System (WISQARS). Accessed online 28 March 2018. http://www.cdc.gov/injury/wisqars/index.html

56. Miller, T.R. 2013. The cost of gun violence. Children's Safety Network, National Injury and Violence Prevention Resource Center. Accessed online 28 March 2018. https://www.childrenssafetynetwork.org/sites/childrenssafetynetwork.org/files/TheCostofGunViolence.pdf

57. Miller, T.R. 2013. The cost of gun violence. Children's Safety Network, National Injury and Violence Prevention Resource Center. Accessed online 28 March 2018. https://www.childrenssafetynetwork.org/sites/childrenssafetynetwork.org/files/TheCostofGunViolence.pdf

58. Belasco, A. 2011. The cost of Iraq,

Afghanistan, and other Global War on Terror operations since 9/11. Congressional Research Service Report for Congress, RL33110, Washington, DC.

59. Klapper, E., et al. 2010. 2010 budget blueprint: Agency by agency. *Washington Post.* Accessed online 28 March 2018. http://www.washingtonpost.com/wp-srv/politics/budget2010/agency_by_agency.html

60. Violence Policy Center. 2011. A shrinking minority: The continuing decline of gun ownership in America. Accessed online 28 March 2018. http://www.vpc.org/studies/ownership.pdf; Anonymous. 2018. Gun ownership in the United States. Statistic Brain Research Institute. Accessed online 28 March 2018. http://www.statisticbrain.com/gun-ownership-statistics-demographics/; Desilver, D. 2013. A minority of Americans own guns, but just how many is unclear. Pew Research Center, 4 June. Accessed online 28 March 2018. http://www.pewresearch.org/fact-tank/2013/06/04/a-minority-of-americans-own-guns-but-just-how-many-is-unclear/; Dimock, M., Doherty, C., & Christian, L. 2013. Perspectives of gun owners, nonowners: Why own a gun? Protection is now top reason. Pew Research Center, 12 March. Accessed online 28 March 2018. http://www.people-press.org/files/legacy-pdf/03-12-13%20Gun%20Ownership%20Release.pdf

61. Hepburn, L., et al. 2007. The U.S. gun stock: Results from the 2004 national firearms survey. *Injury Prevention, 13*, 15–19. Accessed online 28 March 2018. http://www.ncbi.nlm.nih.gov/pmc/articles/PMC2610545/

62. Hepburn, L., et al. 2007. The U.S. gun stock: Results from the 2004 national firearms survey. *Injury Prevention, 13*, 15–19. Accessed online 28 March 2018. http://www.ncbi.nlm.nih.gov/pmc/articles/PMC2610545/

63. Dempsey, C., & Chaniewski, A. 2013. Man who had stockpile of guns, ammo and explosives is arrested, Fairfield police say. *Hartford Courant*, 7 October. Accessed online 28 March 2018. http://www.courant.com/community/fairfield/hc-fairfield-haz-mat-1003-20131002,0,5408331.story

64. Urban Institute. 2018. Accessed online 28 March 2018. http://www.urban.org/

65. Howell, E.M., & Abraham, P. 2013. The hospital costs of firearm assaults. Urban Institute (September). Accessed online 28 March 2018. https://www.urban.org/sites/default/files/publication/23956/412894-The-Hospital-Costs-of-Firearm-Assaults.PDF

66. Howell, E.M., & Abraham, P. 2013. The hospital costs of firearm assaults. Urban Institute (September). Accessed online 28 March 2018. https://www.urban.org/sites/default/files/publication/23956/412894-The-Hospital-Costs-of-Firearm-Assaults.PDF

67. Lichtblau, E., & Motoka, R. 2012. N.R.A. envisions "a good guy with a gun" in every school. *New York Times*, 21 December. Accessed online 28 March 2018. http://www.nytimes.com/2012/12/22/us/nra-calls-for-armed-guards-at-schools.html?pagewanted=all&_r=0

68. Johnson, M.A. 2012. Maryland man found with dozens of weapons, says he's the Joker. NBC News, 27 July. Accessed online 28 March 2018. http://usnews.nbcnews.com/_news/2012/07/27/12993058-maryland-man-found-with-dozens-of-weapons-says-hes-the-joker?lite; Jones, R. 2013. Sacramento tattoo shop owner arrested for assault weapons possession. CBS Sacramento, 27 June. Accessed online 28 March 2018. http://sacramento.cbslocal.com/2013/06/27/convicted-felon-busted-for-possessing-assault-weapons-thousands-of-ammunition-rounds/; Anonymous. 2013. Prosecutor: Man arrested at Kings Island had 4,000 rounds of ammo in truck. WLWT.com, 11 July. Accessed online 28 March 2018. http://www.wlwt.com/article/prosecutor-man-arrested-at-kings-island-had-4-000-rounds-of-ammo-in-truck/3533202; Caniglia, J. 2013. Conviction of Toledo man for stockpiling weapons began with the tracking of camisoles. *Plain Dealer*, 1 September. Accessed online 28 March 2018. http://www.cleveland.com/metro/index.ssf/2013/09/from_camisoles_to_ammunition_a.html; Wohltmann, G. 2013. Father of driver in cyclist death arrested. *Pleasanton Weekly*, 19 July. Accessed online 28 March 2018. https://pleasantonweekly.com/print/story/2013/07/19/father-of-driver-in-cyclist-death-arrested; KAIT Web Staff. 2013. Brothers indicted for having multiple firearms and ammo. KAIT TV (Jonesboro, AR), 12 September. Accessed online 28 March 2018. http://www.kait8.com/story/23294709/brothers-indicted-for-having-multiple-firearms-and-ammo; CBS News. 2009. Man with weapons, ammo arrested near UCLA. 11 February. Accessed online 28 March 2018. http://www.cbsnews.com/2100-201_162-4406019.html; Tennant, P. 2009. Police: Man said 30,000 bullets were for target practice. *Eagle-Tribune*, 16 May. Accessed online 28 March 2018. http://www.eagletribune.com/haverhill/x1650955490/Police-Man-said-30-000-bullets-were-for-target-practice

69. Bergin, B. 2012. How much is 6,000 rounds? Not much, gun advocates say. WNYC, 23 July. Accessed online 28 March 2018. http://www.wnyc.org/story/224666-how-much-6000-rounds/

70. Block, M. 2013. Gun metaphors deeply embedded in English language. National Public Radio, 19 March. Accessed online 28 March 2018. http://www.npr.org/2013/03/19/174767346/gun-metaphors-deeply-embedded-in-english-language); Baker, P. 2013. In gun debate, even language can be loaded. *New York Times,* 15 January. Accessed online 28 March 2018. http://www.nytimes.com/2013/01/16/us/gun-imagery-fills-language-of-debate.html?_r=0

71. ABC News. 2012. Guns in America: A statistical look. 25 August. Accessed online 28 March 2018. http://abcnews.go.com/blogs/headlines/2012/08/guns-in-america-a-statistical-look/

72. Food Marketing Institute. 2012. Supermarket facts—Industry overview 2011–2012. Accessed online 28 March 2018. http://www.fmi.org/research-resources/supermarket-facts

73. Chalabi, M., & Burn-Murdoch, J. 2013. McDonald's 34,492 restaurants: Where are they? *The Guardian,* 17 July. Accessed online 28 March 2018. http://www.theguardian.com/news/datablog/2013/jul/17/mcdonalds-restaurants-where-are-they#data; Chalabi, M., & Burn-Murdoch, J. 2013. McMap of the world, 2013 (map and spreadsheet showing locations of McDonald's fast food restaurants worldwide). Accessed online 28 March 2018. https://docs.google.com/spreadsheet/ccc?key=0At6CC4x_yBnMdG5NcUZTNkkxN2dBRHQzWFVJbHZHMFE#gid=0

Chapter 4

1. Robert A. and Virginia Heinlein Archives. 2016. Opus 29: Beyond this horizon. Accessed online 28 March 2018. http://www.heinleinarchives.net/upload/index.php?_a=viewProd&productId=31

2. Associated Press. 1987. Ex-Lehigh student sentenced to electric chair for murder. *New York Times,* 30 April. Accessed online 28 March 2018. http://www.nytimes.com/1987/04/30/us/ex-lehigh-student-sentenced-to-electric-chair-for-murder.html

3. Brayden, T. 2002. Henry trades appeal rights for life in prison for 1986 rape, murder of Lehigh student. Northampton County judge OKs deal. Death sentence was thrown out in May. *The Morning Call,* 31 August. Accessed online 28 March 2018. http://articles.mcall.com/2002-08-31/news/3417898_1_death-sentence-death-penalty-appeal-rights

4. O'Dell, R., & Ryman, A. 2016. "It means her life was not in vain": The tragedy that gave birth to the Clery Act. *Arizona Republic,* 25 April. Accessed online 28 March 2018. http://www.azcentral.com/story/news/local/arizona-investigations/2016/04/15/tragedy-that-gave-birth-to-clery-act/82811052/

5. Associated Press. 1984. Student at Tulane U. killed. *New York Times,* 5 October. Accessed online 28 March 2018. http://www.nytimes.com/1984/10/05/us/student-at-tulane-u-killed.html

6. Minkin, W. 1985. Westchester opinion: When a daughter is murdered. *New York Times,* 10 March. Accessed online 28 March 2018. http://www.nytimes.com/1985/03/10/nyregion/westchester-opinion-when-a-daughter-is-murdered.html

7. Pennsylvania General Assembly. 1988. College and University Security Information Act, Act 73, 26 May. Accessed online 28 March 2018. http://www.legis.state.pa.us/cfdocs/legis/li/uconsCheck.cfm?yr=1988&sessInd=0&act=73

8. U.S. Public Law 101–542. Accessed online 28 March 2018. https://www.cbc.edu/sites/www/Uploads/STUDENT%20RIGHT%20TO%20KNOW%20ACT%20-%20STATUTE-104-Pg2381.pdf

9. U.S. Public Law 101–542. Accessed online 28 March 2018. https://www.cbc.edu/sites/www/Uploads/STUDENT%20RIGHT%20TO%20KNOW%20ACT%20-%20STATUTE-104-Pg2381.pdf

10. U.S. Department of Justice. 2016. Overview of Title IX of the Education Amendments of 1972, 20 U.S.C. A§ 1681 ET. SEQ. 1972. Accessed online 28 March 2018. https://www.justice.gov/crt/overview-title-ix-education-amendments-1972-20-usc-1681-et-seq

11. U.S. Government Publishing Office. 2016. The Family Educational Rights and Privacy Act. Accessed online 28 March 2018. http://www.ecfr.gov/cgi-bin/text-idx?tpl=/ecfrbrowse/Title34/34cfr99_main_02.tpl; Legal Information Institute. 2016. 20 U.S. Code § 1232g—Family educational and privacy rights. Cornell University Law School. Accessed online 28 March 2018. https://www.law.cornell.edu/uscode/text/20/1232g

12. Legal Information Institute. 2016. 42 U.S. Code Subchapter III—Violence against women. Cornell University Law School. Accessed online 28 March 2018. https://www.law.cornell.edu/uscode/text/42/chapter-136/subchapter-III

13. U.S. Department of Education, Office of Postsecondary Education. 2016. *The Handbook for Campus Safety and Security Reporting* (2016 Edition). Washington, DC. Accessed online 28 March 2018. https://www2.ed.gov/admins/lead/safety/handbook.pdf

14. U.S. Department of Education, Office of Postsecondary Education. 2016. *The Handbook for Campus Safety and Security Reporting* (2016 Edition). Washington, DC. Accessed online 28 March 2018. https://www2.ed.gov/admins/lead/safety/handbook.pdf

15. Federal Register. 2014. Violence Against Women Act: A Rule by the Education Department on 10/20/2014. Accessed online 28 March 2018. https://www.federalregister.gov/documents/2014/10/20/2014-24284/violence-against-women-act

16. U.S. Department of Education, Office of Postsecondary Education. 2016. *The Handbook for Campus Safety and Security Reporting* (2016 Edition). Washington, DC. Accessed online 28 March 2018. https://www2.ed.gov/admins/lead/safety/handbook.pdf

17. U.S. Department of Education, Office of Postsecondary Education. 2016. *The Handbook for Campus Safety and Security Reporting* (2016 Edition). Washington, DC. Accessed online 28 March 2018. https://www2.ed.gov/admins/lead/safety/handbook.pdf

18. U.S. Department of Education, Office of Postsecondary Education. 2016. *The Handbook for Campus Safety and Security Reporting* (2016 Edition). Washington, DC. Accessed online 28 March 2018. https://www2.ed.gov/admins/lead/safety/handbook.pdf

19. U.S. Department of Education, Office of Postsecondary Education. 2016. *The Handbook for Campus Safety and Security Reporting* (2016 Edition). Washington, DC. Accessed online 28 March 2018. https://www2.ed.gov/admins/lead/safety/handbook.pdf

20. U.S. Department of Education, Office of Postsecondary Education. 2016. *The Handbook for Campus Safety and Security Reporting* (2016 Edition). Washington, DC. Accessed online 28 March 2018. https://www2.ed.gov/admins/lead/safety/handbook.pdf

21. National Paralegal College. 2016. Criminal law definitions. Accessed online 28 March 2018. http://nationalparalegal.edu/public_documents/courseware_asp_files/criminalLaw/otherAgainsPersons/Mayhem.asp; Criminal Defense Lawyer. 2016. The crime of mayhem. Accessed online 28 March 2018. http://www.criminaldefenselawyer.com/resources/the-crime-mayhem.htm; Legal Information Institute. 2016. Mayhem. *Wex free legal dictionary and encyclopedia.* Cornell University Law School, Ithaca, New York. Accessed online 28 March 2018. https://www.law.cornell.edu/wex/mayhem

22. Binkley, C., et al. 2014. Reports on college crime are deceptively inaccurate. *Columbus Dispatch*, 30 September. Accessed online 28 March 2018. http://www.dispatch.com/content/stories/local/2014/09/30/campus-insecurity.html; Guffey, J.E. 2013. Crime on campus: Can Clery Act data from universities and colleges be trusted? *ASBBS eJournal, 9*(1), 51–61. Accessed online 28 March 2018. http://0-search.proquest.com.library.uark.edu/docview/1448005586?accountid=8361

23. U.S. Department of Education, Office of Postsecondary Education. 2016. *The Handbook for Campus Safety and Security Reporting* (2016 Edition). Washington, DC. Accessed online 28 March 2018. https://www2.ed.gov/admins/lead/safety/handbook.pdf

24. U.S. Department of Education, Office of Postsecondary Education. 2016. *The Handbook for Campus Safety and Security Reporting* (2016 Edition). Washington, DC. Accessed online 28 March 2018. https://www2.ed.gov/admins/lead/safety/handbook.pdf

25. U.S. Department of Education, Office of Postsecondary Education. 2016. *The Handbook for Campus Safety and Security Reporting* (2016 Edition). Washington, DC. Accessed online 28 March 2018. https://www2.ed.gov/admins/lead/safety/handbook.pdf

26. U.S. Department of Education, Office of Postsecondary Education. 2016. *The Handbook for Campus Safety and Security Reporting* (2016 Edition). Washington, DC. Accessed online 28 March 2018. https://www2.ed.gov/admins/lead/safety/handbook.pdf

27. U.S. Department of Education, Office of Postsecondary Education. 2016. *The Handbook for Campus Safety and Security Reporting* (2016 Edition). Washington, DC. Accessed online 28 March 2018. https://www2.ed.gov/admins/lead/safety/handbook.pdf

28. U.S. Department of Education, Office of Postsecondary Education. 2016. *The Handbook for Campus Safety and Security Reporting* (2016 Edition). Washington, DC. Accessed online 28 March 2018. https://www2.ed.gov/admins/lead/safety/handbook.pdf

29. U.S. Department of Education, Office of Postsecondary Education. 2016. *The Handbook for Campus Safety and Security Reporting* (2016 Edition). Washington, DC. Accessed online 28 March 2018. https://www2.ed.gov/admins/lead/safety/handbook.pdf

30. U.S. Department of Education, Office of Postsecondary Education. 2016. *The Handbook for Campus Safety and Security Reporting* (2016 Edition). Washington, DC. Accessed online 28 March 2018. https://www2.ed.gov/admins/lead/safety/handbook.pdf

31. U.S. Department of Education, Office of Postsecondary Education. 2016. *The Handbook for Campus Safety and Security Reporting* (2016 Edition). Washington, DC. Accessed online 28 March 2018. https://www2.ed.gov/admins/lead/safety/handbook.pdf

32. U.S. Department of Education, Office of Postsecondary Education. 2016. *The Handbook for Campus Safety and Security Reporting* (2016 Edition). Washington, DC. Accessed online 28 March 2018. https://www2.ed.gov/admins/lead/safety/handbook.pdf

33. U.S. Department of Education, Office of Postsecondary Education. 2016. *The Handbook for Campus Safety and Security Reporting* (2016 Edition). Washington, DC. Accessed online 28 March 2018. https://www2.ed.gov/admins/lead/safety/handbook.pdf

34. U.S. Department of Education, Office of Postsecondary Education. 2016. *The Handbook for Campus Safety and Security Reporting* (2016 Edition). Washington, DC. Accessed online 28 March 2018. https://www2.ed.gov/admins/lead/safety/handbook.pdf

35. U.S. Department of Education, Office of Postsecondary Education. 2016. *The Handbook for Campus Safety and Security Reporting* (2016 Edition). Washington, DC. Accessed online 28 March 2018. https://www2.ed.gov/admins/lead/safety/handbook.pdf

36. U.S. Department of Education, Office of Postsecondary Education. 2016. *The Handbook for Campus Safety and Security Reporting* (2016 Edition). Washington, DC. Accessed online 28 March 2018. https://www2.ed.gov/admins/lead/safety/handbook.pdf

37. U.S. Department of Education, Office of Postsecondary Education. 2016. *The Handbook for Campus Safety and Security Reporting* (2016 Edition). Washington, DC. Accessed online 28 March 2018. https://www2.ed.gov/admins/lead/safety/handbook.pdf

38. U.S. Department of Education, Office of Postsecondary Education. 2016. *The Handbook for Campus Safety and Security Reporting* (2016 Edition). Washington, DC. Accessed online 28 March 2018. https://www2.ed.gov/admins/lead/safety/handbook.pdf

39. U.S. Department of Education, Office of Postsecondary Education. 2016. *The Handbook for Campus Safety and Security Reporting* (2016 Edition). Washington, DC. Accessed online 28 March 2018. https://www2.ed.gov/admins/lead/safety/handbook.pdf

40. U.S. Department of Education, Office of Postsecondary Education. 2016. *The Handbook for Campus Safety and Security Reporting* (2016 Edition). Washington, DC. Accessed online 28 March 2018. https://www2.ed.gov/admins/lead/safety/handbook.pdf

41. Stotzer, R.L. 2010. Sexual orientation-based hate crimes on campus: The impact of policy on reporting rates. *Sexuality Research & Social Policy,* 7(3), 147–154; Pérez, Z.J., & Hussey, H. 2014. A hidden crisis: Including the LGBT community when addressing sexual violence on college campuses. Center for American Progress. Accessed online 28 March 2018. https://www.americanprogress.org/issues/lgbt/report/2014/09/19/97504/a-hidden-crisis/

42. U.S. Department of Education, Office of Postsecondary Education. 2016. *The Handbook for Campus Safety and Security Reporting* (2016 Edition). Washington, DC. Accessed online 28 March 2018. https://www2.ed.gov/admins/lead/safety/handbook.pdf

43. U.S. Department of Education, Office of Postsecondary Education. 2016. *The Handbook for Campus Safety and Security Reporting* (2016 Edition). Washington, DC. Accessed online 28 March 2018. https://www2.ed.gov/admins/lead/safety/handbook.pdf

44. Bureau of Justice Assistance. 2001. Hate crimes on campus: The problem and how to confront it. Office of Justice Programs, Department of Justice. Accessed online 28 March 2018. https://www.ncjrs.gov/pdffiles1/bja/187249.pdf; National Center for Education Statistics. 2014. Table 329. 30: On-campus hate crimes at degree-granting postsecondary institutions, by level and control of institution, type of crime, and category of bias motivating the crime: 2009 through 2012. *Digest of Education Statistics.* U.S. Department of Education, Institute of Education Sciences. Accessed online 28 March 2018. http://nces.ed.gov/programs/digest/d14/tables/dt14_329.30.asp; National Center for Education Statistics. 2016. Indicator 23: Hate crime incidents at postsecondary institutions. *Indicators of School Crime and Safety.* U.S. Department of Education, Institute of Education Sciences. Accessed online 28 March 2018. http://nces.ed.gov/programs/crimeindicators/ind_23.asp

45. U.S. Department of Education, Office of Postsecondary Education. 2016. *The Handbook for Campus Safety and Security Reporting* (2016 Edition). Washington, DC. Accessed online 28 March 2018. https://www2.ed.gov/admins/lead/safety/handbook.pdf

46. U.S. Department of Education, Office of Postsecondary Education. 2016. *The Handbook for Campus Safety and Security Reporting* (2016 Edition). Washington, DC. Accessed online 28 March 2018. https://www2.ed.gov/admins/lead/safety/handbook.pdf

47. U.S. Department of Education, Office of Postsecondary Education. 2016. *The Handbook for Campus Safety and Security Reporting* (2016 Edition). Washington, DC. Accessed online 28 March 2018. https://www2.ed.gov/admins/lead/safety/handbook.pdf

48. U.S. Department of Education, Office of Postsecondary Education. 2016. *The Handbook for Campus Safety and Security Reporting* (2016 Edition). Washington, DC. Accessed online 28 March 2018. https://www2.ed.gov/admins/lead/safety/handbook.pdf

49. U.S. Department of Education, Office of Postsecondary Education. 2016. *The Handbook for Campus Safety and Security Reporting* (2016 Edition). Washington, DC. Accessed online 28 March 2018. https://www2.ed.gov/admins/lead/safety/handbook.pdf

50. U.S. Department of Education, Office of Postsecondary Education. 2016. *The Handbook for Campus Safety and Security Reporting* (2016 Edition). Washington, DC. Accessed online 28 March 2018. https://www2.ed.gov/admins/lead/safety/handbook.pdf

51. Gun Violence Archive. Mass shootings. Accessed online 28 March 2018. http://www.gunviolencearchive.org/mass-shooting

Chapter 5

1. Clery Center for Security on Campus. 2016. Jeanne Clery Act text. Accessed online 28 March 2018. http://clerycenter.org/jeanne-clery-act

2. U.S. Department of Education, Office of Postsecondary Education. 2016. Campus Safety and Security Data Analysis Cutting Tool. Accessed online 28 March 2018. http://ope.ed.gov/campussafety/#/

3. U.S. Department of Education, Office of Postsecondary Education. 2016. Campus Safety and Security Data Analysis Cutting Tool. Accessed online 28 March 2018. http://ope.ed.gov/campussafety/#/

4. Federal Bureau of Investigation. 2016. Uniform Crime Reporting (UCR) Program. Accessed online 28 March 2018. https://ucr.fbi.gov/

5. Centers for Disease Control and Prevention. 2018. National Center for Injury and Violence Prevention and Control Web-based Injury Statistics Query and Reporting System (WISQARS). Accessed online 28 March 2018. http://www.cdc.gov/injury/wisqars/index.html

6. U.S. Department of Education, Office of Postsecondary Education. 2016. Campus Safety and Security Data Analysis Cutting Tool. Accessed online 28 March 2018. http://ope.ed.gov/campussafety/#/

7. Virginia Tech Review Panel. 2007. Mass shootings at Virginia Tech April 16, 2007: Report of the review panel presented to Governor Kaine, Commonwealth of Virginia. Accessed online 28 March 2018. https://governor.virginia.gov/media/3772/fullreport.pdf

8. Centers for Disease Control and Prevention. 2018. National Center for Injury and Violence Prevention and Control Web-based Injury Statistics Query and Reporting System (WISQARS). Accessed online 28 March 2018. http://www.cdc.gov/injury/wisqars/index.html

9. Federal Bureau of Investigation. 2016. Uniform Crime Reporting (UCR) Program. Federal Bureau of Investigation. Accessed online 28 March 2018. https://ucr.fbi.gov/

10. Centers for Disease Control and Prevention. 2018. National Center for Injury and Violence Prevention and Control Web-based Injury Statistics Query and Reporting System (WISQARS). Accessed online 28 March 2018. http://www.cdc.gov/injury/wisqars/index.html

11. U.S. Bureau of Justice Statistics. 2014. The nation's two measures of homicide. U.S. Department of Justice, Office of Justice Programs, NCJ 247060 (July). Accessed online 28 March 2018. https://www.bjs.gov/content/pub/pdf/ntmh.pdf

12. Barry, R., & Jones, C. 2014. Hundreds of police killings are uncounted in federal stats. *Wall Street Journal*, 3 December. Accessed online 28 March 2018. http://www.wsj.com/articles/hundreds-of-police-killings-are-uncounted-in-federal-statistics-1417577504

13. U.S. Bureau of Justice Statistics. 2014. The nation's two measures of homicide. U.S. Department of Justice, Office of Justice Programs, NCJ 247060 (July). Accessed online 28 March 2018. https://www.bjs.gov/content/pub/pdf/ntmh.pdf

14. Centers for Disease Control and Prevention. 2018. National Vital Statistics System (NVSS). National Center for Health Statistics. Accessed online 28 March 2018. https://www.cdc.gov/nchs/nvss/

15. U.S. Bureau of Justice Statistics. 2014. The nation's two measures of homicide. U.S. Department of Justice, Office of Justice Programs, NCJ 247060 (July). Accessed online 28 March 2018. https://www.bjs.gov/content/pub/pdf/ntmh.pdf

16. Centers for Disease Control and Prevention. 2018. National Center for Injury and Violence Prevention and Control Web-based Injury Statistics Query and Reporting System (WISQARS). Accessed online 28 March 2018. http://www.cdc.gov/injury/wisqars/index.html

17. U.S. Census Bureau. 2016. Historical pop-

ulation data. U.S. Department of Commerce. Accessed online 28 March 2018. https://www.census.gov/popest/data/historical/

18. Centers for Disease Control and Prevention. 2018. National Center for Injury and Violence Prevention and Control Web-based Injury Statistics Query and Reporting System (WISQARS). Accessed online 28 March 2018. http://www.cdc.gov/injury/wisqars/index.html

19. Centers for Disease Control and Prevention. 2018. National Center for Injury and Violence Prevention and Control Web-based Injury Statistics Query and Reporting System (WISQARS). Accessed online 28 March 2018. http://www.cdc.gov/injury/wisqars/index.html

20. National Center for Education Statistics. 2016. Integrated Post-Secondary Education Data System (IPEDS). U.S. Department of Education, Institute for Education Sciences. Accessed online 28 March 2018. http://nces.ed.gov/ipeds/

21. National Center for Education Statistics. 2016. *Digest of Education Statistics*. U.S. Department of Education, Institute of Education Sciences. Accessed online 28 March 2018. https://nces.ed.gov/programs/digest/

22. National Center for Education Statistics. 2015. Table 314.20: Employees in degree-granting postsecondary institutions, by sex, employment status, control and level of institution, and primary occupation: Selected years, fall 1991 through fall 2013. *Digest of Educational Statistics*. U.S. Department of Education, Institute of Education Sciences. Accessed online 28 March 2018. https://nces.ed.gov/programs/digest/d15/tables/dt15_314.20.asp?current=yes

23. National Center for Education Statistics. 2015. Table 303.20: Total fall enrollment in all postsecondary institutions participating in Title IV programs and annual percentage change in enrollment, by degree-granting status and control of institution: 1995 through 2014. *Digest of Educational Statistics*. U.S. Department of Education, Institute of Education Sciences. Accessed online 28 March 2018. https://nces.ed.gov/programs/digest/d15/tables/dt15_303.20.asp?current=yes

24. Carlisle, N., & Miller, J. 2016. Woman killed by husband at University of Utah planned to leave him, family says. *Salt Lake Tribune*, 30 December. Accessed online 28 March 2018. http://www.sltrib.com/home/4765548-155/woman-killed-in-murder-suicide-at-university

25. Withers, L. 2012. WSU student injured by his own handgun. *Standard Examiner*, 5 January. Accessed online 28 March 2018. http://www.standard.net/Local/2012/01/05/WSU-student-injured-by-his-own-handgun.html

26. Associated Press. 1993. Student opens fire, is shot dead at hearing. *Los Angeles Times*, 9 July. Accessed online 28 March 2018. http://articles.latimes.com/1993-07-09/news/mn-11569_1_university-student

27. Centers for Disease Control and Prevention. 2018. National Center for Injury and Violence Prevention and Control Web-based Injury Statistics Query and Reporting System (WISQARS). Accessed online 28 March 2018. http://www.cdc.gov/injury/wisqars/index.html

28. U.S. Bureau of Justice Statistics. 1997. Age patterns of victims of serious violent crime. U.S. Department of Justice, Office of Justice Programs, Bureau of Justice Statistics Special Report NCJ-162031 (July). Accessed online 28 March 2018. https://www.bjs.gov/content/pub/pdf/apvsvc.pdf; Centers for Disease Control and Prevention. 2013. Homicide rates among persons aged 10–24 years—United States, 1981–2010. *Centers for Disease Control and Prevention Morbidity and Mortality Weekly Report, 62*(27)(12 July), 545–548. Accessed online 28 March 2018. https://www.cdc.gov/mmwr/preview/mmwrhtml/mm6227a1.htm

29. Centers for Disease Control and Prevention. 2018. National Center for Injury and Violence Prevention and Control Web-based Injury Statistics Query and Reporting System (WISQARS). Accessed online 28 March 2018. http://www.cdc.gov/injury/wisqars/index.html

30. Centers for Disease Control and Prevention. 2018. National Center for Injury and Violence Prevention and Control Web-based Injury Statistics Query and Reporting System (WISQARS). Accessed online 28 March 2018. http://www.cdc.gov/injury/wisqars/index.html

31. National Center for Education Statistics. 2015. Table 303.20: Total fall enrollment in all postsecondary institutions participating in Title IV programs and annual percentage change in enrollment, by degree-granting status and control of institution: 1995 through 2014. *Digest of Educational Statistics*. U.S. Department of Education, Institute of Education Sciences. Accessed online 28 March 2018. https://nces.ed.gov/programs/digest/d15/tables/dt15_303.20.asp?current=yes

32. Centers for Disease Control and Prevention. 2018. National Center for Injury and Violence Prevention and Control Web-based Injury Statistics Query and Reporting System (WISQARS). Accessed online 28 March 2018. http://www.cdc.gov/injury/wisqars/index.html

33. Centers for Disease Control and Prevention. 2018. National Center for Injury and Violence Prevention and Control Web-based Injury Statistics Query and Reporting System

(WISQARS). Accessed online 28 March 2018. http://www.cdc.gov/injury/wisqars/index.html

34. Centers for Disease Control and Prevention. 2018. National Center for Injury and Violence Prevention and Control Web-based Injury Statistics Query and Reporting System (WISQARS). Accessed online 28 March 2018. http://www.cdc.gov/injury/wisqars/index.html

35. Benson, A. 2003. Couple dead after apparent murder-suicide at BSU. *The Arbiter*, 11 July. Accessed online 28 March 2018. https://arbiteronline.com/2003/07/11/couple-dead-after-apparent-murder-suicide-at-bsu-2/

36. Johnson, H. 2010. UCSD burning car: Estranged husband arrested on murder, arson charges. *La Jolla Light*, 8 November. Accessed online 28 March 2018. http://www.lajollalight.com/sdljl-ucsd-burning-car-estranged-husband-arrested-on-2010nov08-story.html; Staff. 2011. Man pleads guilty in death of his wife in burning car at UCSD. *La Jolla Light*, 18 November. Accessed online 28 March 2018. http://www.lajollalight.com/sdljl-man-pleads-guilty-in-death-of-his-wife-in-burning-2011nov18-story.html; 10News.com. 2012. Man who strangled wife, burned body in car sentenced. 27 January. Accessed online 28 March 2018. http://www.10news.com/news/man-who-strangled-wife-burned-body-in-car-sentenced

37. Rap News Network. 2004. Hip-hop news: BET & theme park cancel hip hop fest. 17 August. Accessed online 28 March 2018. http://www.rapnews.net/0-202-259384-00.html

38. Daraskevich, J. 2014. Unmarked graves represent Jacksonville homicide victims who have yet to be identified. *Florida Times-Union*, 27 April. Accessed online 4 November 2016. http://jacksonville.com/news/crime/2014-04-27/story/graves-without-names-represent-jacksonville-homicide-victims-who-have; Roland, C. 2004. Body found Sunday at Asylum Lake identified. Western Michigan University, Office of University Relations, 5 May. Accessed online 28 March 2018. http://www.wmich.edu/wmu/news/2004/0405/0304-x242.html; Salisbury, D. 2010. Update: Amanda Ball pleads guilty to manslaughter in death of Andrew Hirst. MLive.com, 23 November. Accessed online 28 March 2018. http://www.mlive.com/news/jackson/index.ssf/2010/11/amanda_ball_pleads_guilty_to_m.html

39. Rocha, V., & Serna, J. 2015. Ventura man jailed on charge he fatally stabbed 1-year-old son. *Los Angeles Times*, 5 January. Accessed online 28 March 2018. http://www.latimes.com/local/lanow/la-me-ln-ventura-man-jailed-in-sons-slaying-20150105-story.html; Anonymous.

2016. Ventura man pleads guilty to stabbing, kidnapping his son. *Ventura County Star*, 15 January. Accessed online 28 March 2018. http://archive.vcstar.com/news/local/ventura/ventura-man-pleads-guilty-to-stabbing-kidnapping-his-son-296a624c-2e3b-509e-e053-0100007fd480-365504821.html.

40. Spain, J. 2013. Changing the narrative of neonaticide. *Indiana Journal of Law and Social Equality*, 2(1), Article 8, 166–181.

41. Spain, J. 2013. Changing the narrative of neonaticide. *Indiana Journal of Law and Social Equality*, 2(1), Article 8, 166–181.

42. Taleb, N.M., Goldstein, D.G., & Spitznagel, M.W. 2009. The six mistakes executives make in risk management. *Harvard Business Review* (October). Accessed online 28 March 2018. https://hbr.org/2009/10/the-six-mistakes-executives-make-in-risk-management; Beddington, J. 2011. Blackett review of high impact low probability risks. Government Office of Science. Accessed online 28 March 2018. https://www.gov.uk/government/uploads/system/uploads/attachment_data/file/278526/12-519-blackett-review-high-impact-low-probability-risks.pdf; Lee, B., Preston, F., & Green, G. 2012. Preparing for high-impact, low-probability events: Lessons from Eyjafjallajökull. Chatman House: The Royal Institute of International Affairs. Accessed online 28 March 2018. https://www.chathamhouse.org/sites/files/chathamhouse/public/Research/Energy,%20Environment%20and%20Development/r0112_highimpact.pdf

43. Centers for Disease Control and Prevention. 2018. National Center for Injury and Violence Prevention and Control Web-based Injury Statistics Query and Reporting System (WISQARS). Accessed online 28 March 2018. http://www.cdc.gov/injury/wisqars/index.html

44. Brady Campaign to Prevent Gun Violence. 2013. Gun death and injury statistics sheet: 3-year average. Data source for this information sheet was the Centers for Disease Control and Prevention National Center for Injury Prevention and Control Web-based Injury Statistics Query and Reporting System (WISQARS), http://www.cdc.gov/injury/wisqars/index.html. Accessed online 28 March 2018. http://www.bradycampaign.org/sites/default/files/GunDeathandInjuryStatSheet3YearAverageFINAL.pdf

45. Delong, K. 2013. UWM student charged in connection with heroin overdose death. *Fox News 6* (Milwaukee, WI), 19 August. Accessed online 28 March 2018. http://fox6now.com/2013/08/19/uwm-student-charged-in-connection-with-heroin-overdose-death/; Kendall, K. 2015. Suspect in overdose investigation sen-

tenced. *The Collegian* (Kansas State University), 15 February. Accessed online 28 March 2018. http://www.kstatecollegian.com/2015/02/15/suspect-in-overdose-investigation-sentenced/; Salisbury, D. 2010. Update: Amanda Ball pleads guilty to manslaughter in death of Andrew Hirst. MLive.com, 23 November. Accessed online 28 March 2018. http://www.mlive.com/news/jackson/index.ssf/2010/11/amanda_ball_pleads_guilty_to_m.html

46. Associate Press. 2002. Driver who hit ASU woman guilty of negligent homicide. *Tucson Citizen*, 29 October. Accessed online 28 March 2018. http://tucsoncitizen.com/morgue2/2002/10/29/145385-driver-who-hit-asu-woman-guilty-of-negligent-homicide/

47. Galvan, A. 2010. A mother's worst nightmare. *Albuquerque Journal*, 25 July. Accessed online 28 March 2018. http://abqjournal.com/news/metro/25233749metro07-25-10.htm

48. Michael, J. 2010. North Dakota Supreme Court upholds Stevie Buckley's manslaughter conviction. *Bismarck Tribune*, 21 December. Accessed online 28 March 2018. http://bismarcktribune.com/news/local/crime-and-courts/north-dakota-supreme-court-upholds-stevie-buckley-s-manslaughter-conviction/article_16d66b70-0d52-11e0-ac99-001cc4c03286.html

49. Associated Press. 2012. Killer used bow and arrow in attack at Casper College; one victim was his father. *New York Daily News*, 1 December. Accessed online 28 March 2018. http://www.nydailynews.com/news/national/killer-bow-arrow-kill-father-article-1.1211499

50. Taylor, S. 2008. Scuba instructor charged in death of UA student. *Tuscaloosa News*, 28 July. Accessed online 28 March 2018. http://www.tuscaloosanews.com/news/20080728/scuba-instructor-charged-in-death-of-ua-student

51. U.S. Department of Education, Office of Postsecondary Education. 2016. Campus Safety and Security Data Analysis Cutting Tool. Accessed online 28 March 2018. http://ope.ed.gov/campussafety/#/

52. Nisbett, R.E., & Cohen, D. 1996. *Culture of honor: The psychology of violence in the South.* Boulder, CO: Westview Press.

53. Google. 2016. Google Earth. Accessed online 28 March 2018. https://www.google.com/earth/

Chapter 6

1. Daly, M., & Wilson, M. 1988. *Homicide.* New York, NY: A. de Gruyter; Yarvis, R.M. 1991. *Homicide: Causative factors and roots.* Lexington, MA: Lexington Books; Jerath, B.K., & Jerath, R. 1993. *Homicide: A bibliography.* Boca Raton, FL: CRC Press; Smith, M.D., & Zahn, M.A. 1999. *Homicide: A sourcebook of social research.* Thousand Oaks, CA: Sage; Smith, M.D., & Zahn, M.A. 1999. *Studying and preventing homicide: Issues and challenges.* Thousand Oaks, CA: Sage; Beeghley, L. 2003. *Homicide: A sociological explanation.* Lanham, MD: Rowman & Littlefield; Miethe, T.D., Regoeczi, W.C., & Drass, K.A. 2004. *Rethinking homicide: Exploring the structure and process underlying deadly situations.* Cambridge, UK: Cambridge University Press; Brookman, F. 2005. *Understanding homicide.* Thousand Oaks, CA: Sage; Daly, M. 2016. *Killing the competition: Economic inequality and homicide.* New Brunswick, NJ: Transaction; Rosenfeld, R. 2016. Documenting and explaining the 2015 homicide rise: Research directions. U.S. Department of Justice, Office of Justice Programs, National Institute of Justice. Accessed online 28 March 2018. https://www.ncjrs.gov/pdffiles1/nij/249895.pdf?ed2f26df2d9c416fbddddd2330a778c6=kvbbjmkbrx-kjbikilv

2. Blumstein, A. 1995. Youth violence, guns, and the illicit-drug industry. *Journal of Criminal Law and Criminology, 86*(1), 10–36; Blumstein, A., & Wallman, J. 2006. *The crime drop in America.* Cambridge, UK: Cambridge University Press; Baumer, E., et al. 1998. The influence of crack cocaine on robbery, burglary, and homicide rates: A cross-city, longitudinal analysis. *Journal of Research in Crime and Delinquency, 35*(3), 316–340; Baumer, E. 1994. Poverty, crack, and crime: A cross-city analysis. *Journal of Research in Crime and Delinquency, 31*(3), 311–327; Blumstein, A., Rivara, F.P., and Rosenfeld, R. 2000. The rise and decline of homicide—and why. *Annual Review of Public Health, 21,* 505–41; McCall, P.L., Parker, K.F., & MacDonald, J.M. 2008. The dynamic relationship between homicide rates and social, economic, and political factors from 1970 to 2000. *Social Science Research, 37*(3), 721–735; Hough, R., & Jones-Brown, D. 2014. Homicide. In D. Jones-Brown, B. Frazier, & M. Brooks (Eds.), *African Americans and criminal justice: An encyclopedia* (pp. 277–281). Westport, CT: Greenwood; LaFree, G. 1999. Declining violent crime rates in the 1990s: Predicting crime booms and busts. *Annual Review of Sociology, 25,* 145–168; Fryer, R.G., et al. 2013. Measuring crack cocaine and its impact. *Economic Inquiry, 51*(3), 1651–1681.

3. Pearson-Nelson, B. 2008. *Understanding homicide trends: The social context of a homicide epidemic.* New York, NY: LFB Scholarly Publishing.

4. Centers for Disease Control and Prevention. 2016. *Principles of epidemiology in public health practice, third edition: An introduction to applied epidemiology and biostatistics: Lesson 1—Introduction to epidemiology; Section 11—Epidemic disease occurrence.* Self-Study Course SS1978. Accessed online 28 March 2018. http://www.cdc.gov/ophss/csels/dsepd/ss1978/lesson1/section11.html

5. Levitt, S.D. 2004. Understanding why crime fell in the 1990s: Four factors that explain the decline and six that do not. *Journal of Economic Perspectives, 18*(1), 163–190. Accessed online 28 March 2018. http://pricetheory.uchicago.edu/levitt/Papers/LevittUnderstandingWhyCrime2004.pdf; Dahlberg, L.L., & Mercy, J.A. 2009. History of violence as a public health issue. *AMA Virtual Mentor, 11*(2), 167–172. Accessed online 28 March 2018. http://www.cdc.gov/violenceprevention/pdf/history_violence-a.pdf

6. Bensing, R.C., & Schroeder, O. 1960. *Homicide in an urban community.* Springfield, IL: Charles C. Thomas Publishers; Neely, C. 2015. *You're dead. So what? Media, police, and the invisibility of black women as victims of homicide.* Lansing, MI: Michigan State University Press; Zack, N. 2015. *White privilege and black rights: The injustice of U.S. police racial profiling and homicide.* Lanham, MD: Rowman & Littlefield; Braithwaite, R.L., Taylor, S.E., & Treadwell, H.M. 2009. *Health issues in the black community.* 3rd edition. San Francisco, CA: Jossey-Bass; Roth, R. 2009. *American homicide.* Cambridge, MA: Harvard University Press; Hough, R., & Jones-Brown, D. 2014. Homicide. In D. Jones-Brown, B. Frazier, & M. Brooks (Eds.), *African Americans and criminal justice: An encyclopedia* (pp. 277–281). Westport, CT: Greenwood; Pearson-Nelson, B. 2008. *Understanding homicide trends: The social context of a homicide epidemic.* New York, NY: LFB Scholarly Publishing.

7. Barry, D., et al. 2012. Race, tragedy and outrage collide after a shot in Florida. *New York Times,* 1 April. Accessed online 28 March 2018. http://www.nytimes.com/2012/04/02/us/trayvon-martin-shooting-prompts-a-review-of-ideals.html

8. Coates, T-N. 2014. On the killing of Jordan Davis by Michael Dunn. *The Atlantic,* 15 February. Accessed online 28 March 2018. http://www.theatlantic.com/politics/archive/2014/02/on-the-killing-of-jordan-davis-by-michael-dunn/283870/

9. Healy, J. 2014. Ferguson, still tense, grows calmer. *New York Times,* 26 November. Accessed online 28 March 2018. http://www.nytimes.com/2014/11/27/us/michael-brown-darren-wilson-ferguson-protests.html

10. Baker, A., Goodman, J.D., & Mueller, B. 2015. Beyond the chokehold: The path to Eric Garner's death. *New York Times,* 13 June. Accessed online 28 March 2018. http://www.nytimes.com/2015/06/14/nyregion/eric-garner-police-chokehold-staten-island.html

11. Eligon, J., & Stolberg, S.G. 2016. Baltimore after Freddie Gray: The "mind-set has changed." *New York Times,* 12 April. Accessed online 28 March 2018. http://www.nytimes.com/2016/04/13/us/baltimore-freddie-gray.html

12. Coscarelli, J. 2014. No charges against Ohio police in John Crawford III Walmart shooting, despite damning security video. *New York Magazine,* 24 September. Accessed online 28 March 2018. http://nymag.com/daily/intelligencer/2014/09/no-charges-john-crawford-iii-walmart-shooting-video.html

13. Smith, M., Capecchi, C., & Furber, M. 2016. Peaceful protests follow Minnesota governor's call for calm. *New York Times,* 8 July. Accessed online 28 March 2018. http://www.nytimes.com/2016/07/09/us/philando-castile-jeronimo-yanez.html

14. Katz, W. 2015. Law enforcement tragedies where nobody pays the price. *New York Times,* 8 April. Accessed online 28 March 2018. http://www.nytimes.com/roomfordebate/2014/11/25/does-ferguson-show-that-cops-who-kill-get-off-too-easily/law-enforcement-tragedies-where-nobody-pays-the-price

15. Coates, T-N. 2013. Trayvon Martin and the irony of American justice. *The Atlantic,* 15 July. Accessed online 28 March 2018. http://www.theatlantic.com/national/archive/2013/07/trayvon-martin-and-the-irony-of-american-justice/277782/; Blow, C.M. 2016. Incandescent with rage. *New York Times,* 27 July. Accessed online 28 March 2018. http://www.nytimes.com/2016/07/28/opinion/incandescent-with-rage.html

16. Centers for Disease Control and Prevention. 2018. National Center for Injury and Violence Prevention and Control Web-based Injury Statistics Query and Reporting System (WISQARS). Accessed online 28 March 2018. http://www.cdc.gov/injury/wisqars/index.html

17. Centers for Disease Control and Prevention. 2018. National Center for Injury and Violence Prevention and Control Web-based Injury Statistics Query and Reporting System (WISQARS). Accessed online 28 March 2018. http://www.cdc.gov/injury/wisqars/index.html

18. Centers for Disease Control and Prevention. 2018. National Center for Injury and

Violence Prevention and Control Web-based Injury Statistics Query and Reporting System (WISQARS). Accessed online 28 March 2018. http://www.cdc.gov/injury/wisqars/index.html

19. Centers for Disease Control and Prevention. 2018. National Center for Injury and Violence Prevention and Control Web-based Injury Statistics Query and Reporting System (WISQARS). Accessed online 28 March 2018. http://www.cdc.gov/injury/wisqars/index.html

20. Centers for Disease Control and Prevention. 2018. National Center for Injury and Violence Prevention and Control Web-based Injury Statistics Query and Reporting System (WISQARS). Accessed online 28 March 2018. http://www.cdc.gov/injury/wisqars/index.html

21. Centers for Disease Control and Prevention. 2018. National Center for Injury and Violence Prevention and Control Web-based Injury Statistics Query and Reporting System (WISQARS). Accessed online 28 March 2018. http://www.cdc.gov/injury/wisqars/index.html

22. Blumstein, A., Rivara, F.P., & Rosenfeld, R. 2000. The rise and decline of homicide—and why. *Annual Review of Public Health, 21*, 505–41.

23. Centers for Disease Control and Prevention. 2018. National Center for Injury and Violence Prevention and Control Web-based Injury Statistics Query and Reporting System (WISQARS). Accessed online 28 March 2018. http://www.cdc.gov/injury/wisqars/index.html

24. Centers for Disease Control and Prevention. 2018. National Center for Injury and Violence Prevention and Control Web-based Injury Statistics Query and Reporting System (WISQARS). Accessed online 28 March 2018. http://www.cdc.gov/injury/wisqars/index.html; Neely, C. 2015. *You're dead. So what? Media, police, and the invisibility of black women as victims of homicide.* Lansing, MI: Michigan State University Press.

25. Centers for Disease Control and Prevention. 2018. National Center for Injury and Violence Prevention and Control Web-based Injury Statistics Query and Reporting System (WISQARS). Accessed online 28 March 2018. http://www.cdc.gov/injury/wisqars/index.html

26. Centers for Disease Control and Prevention. 2018. National Center for Injury and Violence Prevention and Control Web-based Injury Statistics Query and Reporting System (WISQARS). Accessed online 28 March 2018. http://www.cdc.gov/injury/wisqars/index.html

27. Centers for Disease Control and Prevention. 2018. National Center for Injury and Violence Prevention and Control Web-based In-

jury Statistics Query and Reporting System (WISQARS). Accessed online 28 March 2018. http://www.cdc.gov/injury/wisqars/index.html

28. Centers for Disease Control and Prevention. 2018. National Center for Injury and Violence Prevention and Control Web-based Injury Statistics Query and Reporting System (WISQARS). Accessed online 28 March 2018. http://www.cdc.gov/injury/wisqars/index.html

29. Centers for Disease Control and Prevention. 2018. National Center for Injury and Violence Prevention and Control Web-based Injury Statistics Query and Reporting System (WISQARS). Accessed online 28 March 2018. http://www.cdc.gov/injury/wisqars/index.html

30. Centers for Disease Control and Prevention. 2018. National Center for Injury and Violence Prevention and Control Web-based Injury Statistics Query and Reporting System (WISQARS). Accessed online 28 March 2018. http://www.cdc.gov/injury/wisqars/index.html

31. Centers for Disease Control and Prevention. 2018. National Center for Injury and Violence Prevention and Control Web-based Injury Statistics Query and Reporting System (WISQARS). Accessed online 28 March 2018. http://www.cdc.gov/injury/wisqars/index.html

32. Centers for Disease Control and Prevention. 2018. National Center for Injury and Violence Prevention and Control Web-based Injury Statistics Query and Reporting System (WISQARS). Accessed online 28 March 2018. http://www.cdc.gov/injury/wisqars/index.html

33. Centers for Disease Control and Prevention. 2018. National Center for Injury and Violence Prevention and Control Web-based Injury Statistics Query and Reporting System (WISQARS). Accessed online 28 March 2018. http://www.cdc.gov/injury/wisqars/index.html

34. American Academy of Arts & Sciences. 2015. Public research universities: Changes in state funding. The Lincoln Project: Excellence and Access in Public Higher Education. Accessed online 28 March 2018. https://www.amacad.org/multimedia/pdfs/publications/researchpapersmonographs/PublicResearchUniv_ChangesInStateFunding.pdf

35. Watkins, M. 2016. Hutchison, Fenves decry dwindling state support for higher education. *Texas Tribune*, 11 April. Accessed online 28 March 2018. https://www.texastribune.org/2016/04/11/hutchison-fenves-decry-dwindling-state-support-hig/

36. U.S. Department of Education. 2015. 2013 annual report to the president on the results of the participation of historically black colleges and universities in federal programs. White

House Initiative on Historically Black Colleges and Universities. Accessed online 28 March 2018. http://sites.ed.gov/whhbcu/files/2011/12/HBCU-2013-Annual-Report-HBCU-final-.pdf

37. U.S. Department of Education. 2015. 2013 annual report to the president on the results of the participation of historically black colleges and universities in federal programs. White House Initiative on Historically Black Colleges and Universities. Accessed online 28 March 2018. http://sites.ed.gov/whhbcu/files/2011/12/HBCU-2013-Annual-Report-HBCU-final-.pdf

38. U.S. Department of Education. 1991. Historically black colleges and universities and higher education desegregation. Office for Civil Rights. Accessed online 28 March 2018. http://www2.ed.gov/about/offices/list/ocr/docs/hq9511.html

39. University of Arkansas at Pine Bluff. 2016. Historical overview. Accessed online 28 March 2018. https://www.uapb.edu/about/historical_overview.aspx; U.S. Department of Education. 1991. Historically black colleges and universities and higher education desegregation. Office for Civil Rights. Accessed online 28 March 2018. http://www2.ed.gov/about/offices/list/ocr/docs/hq9511.html; Hill, S.T. 1982. The traditionally black institutions of higher education. National Center for Education Statistics, Institute for Education Sciences, U.S. Department of Education. Accessed online 28 March 2018. http://nces.ed.gov/pubs84/84308.pdf

40. U.S. Department of Education, Office of Postsecondary Education. 2016. *The Handbook for Campus Safety and Security Reporting* (2016 Edition). Washington, DC. Accessed online 28 March 2018. https://www2.ed.gov/admins/lead/safety/handbook.pdf

41. U.S. Department of Education, Office of Postsecondary Education. 2016. Campus Safety and Security Data Analysis Cutting Tool. Accessed online 28 March 2018. http://ope.ed.gov/campussafety/#/

42. U.S. Department of Education. 2015. 2013 annual report to the president on the results of the participation of historically black colleges and universities in federal programs. White House Initiative on Historically Black Colleges and Universities. Accessed online 28 March 2018. http://sites.ed.gov/whhbcu/files/2011/12/HBCU-2013-Annual-Report-HBCU-final-.pdf; U.S. Department of Education. 1991. Historically black colleges and universities and higher education desegregation. Office for Civil Rights. Accessed online 28 March 2018. http://www2.ed.gov/about/offices/list/ocr/docs/hq9511.html

43. Anonymous. 2004. A troubling increase in murder rates on black college campuses. *Journal of Blacks in Higher Education* (44)(Summer), 14–17.

44. National Center for Education Statistics. 2016. Integrated Post-Secondary Education Data System (IPEDS). U.S. Department of Education, Institute for Education Sciences. Accessed online 28 March 2018. http://nces.ed.gov/ipeds/

45. National Center for Education Statistics. 2015. Table 313.20: Fall enrollment in degree-granting historically black colleges and universities, by sex of student and level and control of institution: Selected years, 1976 through 2014. *Digest of Education Statistics.* U.S. Department of Education, Institute of Education Sciences. Accessed online 28 March 2018. https://nces.ed.gov/programs/digest/d15/tables/dt15_313.20.asp?current=yes

46. National Center for Education Statistics. 2015. Table 313.20: Fall enrollment in degree-granting historically black colleges and universities, by sex of student and level and control of institution: Selected years, 1976 through 2014. *Digest of Education Statistics.* U.S. Department of Education, Institute of Education Sciences. Accessed online 28 March 2018. https://nces.ed.gov/programs/digest/d15/tables/dt15_313.20.asp?current=yes

47. Centers for Disease Control and Prevention. 2018. National Center for Injury and Violence Prevention and Control Web-based Injury Statistics Query and Reporting System (WISQARS). Accessed online 28 March 2018. http://www.cdc.gov/injury/wisqars/index.html

48. Korff, J., Roussey, T., & Tschida, S. 2012. Bowie State murder trial: Alexis Simpson not guilty of roommate's death. WJLA (Washington, DC), 14 November. Accessed online 28 March 2018. http://wjla.com/news/local/alexis-simpson-best-friend-of-victim-in-bowie-state-murder-trial-testifies—82094; Zapotsky, M. 2012. Woman "scared" before deadly stabbing of roommate. *Washington Post,* 15 November. Accessed online 28 March 2018. https://www.washingtonpost.com/local/crime/woman-scared-before-deadly-stabbing-of-roommate/2012/11/15/67bb2c02-2f3c-11e2-a30e-5ca76eeec857_story.html

49. Stodghill, R. 2015. *Where everybody looks like me: At the crossroads of America's black colleges and culture.* New York, NY: Harper-Collins; Nazaryan, A. 2015. Black colleges matter. *Newsweek,* 18 August. Accessed online 28 March 2018. http://www.newsweek.com/black-colleges-matter-363667

50. Stodghill, R. 2015. *Where everybody looks like me: At the crossroads of America's black colleges and culture.* New York, NY: HarperCollins;

Furious. 2014. 11 historically black colleges & universities that have closed. Urban Intellectuals. Accessed online 28 March 2018. https://urban intellectuals.com/2014/10/17/11-historically-black-colleges-universities-that-have-closed/; Lewis, T. 2015. Here's what you need to know about the plight of HBCUs (and it's getting worse). *Essence Online*, 18 August. Accessed online 28 March 2018. http://www.essence.com/2015/08/18/hbcus-black-colleges-closing-plight

51. National Center for Education Statistics. 2016. Table 306.10: Total fall enrollment in degree-granting postsecondary institutions, by level of enrollment, sex, attendance status, and race/ethnicity of student: Selected years, 1976 through 2015. *Digest of Education Statistics*. U.S. Department of Education, Institute of Education Sciences. Accessed online 28 March 2018. https://nces.ed.gov/programs/digest/d16/tables/dt16_306.10.asp?current=yes

52. Centers for Disease Control and Prevention. 2018. National Center for Injury and Violence Prevention and Control Web-based Injury Statistics Query and Reporting System (WISQARS). Accessed online 28 March 2018. http://www.cdc.gov/injury/wisqars/index.html

53. National Center for Education Statistics. 2015. Table 314.20: Employees in degree-granting postsecondary institutions, by sex, employment status, control and level of institution, and primary occupation: Selected years, fall 1991 through fall 2013. *Digest of Educational Statistics*. U.S. Department of Education, Institute of Education Sciences. Accessed online 28 March 2018. https://nces.ed.gov/programs/digest/d15/tables/dt15_314.20.asp?current=yes; National Center for Education Statistics. 2015. Table 303.20: Total fall enrollment in all postsecondary institutions participating in Title IV programs and annual percentage change in enrollment, by degree-granting status and control of institution: 1995 through 2014. *Digest of Educational Statistics*. U.S. Department of Education, Institute of Education Sciences. Accessed online 28 March 2018. https://nces.ed.gov/programs/digest/d15/tables/dt15_303.20.asp?current=yes

54. Centers for Disease Control and Prevention. 2018. National Center for Injury and Violence Prevention and Control Web-based Injury Statistics Query and Reporting System (WISQARS). Accessed online 28 March 2018. http://www.cdc.gov/injury/wisqars/index.html

55. Centers for Disease Control and Prevention. 2018. National Center for Injury and Violence Prevention and Control Web-based Injury Statistics Query and Reporting System (WISQARS). Accessed online 28 March 2018. http://www.cdc.gov/injury/wisqars/index.html

56. Centers for Disease Control and Prevention. 2018. National Center for Injury and Violence Prevention and Control Web-based Injury Statistics Query and Reporting System (WISQARS). Accessed online 28 March 2018. http://www.cdc.gov/injury/wisqars/index.html

57. Centers for Disease Control and Prevention. 2018. National Center for Injury and Violence Prevention and Control Web-based Injury Statistics Query and Reporting System (WISQARS). Accessed online 28 March 2018. http://www.cdc.gov/injury/wisqars/index.html

58. Centers for Disease Control and Prevention. 2018. National Center for Injury and Violence Prevention and Control Web-based Injury Statistics Query and Reporting System (WISQARS). Accessed online 28 March 2018. http://www.cdc.gov/injury/wisqars/index.html

59. Centers for Disease Control and Prevention. 2018. National Center for Injury and Violence Prevention and Control Web-based Injury Statistics Query and Reporting System (WISQARS). Accessed online 28 March 2018. http://www.cdc.gov/injury/wisqars/index.html

60. Centers for Disease Control and Prevention. 2018. National Center for Injury and Violence Prevention and Control Web-based Injury Statistics Query and Reporting System (WISQARS). Accessed online 28 March 2018. http://www.cdc.gov/injury/wisqars/index.html

61. Centers for Disease Control and Prevention. 2018. National Center for Injury and Violence Prevention and Control Web-based Injury Statistics Query and Reporting System (WISQARS). Accessed online 28 March 2018. http://www.cdc.gov/injury/wisqars/index.html

Chapter 7

1. Anonymous. 2017. Guns on Campus' laws for public colleges and universities: A guide for students, parents, policy makers and journalists. Armed Campuses. Accessed online 28 March 2018. http://www.armedcampuses.org/

2. Jaischik, S., & Lederman, D. 2016. The 2016 Inside Higher Ed Survey of College and University Presidents: A study by Gallup® and *Inside Higher Ed*. Accessed online 28 March 2018. https://www.hobsons.com/res/Whitepapers/2016_IHE_Presidents_Survey_booklet.pdf; Patten, R., Thomas, M., & Wada, J.C. 2013. Packing heat: Attitudes regarding concealed weapons on college campuses. *American Journal of Criminal Justice, 38*(4), 551–569.

3. Bennett, K.J., Kraft, J.R., & Grubb, D. 2011. University faculty attitudes toward guns on campus. *Journal of Criminal Justice Education, 23*(3), 1–20. Accessed online 28 March 2018. https://www.researchgate.net/publication/239790628_University_Faculty_Attitudes_Toward_Guns_on_Campus; Thompson, A., et al. 2013. Faculty perceptions and practices regarding carrying concealed handguns on university campuses. *Journal of Community Health, 38*(2), 366–373; McClennan, B. 2016. UTK "Guns on Campus Poll." Faculty Senate, University of Tennessee, Knoxville. Accessed online 28 March 2018. http://senate.utk.edu/wp-content/uploads/sites/16/2016/04/UTK-Guns-Poll-final.pdf; Brinker, G., Lenneman, B., and Swayne, R. L. 2016. Kansas Board of Regents Council of Faculty Senate Presidents campus employees' weapons survey. Docking Institute of Public Affairs, Fort Hays State University, Fort Hays, Kansas. Accessed online 28 March 2018. http://www.khi.org/assets/uploads/news/14232/regents_facultystaff_gun_survey_2015_(2).pdf; Dahl, P., Bonham, G., Jr, & Reddington, P. 2016. Community college faculty: Attitudes toward guns on campus. *Community College Journal of Research and Practice, 40*(8), 706–717. Accessed online 28 March 2018. https://www.researchgate.net/publication/294874873_Community_College_Faculty_Attitudes_Toward_Guns_on_Campus

4. International Association of Campus Law Enforcement Administrators. 2008. Position statement on concealed carrying of firearms proposals on college campuses. Accessed online 28 March 2018. https://www.okhighered.org/campus-safety/resources/CBP-guns-iaclea-statement.pdf; Thompson, A., et al. 2009. Reducing firearm-related violence on college campuses—Police chiefs' perceptions and practices. *Journal of American College Health, 58*(3), 247–254. Accessed online 28 March 2018. http://0-www.tandfonline.com.library.uark.edu/doi/pdf/10.1080/07448480903293567?needAccess=true

5. Jackson, A., & Gould, S. 2017. 10 states allow guns on college campuses and 16 more are considering it. *Business Insider*, 27 April. Accessed online 28 March 2018. http://www.businessinsider.com/states-that-allow-guns-on-college-campuses-2017-4

6. Kopel, D. 2015. Guns on university campuses: The Colorado experience. *Washington Post*, 20 April. Accessed online 28 March 2018. https://www.washingtonpost.com/news/volokh-conspiracy/wp/2015/04/20/guns-on-university-campuses-the-colorado-experience/?utm_term=.d36c58427a71

7. Associated Press. 2013. Colorado campus gun bans divisive, hard to enforce. CBS TV (Denver), 3 March. Accessed online 28 March 2018. http://denver.cbslocal.com/2013/03/03/colorado-campus-gun-bans-divisive-hard-to-enforce/

8. U.S. Department of Education, Office of Postsecondary Education. 2016. Campus Safety and Security Data Analysis Cutting Tool. Accessed online 28 March 2018. http://ope.ed.gov/campussafety/#/

9. Associated Press. 2013. Colorado campus gun bans divisive, hard to enforce. CBS TV (Denver), 3 March. Accessed online 28 March 2018. http://denver.cbslocal.com/2013/03/03/colorado-campus-gun-bans-divisive-hard-to-enforce/

10. Associated Press. 2013. Colorado campus gun bans divisive, hard to enforce. CBS TV (Denver), 3 March. Accessed online 28 March 2018. http://denver.cbslocal.com/2013/03/03/colorado-campus-gun-bans-divisive-hard-to-enforce/

11. U.S. Department of Education, Office of Postsecondary Education. 2016. Campus Safety and Security Data Analysis Cutting Tool. Accessed online 28 March 2018. http://ope.ed.gov/campussafety/#/

12. Utah. 2006. 2006 Utah Code—63–98–102—Uniform firearm laws. Accessed online 28 March 2018. http://law.justia.com/codes/utah/2006/title63/63_3b003.html

13. Associated Press. 2012. Weber State student accidentally shoots himself. *Daily Herald* (Ogden, UT), 5 January. Accessed online 28 March 2018. http://www.heraldextra.com/news/local/weber-state-student-accidentally-shoots-himself/article_eef6a77c-37d6-11e1-860e-0019bb2963f4.html

14. Carlisle, N., & Parker, N. 2016. Husband and wife die after University of Utah shooting, police say. *Salt Lake Tribune*, 29 December. Accessed online 28 March 2018. http://www.sltrib.com/news/4762770-155/shooting-reported-at-university-of-utah

15. Gavran, J. 2017. Concealed handguns on campus: A multi-year study. *Visions: The Journal of Applied Research for the Association of Florida Colleges, 7*(1), 13–18. Accessed online 28 March 2018. http://keepgunsoffcampus.org/wp-content/uploads/2017/05/Campus-Crime-Report-4.pdf

16. Wisconsin State Legislature. 2011. 2011 Senate Bill 93. Accessed online 28 March 2018. https://docs.legis.wisconsin.gov/2011/related/proposals/sb93

17. Anonymous. 2017. Laws concerning carrying concealed firearms on campus in Wiscon-

sin. Armed Campuses. Accessed online 28 March 2018. http://www.armedcampuses.org/wisconsin/

18. WISN 12 News. 2012. Man dies in UW-Milwaukee dorm room; student arrested. WISN TV 12 (Milwaukee, WI), 6 December. Accessed online 28 March 2018. http://www.wisn.com/article/man-dies-in-uw-milwaukee-dorm-room-student-arrested/6312635

19. Srubas, P. 2015. Man charged in Green Bay murder, drug robbery. *Green Bay Press Gazette* (Green Bay, WI), 15 July. Accessed online 28 March 2018. http://www.greenbay pressgazette.com/story/news/local/2015/07/15/suspect-custody-murder-near-uwgb/30188085/

20. Anonymous. 2017. Laws concerning carrying concealed firearms on campus in Mississippi. Armed Campuses. Accessed online 28 March 2018. http://www.armedcampuses.org/mississippi/

21. Brown, G. 2012. Suspects sought in murder at Mississippi State University. WREG News Channel 3 (Memphis), 25 March. Accessed online 10 July 2017. http://wreg.com/2012/03/25/fatal-shooting-at-mississippi-state-university/

22. Shapiro, T.R. 2015. Delta State University professor told police he killed his "wife" shortly before second shooting. *Washington Post*, 15 September. Accessed online 28 March 2018. https://www.washingtonpost.com/news/grade-point/wp/2015/09/15/history-professor-shot-and-killed-at-delta-state-university-known-as-mentor/?utm_term=.d3469bdc7d45

23. Biemiller, L. 2012. Colorado Supreme Court says state law trumps university's ban on guns. *Chronicle of Higher Education*, 5 March. Accessed online 28 March 2018. http://www.chronicle.com/article/Colorado-Supreme-Court-Says/131076

24. Benson, B. 2012. President Benson's statement on the Colorado Supreme Court ruling on concealed weapons on campus. *CU Boulder Today*, 5 March. Accessed online 28 March 2018. http://www.colorado.edu/today/2012/03/05/president-bensons-statement-colorado-supreme-court-ruling-concealed-weapons-campus

25. Hendrick, T. 2012. Anschutz campus staff member accidentally fires gun. Fox31 (Denver), 12 November. Accessed online 28 March 2018. http://kdvr.com/2012/11/12/anschutz-campus-staff-member-accidentally-fires-gun/

26. Levin, S. 2012. CU-Denver accidental shooting: Now ex-staffer trying to unjam gun when it fired. *Westworld*, 15 November. Accessed online 28 March 2018. http://www.westword.com/news/cu-denver-accidental-shooting-now-ex-staffer-trying-to-unjam-gun-when-it-fired-5909883

27. Kansas Attorney General. 2013. Kansas Personal and Family Protection Act: 2013 legislative changes—frequently asked questions. Accessed online 28 March 2018. http://ag.ks.gov/docs/default-source/documents/2013-concealed-carry-legislative-changes—-faqs.pdf?sfvrsn=6

28. Hancock, P. 2016. University leaders share personal concerns about guns on campus. *Lawrence Journal-World* (Lawrence, KS), 14 September. Accessed online 28 March 2018. http://www2.ljworld.com/news/2016/sep/14/university-chiefs-share-personal-concerns-about-pe/; Kansas Attorney General. 2013. Kansas Personal and Family Protection Act: 2013 legislative changes—frequently asked questions. Accessed online 28 March 2018. http://ag.ks.gov/docs/default-source/documents/2013-concealed-carry-legislative-changes—-faqs.pdf?sfvrsn=6

29. Kansas Attorney General. 2013. Kansas Personal and Family Protection: 2013 legislative changes—frequently asked questions. Accessed online 28 March 2018. http://ag.ks.gov/docs/default-source/documents/2013-concealed-carry-legislative-changes—-faqs.pdf?sfvrsn=6

30. Kansas State Legislature. 2015. An act concerning firearms; relating to the carrying of concealed firearms; relating to the personal and family protection act; amending K.S.A. 2014 Supp. 21–5914, 21–6301, 21–6302, 21–6308, 21–6309, 32–1002, 75–7c01, 75–7c03, 75–7c04, 75–7c05, 75–7c10, 75–7c17,75–7c20 and 75–7c21 and repealing the existing sections; also repealing K.S.A. 2014Supp. 75–7c19. 2015–2016 Legislative Sessions. Accessed online 28 March 2018. http://www.kslegislature.org/li_2016/m/images/pdf.png

31. Winkler, A. 2011. Did the wild west have more gun control than we do today? *Huffington Post*, 9 September. Accessed online 28 March 2018. http://www.huffingtonpost.com/adam-winkler/did-the-wild-west-have-mo_b_956035.html

32. Gorman, M. 2017. Gun found in a Kansas University bathroom two weeks after campus carry legalization. *Newsweek*, 18 July. Accessed online 28 March 2018. http://www.newsweek.com/gun-wichita-state-university-campus-carry-638446

33. Williams, M.R., & Porter, T. 2017. Gun found in bathroom in KU's Wescoe Hall was loaded .38 reported stolen in Olathe. *Kansas City Star*, 5 September. Accessed online 28 March 2018. http://www.kansascity.com/news/local/article171379147.html

34. Arkansas General Assembly. 2013. An act to allow trained and licensed staff and faculty

to carry a concealed handgun on a university, college, or community college campus under certain circumstances; and for other purposes. Accessed online 28 March 2018. http://www.arkleg.state.ar.us/assembly/2013/2013R/Acts/Act226.pdf

35. Hutchinson, A. 2013. Report of the National School Shield Task Force. National School Shield Task Force, National Rifle Association, Arlington, Virginia. Accessed online 28 March 2018. http://www.guns.com/wp-content/uploads/2013/04/National-Shcool-Shield-Safety-report.pdf

36. Reavis, C. 2017. Bicyclist discovers body, police determine death by suicide. *Arkansas Traveler*, 26 October. Accessed online 28 March 2018. http://www.uatrav.com/news/article_fdc0e868-bab5-11e7-9cd3-4bd07b44b41d.html; Riddle, B. 2017. Body found on University of Arkansas–owned property near trail. Accessed online 28 March 2018. http://www.arkansasonline.com/news/2017/oct/26/body-found-university-arkansas-owned-property-deat/

37. Associated Press. 2014. Lawmakers resurrect bill to allow guns on Idaho university campuses. Boise State Public Radio, Boise State University, Boise, Idaho, 24 January. Accessed online 28 March 2018. http://boisestatepublicradio.org/post/lawmakers-resurrect-bill-allow-guns-idaho-university-campuses; Associated Press. 2014. Idaho Education Board votes to fight guns on campus bill. Boise State Public Radio, Boise State University, Boise, Idaho, 3 February. Accessed online 28 March 2018. http://boisestatepublicradio.org/post/idaho-education-board-votes-fight-guns-campus-bill; Associated Press. 2014. Boise police chief says he was blocked from speaking against guns on campus bill. Boise State Public Radio, Boise State University, Boise, Idaho, 12 February. Accessed online 28 March 2018. http://boisestatepublicradio.org/post/boise-police-chief-says-he-was-blocked-speaking-against-guns-campus-bill; Graf, S. 2014. Boise state president says guns on campus bill solves a problem that doesn't exist. Boise State Public Radio, Boise State University, Boise, Idaho, 25 February. Accessed online 28 March 2018. http://boisestatepublicradio.org/post/boise-state-president-says-guns-campus-bill-solves-problem-doesnt-exist

38. Bryce, D. 2014. ISU prof with concealed weapons permit who accidentally shot his foot in class is identified. *Idaho State Journal* (Idaho State University, Pocatello), 4 September. Accessed online 28 March 2018. https://idahostatejournal.com/news/local/isu-prof-with-concealed-weapons-permit-who-accidentally-

shot-his/article_18228ab2-3383-11e4-af7e-001a4bcf887a.html

39. Anonymous. 2017. The UT tower shooting archives. *Texas Monthly*. Accessed online 28 March 2018. http://www.texasmonthly.com/category/topics/ut-tower-shooting/

40. Hamilton, R. 2015. McRaven: Campus carry would create "less safe" environment. *Texas Tribune*, 29 January. Accessed online 28 March 2018. https://www.texastribune.org/2015/01/29/mcraven-campus-carry-would-create-less-safe-enviro/

41. Watkins, M., & Murphy, R. 2016. Where Texas' private universities stand on campus carry. *Texas Tribune*, 29 July. Accessed online 28 March 2018. https://apps.texastribune.org/private-university-campus-carry/

42. Siron, C. 2016. Slain University of Texas student Haruka Weiser was strangled, sexually assaulted, report says. *Dallas News*, 6 April. Accessed online 28 March 2018. https://www.dallasnews.com/news/crime/2016/04/13/slain-ut-austin-student-haruka-weiser-was-strangled-report-says

43. Lee, T. 2016. New Texas law allows college students to carry guns on campus. *U.S. News and World Report*, 1 August. Accessed online 28 March 2018. http://www.nbcnews.com/news/us-news/new-texas-law-allows-college-students-carry-guns-campus-n620911

44. Montgomery, D., & Perez-Pena, R. 2017. Man wielding knife kills one and injures three at University of Texas. *New York Times*, 1 May. Accessed online 28 March 2018. https://www.nytimes.com/2017/05/01/us/texas-austin-stabbing-attack.html; Farmer, L., Mekelburg, M., & Jaramillo, C. 2017. Suspect in UT Austin stabbing charged with murder, had been committed before. *Dallas Morning News*, 3 May. Accessed online 28 March 2018. https://www.dallasnews.com/news/crime/2017/05/01/multiple-people-stabbed-ut-austin-campus

45. Toohey, M. 2017. Viral item debunked: No evidence gun-brandishing student helped subdue UT attacker. *Austin American-Statesman*, 3 May. Accessed online 28 March 2018. http://www.statesman.com/news/local/viral-item-debunked-evidence-gun-brandishing-student-helped-subdue-attacker/z92T0lb56COS9cb6emNGeN/

46. Grinberg, E., & Ellis, R. 2017. Texas Tech police officer fatally shot, freshman student in custody. Cable News Network, 10 October. Accessed online 28 March 2018. http://www.cnn.com/2017/10/09/us/texas-tech-police-officer-fatally-shot/index.html

47. Hendrick, T. 2012. Anschutz campus staff member accidentally fires gun. Fox31 (Denver),

12 November. Accessed online 28 March 2018. http://kdvr.com/2012/11/12/anschutz-campus-staff-member-accidentally-fires-gun/

48. Zuckerman, S. 2014. Idaho professor accidentally shoots himself in the foot in chemistry class. *Reuters*, 3 September. Accessed online 28 March 2018. http://www.reuters.com/article/us-usa-guncontrol-idaho-idUSKBN0GY2E620 140904

49. Associated Press. 2012. Weber State student accidentally shoots himself. *Daily Herald* (Ogden, UT), 5 January. Accessed online 28 March 2018. http://www.heraldextra.com/news/local/weber-state-student-accidentally-shoots-himself/article_eef6a77c-37d6-11e1-860e-0019bb2963f4.html; Carlisle, N., & Parker, N. 2016. Husband and wife die after University of Utah shooting, police say. *Salt Lake Tribune*, 29 December. Accessed online 28 March 2018. http://www.sltrib.com/news/4762770-155/shooting-reported-at-university-of-utah

50. Wikipedia. 2017. Umpqua Community College shooting. Accessed online 28 March 2018. https://en.wikipedia.org/wiki/Umpqua_Community_College_shooting

51. Carlisle, N., & Parker, N. 2016. Husband and wife die after University of Utah shooting, police say. *Salt Lake Tribune*, 29 December. Accessed online 28 March 2018. http://www.sltrib.com/news/4762770-155/shooting-reported-at-university-of-utah; Shapiro, T.R. 2015. Delta State University professor told police he killed his "wife" shortly before second shooting. *Washington Post*, 15 September. Accessed online 28 March 2018. https://www.washingtonpost.com/news/grade-point/wp/2015/09/15/history-professor-shot-and-killed-at-delta-state-university-known-as-mentor/?utm_term=.d3469bdc7d45

52. Violence Policy Center. 2018. Concealed carry killers. Accessed online 28 March 2018. http://concealedcarrykillers.org/

53. Violence Policy Center. 2018. Mass shootings involving concealed handgun permit holders. Accessed online 28 March 2018. http://concealedcarrykillers.org/wp-content/uploads/2017/07/CCW-mass-shooters-7-14-17.pdf

54. State of Tennessee. 2016. Public chapter no. 1061. An act to amend Tennessee Code Annotated, Title 39 and Title 49, relative to permitting certain persons to carry handguns on the property of certain postsecondary institutions. Accessed online 28 March 2018. http://utpolice.utk.edu/wp-content/uploads/sites/48/2016/06/pc1061.pdf

55. Georgia Legislature. 2017. House Bill 280 (as passed House and Senate), now Act 167. Accessed online 28 March 2018. http://www.legis.ga.gov/Legislation/20172018/170679.pdf

56. Coyne, A.C. 2017. Cops: KSU student's gun, wallet stolen in armed robbery at campus dorm. *Atlanta Journal-Constitution*, 25 July. Accessed online 28 March 2018. http://www.ajc.com/news/local/cops-ksu-student-gun-wallet-stolen-armed-robbery-campus-dorm/1IyM6cDukikBYhExsf2qFJ/

57. Li, O. 2016. When Jefferson and Madison banned guns on campus. *The Atlantic*, 6 May. Accessed online 28 March 2018. https://www.theatlantic.com/politics/archive/2016/05/when-jefferson-and-madison-banned-guns-on-campus/481461/; Smith, C., & Huegauburo, N. 2016. Guns on grounds—where did Jefferson stand? How U.Va.'s founder's stance lines up with current policy. *Cavalier Daily*, 20 October. Accessed online 28 March 2016. http://www.cavalierdaily.com/article/2016/10/guns-on-grounds-where-did-jefferson-stand; University of Virginia Board of Visitors. 1824. University of Virginia Board of Visitors Minutes, 4–5 October 1824. Encyclopedia Virginia. Accessed online 28 March 2018. https://www.encyclopediavirginia.org/University_of_Virginia_Board_of_Visitors_Minutes_October_4-5_1824

58. Centers for Disease Control and Prevention. 2018. National Center for Injury and Violence Prevention and Control Web-based Injury Statistics Query and Reporting System (WISQARS). Accessed online 28 March 2018. http://www.cdc.gov/injury/wisqars/index.html

59. Virginia Tech Review Panel. 2007. Mass shootings at Virginia Tech April 16, 2007: Report of the review panel presented to Governor Kaine, Commonwealth of Virginia. Accessed online 28 March 2018. https://governor.virginia.gov/media/3772/fullreport.pdf

60. U.S. Fire Administration. 2008. Northern Illinois University shooting. Federal Emergency Management Administration, Department of Homeland Security Technical Report USFA-TR-167 (February). Accessed online 28 March 2018. https://www.usfa.fema.gov/downloads/pdf/publications/tr_167.pdf; Northern Illinois University. 2010. Report of the February 14, 2008 shootings at Northern Illinois University. Office of the President, Northern Illinois University. Accessed online 28 March 2018. https://webcourses.niu.edu/bbcswebdav/institution/HLC2014RR/CH00/OFFICE-OF-THE-PRESIDENT-February-14-Report-2008-02.pdf

61. Wikipedia. 2017. Umpqua Community College shooting. Accessed online 28 March 2018. https://en.wikipedia.org/wiki/Umpqua_Community_College_shooting

62. Howell, E. 2014. Drake Equation: Estimating the odds of finding E.T. Accessed online 28 March 2018. https://www.space.com/25219-drake-equation.html

63. Anonymous. 2013. What are the odds of being murdered? Discover the Odds, 4 November. Accessed online 28 March 2018. http://discovertheodds.com/what-are-the-odds-of-being-murdered/; Murphy, S., Xu, J., & Kochanek, K. 2013. Deaths: Final data for 2010. *National Vital Statistics Reports, 61*(4), 1–117. Accessed online 28 March 2018. https://www.cdc.gov/nchs/data/nvsr/nvsr61/nvsr61_04.pdf

64. Centers for Disease Control and Prevention. 2018. National Center for Injury and Violence Prevention and Control Web-based Injury Statistics Query and Reporting System (WISQARS). Accessed online 28 March 2018. http://www.cdc.gov/injury/wisqars/index.html

65. Centers for Disease Control and Prevention. 2018. National Center for Injury and Violence Prevention and Control Web-based Injury Statistics Query and Reporting System (WISQARS). Accessed online 28 March 2018. http://www.cdc.gov/injury/wisqars/index.html

66. Boyce, J., & Silver, N. 2017. 2017 March Madness predictions. FiveThirtyEight, 12 March. Accessed online 28 March 2018. https://projects.fivethirtyeight.com/2017-march-madness-predictions/; Miller, J. 2011. Odds versus odds: Betting on March Mania. *Oh! A Blog*, Ohio Lottery's Office of Communications, 24 March. Accessed online 28 March 2018. https://ohiolottery.wordpress.com/2011/03/24/odds-versus-odds/

67. Hand, D.J. 2014. *The improbability principle: Why coincidences, miracles, and rare events happen every day*. New York, NY: Scientific American/Farrar, Straus and Giroux.

68. World Bank. 2017. International homicides (per 100,000 people). Accessed online 28 March 2018. http://data.worldbank.org/indicator/VC.IHR.PSRC.P5?end=2014&start=1995&view=chart&year_high_desc=true

69. National Center for Education Statistics. 2016. *Digest of Education Statistics*. U.S. Department of Education, Institute of Educations Sciences. Accessed online 28 March 2018. https://nces.ed.gov/programs/digest/

70. Anonymous. 2017. Sentry: Earth impact monitoring impact risk data. Center for Near Earth Object Studies, Jet Propulsion Laboratory, NASA, Pasadena, California. Accessed online 28 March 2018. https://cneos.jpl.nasa.gov/sentry/

71. National Weather Service. 2017. How dangerous is lightning? National Oceanic and Atmospheric Administration, Washington, DC. Accessed online 28 March 2018. http://www.lightningsafety.noaa.gov/odds.shtml

72. Anonymous. 2017. Understanding Powerball chances. Missouri Lottery Commission, Jefferson City, Missouri. Accessed online 28 March 2018. http://www.molottery.com/powerball/understanding_chances.jsp

73. Carter, A. 2012. 15 things more likely to happen than winning Mega Millions. *Daily Beast*, 30 March. Accessed online 28 March 2018. http://www.thedailybeast.com/15-things-more-likely-to-happen-than-winning-mega-millions

74. Hand, D.J. 2014. *The improbability principle: Why coincidences, miracles, and rare events happen every day*. New York, NY: Scientific American/Farrar, Straus and Giroux.

75. Hand, D.J. 2014. *The improbability principle: Why coincidences, miracles, and rare events happen every day*. New York, NY: Scientific American/Farrar, Strauss and Giroux.

76. Centers for Disease Control and Prevention. 2018. National Center for Injury and Violence Prevention and Control Web-based Injury Statistics Query and Reporting System (WISQARS). Accessed online 28 March 2018. http://www.cdc.gov/injury/wisqars/index.html

77. National Center for Education Statistics. 2016. *Digest of Education Statistics*. U.S. Department of Education, Institute of Educations Sciences. Accessed online 28 March 2018. https://nces.ed.gov/programs/digest/

78. Anonymous. 2017. Sentry: Earth impact monitoring impact risk data. Center for Near Earth Object Studies, Jet Propulsion Laboratory, NASA, Pasadena, California. Accessed online 28 March 2018. https://cneos.jpl.nasa.gov/sentry/

79. Hand, D.J. 2014. *The improbability principle: Why coincidences, miracles, and rare events happen every day*. New York, NY: Scientific American/Farrar, Straus and Giroux.

Chapter 8

1. Parker, K., et al. 2017. America's complex relationship with guns. Pew Research Center, Social and Demographic Trends. Accessed online 28 March 2018. http://assets.pewresearch.org/wp-content/uploads/sites/3/2017/06/06151541/Guns-Report-FOR-WEBSITE-PDF-6-21.pdf

2. Parker, K., et al. 2017. America's complex relationship with guns. Pew Research Center, Social and Demographic Trends. Accessed on-

line 28 March 2018. http://assets.pewresearch. org/wp-content/uploads/sites/3/2017/06/ 06151541/Guns-Report-FOR-WEBSITE-PDF-6-21.pdf

3. Parker, K., et al. 2017. America's complex relationship with guns. Pew Research Center, Social and Demographic Trends. Accessed online 28 March 2018. http://assets.pewresearch. org/wp-content/uploads/sites/3/2017/06/ 06151541/Guns-Report-FOR-WEBSITE-PDF-6-21.pdf

4. Anonymous. 2016. California's gun violence restraining order law. Law Center to Prevent Gun Violence. Accessed online 28 March 2018. http://smartgunlaws.org/californias-new-gun-violence-restraining-order-law/; Frattaroli, S., et al. 2015. Gun violence restraining orders: Alternative or adjunct to mental health–based restrictions on firearms? *Behavioral Sciences and the Law*, 33(2–3), 290–307.

5. Brady Center to Prevent Gun Violence. 2018. The lifesaving gun law you've never heard of. Accessed online 28 March 2018. http://www. bradycampaign.org/sites/default/files/ERPO-Fact-Sheet_08–2017.pdf

6. Acosta, L. 2015. United States: Gun ownership and the Supreme Court. Law Library of Congress. Accessed online 28 March 2018. https://www.loc.gov/law/help/second-amendment.php

7. Scalia, A. 2008. Opinion of the Court: *District of Columbia, et al., Petitioners v. Dick Anthony Heller*. Supreme Court of the United States No. 07–290. Accessed online 28 March 2018. https://www.law.cornell.edu/supct/pdf/07–290P.ZO

8. Acosta, L. 2015. United States: Gun ownership and the Supreme Court. Law Library of Congress. Accessed online 28 March 2018. https:// www.loc.gov/law/help/second-amendment.php

9. Scalia, A. 2008. Opinion of the Court: *District of Columbia, et al., Petitioners v. Dick Anthony Heller*. Supreme Court of the United States No. 07–290. Accessed online 28 March 2018. https://www.law.cornell.edu/supct/pdf/ 07–290P.ZO

10. Scalia, A. 2008. Opinion of the Court: *District of Columbia, et al., Petitioners v. Dick Anthony Heller*. Supreme Court of the United States No. 07–290. Accessed online 28 March 2018. https://www.law.cornell.edu/supct/pdf/ 07–290P.ZO

11. Anonymous. 2017. Guns on Campus' laws for public colleges and universities: A guide for students, parents, policy makers and journalists. Armed Campuses. Accessed online 28 March 2018. http://www.armedcampuses.org/

12. Associated Press. 2012. Weber State student accidentally shoots himself. *Daily Herald* (Ogden, UT), 5 January. Accessed online 28 March 2018. http://www.heraldextra.com/news/ local/weber-state-student-accidentally-shoots-himself/article_eef6a77c-37d6–11e1–860e-0019bb2963f4.html

13. Carlisle, N., & Parker, N. 2016. Husband and wife die after University of Utah shooting, police say. *Salt Lake Tribune*, 29 December. Accessed online 28 March 2018. http://www.sltrib. com/news/4762770–155/shooting-reported-at-university-of-utah

14. Noble, R., Mims, B., & Piper, R. 2017. University of Utah student shot to death in campus carjacking; hunt underway for "armed and dangerous" suspect. *Salt Lake Tribune*, 31 October. Accessed online 28 March 2018. http://www. sltrib.com/news/2017/10/31/shots-fired-near-university-of-utah/

15. Associated Press. 1993. Student opens fire, is shot dead at hearing. *Los Angeles Times*, 9 July. Accessed online 28 March 2018. http:// articles.latimes.com/1993–07–09/news/mn-11569_1_university-student

16. Whaley, M. 2012. Colorado Supreme Court affirms that CU students with permits can carry concealed guns on campus. *Denver Post*, 5 March. Accessed online 28 March 2018. https://www. denverpost.com/2012/03/05/colorado-supreme-court-affirms-that-cu-students-with-permits-can-carry-concealed-guns-on-campus/

17. Hendrick, T. 2012. Anschutz campus staff member accidentally fires gun. Fox31 (Denver), 12 November. Accessed online 28 March 2018. http://kdvr.com/2012/11/12/anschutz-campus-staff-member-accidentally-fires-gun/

18. Anonymous. 2014. Man killed in officer-involved shooting on Anschutz Medical Campus. *Denver Post*, 19 March. Accessed online 28 March 2018. https://www.denverpost.com/2014/ 03/19/man-killed-in-officer-involved-shooting-on-anschutz-medical-campus/

19. Watkins, M. 2016. Weeks after campus carry went into effect, an accidental misfire at Tarleton State. *Texas Tribune*, 16 September. Accessed online 28 March 2018. https://www.texastribune. org/2016/09/16/campus-carry-accidental-misfire-at-tarleton-state/; Cardona, C.Z. 2016. Tarleton State student accidentally fires gun in campus dorm. *Dallas Morning News*, 16 September. Accessed online 28 March 2018. https://www.dallas news.com/news/higher-education/2016/09/15/ tarleton-state-student-accidentally-discharges-gun-campus-dorm

20. Stranglin, D. 2017. 2 dead at North Lake College in apparent murder-suicide near Dallas.

USA Today, 3 May. Accessed online 28 March 2018. https://www.usatoday.com/story/news/2017/05/03/police-active-shooter-dallas-area-college/101247274/; Steele, T., Chiquillo, J., & de Bruijn, E. 2017. North Lake College gunman was stalking the woman he killed, her family says. *Dallas Morning News*, 4 May. Accessed online 28 March 2018. https://www.dallasnews.com/news/irving/2017/05/03/north-lake-college-lockdown-shooter

21. Svrluga, S. 2017. Texas Tech student faces capital murder charge after allegedly shooting a police officer on campus. *Washington Post*, 10 October. Accessed online 28 March 2018. https://www.washingtonpost.com/news/grade-point/wp/2017/10/10/texas-tech-student-faces-capital-murder-charge-after-allegedly-shooting-a-police-officer-on-campus/?utm_term=.80920f51fc4f

22. Gorman, M. 2017. Gun found in a Kansas University bathroom two weeks after campus carry legalization. *Newsweek*, 18 July. Accessed online 28 March 2018. http://www.newsweek.com/gun-wichita-state-university-campus-carry-638446; Williams, M.R., & Porter, T. 2017. Gun found in bathroom in KU's Wescoe Hall was loaded .38 reported stolen in Olathe. *Kansas City Star*, 5 September. Accessed online 28 March 2018. http://www.kansascity.com/news/local/article171379147.html

23. Spies, M. 2017. Kansas will be first campus-carry state where students won't need permits to tote guns. *The Trace*, 31 March. Accessed online 28 March 2018. https://www.thetrace.org/2017/03/campus-carry-kansas-no-permits-guns/

24. Eldridge, E. 2017. Second robbery in 2017 reported on KSU campus. *Atlanta Journal-Constitution*, 19 September. Accessed online 28 March 2018. http://www.ajc.com/news/local/second-robbery-2017-reported-ksu-campus/oUDuWVyu9VXJu1qqMZnjxO/

25. Coyne, A.C. 2017. Cops: KSU student's gun, wallet stolen in armed robbery at campus dorm. *Atlanta Journal-Constitution*, 25 July. Accessed online 28 March 2018. http://www.ajc.com/news/local/cops-ksu-student-gun-wallet-stolen-armed-robbery-campus-dorm/1IyM6cDukikBYhExsf2qFJ/

26. Reavis, C. 2017. Bicyclist discovers body, police determine death by suicide. *Arkansas Traveler*, 26 October. Accessed online 28 March 2018. http://www.uatrav.com/news/article_fdc0e868-bab5-11e7-9cd3-4bd07b44b41d.html

27. Associated Press. 2017. College student accused of considering mass attack. *Southwest Times Record*, 23 November. Accessed online 28 March 2018. http://www.swtimes.com/news/20171122/john-brown-university-student-accused-of-considering-mass-attack

28. Associated Press. 1993. Student opens fire, is shot dead at hearing. *Los Angeles Times*, 9 July. Accessed online 28 March 2018. http://articles.latimes.com/1993-07-09/news/mn-11569_1_university-student; Associated Press. 1993. Student shoots 3 at hearing in Utah, and is then killed. *New York Times*, 9 July. Accessed online 28 March 2018. http://www.nytimes.com/1993/07/09/us/student-shoots-3-at-hearing-in-utah-and-is-then-killed.html; Cortez, M. 2012. "No one wants to take another life," says former Weber State officer who killed gunman in 1993. *Deseret News*, 19 March. Accessed online 28 March 2018. https://www.deseretnews.com/article/865552494/No-one-wants-to-take-another-life-says-former-Weber-State-officer-who-killed-gunman-in-1993.html

29. Clery Center for Security on Campus. 2018. Summary of the Jeanne Clery Act: A compliance and reporting overview. Accessed online 28 March 2018. http://clerycenter.org/summary-jeanne-clery-act

30. U.S. Department of Education, Office of Postsecondary Education. 2016. Campus Safety and Security Data Analysis Cutting Tool. Accessed online 28 March 2018. https://ope.ed.gov/campussafety/#/

31. University of Central Arkansas. 2008. Information about UCA campus shooting. 27 October. Accessed online 28 March 2018. http://uca.edu/news/information-about-uca-campus-shooting/

32. Arkansas State University. 2010. Student dies from gunshot wound; Chancellor Potts expresses condolences. University Communications Services, Arkansas State University, Jonesboro, Arkansas. Accessed online 28 March 2018. http://asunews.astate.edu/StudentDeath041710.htm

33. U.S. Department of Justice. 2018. Uniform Crime Reporting System. Accessed online 28 March 2018. https://www.bjs.gov/ucrdata/Search/Crime/Crime.cfm

34. U.S. Department of Education, Office of Postsecondary Education. 2016. Campus Safety and Security Data Analysis Cutting Tool. Accessed online 28 March 2018. http://ope.ed.gov/campussafety/#/

35. Bartholemew, D. 2013. Man accidentally shoots self at KUAF radio station in downtown Fayetteville. *Fayetteville Flyer*, 8 February. Accessed online 28 March 2018. http://www.fayettevilleflyer.com/2013/02/08/man-accidentally-shoots-self-at-kuaf-campus-radio-station/

36. Bergan, S., & Miller, S. 2013. Student ac-

cidentally shoots himself on UA campus. 5News KFSM TV, 8 February. Accessed online 28 March 2018. http://5newsonline.com/2013/02/08/man-accidentally-shoots-himself-at-ua-campus-radio-station/

37. Brantley, M. 2013. Legal or not, gun goes off on UA campus. *Arkansas Times*, 8 February. Accessed online 28 March 2018. http://www.arktimes.com/ArkansasBlog/archives/2013/02/08/legal-or-not-gun-goes-off-on-ua-campus

38. Rushing, M. 2013. Student wounded accidentally by gunshot. University Relations Office, University of Arkansas, Fayetteville, Arkansas, 8 February. Accessed online 28 March 2018. http://news.uark.edu/articles/20186/student-wounded-accidentally-by-gunshot

39. SECRANT.com. 2013. Dummy shoots himself at KUAF. Accessed online 28 March 2018. http://www.secrant.com/rant/sec-football/dummy-shoots-himself-at-kuaf/39821372/

40. Taurus Industries. 2017. Taurus Judge® Revolver | 45 Colt/410 GA 3[qm] 5-RDS Matte Stainless. Accessed online 28 March 2018. http://www.taurususa.com/product-details.cfm?id=199&category=Pistol

41. Al-Khateeb, Z. 2017. Arkansas fears SEC membership in jeopardy with new gun law. *Sporting News*, 29 March. Accessed online 28 March 2018. http://www.sportingnews.com/ncaa-football/news/arkansas-razorbacks-gun-law-hb-1249-sec-membership-asa-hutchinson/579s08cli4m9hr481736371r

42. Strauss, C. 2017. The NCAA needs to take a strong stand against Arkansas law that will allow guns in stadiums. Fox Sports, 23 March. Accessed online 28 March 2018. https://www.foxsports.com/college-football/story/the-ncaa-needs-to-take-a-strong-stand-against-arkansas-law-that-will-allow-guns-in-stadiums-032317; Chandler, R. 2017. Here's a good idea—let's give these Arkansas football fans some guns. Sports Grid, 23 March. Accessed online 28 March 2018. https://www.sportsgrid.com/real-sports/ncaa-football/heres-a-good-idea-lets-give-these-arkansas-football-fans-some-guns/; Bolin, E. 2017. Arkansas fans don't seem to care for new law allowing firearms at Hogs games. SEC Country, 22 March. Accessed online 28 March

2018. https://www.seccountry.com/arkansas/arkansas-fans-dont-like-new-gun-law; Kersey, J. 2017. Allowing guns at Arkansas athletic events is a terrible idea. SEC Country. Accessed online 28 March 2018. https://www.seccountry.com/arkansas/arkansas-podcast-guns-in-stadiums; Harper, D. 2017. Arkansas law allowing guns at Razorback games beginning to draw high-powered opposition. SB Nation, 29 March. Accessed online 28 March 2018. https://www.arkansasfight.com/2017/3/29/15105888/arkansas-law-guns-razorback-games-stadium-high-powered-opposition-hb-1249; Kirk, O. 2017. SEC gets involved in the conceal carry controversy in Arkansas. 247Sports, 28 March. Accessed online 28 March 2018. https://247sports.com/college/arkansas/Bolt/SEC-gets-involved-in-the-conceal-carry-controversy-in-Arkansas-52020850; Koster, K. 2017. Opposing teams should boycott playing Arkansas if concealed weapons are allowed at games. The Big Lead, 23 March. Accessed online 28 March 2018. http://thebiglead.com/2017/03/23/opposing-teams-should-boycott-playing-arkansas-if-concealed-weapons-are-allowed-at-games/

43. Jennings, M. 2017. State lawmaker on possibility of sniper teams at Arkansas football games: "Count on it." SEC Country, 31 March. Accessed online 28 March 2018. https://www.seccountry.com/arkansas/lawmaker-sniper-teams-arkansas-razorbacks

44. National Rifle Association Institute for Legislative Action. 2017. Update: Action needed on gun control bill headed to Arkansas House floor despite strong opposition. 29 March. Accessed online 28 March 2018. https://www.nraila.org/articles/20170329/action-needed-gun-control-bill-headed-to-arkansas-house-floor-despite-strong-opposition

45. International Association of Campus Law Enforcement Administrators. 2018. Speakers and topics. International Association of Campus Law Enforcement Administrators Mid-America Regional Conference, Rogers, Arkansas, 8–11 April. Accessed online 28 March 2018. https://uapd.uark.edu/2018-mid-america-iaclea-conference/speakers-and-topics.php

Bibliography

10News.com. 2012. Man who strangled wife, burned body in car sentenced. 27 January. Accessed online 28 March 2018. http://www.10news.com/news/man-who-strangled-wife-burned-body-in-car-sentenced

Abadi, M. 2016. An officer who helped end one of the worst school shootings in US history has a problem with Texas' new gun law. *Business Insider*, 1 August. Accessed online 28 March 2018. http://www.businessinsider.com/ramiro-martinez-opposes-texas-campus-carry-law-2016-8

ABC News. 2012. Guns in America: A statistical look. 25 August. Accessed online 28 March 2018. http://abcnews.go.com/blogs/headlines/2012/08/guns-in-america-a-statistical-look/

Achenbach, J., Wan, W., Berman, M., & Balingit, M. 2016. Five Dallas police officers were killed by a lone attacker, authorities say. *Washington Post*, 8 July. Accessed online 28 March 2018. https://www.washingtonpost.com/news/morning-mix/wp/2016/07/08/like-a-little-war-snipers-shoot-11-police-officers-during-dallas-protest-march-killing-five/

Acosta, L. 2015. United States: Gun ownership and the Supreme Court. Law Library of Congress. Accessed online 28 March 2018. https://www.loc.gov/law/help/second-amendment.php

Al-Khateeb, Z. 2017. Arkansas fears SEC membership in jeopardy with new gun law. *Sporting News*, 29 March. Accessed online 28 March 2018. http://www.sportingnews.com/ncaa-football/news/arkansas-razorbacks-gun-law-hb-1249-sec-membership-asa-hutchinson/579s08cli4m91hr481736371r

American Academy of Arts & Sciences. 2015. Public research universities: Changes in state funding. The Lincoln Project: Excellence and Access in Public Higher Education. Accessed online 28 March 2018. https://www.amacad.org/multimedia/pdfs/publications/research papersmonographs/PublicResearchUniv_ChangesInStateFunding.pdf

American Fact Finder. 2018. United States Census Bureau, Population Division, Annual Estimates of the Resident Population: April 1, 2010 to July 1, 2015. Accessed online 28 March 2018. http://factfinder.census.gov/faces/table services/jsf/pages/productview.xhtml?src=bkmk

Anonymous. 1997. Rates of homicide, suicide, and firearm-related death among children—26 industrialized countries. *Centers for Disease Control and Prevention Morbidity and Mortality Weekly Report, 46*(5)(7 February), 101–105. Accessed online 28 March 2018. http://www.cdc.gov/mmwr/preview/mmwrhtml/00046149.htm

Anonymous. 2004. A troubling increase in murder rates on black college campuses. *Journal of Blacks in Higher Education* (44)(Summer), 14–17.

Anonymous. 2012. Protect children not guns 2012. Children's Defense Fund online report. Accessed online 28 March 2018. https://www.childrensdefense.org/wp-content/uploads/2018/08/protect-children-not-guns-2012.pdf

Anonymous. 2012. Remarks from the NRA press conference on Sandy Hook school shooting, delivered on Dec. 21, 2012 (Transcript). *Washington Post*, 21 December. Accessed online 28 March 2018. https://www.washingtonpost.com/politics/remarks-from-the-nra-press-conference-on-sandy-hook-school-shooting-delivered-on-dec-21-2012-transcript/2012/12/21/bd1841fe-4b88-11e2-a6a6-aabac85e8036_story.html

Anonymous. 2013. Gun violence: A public health issue. *Harvard Magazine*, 9 January. Accessed online 28 March 2018. http://harvardmagazine.com/2013/01/gun-violence-and-public-health

Anonymous. 2013. Prosecutor: Man arrested at

Kings Island had 4,000 rounds of ammo in truck. WLWT.com, 11 July. Accessed online 28 March 2018. http://www.wlwt.com/article/prosecutor-man-arrested-at-kings-island-had-4-000-rounds-of-ammo-in-truck/3533202

Anonymous. 2013. What are the odds of being murdered? Discover the Odds, 4 November. Accessed online 28 March 2018. http://discovertheodds.com/what-are-the-odds-of-being-murdered/

Anonymous. 2014. Man killed in officer-involved shooting on Anschutz Medical Campus. *Denver Post*, 19 March. Accessed online 28 March 2018. https://www.denverpost.com/2014/03/19/man-killed-in-officer-involved-shooting-on-anschutz-medical-campus/

Anonymous. 2016. California's gun violence restraining order law. Law Center to Prevent Gun Violence. Accessed online 28 March 2018. http://smartgunlaws.org/californias-new-gun-violence-restraining-order-law/

Anonymous. 2016. Cuyahoga River fire. Ohio History Connection, Ohio History Central, Cleveland State University. Accessed online 28 March 2018. http://www.ohiohistorycentral.org/w/Cuyahoga_River_Fire?rec=1642

Anonymous. 2016. Ventura man pleads guilty to stabbing, kidnapping his son. *Ventura County Star*, 15 January. Accessed online 28 March 2018. http://archive.vcstar.com/news/local/ventura/ventura-man-pleads-guilty-to-stabbing-kidnapping-his-son-296a624c-2e3b-509e-e053-0100007fd480-365504821.html

Anonymous. 2017. Guns on Campus' laws for public colleges and universities: A guide for students, parents, policy makers and journalists. Armed Campuses. Accessed online 28 March 2018. http://www.armedcampuses.org/

Anonymous. 2017. Laws concerning carrying concealed firearms on campus in Mississippi. Armed Campuses. Accessed online 28 March 2018. http://www.armedcampuses.org/mississippi/

Anonymous. 2017. Laws concerning carrying concealed firearms on campus in Wisconsin. Armed Campuses. Accessed online 28 March 2018. http://www.armedcampuses.org/wisconsin/

Anonymous. 2017. Sentry: Earth impact monitoring impact risk data. Center for Near Earth Object Studies, Jet Propulsion Laboratory, NASA, Pasadena, California. Accessed online 28 March 2018. https://cneos.jpl.nasa.gov/sentry/

Anonymous. 2017. The UT tower shooting archives. *Texas Monthly*. Accessed online 28 March 2018. http://www.texasmonthly.com/category/topics/ut-tower-shooting/

Anonymous. 2017. Understanding Powerball chances. Missouri Lottery Commission, Jefferson City, Missouri. Accessed online 28 March 2018. http://www.molottery.com/powerball/understanding_chances.jsp

Anonymous. 2018. Gun ownership in the United States. Statistic Brain Research Institute. Accessed online 28 March 2018. http://www.statisticbrain.com/gun-ownership-statistics-demographics/

Arkansas General Assembly. 2013. An act to allow trained and licensed staff and faculty to carry a concealed handgun on a university, college, or community college campus under certain circumstances; and for other purposes. Accessed online 28 March 2018. http://www.arkleg.state.ar.us/assembly/2013/2013R/Acts/Act226.pdf

Arkansas State University. 2010. Student dies from gunshot wound; Chancellor Potts expresses condolences. University Communications Services, Arkansas State University, Jonesboro, Arkansas. Accessed online 28 March 2018. http://asunews.astate.edu/StudentDeath041710.htm

Associated Press. 1984. Student at Tulane U. killed. *New York Times*, 5 October. Accessed online 28 March 2018. http://www.nytimes.com/1984/10/05/us/student-at-tulane-u-killed.html

Associated Press. 1987. Ex-Lehigh student sentenced to electric chair for murder. *New York Times*, 30 April. Accessed online 28 March 2018. http://www.nytimes.com/1987/04/30/us/ex-lehigh-student-sentenced-to-electric-chair-for-murder.html

Associated Press. 1993. Student opens fire, is shot dead at hearing. *Los Angeles Times*, 9 July. Accessed online 28 March 2018. http://articles.latimes.com/1993-07-09/news/mn-11569_1_university-student

Associated Press. 1993. Student shoots 3 at hearing in Utah, and is then killed. *New York Times*, 9 July. Accessed online 28 March 2018. http://www.nytimes.com/1993/07/09/us/student-shoots-3-at-hearing-in-utah-and-is-then-killed.html

Associate Press. 2002. Driver who hit ASU woman guilty of negligent homicide. *Tucson Citizen*, 29 October. Accessed online 28 March 2018. http://tucsoncitizen.com/morgue2/2002/10/29/145385-driver-who-hit-asu-woman-guilty-of-negligent-homicide/

Associated Press. 2012. Killer used bow and arrow in attack at Casper College; one victim was his father. *New York Daily News*, 1 December. Accessed online 28 March 2018. http://www.nydailynews.com/news/national/killer-bow-arrow-kill-father-article-1.1211499

Associated Press. 2012. Weber State student accidentally shoots himself. *Daily Herald* (Ogden, UT), 5 January. Accessed online 28 March 2018. http://www.heraldextra.com/news/local/weber-state-student-accidentally-shoots-himself/article_eef6a77c-37d6-11e1-860e-0019bb2963f4.html

Associated Press. 2013. Colorado campus gun bans divisive, hard to enforce. CBS TV (Denver), 3 March. Accessed online 28 March 2018. http://denver.cbslocal.com/2013/03/03/colorado-campus-gun-bans-divisive-hard-to-enforce/

Associated Press. 2014. Boise police chief says he was blocked from speaking against guns on campus bill. Boise State Public Radio, Boise State University, Boise, Idaho, 12 February. Accessed online 28 March 2018. http://boisestatepublicradio.org/post/boise-police-chief-says-he-was-blocked-speaking-against-guns-campus-bill

Associated Press. 2014. Idaho Education Board votes to fight guns on campus bill. Boise State Public Radio, Boise State University, Boise, Idaho, 3 February. Accessed online 28 March 2018. http://boisestatepublicradio.org/post/idaho-education-board-votes-fight-guns-campus-bill

Associated Press. 2014. Lawmakers resurrect bill to allow guns on Idaho university campuses. Boise State Public Radio, Boise State University, Boise, Idaho, 24 January. Accessed online 28 March 2018. http://boisestatepublicradio.org/post/lawmakers-resurrect-bill-allow-guns-idaho-university-campuses

Associated Press. 2017. College student accused of considering mass attack. *Southwest Times Record*, 23 November. Accessed online 28 March 2018. http://www.swtimes.com/news/20171122/john-brown-university-student-accused-of-considering-mass-attack

Baker, A., Goodman, J.D., & Mueller, B. 2015. Beyond the chokehold: The path to Eric Garner's death. *New York Times*, 13 June. Accessed online 28 March 2018. http://www.nytimes.com/2015/06/14/nyregion/eric-garner-police-chokehold-staten-island.html

Baker, P. 2013. In gun debate, even language can be loaded. *New York Times*, 15 January. Accessed online 28 March 2018. http://www.nytimes.com/2013/01/16/us/gun-imagery-fills-language-of-debate.html?_r=0

Barry, D., Kovaleski, S.F., Robertson, C., & Al-varez, L. 2012. Race, tragedy and outrage collide after a shot in Florida. *New York Times*, 1 April. Accessed online 28 March 2018. http://www.nytimes.com/2012/04/02/us/trayvon-martin-shooting-prompts-a-review-of-ideals.html

Barry, R., & Jones, C. 2014. Hundreds of police killings are uncounted in federal stats. *Wall Street Journal*, 3 December. Accessed online 28 March 2018. http://www.wsj.com/articles/hundreds-of-police-killings-are-uncounted-in-federal-statistics-1417577504

Bartholemew, D. 2013. Man accidentally shoots self at KUAF radio station in downtown Fayetteville. *Fayetteville Flyer*, 8 February. Accessed online 28 March 2018. http://www.fayettevilleflyer.com/2013/02/08/man-accidentally-shoots-self-at-kuaf-campus-radio-station/

Baumer, E. 1994. Poverty, crack, and crime: A cross-city analysis. *Journal of Research in Crime and Delinquency, 31*(3), 311–327.

Baumer, E., Lauritsen, J.L., Rosenfeld, R., & Wright, R. 1998. The influence of crack cocaine on robbery, burglary, and homicide rates: A cross-city, longitudinal analysis. *Journal of Research in Crime and Delinquency, 35*(3), 316–340.

Beddington, J. 2011. Blackett review of high impact low probability risks. Government Office of Science. Accessed online 28 March 2018. https://www.gov.uk/government/uploads/system/uploads/attachment_data/file/278526/12-519-blackett-review-high-impact-low-probability-risks.pdf

Beeghley, L. 2003. *Homicide: A sociological explanation*. Lanham, MD: Rowman & Littlefield.

Belasco, A. 2011. The cost of Iraq, Afghanistan, and other Global War on Terror operations since 9/11. Congressional Research Service Report for Congress, RL33110, Washington, DC.

Bennett, K.J., Kraft, J.R., & Grubb, D. 2011. University faculty attitudes toward guns on campus. *Journal of Criminal Justice Education, 23*(3), 1–20. Accessed online 28 March 2018. https://www.researchgate.net/publication/239790628_University_Faculty_Attitudes_Toward_Guns_on_Campus

Benning, T. 2015. Group opposed to "campus carry" says its polling shows most Texans do too. *Dallas Morning News*, 17 March. Accessed online 28 March 2018. http://www.dallasnews.com/news/politics/2015/03/17/group-opposed-to-campus-carry-says-its-polling-shows-most-texans-do-too

Bensing, R.C., & Schroeder, O. 1960. *Homicide in an urban community*. Springfield, IL: Charles C. Thomas Publishers.

Benson, A. 2003. Couple dead after apparent murder-suicide at BSU. *The Arbiter*, 11 July. Accessed online 28 March 2018. https://arbiteronline.com/2003/07/11/couple-dead-after-apparent-murder-suicide-at-bsu-2/

Benson, B. 2012. President Benson's statement on the Colorado Supreme Court ruling on concealed weapons on campus. *CU Boulder Today*, 5 March. Accessed online 28 March 2018. http://www.colorado.edu/today/2012/03/05/president-bensons-statement-colorado-supreme-court-ruling-concealed-weapons-campus

Bergan, S., & Miller, S. 2013. Student accidentally shoots himself on UA campus. 5News KFSM TV, 8 February. Accessed online 28 March 2018. http://5newsonline.com/2013/02/08/man-accidentally-shoots-himself-at-ua-campus-radio-station/

Bergin, B. 2012. How much is 6,000 rounds? Not much, gun advocates say. WNYC, 23 July. Accessed online 28 March 2018. http://www.wnyc.org/story/224666-how-much-6000-rounds/

Biemiller, L. 2012. Colorado Supreme Court says state law trumps university's ban on guns. *Chronicle of Higher Education*, 5 March. Accessed online 28 March 2018. http://www.chronicle.com/article/Colorado-Supreme-Court-Says/131076

Binkley, C., Riepenhoff, J., Wagner, M., & Gregory, S. 2014. Reports on college crime are deceptively inaccurate. *Columbus Dispatch*, 30 September. Accessed online 28 March 2018. http://www.dispatch.com/content/stories/local/2014/09/30/campus-insecurity.html

Block, M. 2013. Gun metaphors deeply embedded in English language. National Public Radio, 19 March. Accessed online 28 March 2018. http://www.npr.org/2013/03/19/174767346/gun-metaphors-deeply-embedded-in-english-language)

Blow, C.M. 2016. Incandescent with rage. *New York Times*, 27 July. Accessed online 28 March 2018. http://www.nytimes.com/2016/07/28/opinion/incandescent-with-rage.html

Blumstein, A. 1995. Youth violence, guns, and the illicit-drug industry. *Journal of Criminal Law and Criminology, 86*(1), 10–36.

Blumstein, A., Rivara, F.P., & Rosenfeld, R. 2000. The rise and decline of homicide—and why. *Annual Review of Public Health, 21*, 505–41.

Blumstein, A., & Wallman, J. 2006. *The crime drop in America*. Cambridge, UK: Cambridge University Press.

Bolin, E. 2017. Arkansas fans don't seem to care for new law allowing firearms at Hogs games. SEC Country, 22 March. Accessed online 28 March 2018. https://www.seccountry.com/arkansas/arkansas-fans-dont-like-new-gun-law

Boyce, J., & Silver, N. 2017. 2017 March Madness predictions. FiveThirtyEight, 12 March. Accessed online 28 March 2018. https://projects.fivethirtyeight.com/2017-march-madness-predictions/

Brady Campaign to Prevent Gun Violence. 2018. Gun death and injury statistics sheet: 3-year average. Accessed online 28 March 2018. http://www.bradycampaign.org/sites/default/files/GunDeathandInjuryStatSheet3YearAverageFINAL.pdf

Brady Center to Prevent Gun Violence. 2018. The lifesaving gun law you've never heard of. Accessed online 28 March 2018. http://www.bradycampaign.org/sites/default/files/ERPO-Fact-Sheet_08–2017.pdf

Braithwaite, R.L., Taylor, S.E., & Treadwell, H.M. 2009. *Health issues in the black community*. 3rd edition. San Francisco, CA: Jossey-Bass.

Brantley, M. 2013. Legal or not, gun goes off on UA campus. *Arkansas Times*, 8 February. Accessed online 28 March 2018. http://www.arktimes.com/ArkansasBlog/archives/2013/02/08/legal-or-not-gun-goes-off-on-ua-campus

Brayden, T. 2002. Henry trades appeal rights for life in prison for 1986 rape, murder of Lehigh student. Northampton County judge OKs deal. Death sentence was thrown out in May. *The Morning Call*, 31 August. Accessed online 28 March 2018. http://articles.mcall.com/2002–08-31/news/3417898_1_death-sentence-death-penalty-appeal-rights

Brinker, G., Lenneman, B., & Swayne, R.L. 2016. Kansas Board of Regents Council of Faculty Senate Presidents campus employees' weapons survey. Docking Institute of Public Affairs, Fort Hays State University, Fort Hays, Kansas. Accessed online 28 March 2018. http://www.khi.org/assets/uploads/news/14232/regents_facultystaff_gun_survey_2015_(2).pdf

Brookman, F. 2005. *Understanding homicide*. Thousand Oaks, CA: Sage.

Brown, G. 2012. Suspects sought in murder at Mississippi State University. WREG News Channel 3 (Memphis), 25 March. Accessed online 10 July 2017. http://wreg.com/2012/03/25/fatal-shooting-at-mississippi-state-university/

Bryce, D. 2014. ISU prof with concealed weapons permit who accidentally shot his foot in class is identified. *Idaho State Journal* (Idaho State University, Pocatello), 4 September. Accessed online 28 March 2018. https://idahostatejournal.com/news/local/isu-prof-with-concealed-weapons-permit-who-accidentally-shot-his/article_18228ab2–3383–11e4–af7e-001a4bcf887a.html

Bureau of Alcohol, Tobacco, and Firearms. 2015. Report on firearms commerce in the U.S. Accessed online 28 March 2018. https://www.atf.gov/about/docs/report/2015-report-firearms-commerce-us/download

Bureau of Alcohol, Tobacco, and Firearms. 2018. Permanent Brady permit chart. Office of Enforcement Programs and Services, Bureau of Alcohol, Tobacco, and Firearms, U.S. Department of Justice. Accessed online 28 March 2018. https://www.atf.gov/rules-and-regulations/permanent-brady-permit-chart

Bureau of Justice Assistance. 2001. Hate crimes on campus: The problem and how to confront it. Office of Justice Programs, Department of Justice. Accessed online 28 March 2018. https://www.ncjrs.gov/pdffiles1/bja/187249.pdf

Campaign to Keep Guns Off Campus. 2018. Accessed online 28 March 2018. http://keepgunsoffcampus.org/state-battles/

Caniglia, J. 2013. Conviction of Toledo man for stockpiling weapons began with the tracking of camisoles. *Plain Dealer*, 1 September. Accessed online 28 March 2018. http://www.cleveland.com/metro/index.ssf/2013/09/from_camisoles_to_ammunition_a.html

Cardona, C.Z. 2016. Tarleton State student accidentally fires gun in campus dorm. *Dallas Morning News*, 16 September. Accessed online 28 March 2018. https://www.dallasnews.com/news/higher-education/2016/09/15/tarleton-state-student-accidentally-discharges-gun-campus-dorm

Carlisle, N., & Miller, J. 2016. Woman killed by husband at University of Utah planned to leave him, family says. *Salt Lake Tribune*, 30 December. Accessed online 28 March 2018. http://www.sltrib.com/home/4765548–155/woman-killed-in-murder-suicide-at-university

Carlisle, N., & Parker, N. 2016. Husband and wife die after University of Utah shooting, police say. *Salt Lake Tribune*, 29 December. Accessed online 28 March 2018. http://www.sltrib.com/news/4762770–155/shooting-reported-at-university-of-utah

Carson, R. 1962. *Silent Spring*. Boston, MA: Houghton Mifflin.

Carter, A. 2012. 15 things more likely to happen than winning Mega Millions. *Daily Beast*, 30 March. Accessed online 28 March 2018. http://www.thedailybeast.com/15-things-more-likely-to-happen-than-winning-mega-millions

Cavanaugh, M.R., Bouffard, J.A., Wells, W., & Nobles, M.R. 2012. Student attitudes toward concealed handguns on campus at 2 universities. *American Journal of Public Health, 102*(12), 2245–2247. Accessed online 28 March 2018. http://www.hhs.iup.edu/rlct/SAFE806HPfl3/MR%20Cavanaugh%20guns%20student%20attitudes%202012.pdf

CBS DFW. 2015. Students & professors sound off on "campus carry" gun bill. 18 March. Accessed online 28 March 2018. http://dfw.cbslocal.com/2015/03/18/students-professors-sound-off-on-campus-carry-gun-bill/

CBS News. 2009. Man with weapons, ammo arrested near UCLA. 11 February. Accessed online 28 March 2018. http://www.cbsnews.com/2100–201_162–4406019.html

Centers for Disease Control and Prevention. 2013. Homicide rates among persons aged 10–24 years—United States, 1981–2010. *Centers for Disease Control and Prevention Morbidity and Mortality Weekly Report, 62*(27)(12 July), 545–548. Accessed online 28 March 2018. https://www.cdc.gov/mmwr/preview/mmwrhtml/mm6227a1.htm

Centers for Disease Control and Prevention. 2016. *Principles of epidemiology in public health practice, third edition: An introduction to applied epidemiology and biostatistics: Lesson 1—Introduction to epidemiology; Section 11—Epidemic disease occurrence.* Self-Study Course SS1978. Accessed online 28 March 2018. http://www.cdc.gov/ophss/csels/dsepd/ss1978/lesson1/section11.html

Centers for Disease Control and Prevention. 2018. National Center for Injury and Violence Prevention and Control Web-based Injury Statistics Query and Reporting System (WISQARS). Accessed online 28 March 2018. http://www.cdc.gov/injury/wisqars/index.html

Centers for Disease Control and Prevention. 2018. National Vital Statistics System (NVSS). National Center for Health Statistics. Accessed online 28 March 2018. https://www.cdc.gov/nchs/nvss/

Chalabi, M., & Burn-Murdoch, J. 2013. McDonald's 34,492 restaurants: Where are they? *The Guardian*, 17 July. Accessed online 28 March 2018. http://www.theguardian.com/news/datablog/2013/jul/17/mcdonalds-restaurants-where-are-they#data

Chalabi, M., & Burn-Murdoch, J. 2013. McMap of the world, 2013 (map and spreadsheet showing locations of McDonald's fast food restaurants worldwide). Accessed online 28 March 2018. https://docs.google.com/spreadsheet/ccc?key=0At6CC4x_ybnMdG5NcUZTNkkxN2dBRHQzWFVJbHZHMFE#gid=0

Chandler, R. 2017. Here's a good idea—let's give these Arkansas football fans some guns. Sports Grid, 23 March. Accessed online 28 March 2018. https://www.sportsgrid.com/real-sports/ncaa-football/heres-a-good-idea-lets-give-these-arkansas-football-fans-some-guns/

Clery Center for Security on Campus. 2016. Jeanne Clery Act text. Accessed online 28 March 2018. http://clerycenter.org/jeanne-clery-act

Clery Center for Security on Campus. 2018. Summary of the Jeanne Clery Act: A compliance and reporting overview. Accessed online 28 March 2018. http://clerycenter.org/summary-jeanne-clery-act

Coates, T-N. 2013. Trayvon Martin and the irony of American justice. *The Atlantic*, 15 July. Accessed online 28 March 2018. http://www.theatlantic.com/national/archive/2013/07/trayvon-martin-and-the-irony-of-american-justice/277782/

Coates, T-N. 2014. On the killing of Jordan Davis by Michael Dunn. *The Atlantic*, 15 February. Accessed online 28 March 2018. http://www.theatlantic.com/politics/archive/2014/02/on-the-killing-of-jordan-davis-by-michael-dunn/283870/

College Presidents for Gun Safety. 2012. Open letter to President Obama. Accessed online 28 March 2018. http://collegepresidentsforgunsafety.org/

Cortez, M. 2012. "No one wants to take another life," says former Weber State officer who killed gunman in 1993. *Deseret News*, 19 March. Accessed online 28 March 2018. https://www.deseretnews.com/article/865552494/No-one-wants-to-take-another-life-says-former-Weber-State-officer-who-killed-gunman-in-1993.html

Coscarelli, J. 2014. No charges against Ohio police in John Crawford III Walmart shooting, despite damning security video. *New York Magazine*, 24 September. Accessed online 28 March 2018. http://nymag.com/daily/intelligencer/2014/09/no-charges-john-crawford-iii-walmart-shooting-video.html

Coyne, A.C. 2017. Cops: KSU student's gun, wallet stolen in armed robbery at campus dorm. *Atlanta Journal-Constitution*, 25 July. Accessed online 28 March 2018. http://www.ajc.com/news/local/cops-ksu-student-gun-wallet-stolen-armed-robbery-campus-dorm/1IyM6cDukikBYhExsf2qFJ/

Criminal Defense Lawyer. 2016. The crime of mayhem. Accessed online 28 March 2018. http://www.criminaldefenselawyer.com/resources/the-crime-mayhem.htm

Dahl, P., Bonham, G., Jr., & Reddington, P. 2016. Community college faculty: Attitudes toward guns on campus. *Community College Journal of Research and Practice*, 40(8), 706–717. Accessed online 28 March 2018. https://www.researchgate.net/publication/294874873_Community_College_Faculty_Attitudes_Toward_Guns_on_Campus

Dahlberg, L.L., & Mercy, J.A. 2009. History of violence as a public health issue. *AMA Virtual Mentor*, 11(2), 167–172. Accessed online 28 March 2018. http://www.cdc.gov/violenceprevention/pdf/history_violence-a.pdf

Daly, M. 2016. *Killing the competition: Economic inequality and homicide*. New Brunswick, NJ: Transaction.

Daly, M., & Wilson, M. 1988. *Homicide*. New York, NY: A. de Gruyter.

Daraskevich, J. 2014. Unmarked graves represent Jacksonville homicide victims who have yet to be identified. *Florida Times-Union*, 27 April. Accessed online 4 November 2016. http://jacksonville.com/news/crime/2014-04-27/story/graves-without-names-represent-jacksonville-homicide-victims-who-have

Delong, K. 2013. UWM student charged in connection with heroin overdose death. *Fox News 6* (Milwaukee, WI), 19 August. Accessed online 28 March 2018. http://fox6now.com/2013/08/19/uwm-student-charged-in-connection-with-heroin-overdose-death/

Dempsey, C., & Chaniewski, A. 2013. Man who had stockpile of guns, ammo and explosives is arrested, Fairfield police say. *Hartford Courant*, 7 October. Accessed online 28 March 2018. http://www.courant.com/community/fairfield/hc-fairfield-haz-mat-1003-20131002,0,5408331.story

Desilver, D. 2013. A minority of Americans own guns, but just how many is unclear. Pew Research Center, 4 June. Accessed online 28 March 2018. http://www.pewresearch.org/fact-tank/2013/06/04/a-minority-of-americans-own-guns-but-just-how-many-is-unclear/

Dimock, M., Doherty, C., & Christian, L. 2013. Perspectives of gun owners, non-owners: Why own a gun? Protection is now top reason. Pew Research Center, 12 March. Accessed online 28 March 2018. http://www.people-press.org/files/legacy-pdf/03-12-13%20Gun%20Ownership%20Release.pdf

Earth Day Network. 2016. The history of Earth Day. Accessed online 28 March 2018. http://

www.earthday.org/earth-day-history-movement

Edwards-Levy, A. 2015. 40 percent of Americans know someone who was killed with a gun. *Huffington Post*, 8 October. Accessed online 28 March 2018. http://www.huffingtonpost.com/entry/americans-know-gun-violence-victims_us_56169834e4b0e66ad4c6bd2b

Eldridge, E. 2017. Second robbery in 2017 reported on KSU campus. *Atlanta Journal-Constitution*, 19 September. Accessed online 28 March 2018. http://www.ajc.com/news/local/second-robbery-2017-reported-ksu-campus/oUDuWVyu9VXJu1qqMZnjxO/

Eligon, J., & Stolberg, S.G. 2016. Baltimore after Freddie Gray: The "mind-set has changed." *New York Times*, 12 April. Accessed online 28 March 2018. http://www.nytimes.com/2016/04/13/us/baltimore-freddie-gray.html

Farmer, L., Mekelburg, M., & Jaramillo, C. 2017. Suspect in UT Austin stabbing charged with murder, had been committed before. *Dallas Morning News*, 3 May. Accessed online 28 March 2018. https://www.dallasnews.com/news/crime/2017/05/01/multiple-people-stabbed-ut-austin-campus

Federal Bureau of Investigation. 2014. Online version of the National Instant Criminal Background Check System (NICS) Operations Report for the 2014 calendar year. Accessed online 28 March 2018. https://www.fbi.gov/file-repository/2014-nics-ops-report-050115.pdf

Federal Bureau of Investigation. 2016. Online version of the National Instant Criminal Background Check System (NICS) Operations Report for the 2016 calendar year. Accessed online 28 March 2018. https://www.fbi.gov/file-repository/2016-nics-operations-report-final-5-3-2017.pdf

Federal Bureau of Investigation. 2016. Uniform Crime Reporting (UCR) Program. Accessed online 28 March 2018. https://ucr.fbi.gov/

Federal Register. 2014. Violence Against Women Act: A Rule by the Education Department on 10/20/2014. Accessed online 28 March 2018. https://www.federalregister.gov/documents/2014/10/20/2014-24284/violence-against-women-act

Firearm and Injury Center at Penn. 2011. Firearm Injury in the U.S. (Resource Book Online). University of Pennsylvania Health System, Philadelphia, Pennsylvania. Accessed online 28 March 2018. http://www.uphs.upenn.edu/ficap/resourcebook/pdf/monograph.pdf

Food Marketing Institute. 2012. Supermarket facts—Industry overview 2011–2012. Accessed online 28 March 2018. http://www.fmi.org/research-resources/supermarket-facts

Frattaroli, S., McGinty E.E., Barnhorst, A., & Greenberg, S. 2015. Gun violence restraining orders: Alternative or adjunct to mental health–based restrictions on firearms? *Behavioral Sciences and the Law, 33*(2–3), 290–307.

Fryer, R.G., Heaton, P.S., Levitt, S.D., & Murphy, K.M. 2013. Measuring crack cocaine and its impact. *Economic Inquiry, 51*(3), 1651–1681.

Furious. 2014. 11 historically black colleges & universities that have closed. Accessed online 28 March 2018. https://urbanintellectuals.com/2014/10/17/11-historically-black-colleges-universities-that-have-closed/

Galvan, A. 2010. A mother's worst nightmare. *Albuquerque Journal*, 25 July. Accessed online 28 March 2018. http://abqjournal.com/news/metro/25233749metro07-25-10.htm

Gavran, J. 2017. Concealed handguns on campus: A multi-year study. *Visions: The Journal of Applied Research for the Association of Florida Colleges, 7*(1), 13–18. Accessed online 28 March 2018. http://keepgunsoffcampus.org/wp-content/uploads/2017/05/Campus-Crime-Report-4.pdf

Georgia Legislature. 2017. House Bill 280 (as passed House and Senate), now Act 167. Accessed online 28 March 2018. http://www.legis.ga.gov/Legislation/20172018/170679.pdf

Giffords Law Center to Prevent Gun Violence. 2018. Gun violence statistics. Accessed online 28 March 2018. http://lawcenter.giffords.org/category/gun-studies-statistics/gun-violence-statistics/

Goard, A. 2015. Hundreds sign petition opposing campus carry at Texas Tech. *Everything Lubbock*, 19 October. Accessed online 28 March 2018. http://www.everythinglubbock.com/news/kamc-news/hundreds-sign-petition-opposing-campus-carry-at-texas-tech

Gonzalez, M.C. 2015. UTEP students rally against campus carry law. *El Paso Times*, 19 October. Accessed online 28 March 2018. http://www.elpasotimes.com/story/news/politics/2015/10/19/utep-students-rally-against-campus-carry-law/74229956/

Google. 2016. Google Earth. Accessed online 28 March 2018. https://www.google.com/earth/

Gorman, M. 2017. Gun found in a Kansas University bathroom two weeks after campus carry legalization. *Newsweek*, 18 July. Accessed online 28 March 2018. http://www.newsweek.com/gun-wichita-state-university-campus-carry-638446

Graf, S. 2014. Boise state president says guns on

campus bill solves a problem that doesn't exist. Boise State Public Radio, Boise State University, Boise, Idaho, 25 February. Accessed online 28 March 2018. http://boisestatepublic radio.org/post/boise-state-president-says-guns-campus-bill-solves-problem-doesnt-exist

Grayson, P., & Meilman, P. 2013. Guns and student safety. *Journal of College Student Psychotherapy, 27*(3), 175–176.

Green, M.S., Swartz, T., Mayshar, E., Lev, B., Leventhal, A., Slater, P.E., & Shemer, J. 2002. When is an epidemic an epidemic? *Israeli Medical Association Journal, 4*, 3–6.

Grinberg, E., & Ellis, R. 2017. Texas Tech police officer fatally shot, freshman student in custody. Cable News Network, 10 October. Accessed online 28 March 2018. http://www.cnn.com/2017/10/09/us/texas-tech-police-officer-fatally-shot/index.html

Guffey, J.E. 2013. Crime on campus: Can Clery Act data from universities and colleges be trusted? *ASBBS eJournal, 9*(1), 51–61. Accessed online 28 March 2018. http://0-search.proquest.com.library.uark.edu/docview/1448005586?accountid=8361

GunPolicy.org. 2018. United States—Gun facts, figures and the law. School of Public Health at the University of Sydney, Australia. Accessed online 28 March 2018. http://www.gunpolicy.org/firearms/region/united-states

Gun Violence Archive. 2018. Mass shootings. Accessed online 28 March 2018. http://www.gunviolencearchive.org/mass-shooting

Hamilton, R. 2015. McRaven: Campus carry would create "less safe" environment. *Texas Tribune*, 29 January. Accessed online 28 March 2018. https://www.texastribune.org/2015/01/29/mcraven-campus-carry-would-create-less-safe-enviro/

Hancock, P. 2016. University leaders share personal concerns about guns on campus. *Lawrence Journal-World* (Lawrence, KS), 14 September. Accessed online 28 March 2018. http://www2.ljworld.com/news/2016/sep/14/university-chiefs-share-personal-concerns-about-pe/

Hand, D.J. 2014. *The improbability principle: Why coincidences, miracles, and rare events happen every day.* New York, NY: Scientific American/Farrar, Straus and Giroux.

Harper, D. 2017. Arkansas law allowing guns at Razorback games beginning to draw high-powered opposition. SB Nation, 29 March. Accessed online 28 March 2018. https://www.arkansasfight.com/2017/3/29/15105888/arkansas-law-guns-razorback-games-stadium-high-powered-opposition-hb-1249

Healy, J. 2014. Ferguson, still tense, grows calmer. *New York Times*, 26 November. Accessed online 28 March 2018. http://www.nytimes.com/2014/11/27/us/michael-brown-darren-wilson-ferguson-protests.html

Hemenway, D., Azrael, D., & Miller, M. 2001. National attitudes concerning gun carrying in the United States. *Injury Prevention, 7*(4), 282–285.

Hemenway, D., & Miller, M. 2000. Firearm availability and homicide rates across 26 high income countries. *Journal of Trauma, 49*, 985–988.

Hendrick, T. 2012. Anschutz campus staff member accidentally fires gun. Fox31 (Denver), 12 November. Accessed online 28 March 2018. http://kdvr.com/2012/11/12/anschutz-campus-staff-member-accidentally-fires-gun/

Hepburn, L., Miller, M., Azrael, D., & Hemenway, D. 2007. The US gun stock: Results from the 2004 national firearms survey. *Injury Prevention, 13*, 15–19. Accessed online 28 March 2018. http://www.ncbi.nlm.nih.gov/pmc/articles/PMC2610545/

Hill, S.T. 1982. The traditionally black institutions of higher education. National Center for Education Statistics, Institute for Education Sciences, U.S. Department of Education. Accessed online 28 March 2018. http://nces.ed.gov/pubs84/84308.pdf

Hough, R., & Jones-Brown, D. 2014. Homicide. In D. Jones-Brown, B. Frazier, & M. Brooks (Eds.), *African Americans and criminal justice: An encyclopedia* (pp. 277–281). Westport, CT: Greenwood.

Howell, E. 2014. Drake Equation: Estimating the odds of finding E.T. Accessed online 28 March 2018. https://www.space.com/25219-drake-equation.html

Howell, E.M., & Abraham, P. 2013. The hospital costs of firearm assaults. Urban Institute (September). Accessed online 28 March 2018. https://www.urban.org/sites/default/files/publication/23956/412894-The-Hospital-Costs-of-Firearm-Assaults.PDF

Hurley, D.J. 2015. Countering the push to put guns on campus. *Public Purpose* (Spring), 14–15. Accessed online 28 March 2018. http://www.aascu.org/MAP/PublicPurpose/2015/Spring/CounteringGuns/

Hutchinson, A. 2013. Report of the National School Shield Task Force. National School Shield Task Force, National Rifle Association, Arlington, Virginia. Accessed online 28 March 2018. http://www.guns.com/wp-content/uploads/2013/04/National-Shcool-Shield-Safety-report.pdf

Idaho Senate Bill 1254. 2014. Legislature of the

State of Idaho, 62nd Session, 2nd Regular Session. Accessed online 28 March 2018. https://legislature.idaho.gov/wp-content/uploads/sessioninfo/2014/legislation/S1254.pdf

Ingraham, C. 2015. There are now more guns than people in the United States. *Washington Post*, 5 October. Accessed online 28 March 2018. https://www.washingtonpost.com/news/wonk/wp/2015/10/05/guns-in-the-united-states-one-for-every-man-woman-and-child-and-then-some/

International Association of Campus Law Enforcement Administrators. 2008. Position statement on concealed carrying of firearms proposals on college campuses. Accessed online 28 March 2018. https://www.okhighered.org/campus-safety/resources/CBP-guns-iaclea-statement.pdf

International Association of Campus Law Enforcement Administrators. 2018. Speakers and topics. International Association of Campus Law Enforcement Administrators Mid-America Regional Conference, Rogers, Arkansas, 8–11 April. Accessed online 28 March 2018. https://uapd.uark.edu/2018-mid-america-iaclea-conference/speakers-and-topics.php

Jackson, A., & Gould, S. 2017. 10 states allow guns on college campuses and 16 more are considering it. *Business Insider*, 27 April. Accessed online 28 March 2018. http://www.businessinsider.com/states-that-allow-guns-on-college-campuses-2017-4

Jaischik, S., & Lederman, D. 2016. The 2016 Inside Higher Ed Survey of College and University Presidents: A study by Gallup® and *Inside Higher Ed*. Accessed online 28 March 2018. https://www.hobsons.com/res/White papers/2016_IHE_Presidents_Survey_book let.pdf

Jennings, M. 2017. State lawmaker on possibility of sniper teams at Arkansas football games: "Count on it." SEC Country, 31 March. Accessed online 28 March 2018. https://www.seccountry.com/arkansas/lawmaker-sniper-teams-arkansas-razorbacks

Jerath, B.K., & Jerath, R. 1993. *Homicide: A bibliography*. Boca Raton, FL: CRC Press.

Johnson, H. 2010. UCSD burning car: Estranged husband arrested on murder, arson charges. *La Jolla Light*, 8 November. Accessed online 28 March 2018. http://www.lajollalight.com/sdljl-ucsd-burning-car-estranged-husband-arrested-on-2010nov08-story.html

Johnson, M.A. 2012. Maryland man found with dozens of weapons, says he's the Joker. NBC News, 27 July. Accessed online 28 March 2018. http://usnews.nbcnews.com/_news/2012/07/27/12993058-maryland-man-found-with-dozens-of-weapons-says-hes-the-joker?lite

Jones, R. 2013. Sacramento tattoo shop owner arrested for assault weapons possession. CBS Sacramento, 27 June. Accessed online 28 March 2018. http://sacramento.cbslocal.com/2013/06/27/convicted-felon-busted-for-possessing-assault-weapons-thousands-of-ammunition-rounds/

KAIT Web Staff. 2013. Brothers indicted for having multiple firearms and ammo. KAIT TV (Jonesboro, AR), 12 September. Accessed online 28 March 2018. http://www.kait8.com/story/23294709/brothers-indicted-for-having-multiple-firearms-and-ammo

Kansas Attorney General. 2013. Kansas Personal and Family Protection Act: 2013 legislative changes—frequently asked questions. Accessed online 28 March 2018. http://ag.ks.gov/docs/default-source/documents/2013-concealed-carry-legislative-changes—-faqs.pdf?sfvrsn=6

Kansas State Legislature. 2015. An act concerning firearms; relating to the carrying of concealed firearms; relating to the personal and family protection act; amending K.S.A. 2014 Supp. 21–5914, 21–6301, 21–6302, 21–6308, 21–6309, 32–1002, 75–7c01, 75–7c03, 75–7c04, 75–7c05, 75–7c10, 75–7c17, 75–7c20 and 75–7c21 and repealing the existing sections; also repealing K.S.A. 2014Supp. 75–7c19. 2015–2016 Legislative Sessions. Accessed online 28 March 2018. http://www.kslegislature.org/li_2016/m/images/pdf.png

Karp, A. 2007. Completing the count: Civilian firearms. In *Small Arms Survey 2007: Guns and the City* (pp. 38–71). Cambridge, UK: Cambridge University Press. Accessed online 28 March 2018. http://www.smallarmssurvey.org/fileadmin/docs/A-Yearbook/2007/en/full/Small-Arms-Survey-2007-Chapter-02-EN.pdf

Karp, A. 2012. Estimating law enforcement firearms. *Small Arms Survey Research Notes* (24)(December). Accessed online 28 March 2018. http://www.smallarmssurvey.org/file admin/docs/H-Research_Notes/SAS-Research-Note-24.pdf

Katz, W. 2015. Law enforcement tragedies where nobody pays the price. *New York Times*, 8 April. Accessed online 28 March 2018. http://www.nytimes.com/roomfordebate/2014/11/25/does-ferguson-show-that-cops-who-kill-get-off-too-easily/law-enforcement-tragedies-where-nobody-pays-the-price

Kendall, K. 2015. Suspect in overdose investigation sentenced. *The Collegian* (Kansas State University), 15 February. Accessed online 28 March 2018. http://www.kstatecollegian.com/2015/02/15/suspect-in-overdose-investigation-sentenced/

Kent State 1970. 2016. Online archive and repository of information, source documents, and history of the 1970 student uprising and Ohio National Guard shootings at Kent State University. Accessed online 28 March 2018. http://www.kentstate1970.org//index2

Kersey, J. 2017. Allowing guns at Arkansas athletic events is a terrible idea. SEC Country. Accessed online 28 March 2018. https://www.seccountry.com/arkansas/arkansas-podcast-guns-in-stadiums

Kirk, C., & Kois, D. 2013. How many people have been killed by guns since Newtown? *Slate*, 16 September. Accessed online 28 March 2018. http://www.slate.com/articles/news_and_politics/crime/2012/12/gun_death_tally_every_american_gun_death_since_newtown_sandy_hook_shooting.html

Kirk, O. 2017. SEC gets involved in the conceal carry controversy in Arkansas. 247Sports, 28 March. Accessed online 28 March 2018. https://247sports.com/college/arkansas/Bolt/SEC-gets-involved-in-the-conceal-carry-controversy-in-Arkansas-52020850

Klapper, E., Lovenheim, S., Amick, J., & Kotecki, E. 2010. 2010 budget blueprint: Agency by agency. *Washington Post*. Accessed online 28 March 2018. http://www.washingtonpost.com/wp-srv/politics/budget2010/agency_by_agency.html

Kopel, D. 2015. Guns on university campuses: The Colorado experience. *Washington Post*, 20 April. Accessed online 28 March 2018. https://www.washingtonpost.com/news/volokh-conspiracy/wp/2015/04/20/guns-on-university-campuses-the-colorado-experience/?utm_term=.d36c58427a71

Korff, J., Roussey, T., & Tschida, S. 2012. Bowie State murder trial: Alexis Simpson not guilty of roommate's death. WJLA (Washington, DC), 14 November. Accessed online 28 March 2018. http://wjla.com/news/local/alexis-simpson-best-friend-of-victim-in-bowie-state-murder-trial-testifies—82094

Koster, K. 2017. Opposing teams should boycott playing Arkansas if concealed weapons are allowed at games. The Big Lead, 23 March. Accessed online 28 March 2018. http://thebiglead.com/2017/03/23/opposing-teams-should-boycott-playing-arkansas-if-concealed-weapons-are-allowed-at-games/

Krouse, W.J. 2012. Gun control legislation. Congressional Research Service Report RL32842, Washington, DC. Accessed online 28 March 2018. http://www.fas.org/sgp/crs/misc/RL32842.pdf

Krug, E.G., Dahlberg, L.L., Mercy, J.A., Zwi, A.B., & Lozano, R. (Eds.). 2002. World report on violence and health. Geneva, World Health Organization. Accessed online 28 March 2018. http://www.who.int/violence_injury_prevention/violence/world_report/en/full_en.pdf

KXAN. 2015. Chief Acevedo stands by statements on campus carry bill. 13 February. Accessed online 28 March 2018. http://kxan.com/2015/02/13/chief-acevedo-stands-by-statements-on-campus-carry-bill/

LaFree, G. 1999. Declining violent crime rates in the 1990s: Predicting crime booms and busts. *Annual Review of Sociology, 25*, 145–168.

Lee, B., Preston, F., & Green, G. 2012. Preparing for high-impact, low-probability events: Lessons from Eyjafjallajökull. Chatman House: The Royal Institute of International Affairs. Accessed online 28 March 2018. https://www.chathamhouse.org/sites/files/chathamhouse/public/Research/Energy,%20Environment%20and%20Development/r0112_highimpact.pdf

Lee, T. 2016. New Texas law allows college students to carry guns on campus. *U.S. News and World Report*, 1 August. Accessed online 28 March 2018. http://www.nbcnews.com/news/us-news/new-texas-law-allows-college-students-carry-guns-campus-n620911

Legal Information Institute. 2016. 20 U.S. Code § 1232g—Family educational and privacy rights. Cornell University Law School. Accessed online 28 March 2018. https://www.law.cornell.edu/uscode/text/20/1232g

Legal Information Institute. 2016. 42 U.S. Code Subchapter III—Violence against women. Cornell University Law School. Accessed online 28 March 2018. https://www.law.cornell.edu/uscode/text/42/chapter-136/subchapter-III

Legal Information Institute. 2016. Mayhem. *Wex free legal dictionary and encyclopedia*. Cornell University Law School, Ithaca, New York. Accessed online 28 March 2018. https://www.law.cornell.edu/wex/mayhem

Lendinara, P. 1991. The world of Anglo-Saxon learning. In E.M. Godden & M. Lapidge (Eds.), *The Cambridge Companion to Old English Literature* (pp. 264–281). Cambridge, UK: Cambridge University Press.

Lennard, N. 2013. Newtown massacre: 155 bullets

in five minutes. *Salon*, 28 March. Accessed online 28 March 2018. http://www.salon.com/2013/03/28/newtown_massacre_155_bullets_in_five_minutes/

Levin, S. 2012. CU-Denver accidental shooting: Now ex-staffer trying to unjam gun when it fired. *Westworld*, 15 November. Accessed online 28 March 2018. http://www.westword.com/news/cu-denver-accidental-shooting-now-ex-staffer-trying-to-unjam-gun-when-it-fired-5909883

Levitt, S.D. 2004. Understanding why crime fell in the 1990s: Four factors that explain the decline and six that do not. *Journal of Economic Perspectives, 18*(1), 163–190. Accessed online 28 March 2018. http://pricetheory.uchicago.edu/levitt/Papers/LevittUnderstandingWhyCrime2004.pdf

Lewis, T. 2015. Here's what you need to know about the plight of HBCUs (and it's getting worse). *Essence Online*, 18 August. Accessed online 28 March 2018. http://www.essence.com/2015/08/18/hbcus-black-colleges-closing-plight

Li, O. 2016. When Jefferson and Madison banned guns on campus. *The Atlantic*, 6 May. Accessed online 28 March 2018. https://www.theatlantic.com/politics/archive/2016/05/when-jefferson-and-madison-banned-guns-on-campus/481461/

Lichtblau, E., & Motoka, R. 2012. N.R.A. envisions "a good guy with a gun" in every school. *New York Times*, 21 December. Accessed online 28 March 2018. http://www.nytimes.com/2012/12/22/us/nra-calls-for-armed-guards-at-schools.html?pagewanted=all&_r=0

Love, J. 2012. Reading fast and slow. *The American Scholar* (Spring). Accessed online 28 March 2018. http://theamericanscholar.org/reading-fast-and-slow/#.UiyX9dKshdI

Loyd, R. 2015. Survey: Majority of UTSA students polled oppose guns on campus. KSAT TV, 24 December. Accessed online 28 March 2018. http://www.ksat.com/news/survey-majority-of-utsa-students-polled-oppose-guns-on-campus

Mackey, M. 2014. Why you shouldn't send your child to an Idaho college. *Fiscal Times*, 9 March. Accessed online 28 March 2018. http://www.thefiscaltimes.com/Articles/2014/03/09/Why-You-Shouldn-t-Send-Your-Child-Idaho-College

Mayors Against Illegal Guns. 2013. Analysis of recent mass shootings. Accessed online 28 March 2018. http://msnbcmedia.msn.com/i/MSNBC/Sections/NEWS/A_U.S.%20news/US-news-PDFs/Analysis_of_Mass_Shootings.pdf

McCall, P.L., Parker, K.F., & MacDonald, J.M. 2008. The dynamic relationship between homicide rates and social, economic, and political factors from 1970 to 2000. *Social Science Research, 37*(3), 721–735.

McCann, M. 2015. Campus carry pushback heats up: More than 800 UT professors oppose guns on campus. *Austin Chronicle*, 30 October. Accessed online 28 March 2018. http://www.austinchronicle.com/news/2015-10-30/campus-carry-pushback-heats-up/

McClennan, B. 2016. UTK "Guns on Campus Poll." Faculty Senate, University of Tennessee, Knoxville. Accessed online 28 March 2018. http://senate.utk.edu/wp-content/uploads/sites/16/2016/04/UTK-Guns-Poll-final.pdf

Michael, J. 2010. North Dakota Supreme Court upholds Stevie Buckley's manslaughter conviction. *Bismarck Tribune*, 21 December. Accessed online 28 March 2018. http://bismarcktribune.com/news/local/crime-and-courts/north-dakota-supreme-court-upholds-stevie-buckley-s-manslaughter-conviction/article_16d66b70-0d52-11e0-ac99-001cc4c03286.html

Miethe, T.D., Regoeczi, W.C., & Drass, K.A. 2004. *Rethinking homicide: Exploring the structure and process underlying deadly situations*. Cambridge, UK: Cambridge University Press.

Miller, J. 2011. Odds versus odds: Betting on March Mania. *Oh! A Blog*, Ohio Lottery's Office of Communications, 24 March. Accessed online 28 March 2018. https://ohiolottery.wordpress.com/2011/03/24/odds-versus-odds/

Miller, T.R. 2013. The cost of gun violence. Children's Safety Network, National Injury and Violence Prevention Resource Center. Accessed online 28 March 2018. https://www.childrenssafetynetwork.org/sites/childrenssafetynetwork.org/files/TheCostofGunViolence.pdf

Minkin, W. 1985. Westchester opinion: When a daughter is murdered. *New York Times*, 10 March. Accessed online 28 March 2018. http://www.nytimes.com/1985/03/10/nyregion/westchester-opinion-when-a-daughter-is-murdered.html

Montgomery, D., & Perez-Pena, R. 2017. Man wielding knife kills one and injures three at University of Texas. *New York Times*, 1 May. Accessed online 28 March 2018. https://www.nytimes.com/2017/05/01/us/texas-austin-stabbing-attack.html

Mozaffarian, D., Hemenway, D., & Ludwig, D.S. 2013. Curbing gun violence: Lessons from public health successes. *Journal of the American Medical Association, 309*(6), 551–552.

Murphy, S., Xu, J., & Kochanek, K. 2013. Deaths:

Final data for 2010. *National Vital Statistics Reports,* 61(4), 1–117. Accessed online 28 March 2018. https://www.cdc.gov/nchs/data/nvsr/nvsr61/nvsr61_04.pdf

National Center for Education Statistics. 2014. Table 329.30: On-campus hate crimes at degree-granting postsecondary institutions, by level and control of institution, type of crime, and category of bias motivating the crime: 2009 through 2012. *Digest of Education Statistics.* U.S. Department of Education, Institute of Education Sciences. Accessed online 28 March 2018. http://nces.ed.gov/programs/digest/d14/tables/dt14_329.30.asp

National Center for Education Statistics. 2015. Table 303.20: Total fall enrollment in all postsecondary institutions participating in Title IV programs and annual percentage change in enrollment, by degree-granting status and control of institution: 1995 through 2014. *Digest of Educational Statistics.* U.S. Department of Education, Institute of Education Sciences. Accessed online 28 March 2018. https://nces.ed.gov/programs/digest/d15/tables/dt15_303.20.asp?current=yes

National Center for Education Statistics. 2015. Table 313.20: Fall enrollment in degree-granting historically black colleges and universities, by sex of student and level and control of institution: Selected years, 1976 through 2014. *Digest of Education Statistics.* U.S. Department of Education, Institute of Education Sciences. Accessed online 28 March 2018. https://nces.ed.gov/programs/digest/d15/tables/dt15_313.20.asp?current=yes

National Center for Education Statistics. 2015. Table 314.20: Employees in degree-granting postsecondary institutions, by sex, employment status, control and level of institution, and primary occupation: Selected years, fall 1991 through fall 2013. *Digest of Educational Statistics.* U.S. Department of Education, Institute of Education Sciences. Accessed online 28 March 2018. https://nces.ed.gov/programs/digest/d15/tables/dt15_314.20.asp?current=yes

National Center for Education Statistics. 2016. *Digest of Education Statistics.* U.S. Department of Education, Institute of Education Sciences. Accessed online 28 March 2018. https://nces.ed.gov/programs/digest/

National Center for Education Statistics. 2016. Indicator 23: Hate crime incidents at postsecondary institutions. *Indicators of School Crime and Safety.* U.S. Department of Education, Institute of Education Sciences. Accessed online 28 March 2018. http://nces.ed.gov/programs/crimeindicators/ind_23.asp

National Center for Education Statistics. 2016. Integrated Post-Secondary Education Data System (IPEDS). U.S. Department of Education, Institute for Education Sciences. Accessed online 28 March 2018. http://nces.ed.gov/ipeds/

National Center for Education Statistics. 2016. Table 306.10: Total fall enrollment in degree-granting postsecondary institutions, by level of enrollment, sex, attendance status, and race/ethnicity of student: Selected years, 1976 through 2015. *Digest of Education Statistics.* U.S. Department of Education, Institute of Education Sciences. Accessed online 28 March 2018. https://nces.ed.gov/programs/digest/d16/tables/dt16_306.10.asp?current=yes

National Paralegal College. 2016. Criminal law definitions. Accessed online 28 March 2018. http://nationalparalegal.edu/public_documents/courseware_asp_files/criminalLaw/otherAgainsPersons/Mayhem.asp

National Rifle Association Institute for Legislative Action. 2017. Update: Action needed on gun control bill headed to Arkansas House floor despite strong opposition. 29 March. Accessed online 28 March 2018. https://www.nraila.org/articles/20170329/action-needed-gun-control-bill-headed-to-arkansas-house-floor-despite-strong-opposition

National Weather Service. 2017. How dangerous is lightning? National Oceanic and Atmospheric Administration, Washington, DC. Accessed online 28 March 2018. http://www.lightningsafety.noaa.gov/odds.shtml

Nazaryan, A. 2015. Black colleges matter. *Newsweek,* 18 August. Accessed online 28 March 2018. http://www.newsweek.com/black-colleges-matter-363667

Neely, C. 2015. *You're dead. So what? Media, police, and the invisibility of black women as victims of homicide.* Lansing, MI: Michigan State University Press.

Nisbett, R.E., & Cohen, D. 1996. *Culture of honor: The psychology of violence in the South.* Boulder, CO: Westview Press.

Noble, R., Mims, B., & Piper, R. 2017. University of Utah student shot to death in campus carjacking; hunt underway for "armed and dangerous" suspect. *Salt Lake Tribune,* 31 October. Accessed online 28 March 2018. http://www.sltrib.com/news/2017/10/31/shots-fired-near-university-of-utah/

Northern Illinois University. 2010. Report of the February 14, 2008 shootings at Northern Illinois University. Office of the President, Northern Illinois University. Accessed online 28 March 2018. https://webcourses.niu.edu/

bbcswebdav/institution/HLC2014RR/CH00/ OFFICE-OF-THE-PRESIDENT-February-14-Report-2008-02.pdf

O'Dell, R., & Ryman, A. 2016. "It means her life was not in vain": The tragedy that gave birth to the Clery Act. *Arizona Republic*, 25 April. Accessed online 28 March 2018. http://www.azcentral.com/story/news/local/arizona-investigations/2016/04/15/tragedy-that-gave-birth-to-clery-act/82811052/

Parker, K., Horowitz, J., Igielnik, R., Oliphant, B., & Brown, A. 2017. America's complex relationship with guns. Pew Research Center, Social and Demographic Trends. Accessed online 28 March 2018. http://assets.pew research.org/wp-content/uploads/sites/3/ 2017/06/06151541/Guns-Report-FOR-WEBSITE-PDF-6-21.pdf

Patten, R., Thomas, M., & Wada, J.C. 2013. Packing heat: Attitudes regarding concealed weapons on college campuses. *American Journal of Criminal Justice, 38*(4), 551–569.

Pearson-Nelson, B. 2008. *Understanding homicide trends: The social context of a homicide epidemic.* New York, NY: LFB Scholarly Publishing.

Pennsylvania General Assembly. 1988. College and University Security Information Act, Act 73, 26 May. Accessed online 28 March 2018. http://www.legis.state.pa.us/cfdocs/legis/li/ uconsCheck.cfm?yr=1988&sessInd=0&act= 73

Pérez, Z.J., & Hussey, H. 2014. A hidden crisis: Including the LGBT community when addressing sexual violence on college campuses. Center for American Progress. Accessed online 28 March 2018. https://www.american progress.org/issues/lgbt/report/2014/09/19/ 97504/a-hidden-crisis/

Price, J.H., Thompson, A., Khubchandani, J., Dake, J., Payton, E., & Teeple, K. 2014. University presidents' perceptions and practice regarding the carrying of concealed handguns on college campuses. *Journal of American College Health, 62*(7), 461–469.

Price, J.H., Thompson, A., Payton, E., Johnson, J., & Brown, O. 2016. Presidents of historically black colleges and universities perceptions and practices regarding carrying of concealed handguns on their campuses. *College Student Journal, 50*(1), 135–144.

Rap News Network. 2004. Hip-hop news: BET & theme park cancel hip hop fest. 17 August. Accessed online 28 March 2018. http://www.rapnews.net/0-202-259384-00.html

Reavis, C. 2017. Bicyclist discovers body, police determine death by suicide. *Arkansas Traveler,* 26 October. Accessed online 28 March 2018. http://www.uatrav.com/news/article_fdc0 e868-bab5-11e7-9cd3-4bd07b44b41d.html

Riddle, B. 2017. Body found on University of Arkansas–owned property near trail. Accessed online 28 March 2018. http://www.arkansasonline.com/news/2017/oct/26/body-found-university-arkansas-owned-property-deat/

Robert A. and Virginia Heinlein Archives. 2016. Opus 29: Beyond this horizon. Accessed online 28 March 2018. http://www.heinleinarch ives.net/upload/index.php?_a=viewProd& productId=31

Rocha, V., & Serna, J. 2015. Ventura man jailed on charge he fatally stabbed 1-year-old son. *Los Angeles Times*, 5 January. Accessed online 28 March 2018. http://www.latimes.com/ local/lanow/la-me-ln-ventura-man-jailed-in-sons-slaying-20150105-story.html

Roland, C. 2004. Body found Sunday at Asylum Lake identified. Western Michigan University, Office of University Relations, 5 May. Accessed online 28 March 2018. http://www.wmich.edu/ wmu/news/2004/0405/0304-x242.html

Rosenfeld, R. 2016. Documenting and explaining the 2015 homicide rise: Research directions. U.S. Department of Justice, Office of Justice Programs, National Institute of Justice. Accessed online 28 March 2018. https://www.ncjrs.gov/pdffiles1/nij/249895.pdf?ed2f26 df2d9c416fbddddd2330a778c6=kvbbjmkbrx-kjbikilv

Roth, R. 2009. *American homicide.* Cambridge, MA: Harvard University Press.

Rushing, M. 2013. Student wounded accidentally by gunshot. University Relations Office, University of Arkansas, Fayetteville, Arkansas, 8 February. Accessed online 28 March 2018. http://news.uark.edu/articles/20186/student-wounded-accidentally-by-gunshot

Russell, B.Z. 2014. Idaho college leaders oppose guns-on-campus bill, but lawmakers press on anyway. *Idaho Statesman*, 3 February. Accessed online 28 March 2018. http://www.spokesman.com/stories/2014/feb/03/idaho-college-leaders-oppose-guns-campus-bill-lawm/

Salisbury, D. 2010. Update: Amanda Ball pleads guilty to manslaughter in death of Andrew Hirst. MLive.com, 23 November. Accessed online 28 March 2018. http://www.mlive.com/ news/jackson/index.ssf/2010/11/amanda_ball_ pleads_guilty_to_m.html

Scalia, A. 2008. Opinion of the Court: *District of Columbia, et al., Petitioners v. Dick Anthony Heller.* Supreme Court of the United States

No. 07–290. Accessed online 28 March 2018. https://www.law.cornell.edu/supct/pdf/07–290P.ZO

Schwarz, H. 2014. Idaho professor shoots himself in foot two months after state legalizes guns on campuses. *Washington Post*, 5 September. Accessed online 28 March 2018. https://www.washingtonpost.com/blogs/govbeat/wp/2014/09/05/idaho-professor-shoots-himself-in-foot-two-months-after-state-legalizes-guns-on-campuses/

SECRANT.com. 2013. Dummy shoots himself at KUAF. Accessed online 28 March 2018. http://www.secrant.com/rant/sec-football/dummy-shoots-himself-at-kuaf/39821372/

Sexton, J. 2004. The university as sanctuary. Reflections of President John Sexton, New York University (November). Accessed online 28 March 2018. https://www.nyu.edu/about/leadership-university-administration/office-of-the-president-emeritus/communications/the-university-as-sanctuary.html

Shapiro, T.R. 2015. Delta State University professor told police he killed his "wife" shortly before second shooting. *Washington Post*, 15 September. Accessed online 28 March 2018. https://www.washingtonpost.com/news/grade-point/wp/2015/09/15/history-professor-shot-and-killed-at-delta-state-university-known-as-mentor/?utm_term=.d3469bdc7d45

Siron, C. 2016. Slain University of Texas student Haruka Weiser was strangled, sexually assaulted, report says. *Dallas News*, 6 April. Accessed online 28 March 2018. https://www.dallasnews.com/news/crime/2016/04/13/slain-ut-austin-student-haruka-weiser-was-strangled-report-says

Skorton, D., & Altschuler, G. 2013. Do we really need more guns on campus? *Forbes*, 21 February. Accessed online 28 March 2018. http://www.forbes.com/sites/collegeprose/2013/02/21/guns-on-campus/#518adeb264c4

Smith, C., & Huegauburo, N. 2016. Guns on grounds—where did Jefferson stand? How U.Va.'s founder's stance lines up with current policy. *Cavalier Daily*, 20 October. Accessed online 28 March 2016. http://www.cavalierdaily.com/article/2016/10/guns-on-grounds-where-did-jefferson-stand

Smith, M., Capecchi, C., & Furber, M. 2016. Peaceful protests follow Minnesota governor's call for calm. *New York Times*, 8 July. Accessed online 28 March 2018. http://www.nytimes.com/2016/07/09/us/philando-castile-jeronimo-yanez.html

Smith, M.D., & Zahn, M.A. 1999. *Homicide: A sourcebook of social research*. Thousand Oaks, CA: Sage.

Smith, M.D., & Zahn, M.A. 1999. *Studying and preventing homicide: Issues and challenges*. Thousand Oaks, CA: Sage.

Spain, J. 2013. Changing the narrative of neonaticide. *Indiana Journal of Law and Social Equality*, 2(1), Article 8, 166–181.

Spies, M. 2017. Kansas will be first campus-carry state where students won't need permits to tote guns. *The Trace*, 31 March. Accessed online 28 March 2018. https://www.thetrace.org/2017/03/campus-carry-kansas-no-permits-guns/

Srubas, P. 2015. Man charged in Green Bay murder, drug robbery. *Green Bay Press Gazette* (Green Bay, WI), 15 July. Accessed online 28 March 2018. http://www.greenbaypressgazette.com/story/news/local/2015/07/15/suspect-custody-murder-near-uwgb/30188085/

Staff. 2011. Man pleads guilty in death of his wife in burning car at UCSD. *La Jolla Light*, 18 November. Accessed online 28 March 2018. http://www.lajollalight.com/sdljl-man-pleads-guilty-in-death-of-his-wife-in-burning-2011nov18-story.html

State of Tennessee. 2016. Public chapter no. 1061. An act to amend Tennessee Code Annotated, Title 39 and Title 49, relative to permitting certain persons to carry handguns on the property of certain postsecondary institutions. Accessed online 28 March 2018. http://utpolice.utk.edu/wp-content/uploads/sites/48/2016/06/pc1061.pdf

Steele, T., Chiquillo, J., & de Bruijn, E. 2017. North Lake College gunman was stalking the woman he killed, her family says. *Dallas Morning News*, 4 May. Accessed online 28 March 2018. https://www.dallasnews.com/news/irving/2017/05/03/north-lake-college-lockdown-shooter

Steffen, J., & Hernandez, E. 2015. Four dead in Colorado Springs officer-involved shooting. *Denver Post*, 31 October. Accessed online 28 March 2018. http://www.denverpost.com/2015/10/31/four-dead-in-colorado-springs-officer-involved-shooting/

Stodghill, R. 2015. *Where everybody looks like me: At the crossroads of America's black colleges and culture*. New York, NY: HarperCollins.

Stotzer, R.L. 2010. Sexual orientation-based hate crimes on campus: The impact of policy on reporting rates. *Sexuality Research & Social Policy*, 7(3), 147–154.

Stranglin, D. 2017. 2 dead at North Lake College in apparent murder-suicide near Dallas. *USA Today*, 3 May. Accessed online 28 March 2018.

https://www.usatoday.com/story/news/2017/05/03/police-active-shooter-dallas-area-college/101247274/

Strauss, C. 2017. The NCAA needs to take a strong stand against Arkansas law that will allow guns in stadiums. Fox Sports, 23 March. Accessed online 28 March 2018. https://www.foxsports.com/college-football/story/the-ncaa-needs-to-take-a-strong-stand-against-arkansas-law-that-will-allow-guns-in-stadiums-032317

Svrluga, S. 2017. Texas Tech student faces capital murder charge after allegedly shooting a police officer on campus. Washington Post, 10 October. Accessed online 28 March 2018. https://www.washingtonpost.com/news/grade-point/wp/2017/10/10/texas-tech-student-faces-capital-murder-charge-after-allegedly-shooting-a-police-officer-on-campus/?utm_term=.80920f51fc4f

Taleb, N.M., Goldstein, D.G., & Spitznagel, M.W. 2009. The six mistakes executives make in risk management. Harvard Business Review (October). Accessed online 28 March 2018. https://hbr.org/2009/10/the-six-mistakes-executives-make-in-risk-management

Taurus Industries. 2017. Taurus Judge® Revolver | 45 Colt/410 GA 3[qm] 5-RDS Matte Stainless. Accessed online 28 March 2018. http://www.taurususa.com/product-details.cfm?id=199&category=Pistol

Taylor, S. 2008. Scuba instructor charged in death of UA student. Tuscaloosa News, 28 July. Accessed online 28 March 2018. http://www.tuscaloosanews.com/news/20080728/scuba-instructor-charged-in-death-of-ua-student

Tennant, P. 2009. Police: Man said 30,000 bullets were for target practice. Eagle-Tribune, 16 May. Accessed online 28 March 2018. http://www.eagletribune.com/haverhill/x165095490/Police-Man-said-30-000-bullets-were-for-target-practice

Thompson, A., Price, J.H., Dake, J., & Teeple, K. 2013. Faculty perceptions and practices regarding carrying concealed handguns on university campuses. Journal of Community Health, 38(2), 366–373.

Thompson, A., Price, J.H., Dake, J.A., Teeple, K., Bassler, S., Khubchandani, J., Kerr, D., Brookins Fisher, J., Rickard, M., Oden, L., & Aduroja, A. 2013. Student perceptions and practices regarding carrying concealed handguns on university campuses. Journal of American College Health, 61(5), 243–253.

Thompson, A., Price, J.H., Mrdjenovich, A.J., & Khubchandani, J. 2009. Reducing firearm-related violence on college campuses—Police chiefs' perceptions and practices. Journal of American College Health, 58(3), 247–254. Accessed online 28 March 2018. https://www.tandfonline.com/doi/pdf/10.1080/07448480903295367?needAccess=true

Toohey, M. 2017. Viral item debunked: No evidence gun-brandishing student helped subdue UT attacker. Austin American-Statesman, 3 May. Accessed online 28 March 2018. http://www.statesman.com/news/local/viral-item-debunked-evidence-gun-brandishing-student-helped-subdue-attacker/z92T0lb56COS9cb6emNGeN/

U.S. Bureau of Justice Statistics. 1997. Age patterns of victims of serious violent crime. U.S. Department of Justice, Office of Justice Programs, Bureau of Justice Statistics Special Report NCJ-162031 (July). Accessed online 28 March 2018. https://www.bjs.gov/content/pub/pdf/apvsvc.pdf

U.S. Bureau of Justice Statistics. 2014. The nation's two measures of homicide. U.S. Department of Justice, Office of Justice Programs, NCJ 247060 (July). Accessed online 28 March 2018. https://www.bjs.gov/content/pub/pdf/ntmh.pdf

U.S. Census Bureau. 2016. Historical population data. U.S. Department of Commerce. Accessed online 28 March 2018. https://www.census.gov/popest/data/historical/

U.S. Department of Education. 1991. Historically black colleges and universities and higher education desegregation. Office for Civil Rights. Accessed online 28 March 2018. http://www2.ed.gov/about/offices/list/ocr/docs/hq9511.html

U.S. Department of Education. 2015. 2013 annual report to the president on the results of the participation of historically black colleges and universities in federal programs. White House Initiative on Historically Black Colleges and Universities. Accessed online 28 March 2018. http://sites.ed.gov/whhbcu/files/2011/12/HBCU-2013-Annual-Report-HBCU-final-.pdf

U.S. Department of Education, Office of Postsecondary Education. 2016. Campus Safety and Security Data Analysis Cutting Tool. Accessed online 28 March 2018. http://ope.ed.gov/campussafety/#/

U.S. Department of Education, Office of Postsecondary Education. 2016. The Handbook for Campus Safety and Security Reporting (2016 Edition). Washington, DC. Accessed online 28 March 2018. https://www2.ed.gov/admins/lead/safety/handbook.pdf

U.S. Department of Justice. 2016. Overview of Title IX of the Education Amendments of 1972,

20 U.S.C. A§ 1681 ET. SEQ. 1972. Accessed online 28 March 2018. https://www.justice.gov/crt/overview-title-ix-education-amendments-1972-20-usc-1681-et-seq

U.S. Department of Justice. 2018. Uniform Crime Reporting System. Accessed online 28 March 2018. https://www.bjs.gov/ucrdata/Search/Crime/Crime.cfm

U.S. Fire Administration. 2008. Northern Illinois University shooting. Federal Emergency Management Administration, Department of Homeland Security Technical Report USFA-TR-167 (February). Accessed online 28 March 2018. https://www.usfa.fema.gov/downloads/pdf/publications/tr_167.pdf

U.S. Government Publishing Office. 2016. The Family Educational Rights and Privacy Act. Accessed online 28 March 2018. http://www.ecfr.gov/cgi-bin/text-idx?tpl=/ecfrbrowse/Title34/34cfr99_main_02.tpl

U.S. Public Law 101–542. Accessed online 28 March 2018. https://www.cbc.edu/sites/www/Uploads/STUDENT%20RIGHT%20TO%20KNOW%20ACT%20-%20STATUTE-104-Pg2381.pdf

University of Arkansas at Pine Bluff. 2016. Historical overview. Accessed online 28 March 2018. https://www.uapb.edu/about/historical_overview.aspx

University of California. 2016. Understanding science. University of California Museum of Paleontology, 3 January. Accessed online 28 March 2018. http://www.understandingscience.org

University of Central Arkansas. 2008. Information about UCA campus shooting. 27 October. Accessed online 28 March 2018. http://uca.edu/news/information-about-uca-campus-shooting/

University of Virginia Board of Visitors. 1824. University of Virginia Board of Visitors Minutes, 4–5 October 1824. Encyclopedia Virginia. Accessed online 28 March 2018. https://www.encyclopediavirginia.org/University_of_Virginia_Board_of_Visitors_Minutes_October_4–5_1824

Utah. 2006. 2006 Utah Code—63–98–102—Uniform firearm laws. Accessed online 28 March 2018. http://law.justia.com/codes/utah/2006/title63/63_3b003.html

Vertuno, J. 2016. Texas private colleges oppose guns on campus. *Christian Science Monitor*, 21 February. Accessed online 28 March 2018. http://www.csmonitor.com/USA/Society/2016/0221/Texas-private-colleges-oppose-guns-on-campus

Violence Policy Center. 2011. A shrinking minority: The continuing decline of gun ownership in America. Accessed online 28 March 2018. http://www.vpc.org/studies/ownership.pdf

Violence Policy Center. 2018. Concealed carry killers. Accessed online 28 March 2018. http://concealedcarrykillers.org/

Violence Policy Center. 2018. Mass shootings involving concealed handgun permit holders. Accessed online 28 March 2018. http://concealedcarrykillers.org/wp-content/uploads/2017/07/CCW-mass-shooters-7-14-17.pdf

Virginia Tech Review Panel. 2007. Mass shootings at Virginia Tech April 16, 2007: Report of the review panel presented to Governor Kaine, Commonwealth of Virginia. Accessed online 28 March 2018. https://governor.virginia.gov/media/3772/fullreport.pdf

Watkins, M. 2016. Hutchison, Fenves decry dwindling state support for higher education. *Texas Tribune*, 11 April. Accessed online 28 March 2018. https://www.texastribune.org/2016/04/11/hutchison-fenves-decry-dwindling-state-support-hig/

Watkins, M. 2016. Weeks after campus carry went into effect, an accidental misfire at Tarleton State. *Texas Tribune*, 16 September. Accessed online 28 March 2018. https://www.texastribune.org/2016/09/16/campus-carry-accidental-misfire-at-tarleton-state/

Watkins, M., & Murphy, R. 2016. Where Texas' private universities stand on campus carry. *Texas Tribune*, 29 July. Accessed online 28 March 2018. https://apps.texastribune.org/private-university-campus-carry/

Whaley, M. 2012. Colorado Supreme Court affirms that CU students with permits can carry concealed guns on campus. *Denver Post*, 5 March. Accessed online 28 March 2018. https://www.denverpost.com/2012/03/05/colorado-supreme-court-affirms-that-cu-students-with-permits-can-carry-concealed-guns-on-campus/

Wikipedia. 2017. Umpqua Community College shooting. Accessed online 28 March 2018. https://en.wikipedia.org/wiki/Umpqua_Community_College_shooting

Williams, M.R., & Porter, T. 2017. Gun found in bathroom in KU's Wescoe Hall was loaded .38 reported stolen in Olathe. *Kansas City Star*, 5 September. Accessed online 28 March 2018. http://www.kansascity.com/news/local/article171379147.html

Winkler, A. 2011. Did the wild west have more gun control than we do today? *Huffington Post*, 9 September. Accessed online 28 March 2018. http://www.huffingtonpost.com/adam-

winkler/did-the-wild-west-have-mo_b_
956035.html

Wisconsin State Legislature. 2011. 2011 Senate Bill 93. Accessed online 28 March 2018. https://docs.legis.wisconsin.gov/2011/related/proposals/sb93

WISN 12 News. 2012. Man dies in UW-Milwaukee dorm room; student arrested. WISN TV 12 (Milwaukee, WI), 6 December. Accessed online 28 March 2018. http://www.wisn.com/article/man-dies-in-uw-milwaukee-dorm-room-student-arrested/6312635

Withers, L. 2012. WSU student injured by his own handgun. *Standard Examiner*, 5 January. Accessed online 28 March 2018. http://www.standard.net/Local/2012/01/05/WSU-student-injured-by-his-own-handgun.html

Wohltmann, G. 2013. Father of driver in cyclist death arrested. *Pleasanton Weekly*, 19 July. Accessed online 28 March 2018. https://pleasantonweekly.com/print/story/2013/07/19/father-of-driver-in-cyclist-death-arrested

World Bank. 2017. International homicides (per 100,000 people). Accessed online 28 March 2018. http://data.worldbank.org/indicator/VC.

IHR.PSRC.P5?end=2014&start=1995&view=chart&year_high_desc=true

World Bank. 2018. Population growth (% annual) for the United States. Accessed online 28 March 2018. http://data.worldbank.org/indicator/SP.POP.GROW?locations=US

Yarvis, R.M. 1991. *Homicide: Causative factors and roots*. Lexington, MA: Lexington Books.

Zack, N. 2015. *White privilege and black rights: The injustice of U.S. police racial profiling and homicide*. Lanham, MD: Rowman & Littlefield.

Zapotsky, M. 2012. Woman "scared" before deadly stabbing of roommate. *Washington Post*, 15 November. Accessed online 28 March 2018. https://www.washingtonpost.com/local/crime/woman-scared-before-deadly-stabbing-of-roommate/2012/11/15/67bb2c02–2f3c–11e2–a30e-5ca76eeec857_story.html

Zuckerman, S. 2014. Idaho professor accidentally shoots himself in the foot in chemistry class. *Reuters*, 3 September. Accessed online 28 March 2018. http://www.reuters.com/article/us-usa-guncontrol-idaho-idUSKBN0GY2E620140904

Index